PRIVACY AND IDENTITY PROTECTION

ONLINE PRIVACY LAWS

EUROPEAN UNION & SELECT FOREIGN COUNTRIES

PRIVACY AND IDENTITY PROTECTION

Additional books in this series can be found on Nova's website under the Series tab.

Additional E-books in this series can be found on Nova's website under the E-book tab.

INTERNET POLICIES AND ISSUES

Additional books in this series can be found on Nova's website under the Series tab.

Additional E-books in this series can be found on Nova's website under the E-book tab.

PRIVACY AND IDENTITY PROTECTION

ONLINE PRIVACY LAWS

EUROPEAN UNION & SELECT FOREIGN COUNTRIES

ETHAN P. WILLIAMS
EDITOR

nova publishers
New York

For permission to use material from this book please contact us:
Telephone 631-231-7269; Fax 631-231-8175
Web Site: http://www.novapublishers.com

Library of Congress Cataloging-in-Publication Data

ISBN: 978-1-62808-623-2

Published by Nova Science Publishers, Inc. † New York

CONTENTS

PREFACE

These reports describe the data protection laws of the European Union (Part I) and of selected foreign countries (Part II). They describe the legal framework for the collection, use, and transfer of data, and examine whether existing laws are adequate to deal with online privacy in an era of rapid technological development and globalization.

Chapter 1 - The right to data protection and the right to privacy are two distinct human rights recognized in the Charter of Fundamental Rights of the European Union, the Treaty on the Functioning of the EU (TFEU), and in two legal instruments of the Council of Europe, to which all the EU Member States are parties.

In January 2012, the European Commission proposed a major overhaul of the existing legislative framework on the protection of personal data. The reform was necessitated mainly by three factors: (a) new challenges posed by globalization and Internet developments in the area of online services, which impact the processing of personal data and endanger the privacy of individuals; (b) a new legal basis in the TFEU; and (c) a dramatic increase in Internet users and serious concerns expressed by 70% of individuals in the EU about the possible misuse of their personal data.

Landmark EU Directive 95/46/EC on the Protection of Individuals with Regard to the Processing of Personal Data on the Free Movement of Such Data, which was adopted in 1995 when the Internet was still in its infancy, met to some extent its twin objectives of safeguarding the personal data of individuals and improving the flow of personal data among EU Member States, but it resulted in diversity of implementation by the twenty-seven EU Members. By contrast, the pending proposal, which is in the form of a draft regulation because of its direct applicability in the legal systems of the Member States of the EU, will bring about greater harmonization of data protection rules, legal certainty, and transparency, and will also remove any obstacles in the flow of personal data within the single market and improve competition. The draft regulation builds upon the fundamental principles on the processing of personal data established by Directive 95/46/EC. Thus, online processing of personal data is prohibited unless it meets necessary safeguards and is based on one of the required legal grounds, such as consent or the protection of vital interests of data subjects. Special categories of data, such as data concerning race, ethnic origin, political affiliations, religion, genetic data, or criminal convictions (the last two added by the Draft Regulation), are granted extra protection. The proposal is designed to enhance the rights of data subjects by introducing two distinct rights: the right to portability and the right to be forgotten. These rights are in addition to those provided for in Directive 95/46/EC, that is, the right to access, object, correct, and erase. The right of portability allows individuals to obtain a copy of their data from one service provider and transfer it easily to another; the right to be forgotten allows individuals to request the elimination of personal data that are no longer needed or wanted. Additional safeguards include new provisions on profiling, and a requirement that data controllers notify individuals in the event of a security breach in order to avoid identity fraud. The privacy of children and their right to personal data protection is also enhanced, because the draft regulation prohibits the processing of personal data of a child below the age of thirteen without the consent of a parent or guardian.

Companies are obliged to implement the principles of privacy by design and privacy by default early in their business practices. The first principle relates to a company's obligation to include data protection safeguards from the very beginning in the development of products or services, whereas the second requires that privacy-friendly default settings must be the norm. The draft regulation also strengthens the enforcement powers of data protection authorities, established under Directive 95/46/EC, by granting them the authority to impose a fine of €250,000 (about US$306,500) on individuals and administrative fines of up to 2% of global annual turnover on companies. Another innovation is that companies that employ more than 250 employees are required to appoint an independent data protection officer. Processors of personal data are required to notify data supervisory authorities within twenty-four hours when there is a security breach of personal data.

The scope of territorial applicability of the Regulation is broad. It will apply when a controller or processor is established in the EU and also to those established outside the EU who offer goods and services to data subjects in the EU or are involved in monitoring the behavior of individuals in the EU. Adequacy decisions verifying that a third country meets the EU standards will be further simplified and clarified. For transfers of personal data outside the EU, contractual clauses and simplified binding corporate rules will ensure that data processed outside the EU are adequately handled and protected.

The draft regulation will be further discussed in the Council and the Parliament and will enter into forcc two years after its publication in the Official Journal of the European Union.

Chapter 2 - The federal Privacy Act 1988 provides the framework for the protection of personal information in the online context in Australia. The law is intended to be technology-neutral and, rather than providing prescriptive rules, it sets out a principle-based approach that can be tailored to apply to different situations. Oversight and complaints functions are performed by an independent Privacy Commissioner. The legislation also provides for a degree of self-regulation on the part of industry groups and for the Privacy Commissioner to produce education and guidance material for businesses, government agencies, and the public. There is no established cause of action for invasion of privacy in Australian constitutional, statutory, or common law.

Major privacy reforms are being considered by the Australian parliament following a complete review of the legislation by the Australian Law Reform Commission in 2008. In 2011, a Senate committee also expressed some concerns about the adequacy of the current framework to protect online privacy following an investigation and submission process on this issue. Further proposals not in the present bill that may be developed by the government include a statutory cause of action for invasion of privacy, data retention requirements, new obligations relating to children and young people, and a mandatory data breach notification system.

In: Online Privacy Laws
Editor: Ethan P. Williams

ISBN: 978-1-62808-623-2

Chapter 1

ONLINE PRIVACY LAW (PART ONE): EUROPEAN UNION*

Theresa Papademetriou

EXECUTIVE SUMMARY

The right to data protection and the right to privacy are two distinct human rights recognized in the Charter of Fundamental Rights of the European Union, the Treaty on the Functioning of the EU (TFEU), and in two legal instruments of the Council of Europe, to which all the EU Member States are parties.

In January 2012, the European Commission proposed a major overhaul of the existing legislative framework on the protection of personal data. The reform was necessitated mainly by three factors: (a) new challenges posed by globalization and Internet developments in the area of online services, which impact the processing of personal data and endanger the privacy of individuals; (b) a new legal basis in the TFEU; and (c) a dramatic increase in Internet users and serious concerns expressed by 70% of individuals in the EU about the possible misuse of their personal data.

Landmark EU Directive 95/46/EC on the Protection of Individuals with Regard to the Processing of Personal Data on the Free Movement of Such Data, which was adopted in 1995 when the Internet was still in its infancy, met to some extent its twin objectives of safeguarding the personal data of individuals and improving the flow of personal data among EU Member States, but it resulted in diversity of implementation by the twenty-seven EU Members. By contrast, the pending proposal, which is in the form of a draft regulation because of its direct applicability in the legal systems of the Member States of the EU, will bring about greater harmonization of data protection rules, legal certainty, and transparency, and will also remove any obstacles in the flow of personal data within the single market and improve competition.

The draft regulation builds upon the fundamental principles on the processing of personal data established by Directive 95/46/EC. Thus, online processing of personal data is prohibited

---

* This report was released by The Law Library of Congress, Global Legal Research Center, June 2012.

unless it meets necessary safeguards and is based on one of the required legal grounds, such as consent or the protection of vital interests of data subjects. Special categories of data, such as data concerning race, ethnic origin, political affiliations, religion, genetic data, or criminal convictions (the last two added by the Draft Regulation), are granted extra protection.

The proposal is designed to enhance the rights of data subjects by introducing two distinct rights: the right to portability and the right to be forgotten. These rights are in addition to those provided for in Directive 95/46/EC, that is, the right to access, object, correct, and erase. The right of portability allows individuals to obtain a copy of their data from one service provider and transfer it easily to another; the right to be forgotten allows individuals to request the elimination of personal data that are no longer needed or wanted. Additional safeguards include new provisions on profiling, and a requirement that data controllers notify individuals in the event of a security breach in order to avoid identity fraud. The privacy of children and their right to personal data protection is also enhanced, because the draft regulation prohibits the processing of personal data of a child below the age of thirteen without the consent of a parent or guardian.

Companies are obliged to implement the principles of privacy by design and privacy by default early in their business practices. The first principle relates to a company's obligation to include data protection safeguards from the very beginning in the development of products or services, whereas the second requires that privacy-friendly default settings must be the norm.

The draft regulation also strengthens the enforcement powers of data protection authorities, established under Directive 95/46/EC, by granting them the authority to impose a fine of €250,000 (about US$306,500) on individuals and administrative fines of up to 2% of global annual turnover on companies. Another innovation is that companies that employ more than 250 employees are required to appoint an independent data protection officer. Processors of personal data are required to notify data supervisory authorities within twenty-four hours when there is a security breach of personal data.

The scope of territorial applicability of the Regulation is broad. It will apply when a controller or processor is established in the EU and also to those established outside the EU who offer goods and services to data subjects in the EU or are involved in monitoring the behavior of individuals in the EU. Adequacy decisions verifying that a third country meets the EU standards will be further simplified and clarified. For transfers of personal data outside the EU, contractual clauses and simplified binding corporate rules will ensure that data processed outside the EU are adequately handled and protected.

The draft regulation will be further discussed in the Council and the Parliament and will enter into force two years after its publication in the Official Journal of the European Union.

I. LEGAL FRAMEWORK

Under European Union (EU) law, the right to privacy and the right to protection of personal data are two distinct fundamental human rights.[1] The Charter of Fundamental Rights of the European Union (CFR), which acquired binding status on December 1, 2009, recognizes the right to privacy in article 7 and the right to the protection of one's personal data in article 8.[2] Furthermore, article 8 reaffirms the principle that personal data must be processed fairly and for specific purposes, based on the consent of the individual concerned or some other legitimate purposes laid down by law. It also recognizes the right of individuals to access the data collected and the right to have it rectified, in case of inaccuracy or incompleteness. Compliance with such rules is entrusted to the control of an independent authority established by EU Member States.[3] In a society, the right to personal data may be restricted by law in order to strike a balance with the freedoms and rights of others and with the general interest, subject to the principle of proportionality, which is established in the EU and legal systems of the Member States.[4]

In addition, the Treaty on the Functioning of the European Union (TFEU), recognizes the right of every individual to his/her personal data.[5] It also introduced a new and specific legal basis for the adoption of rules on data protection and grants the authority to the EU legislative bodies (Parliament and Council) to adopt rules concerning the processing of personal data by EU institutions, bodies, and Member States, and to ensure that compliance with such rules is assigned to the control and review of independent authorities.[6]

II. Current EU Law

A. Directives

Social networking, or "online services" as it is referred to in EU terminology, falls within the scope of the basic framework of Directive 95/46/EC on the Protection of Individuals with Regard to the Processing of Personal Data and on the Free Movement of Such Data[7] (hereafter the Data Protection Directive) because it involves the processing of personal data of users. The Data Protection Directive was designed to achieve two basic objectives: (1) protect the fundamental right to the personal data of data subjects; and (2) ensure the free flow of personal data in the internal market.

The Data Protection Directive was transposed by the twenty-seven EU Member States[8] and the three European Economic Area States: Iceland, Liechtenstein, and Norway.[9] Switzerland has also implemented the Directive in the areas related to the Schengen Agreement[10]. The Commission's 2002 report on the transposition of Directive 95/46/EC and its subsequent Communication in 2007[11] concluded that the Data Protection Directive had partially achieved its twin objectives of safeguarding the right to personal data and facilitating the flow of such data within the EU.[12] The Commission noted that the Directive "did not manage to fully achieve its internal market policy objective," or to remove obstacles in implementation across the EU. Existing divergences among EU Members relate to the interpretation of such key terms as "controller," "personal data," and "in enforcement."[13]

In addition to the Data Protection Directive, online services are also governed by the following Directives:

- Directive 2002/58/EC Concerning the Processing of Personal Data and the Protection of Privacy in the Electronic Communications Sector (Directive on Privacy and Electronic Communications)[14]

- Directive 2006/24/EC on the Retention of Data Generated in Connection with the Provision of Publicly Available Electronic Communications Services or of Public Communications Networks and Amending Directive 2002/58/EC[15]
- Directive 2009/136/EC Amending Directive 2002/58/EC on Universal Service and Users' Rights Relating to Electronic Communications Networks and Services[16]

B. Regulation

EU institutions are also bound to protect the fundamental rights and freedoms of individuals, in particular their right to privacy and personal data protection, by virtue of Regulation (EC) No. 45/2001 on the Protection of Individuals with Regard to the Processing of Personal Data by the Community Institutions and Bodies and on the Free Movement of Such Data.[17]

C. Definitions

The Data Protection Directive introduced some key concepts that have been used in subsequent EU legislation on personal data protection. It defines "personal data" as "any information relating to an identified or identifiable natural person ('data subject')."[18] The broad definition has resulted in differences of interpretation among EU Members. The Commission has noted that IP addresses, which identify computers on networks; digital pictures; geo-location data; and telephone numbers are considered to be personal data by some EU Members, while others define them as such only under certain conditions.[19] An "identifiable person" is a natural person who can be identified either by an identifiable number or on the basis of some elements, including his/her physical, physiological, mental, economic, cultural, or social identity.[20] "Processing of personal data" means "any operation or set of operations which is performed upon personal data, whether or not by automatic means."[21]

The Data Protection Directive provides a nonexhaustive list of what constitutes processing. Thus, "processing" is a very broad term and includes the following: collection, recording, storage, organization, alteration or adaptation, use, disclosure, retrieval, alignment, combination, blocking, erasure, or dissemination or otherwise making data available.[22]

The Data Protection Directive also differentiates between "controller" and "processor." The term "controller" means any natural or legal person, public authority, agency, or any other body that jointly with others or alone determines the purposes and means of processing of personal data.

"Processor" is defined as a natural or legal person or public authority, agency, or other body that "processes personal data on behalf of the controller."[23] In many instances, the roles of the controller and processor are not easily distinguishable. Whether an organization is a controller or a processor and the applicable criteria for each designation were clarified by the Article 29 Working Party, which was established by the Data Protection Directive in Opinion 1/2010 on the Concepts of "Controller" and Processor."[24]

D. Fundamental Principles Governing Personal Data Processing

Under the Data Protection Directive, all processing of personal data must (subject to some exceptions provided in article 13) comply with the principles related to data quality prescribed in article 6 and with one of the six grounds for making data processing legitimate, as contained in article 7. Article 7 contains an exhaustive and restrictive list of grounds.

Specifically, in compliance with article 6 of the Data Protection Directive, controllers of online services who deal with personal data must ensure that personal data are

- processed fairly and lawfully;
- gathered for specific, explicit, and legitimate purposes and not further processed in a manner incompatible with those purposes (processing for historical, statistical, or scientific purposes shall not be deemed in violation of the directive, if the EU Members provide further safeguards);
- adequate, relevant, and not excessive to the purpose the data were initially collected;
- accurate and current, where possible (inaccurate data must be either corrected or deleted; and
- kept in a form that allows identification of the data subject for no longer than is necessary for the purposes for which the data were gathered or for which they are further processed.[25]

E. Grounds for Processing of Personal Data

As stated above, processing—that is, collection, storage, and use of personal data—by online media or services is prohibited. The Data Protection Directive provides six legal grounds for processing. Consequently, processing is lawful in the following instances:

- Where the data subject has granted its unambiguous consent
- To perform a contract in which one of the parties is the data subject
- To enable the controller to comply with a legal obligation
- To protect the vital interests of the data subject
- To perform a task for the public interest or in the exercise of an official authority vested in the controller
- To pursue legitimate interests by the controller or third parties who have become privy to such data, unless the protected interests of the data subject override those of the controller or third parties[26]

The last ground requires a balancing act between the interests of the data subject and those of the controller or third parties to whom the data have been disclosed. The Commission's First Report on Implementation of the General Directive has clarified that the factors to be taken under consideration in such a case include the nature of the data, the nature of processing, and whether the action is carried out by the private or public sector.

The Commission also indicates that implementation of this test differs among EU Members.[27] Several EU Member States adopt a strict interpretation of this ground and decide in favor of the data subject or limit its application to certain categories of data.[28]

F. Processing of Special Categories of Data

Online services are not permitted to process certain data because of their sensitive nature. These data relate to one's racial or ethnic origin, political opinions, religious or philosophical beliefs, trade-union membership, and the processing of data related to one's health or sex life.[29]

However, the Data Protection Directive allows the processing of such data, inter alia, where

- the data subject has granted explicit consent;
- processing is necessary so that the controller can carry out obligations and rights in the field of employment, and is authorized by national law;
- processing is necessary to protect the vital interests of the data subject;
- processing is carried out in the course of legitimate activities by a foundation or association that has political, philosophical, religious, or trade-union objectives, with appropriate guarantees and with the condition that such processing relates to the entity's members or those having regular contact with the entity; or
- processing relates to data made public by the data subject or is necessary in connection with a legal claim.[30]

In case of offenses or criminal convictions or security measures, data can be processed only by an official authority[31]

G. Exemptions

The Data Protection Directive permits EU Member States to adopt legislation to restrict the rights of data subjects for the following reasons, including

- national security, public security, and defense;
- prevention, investigation, detection, and prosecution of criminal offenses or violations related to codes of ethics of regulated professions;
- important economic or financial interests of the EU or a Member State; and
- the protection of data subjects or the rights and freedoms of others.[32]

In addition, the Privacy and Electronic Communications Directive allows the adoption of legislative measures by the EU Members to retain personal data for a limited period and for the purposes stated above.[33]

H. Consent

The Data Protection Directive defines "the data subject's consent" as "any freely given specific and informed indication" of the data subject's wishes that signifies his or her agreement to the processing of personal data.[34] Thus, consent must meet the requirements of being (a) freely given, (b) specific, and (c) informed. In Opinion 15/2011 on the Definition of Consent, the Article 29 Working Party emphasized the significance of consent in the processing of personal data.[35] It clarified that in many instances, consent cannot be granted freely—for instance, due to the relationship between the data subject and the controller or in cases of personal data provided to public authorities. Under those circumstances the word "freely" means that it must be given free of intimidation or deception. On the other hand, "informed" consent means the data subject understands well the context and substance of what it means to his or her personal data.[36] The Directive on Privacy and Electronic Communications builds upon these principles and clarifies in recital 17 that "[c]onsent may be given by any appropriate method enabling a freely given specific and informed indication of the user's wishes, including by ticking a box when visiting an Internet website."[37]

I. Rights of Data Subjects

1. Right of Access

One of the basic rights of data subjects is the right to access their personal data. The right to access involves the right to receive, free of charge, notification as to whether data are being processed and information on the purpose of processing, categories of data being processed, and individuals or organizations to whom the data are disclosed.[38]

Data subjects also have the right to rectify, erase, or block the processing of data that are incompatible with the provisions of the Data Protection Directive, or of data that are incomplete and inaccurate.[39] Furthermore, they have the right to request that the controller notify third parties who are recipients of personal data about the correction.[40]

2. Right to Object

Data subjects have the right to object

- at any time on "compelling legitimate grounds" regarding the processing of their personal data carried out for the performance of a task for public interest reasons, in the exercise of official authority exercised by the controller, or when processing is necessary for the legitimate interests of the controller; and
- where processing is for the purpose of direct marketing.[41]

J. Installation of Technical and Organizational Security Measures

The Personal Data Protection Directive introduced the general requirement that the controller must put in place "appropriate technical and organizational measures" designed to safeguard personal data against unlawful destruction, accidental loss, alteration, unauthorized access, or disclosure, especially where the processing entails the transmission of data over a network.[42] The measures must be appropriate to the risk involved and to the nature of data processed, taking into account the state of the art available and the cost of implementing such measures.[43]

In addition, when processing is performed by a processor on behalf of a controller, the processor must also provide guarantees that the processing will be done in compliance with technical and organizational measures.[44] In such a case, the working relationship between the controller and processor must be dealt with through a contract specifying that the processor must only act based on instructions by the processor.[45]

The Privacy and Electronic Communications Directive contains the same language, requiring providers of publicly available electronic communications services to adopt organizational and technical measures in order to provide security for its services.[46] Directive 2009/136/EC, which amended the E-Privacy Directive, added the following additional requirements that the adopted security measures must meet:

- Ensure that only authorized people can access personal data for lawful purposes
- Protect personal data that are stored or transmitted against accidental loss or unlawful destruction
- Ensure the implementation of security policy[47]

In case of a breach of personal data, the provider of publicly available electronic communications services must notify (a) the competent national authority, and (b) the subscriber or individual if the breach is likely to adversely affect his or her personal data or privacy.[48]

The Data Retention Directive (discussed below) also requires the adoption of appropriate technical and organizational measures in order to safeguard data that have been retained against accidental loss; accidental destruction; or unauthorized storage, processing, access, or disclosure. These measures must also ensure that such data can only be accessed by authorized personnel.[49]

K. Data Collection by Smartphone Applications

The relevant legal framework on data collection by smartphone applications is the Personal Data Protection Directive. In Opinion 13/2011 on Geolocation Services on Smart Mobile Devices the Article 29 Working Party expressed the view that the Personal Data Protection Directive applies in all cases where personal data are being processed as the result of the processing of location data.[50]

The Privacy and Electronic Communications Directive, as revised by Directive 2009/136/EC, only applies to the processing of base station data by telework operators. Telework operators process base station data within the framework of offering public electronic communications services. Article 2(c) of Directive 2009/136 defines "location data" as "any data processed in an electronic communications network or by an electronic communications service, indicating the geographic position of the terminal equipment of a user of a publicly available electronic communications service."[51] Consequently, because location data derived from base stations relate to an identified or identifiable natural person, they are subject to the Data Protection Directive.

Users have the right to receive from different controllers access to location data collected from their smart mobile devices as well as information on the purpose of processing including recipients to whom the data are disclosed.[52] The E-Privacy Directive introduced a mandatory notification requirement where personal data is breached.[53]

L. Limits on Geodata

The processing of location data from smart mobile devices is not allowed unless the data subject has granted his or her prior informed consent. The consent must also meet the requirements of being specific to the type of purposes for which the data are processed, and the subject must be given the option of withdrawing consent. The data subject must also have the same rights provided by the Data Protection Directive—i.e., the right to access, rectify, or erase any profiles created based on the collection and processing of location data.[54] When location data other than the traffic data of users of publicly available electronic communications services are processed, such data may only be processed if they are made anonymous or with the consent of the users, to the extent and for the duration necessary to provide value-added service.[55]

Moreover, the service provider is responsible for notifying users, prior to obtaining their consent, of the type of location data (other than traffic data), the purposes and duration of the processing, and whether their location data will be forwarded to a third party. Users must be given the option to withdraw their consent at any time.[56]

M. Protection of Minors

Although the privacy right of children is enshrined in several international legal instruments,[57] there are no specific rules pertaining to the personal data of children in either the Data Protection Directive or the Privacy and Electronic Communications Directive. Because the scope of both Directives extends to the data of "every natural person," however, the built-in safeguards arguably apply to both children and adults. Consequently, the general principles on data quality contained in the Personal Data Protection Directive, such as fairness, proportionality, and relevance, apply to children. In addition, the general obligations that only adequate, relevant, and nonexcessive data can be collected and processed govern the processing of the personal data of children. In general, controllers must take into account the circumstances of a child and his/her best interests. Moreover, the personal data of children must be accurate and current; inaccurate or incomplete data must either be erased or corrected.

The Data Protection Directive's article 7 on the legality of processing and article 9 on the processing of personal categories of data are also applicable to children. As far as the right of access, it can be exercised either by the child based on his/her maturity level, or by the child's representative. Children's data cannot be used for purposes other than those for which they were collected.

The Article 29 Data Protection Working Party has issued a number of opinions on the protection of personal data of children, including an opinion addressed to school authorities, Opinion 2/2009 on the Protection of Children's Personal Data (General Guidelines and the Special Case of Schools).[58]

N. Retention of Data

Directive 2006/24/EC on the Retention of Data Generated or Processed in Connection with the Provision of Publicly Available Electronic Communications Services or of Public Communications Networks and Amending Directive 2002/58/EC[59] (hereafter, the Data Retention Directive) requires EU Members to adopt legislation ensuring that operators of publicly available electronic communications services or networks retain traffic and location data generated from fixed and mobile telephony, Internet access, and Internet email and telephony for a period of six months and up to two years to investigate, detect, and prosecute serious crime. [60]

Article 5 of the Date Retention Directive specifies that the following categories of data must be retained, with specific data types depending on whether it is fixed network or mobile telephony, or Internet email and Internet telephony:

- Data necessary to trace and indentify the source of a communication
- Data necessary to identify the destination of a communication

EU Members were obliged to transpose Directive 2006/24/EC by September 15, 2007, with the option of postponing certain obligations related to Internet access, email, and telephony by a March 15, 2009, deadline. In April 2011, the Commission published its evaluation report on implementation of the Data Retention Directive.[61] EU Members responded that data retention is "very valuable and in some cases indispensable, for preventing and combating crime, for protecting victims and for the acquittal of the innocent in criminal cases."[62]

The Commission also noted that requests to access stored data by law enforcement authorities is constantly increasing and that the number of requests varies considerably among the EU Member States.[63]

As of April 2011, twenty-five EU Members had notified the Commission of their transposition of the Data Retention Directive; however, in Romania, Germany, and the Czech Republic, the transposition laws have been annulled by the respective constitutional courts.[64] On May 31, 2012, the Commission referred Germany to the European Court of Justice for not complying with its obligation to transpose the Data Retention Directive after the initial transposition law adopted by Germany was annulled by the German Federal Constitutional Court in 2010.

The Commission suggested that the ECJ impose a daily penalty payment of €315,036.54 (about US$396,260).[65] In addition, the Commission announced its intention to discontinue its proceedings against Austria based on Austria's notification of measures that fully transpose the Data Retention Directive into national law, and to partially withdraw charges against Sweden.[66]

O. Remedies and Sanctions

EU Members are required to provide means of redress to data subjects whose personal data have been infringed. Thus, the Personal Data Protection Directive provides data subjects with the following rights:

- Administrative remedies before the national supervisory authority[67]
- Judicial remedies for any breach of rights guaranteed by national law[68]
- Compensation by the controller for the damage suffered for any processing in violation of the rules; a controller may avoid liability in whole or in part, however, by proving that he/she is not responsible for the violation[69]

When implementing EU law, Member States are also obliged to make provisions in their national legislation for sanctions to be imposed in case of infringement.[70]

Users of online services whose personal data are unlawfully processed also have the same remedies on the basis of the Privacy and Electronic Communications Directives.[71] Moreover, data subjects whose personal data have been retained in violation of the Data Retention Directive enjoy the same remedies as those provided to data subjects based on the Personal Data Protection Directive.[72]

P. Transfer of Personal Data to Third Countries outside the EU

The Data Protection Directive has extraterritorial application and prohibits the transfer of personal data that are undergoing processing, or will be processed after the transfer, to third countries (outside the EU) that do not meet the standard of "an adequate level of protection."[73] In the case of transfers, the preliminary question that must be examined is what constitutes a transfer, within and outside the EU. The Data Protection Directive does not provide a definition of "transfer," but the concept of international transfer was clarified in the *Bodil Lindqvist* case heard before the European Court of Justice. The ECJ held that the mere publication of data on the Internet is not a transfer of data to a third country outside the EU, even though the data is accessible to Internet users in other countries.[74] The ECJ reasoned that the data were not sent automatically from the server to other Internet users, but users instead had to access the data on their own, and that there was no direct transfer of personal data between the person who loaded the information and the persons accessing it on the Internet.[75] Thus, the criterion is whether data have actually been received in a third country. It is not sufficient that the data were available on the Internet.[76]

The adequacy standard is assessed based on a number of factors related to the transfer, including the nature of the data, the purpose and duration of processing of the data, the country of origin and country of final destination, and the existing general or sectoral rules of law in the third country or international commitments assumed by the third country.[77] EU Members are required to notify each other and the Commission if a country does not meet the adequacy criterion.[78] If the Commission finds that the third country does not meet the criterion, the EU Members are required to prohibit any transfer. The Directive empowered the

Commission to enter into negotiations with a third country to remedy the situation, however.[79]

The Article 29 Working Party established a functional test to review the adequacy criterion. In its 1998 Opinion on transfers, it developed a number of substantive and procedural criteria to reach a conclusion that a particular country meets the adequacy standard, including

- purpose limitation;
- data quality and proportionality;
- transparency and security;
- rights to access, rectify, and object; and
- existing enforcement mechanisms.[80]

The Data Protection Directive contains a number of derogations to the general prohibition on transfers to a third country. Thus, national law may provide that a transfer of personal data to a third country that does not meet the adequacy criterion is possible on several grounds, including, inter alia, the following:

- Where the individual has granted his unambiguous consent to the proposed transfer
- Where the transfer is necessary for the performance of a contract between the individual and the controller
- Where the transfer is necessary for the protection of the vital interests of the individual
- Where the transfer is necessary or is required by law based on significant public interest grounds[81]

Q. EU Members' Authorization

EU Members may also authorize a transfer of personal data to a third country that does not meet the adequacy criterion if the controller adopts one of two options to ensure that personal data are protected: (a) contractual clauses, or (b) corporate binding rules.[82] A controller who intends to use contractual clauses may avail him or herself of standard contractual clauses adopted by the Commission or other customized clauses. No prior authorization is needed for a transfer of data if standard contractual clauses are used. Corporate binding rules are designed to be used by multinational corporations that transfer tremendous amounts of data within a group of companies when some are outside the EU.[83] EU Members must notify the Commission and other EU Members of authorizations granted.

R. Safe Harbor Agreement

The US Department of Commerce and the European Commission have concluded a Safe Harbor Agreement to ensure that personal data transfers from the EU to the US meet the required adequacy criterion. US corporations that are or will be engaged in the processing of

EU data are legally obliged to adhere to the standards, as contained in the Directive. The Safe Harbor Agreement contains the Safe Harbor Principles[84] and a set of "Frequently Asked Questions."[85] The European Commission has issued decisions on the adequacy of the protection of personal data in third countries with regard to the domestic law of the following countries and the listed arrangements: Andorra, Argentina, Australia, Canada, Switzerland, the Faeroe Islands, Guernsey, the State of Israel, the Isle of Man, Jersey, the US Department of Commerce's Safe Harbor Privacy Principles, and the transfer of Air Passenger Name Record Data to US Customs and Border Protection.[86]

III. European Court of Justice Decisions

A. Limitations on the Right to Personal Data

In general, the right to privacy and right to protection of personal data are subject to limitations imposed by the principle of proportionality and the case law of the European Court of Justice (ECJ). Most of the legal issues on data protection that reach the ECJ are in the form of requests for a preliminary ruling forwarded by the national courts.

The European Court of Justice (ECJ) held in the case of *Volker und Markus Schecke v. Land Hessen* that the right to protection of personal data is not an absolute right, but must be viewed in relation to its function in society and be balanced against any other fundamental human rights based on the principle of proportionately.[87] Proportionality, a well-established principle in the legal order of the EU Members and the case law of the ECJ, allows limitations on the exercise of fundamental rights as long as they are provided by law and respect the core of such rights. Article 52(1) of the Charter of Fundamental Rights provides that "subject to the principle of proportionality, limitations may be made only if they are necessary and genuinely meet the objectives of general interest recognized by the Union or the need to protect the rights and freedoms of others."[88] In the *Schecke* judgment, the ECJ held that the pursuit of the objectives of the EU must be balanced with the fundamental rights of article 7 and 8 of the Charter, dealing with privacy and personal data protection. Specifically, the ECJ held that the Council and Commission must balance the European Union's interest in increasing security by fighting crime against "the interference with the right of the beneficiaries concerned to respect for their private life in general and to the protection of their personal data in particular."[89]

B. Downloading Songs Illegally

On February 16, 2012, the ECJ rendered an important judgment on the illegal downloading of songs by Internet users. The ECJ held that online social networking sites cannot be forced to take measures, such as installing filtering systems, in order to prevent users from downloading songs illegally.[90] The case arose in 2009 when Sabam, a Belgian national music royalty collecting society, sought an injunction from the Court of First Instance in Belgium to require Netlog—a social networking site similar to Twitter and Facebook—to take measures in order to prevent users from downloading songs illegally or pay a penalty of €1,000 daily in the case of noncompliance. The Belgian Court asked for a preliminary ruling on whether European Union law precludes a national court from issuing an injunction against an Internet service hosting provider that obliges it to install a filtering system at its own expense and for an unlimited period, which would apply indiscriminately to all of its users.

The ECJ first confirmed that Netlog meets the requirements of a hosting service provider, that the filtering system would enable Netlog to identify all the files stored on its servers by the service users, and that those files may contain works that belong to copyright holders. Consequently, the ECJ reasoned, hosting service providers such as Netlog would have to ascertain which of these stored files contain works that are unavailable to the users unlawfully and would have to prevent such files through filtering systems.[91]

The ECJ noted that national authorities, in protecting the rights of copyright holders, must balance the rights of such holders against the fundamental rights of users, such as the right to their personal data and the right to receive and impart information, which would likely be impacted by such measures. The ECJ affirmed that the e-Commerce Directive prohibits the "general monitoring of the information stored on its servers." The ECJ held that

> in adopting an injunction requiring the hosting service provider to install such a filtering system, the national court would not be respecting the requirement that a fair balance be struck between the right to intellectual property, on the one hand, and the freedom to conduct business, the right to protection of personal data and the freedom to receive or impart information, on the other.[92]

C. Annulment of the US-EU Passenger Name Record Agreement

On May 30, 2006, the ECJ annulled the Commission's Decision of the adequacy finding and the Council Decision related to the conclusion of a Passenger Name Record Agreement between the US and the EU.[93]

On December 11, 2011, the Council of the EU adopted a decision on the Conclusion of the Agreement between the United States of America and the European Union on the Use and Transfer of Passenger Name Records to the United States Department of Homeland and Security.[94]

IV. Public and Scholarly Opinion

A public consultation was initiated by the Commission following the publication of its 2010 Communication, "A Comprehensive Approach on Personal Data Protection in the European Union," with a deadline of January 2011.[95] The Commission received a total of 305 responses—54 from citizens, 31 from public authorities and 220 from business associations, and nongovernmental organizations. The respondents provided opinions on issues identified as critical by the Commission. On improving individuals' rights, the majority of stakeholders felt that "the current lack of harmonization is detrimental to economic activity within the EU."[96]

Big companies were keen on having a uniform framework. On increasing transparency of the processing of personal data, even though this principle is embedded in the Personal Data Directive, some respondents called for improvement of the current status. The protection of children from online activities was of paramount importance to citizens. Many respondents urged the adoption of a cut-off age and specific requirements for the processing of children's data, while others called for no specific and detailed provisions on children based on differing rules for the definition of a child among EU Members and the divergence in maturity levels in children.

In particular, the issue of data protection authorities was among other issues that drew concern, including data minimization, the right to be forgotten, data portability, and ensuring informed and free consent. Data protection authorities, public institutions and the European Data Protection Supervisor (EDPS) endorsed the initiative of introducing data protection officers, albeit with some skepticism due to the financial and administrative burdens associated with them.[97]

Eurobarometer, the Commission's public opinion analysis section, conducted a large-scale survey of attitudes of European citizens toward the processing of personal data protection and privacy issues.[98] Some notable highlights include the following:

- Six out of ten Internet users usually read privacy statements and 70% of those modify their decisions accordingly[99]
- 62% of Europeans provide the minimum data required
- 70% of Europeans believe that their personal data held by companies could be used for other purposes than those originally collected[100]
- 74% of Europeans view the disclosure of personal data as part of technological developments and globalization
- The majority of Europeans feel uncomfortable about internet profiling 101
- 98% of the participants in Greece and Cyprus; 97% in the Czech Republic; and 96% in Ireland, Malta, and Slovakia responded that specific consent is required prior to processing[102]

During a conference in Luxembourg in May 2012, the European Union Data Protection Commissioners (130 commissioners from thirty-eight European countries) adopted a Resolution on the pending EU and Council of Europe reforms. The Resolution endorsed the following proposals from the EU proposed legislative package:

- Codification of the principle of data minimization
- More options for redress granted to data subjects whose data are violated
- Specific provisions on children, the right to be forgotten, and the right of portability
- Strengthening the right of access and the right to object[103]

V. Pending Reforms

Since 1995, when the EU put in place fundamental rules on personal data protection, technology and globalization have drastically affected the processing of personal data. Social networks altered the methods of sharing information and the advent of cloud computing, by which more data is stored on remote servers rather than personal computers, poses new challenges.[104] At the same time, the 1995 Data Protection Directive did not achieve the anticipated level of harmonization of data protection rules in the EU. Meanwhile, according to estimates, 250 million people are daily users of the Internet in Europe,[105] and European citizens are becoming increasingly aware of risks to their privacy and personal data posed by online activities. The Commission's 2010 Communication, A Comprehensive Approach on Personal Data Protection in the European Union, emphasized that the EU "needs a more comprehensive and coherent policy on the fundamental right to personal data protection."[106] The Commission's efforts have garnered support from the Parliament[107] and the Justice and Home Affairs Council of the EU. The latter, in its February 2011 conclusions, agreed with a number of the proposed changes.[108]

On January 25, 2012, the European Commission published its proposal for the reform of EU legislation on data protection. The twin objectives of the proposal remain the same as that of the Data Protection Directive. The pending reform is designed to meet the challenges posed by contemporary Internet developments and to safeguard personal data irrespective of future changes in technology and the digital environment.

The Commission's reform package contains two legislative pieces: (a) a draft regulation on the Processing of Individuals with Regard to the Processing of Personal Data and on the Free Movement of Such Data (General Data Protection Regulation),[109] and (b) a Directive on the Protection of Individuals with Regard to the Processing of Personal Data by Competent Authorities for Criminal Offenses.[110] The Commission opted for a regulation because of its direct applicability in the legal order of the EU Member States and because, once it is enforced, it will result in greater legal certainty and improve the protection of personal data of individuals. The draft regulation is based on the new legal basis established by article 16 of the TFEU, and once adopted by the Council and the Parliament it will repeal the Data Protection Directive.

In its March 2012 Opinion on the Data Protection Reform Proposals,[111] the Article 29 Data Working Party endorsed certain proposals contained in the draft regulation that are designed to improve data subjects' rights, enhance the responsibility of controllers, and strengthen the position of supervisory authorities at the national and international levels.[112] However, it criticized the introduction of a separate Directive to protect personal data in the area of police and criminal justice because of its potential to result in less consistency and less protection of data subjects.[113] Moreover, it opined that the provisions of the Directive need to be aligned with those of the Regulation, so that personal data are well safeguarded. The Data Protection Working Party expressed its regret that neither instrument deals with the issue of the collection and transfer of data by private parties or non-law enforcement public authorities for law enforcement purposes. It also expressed its reservations regarding the Commission's authority, granted by the draft regulation, to adopt delegated and implementing acts to fully implement the regulation.[114]

A. Definitions and Basic Principles

The draft regulation incorporates the same definitions introduced by the Data Protection Directive, while modifying and improving others. It also defines new terms, such as "genetic data," "biometric data," "data concerning health," "group of undertakings," "binding corporate rules," "child," and "supervisory authority."[115] In general, the draft regulation applies the same principles on data protection as those introduced by article 6 of the Data Protection Directive. The draft regulation adds the principles of transparency, clarifies the data minimization principle, and reinforces a comprehensive scheme of responsibilities and liabilities of the controller. The draft regulation requires controllers and processors to implement a number of policies and technical and organizational measures to ensure data security.[116] A significant innovation is the requirement of notification of the supervisory authority within twenty-four hours in case of a personal data breach,[117] and notification of the data subject if the breach will adversely affect the privacy and personal data of individuals.[118] Moreover, it also imposes an obligation on controllers and processors to maintain documentation of all processing operations under their responsibility.[119]

B. Processing of Special Categories of Data

The draft regulation prohibits the processing of personal data that indicate race or ethnic origin, political opinions, religion or beliefs, and trade union membership, and the processing of genetic data or data concerning the subject's health or sex life, criminal convictions, or related security measures.[120] The list of special categories of data is broader than that of the Data Protection Directive because it includes genetic data, criminal convictions, and related security measures.

The Regulation permits the processing of sensitive data under safeguards similar to those provided for in article 8 of the Data Protection Directive.

C. Processing of Health Data

The processing of health data is given added protection by the draft regulation. Thus, processing of such data is permitted on the basis of EU law or Member State law, which must include suitable safeguards to protect the interests of the data subjects, and for the following reasons:

- For preventive or occupational medicine, medical diagnosis, or health care services subject to professional secrecy[121]
- Public interest reasons in the field of public health or in areas such as social protection[122]
- For historical, statistical, or scientific research purposes with the proviso that such purposes cannot otherwise be fulfilled[123]

D. Conditions for Consent

The draft regulation provides a more comprehensive definition of consent than that of the Data Protection Directive through the addition of the word "explicit." This means "any freely given specific, informed and *explicit* indication" of the data subject's wishes that is either provided in a statement or in a clear affirmative action indicates agreement to personal data being processed.[124]

The Regulation places the burden of proof of the data subject's consent on the controller who processes the personal data for specified purposes. Individuals have the right to withdraw their consent at any time. When there is a significant imbalance between the position of the data subject and the controller, mere consent given by an individual will not provide the basis for processing.[125]

E. Data Protection by Design and by Default

An innovation of the draft regulation is the requirement that controllers must incorporate appropriate technical and organizational measures at an early stage when they determine the means of processing and also at the time of processing itself.[126] Moreover, processors will be required to ensure that, by default, only those data are processed "which are necessary for each specific purpose of the processing," and that such data are not retained in larger quantities or for a longer period of time than is necessary.[127]

The privacy by design principle is also espoused by the US Federal Trade Commission, which incorporates this principle as one of its key recommendations to companies in a March 2012 report on protecting consumer privacy.[128]

F. Rights of the Data Subject

The draft regulation introduces a new requirement for controllers to provide transparent, easily accessible, and understandable information on personal data protection.[129] Controllers are obliged to inform the data subjects without delay and at the latest within one month of receipt of the request whether any action has been taken regarding any rectification or erasure pertaining to his/her personal data.[130]

G. Right to Rectification

Data subjects have the right to request that the controller rectify personal data that are inaccurate and communicate such rectification to the data subject.[131]

H. Right to Be Forgotten and to Erase

Data subjects have the right to obtain from the controller the erasure of personal data and assurance that the controller will abstain from further dissemination of such data, especially of data made available by the data subject related to his/her childhood and when one of the following reasons apply:

- The data are no longer needed in relation to the purpose for which they were initially collected or processed
- The data subject has withdrawn his/her consent on which the processing was based, or the storage period has expired
- The data subject objects to the processing of personal data on grounds related to his/her particular situation
- The processing of data is not compatible with the Regulation for other reasons132

I. Right to Data Portability

The draft regulation provides for a new right for data subjects not previously included in the Data Protection Directive: the right of data portability.[133] This right grants the data subject, when personal data are processed by electronic means, the right to obtain from the controller a copy of data that are processed in an electronic and structured format and, which allows for further use by the data subject.[134]

J. Right to Object

The right to object is entrusted to data subjects at any time during processing where the objection is based on grounds such as safeguarding the vital interests of the data subject, performing a task carried out in the public interest, or for purposes of the legitimate interests of the controller. As far as direct marketing, the data subject will have the right to object free of charge. Such a right will be available to the data subject in a manner that is easily understood and is distinct from other information.[135]

K. Profiling

The draft regulation introduces a distinct article related to profiling measures, in contrast to the Data Protection Directive, which did not specifically address this issue. Article 20 of the draft regulation states that every data subject

> [s]hall have the right not to be subject to a measure which produces legal effects concerning this natural person or significantly affects this natural person, and which is based solely on automated processing intended to evaluate certain personal aspects relating to this natural person or to analyze or predict in particular the natural person's performance at work, economic situation, location, health, personal preferences, reliability or behavior.[136]

Profiling of a data subject is possible in the following instances:

- Processing of personal data is necessary for entering into or performing a contract that was initiated by the data subject and suitable safeguards have been added

- Processing is expressly authorized either in the laws of EU Member States or in EU legislation (national legislation must also provide additional safeguards to protect the legitimate interests of a data subject)
- The data subject has given his/her consent, subject to the specific requirements pertaining to consent, as included in article 7[137]

The Article 29 Working Party, in its Opinion 01/2012, agreed with the conditions on profiling.[138] However, it opined that the issue of profiling is a complex one in an online environment, that profiling should not be limited to automated processing, and that the term "significantly affects" is vague. It also opined that profiling should cover the creation of personal profiles by social networks or the creation of motion profiles by mobile applications.[139]

L. Protection of Minors

Article 8, paragraph 1 of the draft regulation requires that consent be given or authorized by a child's parent or legal guardian when the information society offers services directly to a child and the child concerned is below the age of thirteen. Only upon consent by the appropriate parent or legal guardian is the processing of a child's personal data lawful.[140] General contract law provisions of the EU Members with regard to the formation, validity, or effect of a contract as it relates to a child remain unaffected. The Commission has the power to adopt delegated acts regarding specific criteria and requirements in order to obtain "verifiable consent," and the Commission may also establish standard forms for specific ways to obtain verifiable consent.[141]

VI. Role of Data Protection Authorities

A. EU Level: European Data Protection Supervisor

Similarly to the EU Member States, which are bound by the EU legislation on data protection, EU institutions and bodies are required to ensure that the right to privacy and the right of personal data protection are respected. The European Data Protection Supervisor, an independent supervisory authority, was established on the basis of article 41 of Regulation 45/2001,[142] and is in charge of ensuring that EU institutions adhere to the rules on protection of personal data. It also monitors the application of the said Regulation and other EU legislation on personal data and advises the Community institutions on any aspect affecting personal data.[143]

The draft regulation proposes the establishment of a European Data Protection Board (EDPB). The EDPB will be an independent body and will play an advisory role to the Commission. It will consist of the head of the supervisory authority of each Member State and the European Data Protection Supervisor.[144] It will replace the Article 29 Working Party on the Protection of Individuals with Regard to the Processing of Personal Data, created under the Personal Data Protection Directive. National supervisory authorities will be required to communicate any draft measure that may, inter alia, affect the free movement of personal data to the EDPB and the Commission.[145]

B. Member States

Similarly to the Data Protection Directive, the draft regulation requires each Member to designate one or more public authorities to monitor the application of the rules of the Regulation. One supervisory authority will act as a contact point and participate in the EDPB. Members of national supervisory authorities must be appointed by the parliament or the government of each EU Member and be selected from among individuals whose independence is beyond any doubt.

The draft regulation expands the role of the supervisory authorities to cooperate with each other and with the Commission. Based on the decision of the ECJ in the case of *Commission v. Germany*, which dealt with the independence of supervisory authorities, the Draft Regulation also expands on the independence of supervisory authorities.[146] Each supervisory authority has competence within the territory of the Member State where it is located. The draft regulation proposes a "one-stop shop" by which a supervisory authority is granted additional competence when a controller or a processor is established in several Member States.[147] The supervisory authority is required to prepare annual reports describing the application and enforcement of data protection rules in the individual Member States.

The draft regulation makes a distinction between duties assigned to the supervisory authorities and powers bestowed on them. Supervisory authorities have the following duties:

- Monitoring the application of the provisions of the draft regulation
- Hearing and investigating complaints either on its own initiative or based on complaints by the data subject, which must be handled free of charge
- Approving binding rules
- Issuing opinions on the draft codes of conduct adopted pursuant to article 38(2)
- Promoting public awareness of the risks, rules, safeguards, and rights of individuals[148]

Some of the key powers of the supervisory authorities are the following:

- Notifying the controller or the processor of an alleged breach of the rules on processing of personal data and ordering both to remedy the situation
- Imposing a definite or temporary ban on processing
- Bringing to the attention of judicial authorities violations of the rules contained in the regulation
- Engaging in legal proceedings, in case an individual or a legal person initiates legal action against a decision of a supervisory authority
- Ordering the controller and processor to comply with the requests of data subjects
- Ordering the rectification, erasure, or destruction of data processed in violation of the draft regulation
- Imposing a ban on processing

- Suspending data flows to a recipient in a third country or to an international organization
- Issuing opinions on issues involving personal data protection[149]

C. Designation of Data Protection Officers

An additional safeguard envisioned by the draft regulation is the designation of a data protection officer by controllers or processors when the processing of personal data is carried out by a public authority or by an enterprise that employs 250 persons or more, or when the processing requires the regular and systematic monitoring of data subjects because of its scope and purpose.[150]

VII. Remedies, Liabilities, and Sanctions

In general, the rights of data subjects are clarified and improved by the draft regulation. Chapter VIII of the Draft Regulation is composed of seven articles and lists the following rights of data subjects: (a) to file a complaint with a supervisory authority, (b) to a judicial remedy against a supervisory authority, (c) to a judicial remedy against a controller or a processor, and (d) to compensation and liability. It also introduces common rules on court proceedings.[151]

Moreover, the draft regulation empowers supervisory authorities to impose effective, proportionate, and dissuasive penalties.[152] A supervisory authority is authorized to impose an administrative fine of €250,000 (about US$ 306,500) to a natural person who processes personal data without a commercial interest after a repeat noncompliance with the Draft Regulation. If it is an enterprise, or an organization that employs less than 250 persons, the fine will be up to 0.5% of its annual worldwide turnover.[153] A warning is issued with no fine to first time offenders, either individuals or companies.[154]

Another positive aspect is that the draft regulation reinforces the right of organizations and associations engaged in protecting the rights of data subjects to lodge a complaint with a supervisory authority.[155] This right can be exercised irrespective of a complaint initiated by a data subject.[156]

VIII. Territorial and Extraterritorial Application of the Draft Regulation

The territorial scope of the draft regulation extends to the processing of personal data when a controller or processor is established in the European Union.[157] It also has extraterritorial application when the processing of personal data of individuals who reside within the EU is undertaken by a processor who is not established in the EU, but the processing relates to one of the following two activities: (a) the provision of services and goods to individuals within the EU, or (b) the monitoring of their behavior.[158]

Similarly to the Data Protection Directive, a transfer of personal data to a third country or an international organization may take place, provided that the Commission has issued an adequacy decision. In such a case there is no need for further authorization.[159] Adequacy decisions will be published in the Official Journal of the European Union. The United States has already expressed its concern that US companies would be subject to stricter data protection rules.[160]

In the absence of an adequacy decision, a controller or processor may transfer personal data to a third country, provided that additional safeguards have been taken in a legally binding instrument, such as binding corporate rules or standard data protection clauses adopted by the Commission.[161]

End Notes

[1] The right to privacy is also protected by article 8 of the European Convention of Human Rights and Fundamental Freedoms, to which all the EU Member States are states parties, as members of the Council of Europe. In addition, automatic processing of personal data is protected and governed by the 1981 Council of Europe Convention for the Protection of Individuals with Regard to Automatic Processing of Personal Data and Its Protocol. Recently, the Council of Europe began revising the 1981 Convention to bring it in line with contemporary technology and ensure harmonization with EU legal reform.

[2] Charter of Fundamental Rights of the European Union, 2010 O.J. (C 83) 02, http://eurlex.europa.eu/LexUriServ/LexUriServ.do?uri=OJ:C:2010:083:0389:0403:EN:PDF.

[3] Id. art. 8.

[4] Id. art. 52(1).

[5] Consolidated Version of the Treaty on the Functioning of the European Union [TFEU], art. 16, 2010 O.J. (C 83) 47, http://eur-lex.europa.eu/LexUriServ/LexUriServ . do?uri=OJ:C:2010:083:0047:0200:EN:PDF.

[6] Id.

[7] Directive 95/46/EC of the European Parliament and of the Council of 24 October 1995 on the Protection of Individuals with Regard to the Processing of Personal Data and on the Free Movement of Such Data, 1995 O.J. (L 281) 31, http://eur-lex.europa.eu/LexUriServ/LexUriServ.do?uri=OJ:L:1995:281:0031:0050:EN:PDF.

[8] The European Commission initiated legal action against Luxembourg before the European Court of Justice (ECJ) for failing to transpose the Data Protection Directive within the prescribed period (by October 24, 1998). The ECJ issued its decision in 2001, found against Luxembourg, and ordered it to pay the costs. Case C450/00, Judgment of the Court (Grand Chamber), European Commission v. Grand Duchy of Luxembourg, http://eur-lex.europa.eu/LexUriServ/LexUriServ.do?uri=CELEX:62000CJ0450:EN:PDF.

[9] Decision of the European Economic Area Joint Committee No. 83/1999 Amending Protocol 37 and Annex XI (Telecommunications Services) to the EEA Agreement, 2000 O.J. (L 296) 41, http://eurlex.europa.eu/Result.do?aaaa=2000&mm=&jj=&type=l&nnn=296&pppp=41&RechType=RECH_reference_pub&Submit=Search.

[10] Annex B (Article 2(2)), Agreement Between the European Union, the European Community and the Swiss Confederation on the Swiss Confederation's Association with the Implementation, Application and Development of the Schengen Acquis, 2008 O.J. (L 53) 52, http://eur-lex.europa.eu/LexUriServ/LexUriServ.do?uri=OJ:L:2008:053:0052:0079:EN:PDF.

[11] Communication from the Commission to the European Parliament and the Council on the Follow-up of the Work Programme for the Better Implementation of the Data Protection Directive, COM (2007) 87 final (Mar. 7, 2007), http://eur-lex.europa.eu/LexUriServ/LexUriServ.do?uri=COM:2007:0087:FIN:EN:PDF.

[12] Report from the Commission: First Report on the Implementation of the Data Protection Directive (95/46/EC) COM (2003) 265 final (May 15, 2003), http://eur-lex.europa.eu/LexUriServ/LexUriServ.do?uri=CELEX:52003DC0265:EN:NOT.

13 For an in-depth analysis of transposition of Directive 95/46/EC by EU Member States, see DOUWE KORFF, EC STUDY ON IMPLEMENTATION OF DATA PROTECTION DIRECTIVE: COMPARATIVE SUMMARY OF NATIONAL LAWS (Sept. 2002), available at http://www.garanteprivacy.it/ garante/ document?ID=455584. See also Annex 2 to the Impact Assessment Evaluation on the Implementation of the

Data Protection Directive, http://ec.europa.eu/ justice/data-protection/document/ review2012/sec_2012_72_annexes_en.pdf (last visited June 30, 2012).

[14] Directive 2002/58/EC of the European Parliament and of the Council of 12 July 2002 Concerning the Processing of Personal Data and the Protection of Privacy in the Electronic Communications Sector (Directive on Privacy and Electronic Communications), 2002 O.J. (L 201) 37, http://eur-lex.europa.eu/LexUriServ/LexUriServ.do?uri=OJ:L:2002:201:0037:0047:EN:PDF.

[15] Directive 2006/24/EC of the European Parliament and of the Council of 15 March 2006 On the Retention of Data Generated or Processed in Connection with the Provision of Publicly Available Electronic Communications Services or of Public Communications Networks and Amending Directive 2002/58/EC, 2006 O.J. (L 105) 54, http://eur-lex.europa.eu/LexUriServ/LexUriServ.do?uri=OJ:L:2006:105:0054:0063:EN:PDF.

[16] Directive 2009/136/EC of the European Parliament and of the Council of 25 November 2009 Amending Directive 2002/22/EC on Universal Service and Users' Rights Relating to Electronic Communications Networks and Services, Directive 2002/58/EC Concerning the Processing of Personal Data and the Protection of Privacy in the Electronic Communications Sector and Regulation (EC) No 2006/2004 on Cooperation Between National Authorities Responsible for the Enforcement of Consumer Protection Laws, 2009 O.J. (L 377) 11, http://eur-lex.europa.eu/LexUriServ/LexUriServ.do?uri=OJ:L:2009:337:0011:0036:EN:PDF.

[17] Regulation (EC) No. 45/2001 of the European Parliament and of the Council of 18 December 2000 on the Protection of Individuals with Regard to the Processing of Personal Data by the Community Institutions and Bodies and on the Free Movement of Such Data, 2001 O.J. (L 8) 1, http://eur-lex.europa.eu/LexUriServ/LexUriServ.do?uri=OJ:L:2001:008:0001:0022:EN:PDF.

[18] Directive 95/46/EC, supra note 7, art. 2(a).

[19] Annexes to the Impact Assessment, European Commission, Annex I Current EU Legal Instruments for the Protection of Personal Data, http://ec.europa.eu/justice/data-protection/document/review2012/sec_2012_72_annexes_en.pdf (last visited June 30, 2012).

[20] Directive 95/46/EC, supra note 7, art. 2(a).

[21] Id. art. 2(b).

[22] Id.

[23] Id. art. 2(d)–(e).

[24] Article 29 Data Protection Working Party, Opinion 1/2010 on the Concepts of "Controller" and "Processor", 00264/10/EN, WP 169 (Feb. 16, 2010), http://ec.europa.eu/justice/policies/privacy/docs/wpdocs/2010/ wp169 en.pdf.

[25] Directive 95/46/EC, supra note 7, art. 6.

[26] Id. art. 7.

[27] European Commission, First Report on the Implementation of the Data Protection Directive (95/46/EC), COM (2003) 265 final,http://eur-lex.europa.eu/LexUriServ/LexUriServ.do?uri=COM:2003:0265:FIN:EN:PDF. See also Analysis and Impact Study on the Implementation of Directive 95/46/EC in Member States, http://ec.europa. eu/justice/policies/privacy/docs/lawreport/consultation/technical-annex_en.pdf.

[28] Id.

[29] Directive 95/46/EC, supra note 7, art. 8.

[30] Id. art. 8(2)(a)–(e).

[31] Id.

[32] Id. art. 13.

[33] Directive 2002/58/EC, supra note 14, art. 15.

[34] Directive 95/46/EC, supra note 7, art. 2(h).

[35] Article 29 Data Protection Working Party, Opinion 15/2011 on the Definition of Consent, 01197/11/EN WP187 (July 13, 2011), http://ec.europa.eu/justice/policies/privacy/docs/wpdocs/2011/wp187_en.pdf.

[36] Id. at 12.

[37] Directive 2002/58/EC, supra note 14, recital 17.

[38] Directive 95/46/EC, supra note 7, art. 12.

[39] Id.

[40] Id.

[41] Id. art. 14.

[42] Id. art. 17.

[43] Id.

[44] Id. art. 17, para. 2.

[45] Id. art. 17, para. 3.

[46] Directive 2002/58/EC, supra note 14, art. 4.

[47] Directive 2009/136/EC, supra note 16, art. 4(b).
[48] Id. art. 4(c)(3).
[49] Directive 2006/24/EC, supra note 15, art. 7(b), (c).
[50] Article 29 Data Protection Working Party, Opinion 13/2011 on Geolocation Services on Smart Mobile Devices 19, 881/11/EN, WP 185 (May 16, 2011), http://ec.europa.eu/justice/policies/privacy/docs/wpdocs/2011/wp185_en.pdf.
[51] Directive 2009/136/EC, supra note 16, at 29, amending Directive 2002/58/EC, supra note 14, art. 2(c).
[52] Article 29 Data Protection Working Party, Opinion 13/2011, supra note 50.
[53] Directive 2002/58/EC, supra note 14, art. 4(c)(3), as amended by Directive 2009/136/EC, supra note 16.
[54] For an analysis on the applicable law and limitations on processing of location data collected through smart mobile devices, see Article 29 Data Protection Working Party, Opinion 13/2011, supra note 50.
[55] Directive 2002/58/EC, supra note 14, art. 9.
[56] Id.
[57] For example, article 16 of the Convention on the Rights of the Child provides that no child shall be subject to arbitrary or unlawful interference with his or her privacy, family, home, or correspondence, nor to unlawful attacks on his or her honor and reputation. Convention on the Rights of the Child, entered into force Sept. 2, 1990, U.N. Doc. A/44/49 (1989), http://www2.ohchr.org/english/law/crc.htm.
[58] Article 29 Data Protection Working Party, Opinion 2/2009 on the Protection of Children's Personal Data (General Guidelines and the Special Case of Schools), 398/09/EN, WP 160 (Feb. 11, 2009), http://ec.europa.eu/justice/policies/privacy/docs/wpdocs/2009/wp160_en.pdf.
[59] Directive 2006/24/EC, supra note 15.
[60] Id. arts. 1, 6.
[61] Frequently Asked Questions: Evaluation Report of the Data Retention Directive, Memo/11/251 (Apr. 18, 2011), http://europa.eu/rapid/pressReleasesAction.do?reference=MEMO/11/251&format=HTML&aged=0&language=EN&guiLanguage=en.
[62] Id. at 2 (PDF version).
[63] Id. at 3.
[64] Id.
[65] Id.
[66] Press Release, European Commission, Data Retention: Commission Takes Germany to Court Requesting That Fines Be Imposed (May 31, 2012), http://www.statewatch.org/news/2012/jun/eu-com-germany-mand-ret.pdf.
[67] Directive 95/46/EC, supra note 7, art. 28, para. 4.
[68] Id. art. 22.
[69] Id. arts. 22–23.
[70] Id. art. 24.
[71] Directive 2002/58/EC, supra note 14, art. 15, para. 2.
[72] Directive 2006/24/EC, supra note 15, art. 13(1).
[73] Directive 95/46/EC, supra note 7, art. 25(1).
[74] Case C-101/01, Judgment of the Court of 6 November 2003, Criminal Proceedings Against Bodil Lindqvist, http://curia.europa.eu/juris/showPdf.jsf?text=&docid=48382&pageIndex=0&doclang=en&mode=doc&dir=&occ=first&part=1&cid=42578.
[75] Id.
[76] Christopher Kuner, European Data Protection Law: Corporate Compliance And Regulation 186 (2007).
[77] Directive 95/46/EC, supra note 7, art. 25(2).
[78] Id. art. 25(3).
[79] Id.
[80] Working Document, Working Party on the Protection of Individuals with Regard to the Processing of Personal Data, Transfers of Personal Data to Third Countries: Applying Articles 25 and 26 of the EU Data Protection Directive, DG XV D/5025/98, WP 12 (July 24, 1998), http://ec.europa.eu/justice/policies/privacy/docs/wpdocs/1998/wp12_en.pdf.
[81] Directive 95/46/EC, supra note 7, art. 26, para. 1.
[82] Id. art. 26, para. 2.
[83] The Article 29 Working Party has published three papers on the procedure for approval of Binding Corporate Rules (BCRs): (a) Working Document: Binding Corporate Rules (2003); (b) Model Checklist: Application for Approval of Binding Corporate Rules (2004); and (c) Working Document Setting Forth a Cooperation Procedure for Issuing Common Opinion on Adequate Safeguards Resulting from "Binding Corporate Rules"

(2005). See list of documents prepared by the Working Party, http://ec.europa.eu/justice/policies/privacy/workinggroup/wpdocs/index_en.htm (last visited June 30, 2012).

[84] Safe Harbor Privacy Principles, US DEPARTMENT OF COMMERCE (July 21, 2000), http://export.gov/safeharbor/eu/eg_main_018475.asp.

[85] Frequently Asked Questions, US DEPARTMENT OF COMMERCE http://export.gov/faq/index.asp (last updated Mar. 21, 2012). See also Commission Decision (EC) 2000/520 of 26 July 2000 Pursuant to Directive (EC) 95/46 On the Adequacy of the Protection Provided by the Safe Harbor Privacy Principles and Related Frequently Asked Questions Issued by the US Department of Commerce, 2000 O.J. (L 215) 7, http://eur-lex.europa.eu/LexUriServ/LexUriServ.do?uri=OJ:L:2000:215:0007:0047:EN:PDF.

[86] Commission Decisions on the Adequacy of the Protection of Personal Data in Third Countries, EUROPEAN COMMISSION, http://ec.europa.eu/justice/data-protection/document/internationaltransfers/adequacy/_index_en.htm (last updated Oct. 4, 2012).

[87] Joint Cases C-92/09 and C-93/09, Volker und Markus Schecke GbR, Hartmut Eifert v. Land Hessen, Judgment of the Court (Grand Chamber) (Nov. 9, 2010), http://curia.europa.eu/juris/liste.jsf?language=en&jur=C,T,F&num=C-92/09&td=ALL.

[88] Article 52(1) of the Charter of Fundamental Rights of the EU, supra note 2, provides for limitations only when they are provided by law and observe the essence of those rights and freedoms.

[89] Volker und Markus Schecke GbR, Hartmut Eifert v. Land Hessen, ¶¶ 76, 77.

[90] Press Release, Court of Justice of the European Union, The Owner of an Online Social Network Cannot be Obliged to Install a General Filtering System, Covering All Its Users, in Order to Prevent the Unlawful Use of Musical and Audio-Visual Work (Feb. 16, 2012), http://curia.europa.eu/jcms/upload/docs/ application/pdf/2012- 02/cp120011en.pdf.

[91] Id.

[92] Case C360/10, Judgment of the ECJ (Third Chamber), Feb. 16, 2012, Belgische Vereniging van Auteurs, Componisten en Uitgevers CVBA (SABAM) v. Netlog, NV, para. 52, http://curia.europa.eu/juris/document/document.jsf?text=&docid=119512&pageIndex=0&doclang=en&mode=req&dir=&occ=first&part=1&cid=44646.

[93] Cases C-317/04 & C-318/04, European Parliament v. Council of the European Union and Commission of the European Communities, 2006 E.C.R. I-04721, http://eur-lex.europa.eu/LexUriServ/Lex UriServ.do?uri=CELEX:62004CJ0317:EN:PDF.

[94] Council of the European Union, Agreement Between the United States of America and the European Union on the Use and Transfer of Passenger Name Records to the United States Department of Homeland Security, 17434/11 (Dec. 8, 2011), http://register.consilium.europa.eu/pdf/en/11/st17/st17434.en11.pdf.

[95] Communication from the Commission to the European Parliament, the Council, the Economic and Social Committee and the Committee of the Regions, A Comprehensive Approach on Personal Data Protection in the European Union, COM (2010) 609 final (Nov. 4, 2010), http://ec.europa.eu/justice/news/consulting_public/0006/com_2010_609_en.pdf.

[96] Annex 4, Summary of Replies to the Public Consultation on the Commission's Communication on a Comprehensive Approach on Personal Data Protection in the European Union, at 54, http://ec.europa.eu/justice/data-protection/document/review2012/sec_2012_72_annexes_en.pdf.

[97] Id. at 64.

[98] EUROPEAN COMMISSION, SPECIAL EUROBAROMETER 359: ATTITUDES ON DATA PROTECTION AND ELECTRONIC IDENTITY IN THE EUROPEAN UNION (June 2011), http://ec.europa.eu/public_opinion/archives/ebs/ ebs_359_en.pdf.

[99] Id. at 115.

[100] Id. at 146.

[101] Id. at 74.

[102] Id. at 149.

[103] Spring Conference 2012 of the European Data Protection Commissioners, Resolution on the European Data Protection Reform (Luxembourg, May 3–4, 2012), http://www.edps.europa.eu/EDPSWEB/webdav/site/mySite/shared/Documents/Cooperation/Conference EU/12-05-04 Spring conference Resolution EN.pdf.

[104] On July 20, 2012, the European Commission announced that a communication addressing a variety of aspects of cloud computing will be published soon. According to the announcement, the communication will be divided into three sections: personal data protection and security, copyright, and standardization. As far personal data, the communication will address issues such as whether cloud providers should be required to provide a backup copy, applicable law when the user of a cloud service is a non-EU citizen, and transfers of personal data

outside the EU. News Release, EurActiv, Brussels to Unveil EU Cloud Computing Strategy (July 20, 2012), http://www.euractiv.com/infosociety/brussels-unveil-eu-cloud-computi-news-514012.

[105] European Commission, How Does the Data Protection Reform Strengthen Citizen's Rights? http://ec.europa.eu /justice/data-protection/document/review2012/factsheets/2_en.pdf (last visited June 25, 2012).

[106] COM (2010) 609 final, supra note 95.

[107] European Parliament: Resolution of July 6, 2011 on a Comprehensive Approach on Personal Data Protection in the European Union (2011/2025(INI)), http://www.europarl.europa.eu/sides/getDoc.do?pubRef=-//EP//TEXT+TA+P7-TA-2011-0323+0+DOC+XML+V0//EN.

[108] Council of the EU, Council Conclusions on the Communication from the Commission to the European Parliament and the Council – A Comprehensive Approach on Personal Data Protection in the EU, 3071st Justice and Home Affairs Council Meeting, Brussels, 24 and 25 February 2011, http://www.consilium. europa.eu/ uedocs/cms_data/docs/pressdata/en/jha/119461.pdf.

[109] Proposal for a Regulation of the European Parliament and of the Council on the Protection of Individuals with Regard to the Processing of Personal Data and on the Free Movement of Such Data (General Data Protection Regulation) [hereinafter Draft Regulation], COM (2012) 11 final (Jan. 15, 2012), http://eur-lex.europa.eu/LexUriServ/LexUriServ.do?uri=COM:2012:0011:FIN:EN:PDF.

[110] Proposal for a Directive of the European Parliament and of the Council on the Protection of Individuals with Regard to the Processing of Personal Data by Competent Authorities for the Purposes of Prevention, Investigation, Detection or Prosecution of Criminal Offenses or the Execution of Criminal Parties and the Free Movement of Such Data, COM (2012) 10 final (Jan. 25, 2012), http://eur-lex.europa.eu/LexUriServ /LexUriServ.do?uri=COM:2012:0010:FIN:EN:PDF.

[111] Article 29 Data Protection Working Party, Opinion 01/2012 on the Data Protection Reform Proposals, 00530/12/EN, WP 191 (Mar. 23, 2012), http://ec.europa.eu/justice/data-protection opinion-recommendation/files/2012/wp191_en.pdf.

[112] Id. at 4.

[113] Id. at 5.

[114] Id. at 7.

[115] Draft Regulation, supra note 109, art. 4.

[116] Id. art. 22.

[117] Id. art. 31, para. 1.

[118] Id. art. 32, para. 1.

[119] Id. art. 28.

[120] Id. art. 9.

[121] Id. art. 81.

[122] Id.

[123] Id. art. 83.

[124] Id. art. 4, para. 8 (emphasis added).

[125] Id. art. 7.

[126] Id. art. 23, para. 1.

[127] Id. art. 23, para. 2.

[128] FEDERAL TRADE COMMISSION, PROTECTING CONSUMER PRIVACY IN AN ERA OF RAPID CHANGE: RECOMMENDATIONS FOR BUSINESSES AND POLICYMAKERS (Mar. 2012), http://www.ftc.gov/os/2012/03/120326 privacyreport.pdf. Other recommendations include the "do not track mechanism," which can be used by consumers who do not want their online activities to be followed, and greater transparency by companies to disclose what type of data and for what purpose it is used.

[129] Draft Regulation, supra note 109, art. 11.

[130] Id. art. 12, para. 2.

[131] Id. art. 16.

[132] Id. art. 17, para. 1.

[133] Id. art. 18.

[134] Id. para. 1.

[135] Id. art. 19, paras. 1–2.

[136] Id. art. 20, para. 1.

[137] Id. para. 2

[138] Article 29 Data Protection Working Party, Opinion 01/2012, supra note 111. 139 Id.

[140] Draft Regulation, supra note 109, art. 8, para. 1.

[141] Id. paras. 3–4.

[142] Regulation (EC) No. 45/2001 of the European Parliament and of the Council of 18 December 2000 On the Protection of Individuals with Regard to the Processing of Personal Data by the Community Institutions and Bodies and on the Free Movement of Such Data, 2001 O.J. (L 8) 1, http://eur-lex.europa.eu/LexUriServ/LexUriServ.do?uri=OJ:L:2001:008:0001:0022:EN:PDF.

[143] See EUROPEAN DATA PROTECTION SUPERVISOR, http://www.edps.europa.eu/EDPSWEB/edps/EDPS?lang=en (last visited June 25, 2012).

[144] Draft Regulation, supra note 109, art. 64.

[145] Id. art. 58.

[146] Case C-518/07, Judgment of the ECJ, Grand Chamber, March 9, 2010, European Commission v. Federal Republic of Germany, http://curia.europa.eu/juris/liste.jsf?language=en&num=C-518/07.

[147] Draft Regulation, supra note 109, art. 51.

[148] Id. art. 52.

[149] Id. art. 53.

[150] Id. art. 35.

[151] Id. arts. 73–79.

[152] Id. art. 79, paras. 1–2.

[153] Id. art. 79, paras. 3–4.

[154] Id.

[155] Id. art. 73, para. 2.

[156] Id. art. 73, para. 3.

[157] Id. art. 3, para. 1.

[158] Id. art. 3.

[159] Id. art. 41.

[160] US Lobbying Waters Down EU Data Protection Reform, EURACTIV (Feb. 21, 2012), http://www.euractiv.com/specialreport-data-protection/us-lobbying-waters-eu-data-prote-news-510991.

[161] Draft Regulation, supra note 109, art. 42.

In: Online Privacy Laws
Editor: Ethan P. Williams

ISBN: 978-1-62808-623-2

Chapter 2

ONLINE PRIVACY LAW (PART TWO): AUSTRALIA, CANADA, FRANCE, GERMANY, ISRAEL, ITALY, JAPAN, NETHERLANDS, PORTUGAL, SPAIN, SWEDEN, AND THE UNITED KINGDOM*

Kelly Buchanan, Tariq Ahmad, Nicole Atwill, Edith Palmer, Ruth Levush, Laura Andriulli, Sayuri Umeda, Wendy Zeldin, Eduardo Soares, Graciela Rodriguez-Ferrand, Elin Hofverberg and Clare Feikert-Ahalt

AUSTRALIA ONLINE PRIVACY LAW

Executive Summary

The federal Privacy Act 1988 provides the framework for the protection of personal information in the online context in Australia. The law is intended to be technology-neutral and, rather than providing prescriptive rules, it sets out a principle-based approach that can be tailored to apply to different situations. Oversight and complaints functions are performed by an independent Privacy Commissioner. The legislation also provides for a degree of self-regulation on the part of industry groups and for the Privacy Commissioner to produce education and guidance material for businesses, government agencies, and the public. There is no established cause of action for invasion of privacy in Australian constitutional, statutory, or common law.

Major privacy reforms are being considered by the Australian parliament following a complete review of the legislation by the Australian Law Reform Commission in 2008. In 2011, a Senate committee also expressed some concerns about the adequacy of the current

* This report was released by The Law Library of Congress, Global Legal Research Center, June 2012.

framework to protect online privacy following an investigation and submission process on this issue. Further proposals not in the present bill that may be developed by the government include a statutory cause of action for invasion of privacy, data retention requirements, new obligations relating to children and young people, and a mandatory data breach notification system.

I. Legal Framework

The federal Privacy Act 1988 provides the primary legislative framework for the protection of privacy (including online data protection) by private organizations in Australia.[1]

The Australian Constitution and state constitutions do not contain provisions relating to the protection of privacy, and there is no entrenched bill of rights at the federal level.[2]

The Privacy Act is primarily a principle-based framework that applies to the collection, use, storage, and destruction of "personal information." Such information is defined as "information or an opinion (including information or an opinion forming part of a database), whether true or not, and whether recorded in a material form or not, about an individual whose identity is apparent, or can reasonably be ascertained, from the information or opinion."[3] In addition, the Act contains protections relating to the collection and use of a subset of personal information referred to as "sensitive information," covering information or opinions about such things as an individual's racial or ethnic origin, political opinions, and religious beliefs.[4]

The relevant provisions of the Privacy Act for the purposes of this report apply to "organisations." These are defined in section 6C as including individuals, body corporates, partnerships, any other unincorporated associations, and trusts. "Small business operators" are generally excluded from the definition and therefore from the application of the Privacy Act requirements.[5] Such entities are defined in section 6D as businesses with annual sales of less than AU$3 million (about US$3 million).[6] However, a small business that holds health information; "discloses personal information about another individual to anyone else for a benefit, service or advantage"; or "provides a benefit, service or advantage to collect personal information about another individual from anyone else" would be subject to the relevant provisions in the Act.[7] Other businesses are also able to opt into Privacy Act coverage.[8]

Organizations subject to the Privacy Act are required to operate in accordance with the National Privacy Principles (NPPs),[9] which are set out in Schedule 3 of the Act. The NPPs cover the collection, use, and disclosure of personal information, as well as data quality, data security, openness, access and correction, the use of identifiers, anonymity, transborder data flows, and the collection of sensitive information. The NPPs and the public sector equivalent, the Information Privacy Principles (IPPs), were largely based on the Organisation for Economic Co-operation and Development (OECD) privacy principles developed in 1980, with some additions.[10] They are essentially the "minimum standards" for how businesses and other private sector organizations should collect personal information, for use and disclosure of personal information, and in relation to "ensuring that the personal information they hold is accurate and secure."[11]

The Act also makes provisions for privacy codes to be developed by industry organizations.[12] Such codes must provide at least as much protection as the NPPs. Once a code has been approved by an independent regulator—the Privacy Commissioner[13]—it becomes binding on entities that are registered with the relevant organization.[14] The Privacy Codes Register currently cites only two approved privacy codes: the Market and Social Research Privacy Code and the Queensland Club Industry Privacy Code.[15] A draft Internet Industry Privacy Code, developed by the Internet Industry Association and submitted for registration in 2003, is currently under consideration by the Privacy Commissioner.[16]

II. Current Law

The provisions in the Privacy Act relating to private sector organizations, including the NPPs and the privacy code provisions, were enacted in 2000[17] as "part of the Commonwealth Government's commitment to enacting balanced privacy legislation for the private sector to ensure that full advantage may be taken of the opportunities that electronic commerce presents for Australian business within Australia and overseas."[18] In particular, one of the objectives of the reforms was to ensure that the system for handling personal information in the private sector is compatible with the European Union Directive on the Protection of Individuals with Regard to the Processing of Personal Data and on the Free Movement of Such Data (Directive 95/46/EC)[19] in order to remove "any potential barriers to international trade."[20]

Since the introduction of the NPPs, the wording and application of the law in relation to developments in the capabilities and use of online technologies[21] have been the subjects of various reviews and discussions, including an investigation into the adequacy of online privacy protection for Australians by the Senate's Environment and Communications References Committee, completed in April 2011,[22] and a report proposing large-scale privacy law reform completed by the Australian Law Reform Commission (ALRC) in 2008.[23]

As indicated in the overview of the legal framework above, the Privacy Act sets out standards for the management and use of personal information by way of broad principles, rather than a large number of prescriptive rules.[24] According to the explanatory memorandum to the Privacy Amendment (Private Sector) Bill 2000, the NPPs were intended to be technologyneutral.[25] There are therefore no provisions that apply specifically to different methods or technologies for obtaining and storing information.

Various self-regulatory instruments and guidance material relating to online privacy have been produced by industry groups as well as by the Privacy Commissioner and other government entities. The Privacy Commissioner is of the view that Australia should take a multifaceted approach to online privacy protection that includes a range of formal and informal mechanisms. The Senate committee expressed general agreement, stating that "given jurisdictional boundaries and the transnational nature of the Internet, it would be impossible for legislation alone to adequately protect the privacy of Australians online, and accordingly it is clear that educational programs and international engagement must form part of any successful approach to privacy," and also that "[s]elf-regulation will have a key role in this regard in setting industry best-practice benchmarks."[26]

The following sections provide information on how the various aspects of the NPPs can be seen to apply in relation to the protection of privacy in the context of developments in online technologies. Information is also provided on some of the areas where there has been a focus on education and self-regulation.

A. Key Principles Relating to Online Data Protection

The NPPs are not expressed as positive individual privacy rights but rather as general standards for data collection and protection that should be applied by different organizations. Many of the principles include limitations or exceptions to the general concepts. The following are some the core concepts reflected in the NPPs:

- The collection of a data subject's personal information must be necessary for one or more of an organization's functions.
- Personal information must be collected "only by lawful and fair means and not in an unreasonably intrusive way."[27]
- An organization must "take reasonable steps" to ensure that a data subject whose personal information is collected is aware of "the identity of the organization and how to contact it; the fact that he or she is able to gain access to the information; the purposes for which the information is collected"; the organizations (or types of organizations) to which information could be disclosed; any law that requires the information to be collected; and the consequences to the individual if all or part of the information is not collected.[28]
- Unless certain criteria apply, an organization must not use or disclose a data subject's personal information for a purpose other than the primary purpose of collection.
- An organization "must take reasonable steps to make sure that the personal information it collects, uses or discloses is accurate, complete and up-to-date"[29] and must protect it from misuse, loss, and unauthorized access, modification, or disclosure.
- If personal information is no longer needed for the purpose for which it was collected, an organization must take reasonable steps to destroy or "permanently de-identify" that information.[30]

1. Principles Relating to Behavioral Advertising

The opportunities to conduct targeted or behavioral online advertising have expanded greatly in recent years due to developments in online technologies and the way that people use them. Various principles may be relevant to this practice, including NPP 2.1(c), which allows for personal information (but not sensitive information) to be used for the secondary purpose of direct marketing, provided that it is impracticable to get the data subject's consent before using the information; the data subject is given the opportunity to opt out from further communications; and the data subject has not already requested not to be sent direct marketing material.

Australian government entities have identified that this and other principles may not provide for comprehensive regulation of, for example, the tracking of users' web browsing or key words in emails in order to conduct online behavioral advertising. The Attorney-General's Department, cited in the Senate committee's 2011 report, has stated that "there is nothing to prevent web-based email service providers filtering emails in such a manner under Australia's telecommunications interception legislation, because of the fact that users agree to the filtering when they sign up to the email service."[31] Furthermore, not all information collected would be considered "personal information" under the Privacy Act, although the Privacy Commissioner is of the view that, over time, the aggregation of the data may enable identification of individuals.[32] The Commissioner stated:

> What we would like to see as much as possible in that context is choice—choice for the individual to know what is happening and choice to be able to at least opt out if not opt in to that sort of marketing, where it is effective and will work.[33]

The Senate committee's report also noted that while search engines such as Google may currently provide a choice to opt out, the relevant policies and procedures are often complex and difficult for users to navigate,[34] and pointed out various industry groups' efforts at self-regulation through the development of guidelines related to online behavioral advertising standards.[35] These guidelines include the need for explicit consent prior to engaging in third-party online behavioral advertising as well as the option to withdraw such consent.[36] Having also considered the US Federal Trade Commission's (FTC's) investigation of the issue, the committee recommended that the Privacy Commissioner work with interested parties to "develop and impose a code which includes a 'Do Not Track' model."[37]

2. Principles Relating to the Protection of Minors

The Privacy Act does not contain specific provisions regarding the rights or protection of information relating to minors. The ALRC noted:

> There is no federal legislation specifically addressing the privacy of children and young people. While the Privacy Act 1988 (Cth) applies to individuals under the age of 18, there is no provision dealing explicitly with the particular needs of children and young people. It is not always clear how the Act applies to these individuals, or who can and should make decisions about privacy on behalf of an individual under the age of 18.[38]

With regard to young people, the Privacy Commissioner's guidelines on the application of the NPPs state:

> The Privacy Act does not specify an age after which individuals can make their own privacy decisions. Determining the decision-making capabilities of a young person can be a complex matter, often raising other ethical and legal issues. Organisations will need to address each case individually.[39]

There is a range of educational programs and guidance material available in Australia to assist organizations, families, and young people themselves to take appropriate action with regard to the personal information of minors. Resources include targeted websites on Internet safety and privacy, guidance to advertisers on managing images of children in the online context, and guidance documents produced by the Privacy Commissioner on matters such as social networking. The Senate committee received submissions stating that online privacy is a strong focus in most schools, although it is not currently a mandatory requirement in the curriculum.[40]

The ALRC considered issues related to young people and privacy in its 2008 report, including developments in the use of online social networking sites by young people.[41] It noted that the various sites have age restrictions, but found that these are regularly ignored by young people. In the context of social networking sites, it recommended the expansion of programs targeting young people as well as self-regulation, rather than the development of a regulatory approach such as that contained in the Children's Online Privacy Protection Act in the US.

The ALRC also examined issues relating to the capacity of young people to consent and make decisions regarding their personal information. It recommended that a system of individual assessment be formally incorporated into the Privacy Act, along with a minimum age of presumption of capacity,[42] and that the "Direct Marketing" principle referred to above include additional protections for children under the age of fifteen.[43]

3. Smartphone Applications and Location Information

Some of the educational materials produced by the Privacy Commissioner and other agencies highlight the need for individuals to consider privacy issues when using smartphones. The Australian government also has a range of initiatives relating to cyber security,[44] cyber safety, and the digital economy[45] that include consideration of issues relating to developments in smartphone technology, such as the ability to track, record, and share location information. The privacy issues relating to smartphone use as well as social networking were a particular focus of Privacy Awareness Week 2012, when Australians were "urged to take stock of their web privacy settings and to pay more attention to the terms and conditions attached to smartphone applications before they sign up."[46]

B. Consent

There is no distinct privacy principle requiring that an organization obtain the consent of a data subject in relation to the collection, storage, and use of their personal information. However, consent is relevant to the operation of some of the NPPs. According to the ALRC,

> Consent is either framed as an exception to a general prohibition against personal information being handled in a particular way or as a basis to authorise the handling of personal information in a particular way. Significantly, in each case, consent is not the only exception to a stated prohibition, nor the only basis for permitting the handling of personal information in a particular way.[47]

The Privacy Act 1988 contains a broad definition of consent, which includes either "express consent or implied consent."[48] The Privacy Commissioner has stated:

> Consent means voluntary agreement to some act, practice or purpose. It has two elements: knowledge of the matter agreed to, and voluntary agreement. Consent can be express or implied. Express consent is given explicitly, either orally or in writing. Implied consent arises where consent may reasonably be inferred in the circumstances from the conduct of the individual and the organisation. Consent is invalid if there is extreme pressure or coercion.
>
> Only a competent individual can give consent although an organisation can ordinarily assume capacity unless there is something to alert it otherwise. Competence means that individuals are capable of understanding issues based on reasoned judgments and communicating their decisions. The general law about competence and incapacity will apply to the issue of consent.[49]

The Senate committee's report on online privacy protection noted that "people are often required to consent to numerous pages of legalese, waiving their privacy rights, in order to use web-based services,"[50] and that

> [w]hile the Privacy Act has long allowed consent to justify the waiver of privacy rights in the offline sphere, it seems to the committee that the over-use of complex consent forms has increased exponentially with the expansion of online services.[51]

The committee also considered, and agreed with, the views expressed by the FTC regarding the ineffectiveness of online privacy notices and consent forms, and recommended legislative changes as well as practical guidance to address the issue.[52]

C. Transparency

NPP 5 requires organizations to set out, in a document that is available to anyone on request, "clearly expressed policies" on the management of personal information. It also requires that an organization, on request, take "take reasonable steps" to let a data subject know what sort of personal information it holds, for what purposes, and how it is collected and used. In addition, NPP 1.3 requires that, at or before the time that an organization collects personal information, it must take reasonable steps to make the data subject aware of a list of matters, including the identity of the organization, the fact that the data subject can gain access to the information, the purposes for which the information is collected, and the organizations to which such information is usually disclosed.

The Explanatory Memorandum to the 2000 Amendment Bill explicitly noted these latter transparency requirements with respect to collecting information online:

> Where information is collected via the internet, NPP 1.3 would require that a policy statement appear on the web page notifying the individual of contact details of the organisation collecting the information and outlining in what circumstances, and for what purposes personal information (such as an email address, name or other personal details including purchasing habits linked to an email address) is collected.[53]

The Privacy Commissioner's guidance document on the NPPs includes the following advice to organizations that collect information online: "If an organisation collects personal information using a cookie, web bug or other means, it could give the NPP 1.3 information in a statement clearly available on the web site; for example, it could be linked directly from the homepage and other pages that make use of the devices."[54]

D. Anonymity

NPP 8 requires that, "[w]herever it is lawful and practicable, individuals must have the option of not identifying themselves when entering transactions with an organisation." According to the ALRC, this principle was "intended to affect the design of new technologies that collect more information than is necessary when an organisation transacts with individuals."[55] However, an organization could argue that allowing for an individual to remain anonymous is impracticable for various reasons, including their own systems and needs in terms of being able to identify people conducting transactions. The Privacy Commissioner's guidelines simply state that "[a]nonymity is an important element of privacy. In some circumstances, it will not be practicable to do business anonymously. In others there will be legal obligations that require identification of the individual. This principle is not intended to facilitate illegal activity."[56]

E. Security

NPP 4 requires that an organization take reasonable steps to protect personal information from "misuse and loss" and from "unauthorized access, modification or disclosure." Organizations must also seek to destroy or "permanently de-identify" information that is no longer needed. The Privacy Commissioner's guidelines refer to the protection of personal information through maintaining measures relating to physical security of premises, computer and network security, communications security, and personnel security.[57] "Reasonable steps" will depend on the circumstances of the organization and the type of information held, including the possible harm that would arise from a security breach.[58]

F. Complaints Mechanisms

The Privacy Commissioner handles complaints relating to private organizations and government agencies. The Privacy Act provides that "an individual may complain to the Commissioner about an act or practice that may be an interference with the privacy of the individual."[59]

The Privacy Commissioner can only investigate complaints if the complainant has already complained to the respondent organization, unless the Commissioner determines that it was not appropriate for the individual to make such a complaint.[60] The Commissioner may decide not to investigate a complaint in certain circumstances,[61] for example if the Commissioner considers that the respondent has adequately dealt with the complaint or has not yet had adequate opportunity to do so.[62] Representative complaints may be made where an act or practice may interfere with the privacy of two or more people. 63

Various requirements and powers are relevant to the conduct of investigations by the Commissioner, including natural justice principles and the ability to examine people under oath. In addition to the Privacy Commissioner, the Australian Communications and Media Authority and the Telecommunications Industry Ombudsman may receive privacy complaints such as those relating to spam and some other Internet-related complaints.[64] The Human Rights Commission can also receive complaints or have these referred to them by the Privacy Commissioner if the issue relates to the functions of that entity under various statutes.[65]

G. Sanctions and Remedies

Following the investigation of a complaint, the Commissioner can either make a determination dismissing the complaint or can find the complaint substantiated and make a declaration that may specify various remedies. For instance, the Commissioner may rule that the respondent organization interfered with the privacy of an individual and should not repeat or continue the relevant conduct; that the respondent should take a particular course of action to redress any loss suffered by the complainant; or that the complainant is entitled to a specific amount of compensation. However, the Privacy Commissioner has apparently only once considered a claim for compensation in making a determination relating to a breach of the NPPs.[66]

Enforcement proceedings relating to a determination can be brought in the Federal Court or Federal Magistrates Court by the complainant or the Privacy Commissioner.[67] There is no right of appeal in relation to determinations made by the Commissioner, although it is possible to seek judicial review of the administrative actions of the Commissioner in reaching a determination (for example, on the grounds of a breach of natural justice, abuse of power, or unreasonableness).[68]

Some criminal sanctions are available under the Privacy Act, primarily in relation to breaches of credit reporting rules.[69] The Privacy Act also allows any party to take an action directly to the Federal Court to obtain an injunction against breach of one of the NPPs without first complaining to the Privacy Commissioner. However, this avenue has only been utilized twice.[70]

The ALRC report includes a discussion of developments in Australian courts in relation to a tort of invasion of privacy. There is currently no statutory recognition of such a cause of action, but the High Court has left open the possibility of the development of the tort at common law, and two lower courts have held that it is a part of the common law of Australia.[71] The ALRC has proposed the formulation of a statutory cause of action for breach of privacy.

H. Cross-border Application

Section 5B of the Privacy Act specifies that the provisions of the Act, including the NPPs and the functions and powers of the Privacy Commissioner, may be applied extraterritorially, provided that there is an organizational or an operational link with Australia.

- Organizational link: the Act applies to organizations that are Australian citizens or residents, or a partnership, trust, or company that is formed in Australia, or an unincorporated association that is managed or controlled in Australia
- Operational link: where an organization carries on business in Australia or the personal information was collected and held in Australia[72]

The intent of this provision was to prevent companies from avoiding the requirements of the legislation by moving personal information overseas.

The Act only applies to personal information about an Australian citizen or resident and therefore does not cover information transferred into Australia that relates to overseas individuals. As stated in the Explanatory Memorandum to the 2000 Amendment Bill,

> Where a foreign organisation collects personal information about Australians outside Australia, the Act will only apply if the information is transferred into Australia. Once the information is held in Australia, the Act will apply to acts and practices outside Australia in relation to that information.
>
> Where a foreign organisation collects personal information about Australians overseas and holds that information overseas, the Act will not apply except to the extent that National Privacy Principle 9 applies to the transfer of personal information to that organisation from an organisation in Australia.[73]

In relation to the latter point made in the above excerpt, NPP 9 on data transfers specifies that the act of exporting or transferring personal data by an organization within Australia to a foreign country is a breach of privacy unless certain criteria are met. The principle is based on the restrictions on international data transfers set out in European Union Directive 95/46.[74]

In order to enhance cross-border enforcement efforts, the Privacy Commissioner is involved in a range of international forums aimed at improving relationships with privacy regulators in other jurisdictions. In terms of legal questions, however, the Privacy Commissioner's report to the Senate committee stated that "there is uncertainty as to how this provision [section 5B] operates with respect to personal information submitted over the internet by an individual in Australia to an organisation based overseas."[75] In particular, the Privacy Commissioner suggested that the requirement to collect information *in* Australia was ambiguous in the context of online transactions where the point of uploading the information is Australia but the point of receipt is overseas.[76]

I. Data Retention Requirements

In the past two years, there has been some discussion and speculation about the possible introduction of a data retention framework similar to the European Directive on Data Retention.[77] Such a framework would require entities to retain certain information and enable access to law enforcement agencies on request. The April 2011 Senate committee report considered the issue and potential proposal in detail and included an explanation of existing practices in Australia, particularly under the Telecommunications (Interception and Access) Act 1979.[78] The report explained that there is currently no requirement for an Internet service provider (ISP) to retain metadata relating to the online communications of its customers, although law enforcement agencies do have the power to authorize the disclosure of such data by the ISP if it has been retained. To obtain the content of online communications, the relevant agency must present a warrant.[79]

A representative of the Attorney-General's Department was quoted by the Senate committee as stating that the government had not made a firm decision about a data retention proposal.[80] The Committee considered a number of submissions on the possible proposal and stated that it had a number of concerns about the proposal itself as well as the way it had been handled by the government.[81]

The Cybercrime Legislation Amendment Bill[82] introduced in June 2011 seeks to amend the Telecommunications (Interception and Access) Act 1979 and other relevant legislation "to ensure that Australian legislation is compliant with the Council of Europe Convention on Cybercrime requirements in order to facilitate Australia's accession to the Convention."[83] The amendment bill contains provisions relating to the preservation of stored communications upon receipt of a request from the Australian Federal Police on behalf of certain foreign countries.[84] However, it does not seek to introduce a complete system for mandatory data retention or to allow warrantless access by law enforcement officials.[85]

Some documents relating to the government's development of a data retention proposal were released later in 2011.[86] Most recently, in May 2012, it was reported that public consultation on the issue of data retention and access by law enforcement officials would be conducted by a parliamentary joint committee that has been tasked with reviewing national security legislation.[87] So far, full details of the possible proposal have not been released, and the government has said that it will decide whether to pursue reforms once it has examined the Senate committee's findings.[88]

III. Role of Data Protection Agencies

As stated by the ALRC in its review of the privacy law framework in Australia, in a principles-based system "the regulator plays a particularly significant role."[89] The Privacy Commissioner is an individual, independent regulator supported by an office.[90] The Privacy Act 1988's broad approach involves setting out the functions of the Privacy Commissioner (primarily in Parts IV and V) and then providing the "powers" to do all things necessary for the performance of those functions.[91] In addition to receiving and investigating complaints about acts or practices of both public and private sector entities, the Commissioner's functions include

- approving privacy codes and reviewing their operation;
- examining and reporting to the government on proposed enactments that might authorize interference with the privacy of individuals or otherwise have an adverse effect on privacy;
- monitoring developments in data processing and computer technology to ensure that any adverse effects on privacy are minimized;
- promoting an understanding and acceptance of the privacy principles and publishing guidelines on various matters relating to privacy;
- undertaking educational programs for the purpose of promoting the protection of individual privacy; and
- making recommendations to the government regarding the need for legislative or administrative action in the interests of privacy of individuals.[92]

The Privacy Act provides some scope for the Privacy Commissioner to initiate investigations on his or her own motion.[93] However, such investigations cannot result in enforceable determinations.[94] The Privacy Commissioner also has the power to issue Public Interest Determinations following a request from a public or private entity. These determinations state that "an act or practice of an Australian or ACT Government agency, or a private sector organisation, which may constitute a breach of an Information Privacy Principle, a National Privacy Principle or an approved privacy code, shall be regarded as not breaching that principle or approved code for the purposes of the Act."[95]

When carrying out his or her duties and exercising power under the Act, the Privacy Commissioner must have regard to the "protection of human rights and social interests that compete with privacy, including the general desirability of a free flow of information" and take into account Australia's international obligations and international guidelines that are being developed in relation to the protection of individual privacy.[96]

IV. Court Decisions

As there is no constitutional or statutory cause of action relating to breaches of privacy, and no confirmed privacy tort at common law, matters relating specifically to online privacy have generally not come before the Australian courts.[97]

V. Public and Scholarly Opinion

Developments in online technology, their impact on personal privacy, and the regulatory response are subjects of considerable discussion in Australia by the executive and parliamentary bodies at the federal and state levels, as well as the Privacy Commissioner and other independent agencies, the business and technology sectors, academics, the media, and the public. There have been various public surveys in recent years regarding attitudes to privacy,[98] including in relation to the online environment. The following are some of the areas of comment and concern in surveys, the media, and scholarly articles.

A. Data Breaches

There have been several significant data breaches by various entities in recent years that have affected Australians.[99] Such breaches have been widely covered by the media. The importance and extent of this issue led to the Privacy Commissioner recently releasing new guidelines regarding the handling of personal information security breaches by agencies and organizations.[100]

One survey indicates that Australians are most concerned about data security in the context of the privacy of their financial information and identity theft.[101] The survey also indicated that the public strongly favors the introduction of compulsory data breach notification rules, which were also recommended by the ALRC in its 2008 report.[102] Other criticisms of the current framework include that the Privacy Commissioner lacks sufficient powers, or has not made sufficient use of existing powers, to penalize organizations financially for serious data security and other NPP breaches.[103]

B. Online Behavioral Advertising

Another area of increasing discomfort on the part of the public is online behavioral advertising.[104] Discussions of this issue include references to the complexity of privacy policies, the ability for companies to easily obtain consent to collect information, and the weaknesses of the NPPs in terms of regulating the collection of information using cookies.[105] In one survey, 95% of people preferred that "do not track" rules be developed.[106]

C. Notification, Consent, Access, and Deletion

In surveys, members of the public have expressed a desire to be notified and have control over what information is collected about them online as well as to be able to access what is held about them and request deletion.[107] There is also quite a high level of awareness about the privacy implications of sharing information online, including through social networking sites, with people seeking to opt out of having their information collected. For example, 69% of respondents in a survey said that they have "refused to use an application or Web site because it collects too much personal information, with 79% simply refusing to provide personal information."[108]

Academics have also discussed the issue of consent in relation to the "borderless" nature of the Internet.[109] One commentator noted the ease with which consent can be used as a "miracle cure" for breaches of the NPPs in this and other contexts.[110] In the Privacy Commissioner's 2007 survey of attitudes to privacy, 90% of respondents were concerned about their personal information being sent overseas without their knowledge or consent.[111]

VI. Pending Reforms

The government produced its "first stage response" to 197 of the ALRC's 295 recommendations in October 2009 and agreed to develop legislation to implement many of the proposals.[112] Following a release of an exposure draft of new privacy principles, the Senate Finance and Public Administration Committee completed an inquiry and public submission process in June 2011.[113] On May 23, 2012, the government introduced the Privacy Amendment (Enhancing Privacy Protection) Bill 2012,[114] which implements more than half of the ALRC's recommendations. In her speech on the bill to the parliament, the Attorney-General stated that

> [i]n an online world, we are increasingly sharing our personal information on social networking sites and paying our bills and buying [sports] tickets over the internet. While these technological changes bring immense benefits to working families, there are risks. That's why Labor is tightening up the rules around how companies and organisations can collect, use and disclose personal information.[115]

The model of using principle-based law with a small number of prescriptive rules, together with guidance and oversight by a regulatory body, is maintained in the bill. Key amendments that are relevant to the protection of privacy online[116] include the following:

- A single set of principles that will apply to both the public and private sectors, to be known as the Australian Privacy Principles (APPs). These will also be restructured to better reflect the "life cycle" of personal information.[117]
- An amendment to the definition of "personal information" to include the notion of a "reasonably identifiable individual." This is aimed at bringing the definition into line with international standards and precedents while ensuring that it remains technology-neutral and flexible.[118]
- A new division ("APP codes") will provide for the development of codes of practice regarding how one or more of the APPs will be applied or complied with by a particular sector. The Privacy Commissioner may request that such a code be developed and breaches will be investigated along with breaches of the APPs.[119]
- A new privacy principle on direct marketing will require companies to provide a clear and simple way for opting out of receiving direct marketing materials.[120]
- Changes to the protections for individuals when companies disclose personal information overseas, including requiring that Australian entities take reasonable steps to ensure that an overseas recipient does not breach the APPs. The accountability approach is based on the APEC Privacy Framework[121] and OECD Guidelines, rather than the EU Data Protection Directive of 1996, which the current NPP 9 is based on.[122]
- A new requirement for organizations to develop detailed privacy policies that are clear and accessible. The policies will be required to be kept up-to-date and state whether information is likely to be disclosed to overseas recipients, and if so, in which countries.[123]
- A higher standard of protection will apply in relation to sensitive information.[124]
- Enhanced functions and powers for the Privacy Commissioner, including allowing him or her to make determinations to direct organizations to take specific steps to stop certain conduct or take reasonable action to redress any loss or damages suffered.[125]

- The ability for the Privacy Commissioner to obtain "enforceable undertakings" from organizations, following which a court can issue appropriate orders, including for compensation to be paid.[126]
- The Privacy Commissioner will be able to apply to the court for a civil penalty order against organizations for serious or repeated breaches of privacy.[127]
- The Privacy Commissioner will be able to conduct privacy performance assessments of organizations.[128]

The bill has been referred to the House Standing Committee on Social Policy and Legal Affairs for consideration and public consultation.[129] Once the bill is passed, the government will turn to its second stage response to the ALRC's report, which will include the recommendations relating to children and young people, a system of compulsory notification of serious data breaches, and a statutory cause of action for serious invasions of privacy. This latter issue has already been the subject of a government discussion paper released in September 2011.[130] The government is now considering submissions received in response to the paper.[131]

Prepared by Kelly Buchanan
Chief, Foreign, Comparative,
and International Law Division I
June 2012

CANADA
ONLINE PRIVACY LAW

Executive Summary

Canadian courts have relied on rights contained in the Canadian Charter of Rights and Freedoms to protect citizens against unreasonable invasions of privacy. Personal data protection is primarily regulated on the federal level by the Personal Information Protection and Electronic Documents Act (PIPEDA), but existing provincial-level statutes may take precedence over the federal law.

PIPEDA has adopted ten privacy principles, which include obligations as well as recommended practices. These principles regulate privacy issues in respect to consent, transparency, security measures, and data retention. Though there are no specific rules for regulating social networks, smartphone apps, and other online activities, PIPEDA applies to the online activities of companies such as Facebook and Google.

PIPEDA doesn't offer any specific provisions on protecting the personal data of minors. However, new reform proposals are being considered to strengthen the law in this area.

Oversight and enforcement of PIPEDA is shared between the Privacy Commissioner of Canada and the Federal Court of Canada. The Privacy Commissioner has authority to (1) investigate complaints filed by individual citizens, (2) mediate privacy disputes, (3) audit personal information practices of organizations, (4) report on abuses or violations of PIPEDA, (5) seek remedies in Federal Court, and (6) publish research and promote public awareness on privacy issues. The Federal Court of Canada, on the other hand, can order organizations to comply with PIPEDA, publish notices or corrections, and award damages.

PIPEDA has predominantly attracted criticism from scholars and other commentators over its weak oversight and enforcement mechanisms. The general nature of the Act's provisions has also been criticized. Public surveys prior to and after the passing of PIPEDA reveal that Canadians have consistently shown a high level of interest and concern over privacy issues.

I. Legal Framework

Canadian courts have interpreted various sections of the Canadian Charter of Rights and Freedoms,[1] including the right to life, liberty, and security,[2] and the protection against unreasonable search and seizure,[3] as protecting against unreasonable invasions of privacy. Moreover, the Supreme Court of Canada has recognized the essential role of privacy in a democratic state, stating that

> society has come to realize that privacy is at the heart of liberty in a modern state. . . . Grounded in a man's physical and moral autonomy, privacy is essential for the wellbeing of the individual. . . . The restraints imposed on government to pry into the lives of the citizen go to the essence of a democratic state.[4]

On the federal level, Canada has two major pieces of data protection legislation. The Privacy Act 1980[5] was the first law adopted to regulate the collection, use, and disclosure of personal information by public or government bodies. However, as noted by the PRIVIREAL (Privacy in Research Ethics & Law) project, "rapid advances in information technology and the pressure to conform to European standards to facilitate cross-continental trade meant that new legislation was soon required."[6]

The Personal Information Protection and Electronic Documents Act (PIPEDA)[7] regulates the private sector. PIPEDA provisions are general in nature, and are not limited to online-related activities. PIPEDA does not apply to "organizations" subject to the federal Privacy Act or that are regulated by the public sector at a provincial level, nor to non-profit organizations and charitable activities, unless they are of a "commercial" nature, as defined by PIPEDA (see section II, "Current Law"). Similarly, it does not cover employment data used for noncommercial purposes other than that relating to employees in the federally regulated private sector.

The Act was passed by Parliament in 2000, but was implemented in three stages before it fully came into force on January 1, 2004. PIPEDA seeks to "support and promote electronic commerce by protecting personal information that is collected, used or disclosed"[8] in the course of commercial transactions in the private sector. According to an assistant professor of law, Tina Piper, "[t]he Act was promulgated as a result of the inadequacy of the [prior] privacy regime in Canada to protect personal information in the private sector."[9] Another principal aim of the law was to bring Canada's privacy legislation into conformity with the European Union's directive on data protection, Council Directive 95/46/EC.[10] The Directive prohibits EU member states from trading personal data with countries that do not ensure an "adequate level"[11] of privacy protection, "protection equal to or greater than provided by the

Directive."[12] In 2002, the European Commission confirmed that "Canada is considered as providing an adequate level of protection for personal data transferred from the Community to recipients subject to the Personal Information Protection and Electronic Documents Act"[13] in accordance with Council Directive 95/46.

The provinces of British Columbia,[14] Alberta,[15] and Quebec[16] have their own privacy legislation regulating the private sector. Moreover, Alberta,[17] Saskatchewan,[18] Manitoba,[19] Ontario,[20] and New Brunswick[21] have private sector laws relating specifically to health information.

Pursuant to section 26(2) of the Act, the federal cabinet has the power to grant organizations an exemption for activities covered by provincial privacy legislation: the Governor in Council can issue an order,

> if satisfied that legislation of a province that is substantially similar to this Part applies to an organization, a class of organizations, an activity or a class of activities, exempt[ing] the organization, activity or class from the application of this Part in respect of the collection, use or disclosure of personal information that occurs within that province.

However, organizations or activities would only be exempted for transactions occurring within the province, and PIPEDA would still apply for interprovincial and cross-border activities.

II. Current Law

PIPEDA is divided into two parts. The first part regulates the collection, use, and disclosure of personal information in the private sector. The second part deals with electronic documents and evidence.

Under PIPEDA "'personal information' may not be collected, used or disclosed in the context of a 'commercial activity' without the consent of the individual to whom the information relates."[22] The Act defines personal information as "information about an identifiable individual, but does not include the name, title or business address or telephone number of an employee of an organization"; commercial activity as "any particular transaction, act or conduct or any regular course of conduct that is of a commercial character, including the selling, bartering or leasing of donor, membership or other fundraising lists"; and organization as "a term that includes persons, associations, partnerships and trade unions."[23] According to the Industry Canada website, maintained by the Canadian Minister of Industry, "[t]he term 'persons' includes corporations as well as individuals."[24]

Schedule 1 of the Personal Information Protection and Electronic Documents Act sets out a list of ten principles that organizations "must follow when collecting, using and disclosing personal information in the course of commercial activity."[25] These principles were originally laid down in the Canadian Standards Association Model Code for the Protection of Personal Information.[26] The principles "contain both mandatory obligations that must be complied with as well as recommended practices that should be adopted."[27] The PIPEDA principles, as summarized in an Industry Canada FAQ, are as follows:

- **Accountability**: An organization is responsible for personal information under its control and shall designate an individual or individuals who are accountable for the organization's compliance with the following principles.
- **Identifying Purposes**: The purposes for which personal information is collected shall be identified by the organization at or before the time the information is collected.
- **Consent**: The knowledge and consent of the individual are required for the collection, use or disclosure of personal information, except where inappropriate.
- **Limiting Collection**: The collection of personal information shall be limited to that which is necessary for the purposes identified by the organization. Information shall be collected by fair and lawful means.
- **Limiting Use, Disclosure, and Retention**: Personal information shall not be used or disclosed for purposes other than those for which it was collected, except with the consent of the individual or as required by law. Personal information shall be retained only as long as necessary for the fulfillment of those purposes.
- **Accuracy**: Personal information shall be as accurate, complete, and up-to-date as is necessary for the purposes for which it is to be used.
- **Safeguards**: Personal information shall be protected by security safeguards appropriate to the sensitivity of the information.
- **Openness**: An organization shall make readily available to individuals specific information about its policies and practices relating to the management of personal information.
- **Individual Access**: Upon request, an individual shall be informed of the existence, use and disclosure of his or her personal information and shall be given access to that information. An individual shall be able to challenge the accuracy and completeness of the information and have it amended as appropriate.
- **Challenging Compliance**: An individual shall be able to address a challenge concerning compliance with the above principles to the designated individual or individuals accountable for the organization's compliance.[28]

A. Consent

Principle 3 stipulates that "knowledge and consent of the individual are required for the collection, use, or disclosure of personal information, except where inappropriate."[29] The organization must "make a reasonable effort to ensure that the individual is advised of the purposes for which the information will be used."[30] Consent must be obtained before or at the time of collection, as well as when a new use of the personal information is identified.[31] Both the way in which an organization seeks consent and the form of the consent sought by the organization "may vary, depending on the circumstances and the type of information collected."[32] If the information is considered sensitive, the organization should seek express consent from the individual;[33] "[i]mplied consent would generally be appropriate when the information is less sensitive."[34] Consent can also be given by an authorized representative (such as a legal guardian or a person having power of attorney).[35]

Individuals can give consent in many ways. For example,

a) an application form may be used to seek consent, collect information, and inform the individual of the use that will be made of the information. By completing and signing the form, the individual is giving consent to the collection and the specified uses;
b) a checkoff box may be used to allow individuals to request that their names and addresses not be given to other organizations. Individuals who do not check the box are assumed to consent to the transfer of this information to third parties;
c) consent may be given orally when information is collected over the telephone; or
d) consent may be given at the time that individuals use a product or service.[36]

The Act also stipulates certain specific circumstances or exceptions in which a private sector organization may collect, use, or disclose personal information where knowledge or consent is not required.[37] According to section 5(3), "[a]n organization may collect, use or disclose personal information only for purposes that a reasonable person would consider are appropriate in the circumstances."

B. Transparency

Principle 8 requires organizations to be open about their management of personal information: "An organization shall make readily available to individuals specific information about its policies and practices relating to the management of personal information."[38] Organizations should be "open about their policies and practices"[39] and individuals should be "able to acquire information about an organization's policies and practices without unreasonable effort."[40] Moreover, the information must be made "available in a form that is generally understandable"[41] and must include

a) the name or title, and the address, of the person who is accountable for the organization's policies and practices and to whom complaints or inquiries can be forwarded;
b) the means of gaining access to personal information held by the organization;
c) a description of the type of personal information held by the organization, including a general account of its use;
d) a copy of any brochures or other information that explain the organization's policies, standards, or codes; and
e) what personal information is made available to related organizations (e.g., subsidiaries).[42]

No particular method is prescribed for how an organization should make its policies and practices available. Instead, the principle stipulates that it can be "available in a variety of ways," depending on the "nature of its business and other considerations."[43] For example, principle 8 advises that "an organization may choose to make brochures available in its place of business, mail information to its customers, provide online access, or establish a toll-free telephone number."[44]

In addition, principle 2 requires that the "purpose for which personal information is collected" is identified by the organization "at or before the time the information is collected."[45] The purpose has to be documented in order to comply with the above openness principle.[46] Moreover, "[w]hen personal information that has been collected is to be used for a purpose not previously identified, the new purpose shall be identified prior to use."[47] The principle also requires that the identified purposes should be specified to the person from whom the personal information is being collected, either "orally or in writing."[48]

C. Safeguards and Security Measures

Principle 7 requires that personal information must be "protected by security safeguards appropriate to the sensitivity of the information."[49] The measures must protect against "loss or theft, as well as unauthorized access, disclosure, complying, use or modification" and "regardless of the format in which [the information] is held."[50] Principle 7 states:

> The nature of the safeguards will vary depending on the sensitivity of the information that has been collected, the amount, distribution, and format of the information, and the method of storage. More sensitive information should be safeguarded by a higher level of protection.[51]

The principle requires due care in the process of "disposal or destruction of personal information, to prevent unauthorized parties from gaining access to the information,"[52] and stipulates certain methods of protection, which should include

> a) physical measures, for example, locked filing cabinets and restricted access to offices;
> b) organizational measures, for example, security clearances and limiting access on a "need-to-know" basis; and
> c) technological measures, for example, the use of passwords and encryption.[53]

Organizations are also required to "make their employees aware of the importance of maintaining the confidentiality of personal information."[54]

D. Anonymity and Data Retention

The implementation of guidelines and procedures for retention of personal information appears to be a recommendation rather then a statutory requirement. According to principle 5,

> [o]rganizations should develop guidelines and implement procedures with respect to the retention of personal information. These guidelines should include minimum and maximum retention periods. Personal information that has been used to make a decision about an individual shall be retained long enough to allow the individual access to the information after the decision has been made. An organization may be subject to legislative requirements with respect to retention periods.[55]

Furthermore, personal information "that is no longer required to fulfill the identified purposes should be destroyed, erased, or made anonymous."[56] The only requirement appears to be that "[o]rganizations shall develop guidelines and implement procedures to govern the destruction of personal information."[57]

E. Protection Related to Social Networking and Other Online Activities

Besides the general obligations and guidelines stipulated in Schedule 1 of PIPEDA, there do not appear to be specific regulations on data protection in respect to social networking, smartphone applications, or geographic data. However, according to a report by the current

Privacy Commissioner, Jennifer Stoddart (more on the role of the Privacy Commission can be found in section III of this report), "PIPEDA would apply to the personal information handling practices of private sector organizations engaged in online tracking, profiling and targeting, and cloud computing."[58] The Privacy Commissioner has been particularly critical of the role of social media websites. While testifying before a House of Commons committee, she stated, "I have become very concerned about the apparent disregard that some of these social media companies have shown for Canadian privacy laws."[59] She also said, "We have very limited power in that regard, and I believe more respect would be shown to Canada's laws if we did have that power."[60]

In 2010, an investigation by the Office of the Privacy Commissioner found that Facebook violated Canadian privacy law, and this led to significant changes in the social networking company's privacy policies. More recently, Stoddart has released additional findings of three complaint investigations involving Facebook and stated that Facebook "has shown greater awareness of users' privacy rights."[61] However, she affirms that the company "still needs to do a better job of considering privacy issues before rolling out new features."[62]

Google has also faced investigations in respect to its former social networking feature Google Buzz and its Street View feature. The Privacy Commission found Google in breach of Canada's privacy laws "after being made aware that Google Street View cars had been collecting payload data from unencrypted WiFi networks during their collection of publicly broadcast WiFi signals."[63] Google was also chastised by the Privacy Commissioner when it automatically integrated its Google Buzz feature with its email service. According to a letter cosponsored by the Privacy Commissioner, concern was raised that the personal information of Google's email users "was being disclosed."[64] According to the letter, "Google automatically assigned users a network of 'followers' from among people with whom they corresponded most often on Gmail, without adequately informing Gmail users about how this new service would work or providing sufficient information to permit informed consent decisions."[65]

F. Data Protection and Minors

In Canada, there is no legislation that deals specifically with children's privacy or data protection, nor are there specific provisions in PIPEDA that address this issue. A report by the Office of the Privacy Commissioner has noted that the "average age of children who use the Internet appears to be dropping, and the implications on their privacy need careful attention from public policy makers. . . . Many experts have stated that ensuring children's personal information is protected is an area that needs more attention."[66]

According to the Office of the Privacy Commissioner, consent for a minor, for the purposes of PIPEDA, may be obtained from a legal guardian.[67]

Currently, proposed amendments to PIPEDA "include measures to better protect the privacy of minors online."[68] There is a proposal to expand the requirements for consent by placing "an additional onus on the organization collecting, using or disclosing information to ensure that the person providing the information 'understands' that he or she is providing the information and the manner in which it may be used."[69] The provision is expected "to provide increased protection to minors due to the fact that it is . . . expected that an individual's capacity to understand will vary with age."[70]

In 2011, Canada's Privacy Commissioner unveiled a series of new guidelines "for advertisers designed to restrict how marketers can track users, including children, on the Internet."[71]

G. Enforcement

The Federal Court of Canada can only provide civil remedies or damages for violations of PIPEDA provisions.[72] There are no criminal sanctions or offenses under the Act.

H. Anti-Spam Legislation

Anti-spam legislation[73] was recently passed that targets spam, unwanted commercial email, spyware, malware, and phishing. Bill C-12 also provides for a private right of action, which would allow individuals to take civil action against violators. Moreover, under the new law, the Canadian Radio-television and Telecommunications Commission (CRTC) and Competition Bureau can impose penalties on individuals and businesses.

III. Role of Data Protection Agencies

Enforcement of data protection laws is the responsibility of the Privacy Commissioner and the Federal Court of Canada. The Privacy Commissioner of Canada is a federal ombudsman established to investigate privacy complaints against both public and private bodies. The Privacy Commissioner was established under the Privacy Act, which came into force on July 1, 1983. With the enactment of PIPEDA, the Privacy Commissioner was given authority to investigate complaints against private organizations.

The Commissioner's powers to further the privacy rights of Canadians include

- investigating complaints, conducting audits and pursuing court action under two federal laws;
- publicly reporting on the personal information-handling practices of public and private sector organizations;
- supporting, undertaking and publishing research into privacy issues; and
- promoting public awareness and understanding of privacy issues.[74]

PIPEDA does not give complainants the automatic right to sue for violations of the obligations stipulated under the Act. Under Section 11(1) of PIPEDA, "[a]n individual may file with the Commissioner a written complaint against an organization for contravening" a provision or obligation under the Act.[75] Moreover, "[i]f the Commissioner is satisfied that there are reasonable grounds to investigate a matter,"[76] he or she may initiate the complaint.

According to PIPEDA,

[t]he Commissioner shall conduct an investigation in respect of a complaint, unless the Commissioner is of the opinion that

a) the complainant ought first to exhaust grievance or review procedures otherwise reasonably available;
b) the complaint could more appropriately be dealt with, initially or completely, by means of a procedure provided for under the laws of Canada, other than this Part, or the laws of a province; or
c) the complaint was not filed within a reasonable period after the day on which the subject matter of the complaint arose.[77]

A decision to not review a complaint can be reconsidered if the complainant provides compelling reasons to do so.[78] Also, the Commissioner may discontinue an investigation for a number of reasons, for example if there is insufficient evidence to pursue the investigation or if the complaint is trivial or frivolous.[79]

After concluding the investigation, the Commissioner is required to produce a report of findings and recommendations, which must be sent to the complainant and the organization. It should be noted that the Commissioner has no authority to order compliance, award damages, or impose penalties.[80] However, under section 14 of the Act, "[a] complainant may, after receiving the Commissioner's report or being notified . . . that the investigation of the complaint has been discontinued, apply to the Court [Federal Court of Canada] for a hearing in respect of any matter in respect of which the complaint was made, or that is referred to in the Commissioner's report."[81] The Act furthermore provides the Federal Court of Canada the authority to order an organization to "correct its practices"; "publish a notice of any action taken or proposed to be taken to correct practices"; and "award damages to the complainant, including damages for any humiliation that the complainant has suffered."[82]

In testimony referred to earlier in the report, Privacy Commissioner Stoddart informed the House of Commons committee that Canada's Personal Information Protection and Electronic Documents Act is far too weak and reforms are necessary to provide stricter penalties and fines.[83]

IV. Court Decisions

The first time the Federal Court of Canada awarded damages under PIPEDA was in the case of *Nammo v. TransUnion*.[84] The landmark decision signaled "the court's willingness to award damages for privacy violations in certain egregious circumstances."[85]

Canadian courts have noted that PIPEDA "was not intended to apply extraterritorially,"[86] with the Federal Court holding that "Parliament cannot have intended that PIPEDA govern the collection and use of personal information worldwide."[87] However, the Court held that PIPEDA "could still cover foreign entities that either receive or transmit communications to and from Canada, and that collect and disclose personal information about individuals in Canada."[88]

In another significant ruling, *State Farm Mutual v. Privacy Commissioner*,[89] the Federal Court of Canada held, as summarized by the Office of the Privacy Commissioner, that "State Farm was not engaged in 'commercial activities' when it collect[ed], use[d] or disclose[d] personal information in the course of defending its insured against litigation,"[90] and hence is not subject to PIPEDA.

V. Scholarly Opinion and Commentary

According to legal scholar Jeremy Warner, PIPEDA has "attracted criticism over its level of generality and over ineffective oversight and enforcement mechanisms."[91] Other criticisms include the lack of a reporting mechanism that would require a company to report a privacy breach to the Privacy Commissioner's Office or to consumers. The Privacy Commissioner has noted that "with barely any penalties for breaching provisions in PIPEDA, there is little incentive for companies to invest in better data protection systems."[92]

Commentators have criticized the overlap between the role of Privacy Commissioners at the federal and provincial level, since "this apparent overlap is likely to create a degree of confusion over which body—federal or provincial—has jurisdiction where data flows outside a province are concerned."[93]

Certain scholars have also shown disapproval of Canada's approach to data protection, and PIPEDA in particular, for putting business interests ahead of privacy rights. According to Tina Piper, the serious concerns of Canadians in respect to the "proliferation and commercial importance of personal information" was not adequately addressed by PIPEDA. Business interests and "the characterization of privacy in market terms rather than in the language of human rights and long-term policy objectives" prevented Canadians' concerns from being adequately addressed.[94]

Other scholars have assessed Canada's data protection laws by looking at how they embody different personal rights. The Canadian legal framework for privacy, in comparison to the ones in the US and Europe, takes the middle ground between conceptualizing privacy protection as protecting personal autonomy and protecting personal dignity (the individual's right to control access to personal identifiable information).[95]

VI. Public Opinion

According to Tina Piper, "[p]ublic surveys of Canadians have consistently revealed a remarkably high level of concern over the issue of privacy."[96] Prior to the enactment of PIPEDA in 2000, several reports, surveys, and polls indicated serious apprehension over the issue of privacy and data protection.[97] A 1992 Canadian Privacy Survey by Ekos Research found that 92% of the three thousand Canadians interviewed "believed privacy to be an important issue and that 60 percent believed they have less personal privacy now than a decade ago."[98] A 1994 Gallup Canada survey conducted by Andersen Consulting showed that "over 80 percent of the Canadians polled expressed concern about the personal information about them that might be collected by companies through the information highway."[99] Another study by Ekos in 1998 revealed that "94 percent of Canadians believe it is increasingly important to have safeguards for personal information on the Internet. Canadians, moreover, are becoming much more knowledgeable about privacy issues."[100] Piper notes that "[t]hese studies suggest a pervasive belief that personal privacy is under siege from a range of technological, commercial and social threats and that something must be done about it."[101]

A 1997 study, conducted by the House of Commons Standing Committee on Human Rights, attempted to gauge public opinion of privacy by having surveyors travel across the country and hold meetings with citizens. According to the study,

> Canadians see privacy . . . not just as an individual right, but as part of our social or collective value system. As we struggled with the impact of new technologies on our understanding of privacy, we realized that, ultimately, we were talking about what kind of society we want for our future. Canadians view privacy as far more than the right to be left alone, or to control who knows what about us. It is an essential part of the consensus that enables us not only to define what we do in our own space, but also to determine how we interact with others—either with trust, openness and a sense of freedom, or with distrust, fear and a sense of insecurity.[102]

The study concluded that "we could not but be amazed by the degree of consensus that emerged in each of our meetings . . . they [citizens] all believe that privacy matters."[103]

According to a more recent survey, published in a 2011 report issued by the Office of the Privacy Commissioner of Canada,[104] "[p]rivacy protection is seen as important but perhaps not an issue Canadians feel they have control over." According to the report,

> [a]lmost two thirds of Canadians (65%) agreed that protecting the personal information of Canadians will be one of the most important issues facing the country in the next ten years. . . . Six in ten Canadians agreed that they felt they had less protection of their personal information in their daily lives than they did ten years ago. . . . Most Canadians did not feel confident that they had enough information to know how new technologies might affect their personal privacy: While 43% said they did have enough information about this, three in ten (31%) said they did not, while a quarter (24%) neither agreed nor disagreed with this premise.[105]

According to the same report, "[t]he awareness of federal privacy institutions and privacy laws remains steady. . . . Most felt that their knowledge of personal privacy rights under the laws protecting their personal information was either poor (36%) or somewhere in neutral territory— neither good nor bad (33%)."[106] Moreover, "[t]hree in ten Canadians were aware of a federal institution that helps them with privacy and the protection of personal information from inappropriate collection, use and disclosure."[107]

VII. Pending Reforms

On September 29, 2011, the federal government of Canada reintroduced a bill amending PIPEDA.[108] Proposed changes in Bill C-12 include the following:

- Redefining "personal information" to remove the provision that business contact information is not personal information.[109]
- Inserting a provision "that would expand the requirements for consent under the legislation. The provision would provide that consent will be valid only if it is reasonable to expect that the individual providing it understands 'the nature, purpose and consequences of the collection, use or disclosure of personal information' to which they are consenting."[110]
- Imposing "important new mandatory reporting obligations on organizations subject to PIPEDA, requiring them to report any 'material breach of security safeguards involving personal information under its control' to the federal Privacy

Commissioner as soon 'as feasible after the organization determines that a material breach of its security safeguards' has occurred."[111]

- Adding new exceptions, including "business transactions" and "employment relationship" exceptions, to the requirement for informed consent to use and disclose personal information.[112]

Tariq Ahmad
Legal Research Analyst
June 2012

France
Online Privacy Law

Executive Summary

France's data protection law dates back to 1978 with the enactment of Law 78-17 on Information Technologies, Data Files and Civil Liberties. This Law is said to have inspired the drafting of European Union Directive 95/46/EC on personal data protection. The 1978 Law has been amended on several occasions to comply with more recent European Union Directives. Personal data must be collected and processed fairly and lawfully for specified, explicit, and legitimate purposes, and with the consent of the data subject. In addition to the right to consent, data subjects have been given the following rights: right to be informed, right to object, right of access, right to correct and delete information, and right to be forgotten.

The 1978 Law does not explicitly mention the privacy rights of minors. France favors informing parents and children about responsible Internet use by way of major communication campaigns and education in school. Electronic communications providers must erase or render anonymous electronic communications traffic and location data. There are, however, several exceptions to this rule for purposes of the investigation and prosecution of criminal offenses and for protecting intellectual property. In such cases data may be kept for a maximum of one year. Violations of the 1978 Law may result in criminal, civil, or administrative sanctions.

The 1978 Law also created an independent data protection commission whose powers were further increased in 2004. The primary mission of the commission is to inform data subjects and controllers of their rights and obligations and to monitor compliance with the 1978 Law. To perform its mission, the commission may act by way of recommendations, guidance, individual or regulatory decisions, and on-site inspections. It also has the power to impose administrative sanctions and fines. A draft law further strengthening personal data protection has been pending before Parliament since March 2010. The adoption by the EU of the new data protection regulation currently under consideration may render this draft law obsolete.

I. Legal Framework

There is no specific personal data protection guarantee in the 1958 Constitution. The primary text on data protection is Law 78-17 of January 6, 1978, on Information Technologies, Data Files and Civil Liberties, as amended (1978 Law).[1] Its first article sets forth the principle that information technology is at the service of each citizen and cannot violate human identity, human rights, privacy, or individual or public liberties.[2]

France, together with Sweden and the German State of Hessen, was one of the first countries in Europe to adopt a data protection law. The 1978 Law is said to have inspired the drafting of Directive 95/46/EC on personal data protection.[3] The 1995 Directive intended to harmonize the protection of the right to the privacy of individuals with respect to the processing of personal data among Member States.[4]

France transposed this Directive by Law 2004-801 of August 6, 2004 (2004 Law).[5] As the 1978 Law was largely compatible with the 1995 Directive, most of its articles remained unchanged and it has kept its original number and is generally referred to as Law 1978 of January 6, 1978, as amended by Law 2004-801 of August 6, 2004. Law 2004-801 also transposed parts of Directive 2002/58/EC on privacy and electronic communications, notably its provisions on cookies.[6] The remaining portions of the Directive were directly transposed in France's Post Offices and Electronic Communications Code.

The 1978 Law was also implemented by Decree 2005-1309 of October 2005, as amended by Decree 2007-451 of March 25, 2007.[7] The Law was further modified in 2009,[8] 2010,[9] and 2011.[10] The latest modification resulted from the transposition of two EU directives referred to as the "Telecom Package" by Ordinance 2011-1012.[11] These directives reform the EU framework on electronic communications.

In addition, France has signed and ratified the Council of Europe Convention for the Protection of Individuals with regard to Automatic Processing of Personal Data, signed in Strasbourg in January 1981.[12]

II. Current Law

The 1978 Law provides for procedures ensuring the confidentiality of personal information held by government agencies and private entities. It also created an independent data protection authority, the National Data Processing and Liberties Commission (Commission Nationale de l'Informatique et des Libertés, CNIL). The CNIL's primary mission is to ensure that the development of information technology remains at the service of each citizen and does not infringe upon human identity, the rights of man, or individual or public liberties.

The 1978 Law does not contain any specific rules regarding its application to the Internet. The CNIL, however, has provided extensive information on several matters related to the Internet in a series of articles published on its website. The articles include "Ten Recommendations on PC Security," "The Duties of Bloggers," "Targeted Marketing on the Internet," "Search Engines and Privacy," "Street View: CNIL Review," "The Status of IP Addresses", and "Social Networks."[13] The CNIL has also published a study on security regarding the latest generation of smartphones, providing ten recommendations on how to protect personal data, including one's geographic position.[14] Its recommendations include avoiding the recording of confidential information in a smartphone, choosing a complicated code, adding an automatic lock to the code, installing antivirus software, and turning off the GPS or Wi-Fi feature when not using a location-based application.[15] In addition, the CNIL recently reissued guidance on cookies.[16]

A. Scope of Application

The 1978 Law applies to the processing, automated or not, of personal data contained or intended to be part of a personal data filing system. It applies to the processing of personal data (automated or not) from the private and public sectors carried out by a natural person or legal entity.[17] Processing undertaken exclusively for private (personal or household) activities is excluded. The Law also expressly excludes "cache" copies, described as

> temporary copies made in the context of technical operations of transmission and access provision to a digital network for the purpose of automatic, intermediate and transitory storage of data and with the sole aim of allowing other recipients of the service to benefit from the best access possible to the transmitted information.[18]

B. Territorial Application of French Law

The 1978 Law applies to the processing of personal data where the data controller is established on French territory. The data controller who carries out his activity on French territory within an establishment, whatever its legal form, is considered established on French territory.[19] The Law also applies where the data controller, although not established on French territory or in any other Member State of the European Union, uses means of processing located on French territory, with the exception of processing used only for the purposes of transit through the territory or that of any other Member State of the European Union.[20]

In addition, the question of under what circumstances French law applies to the Internet where the data controller is not on French territory, but the personal data are posted online by an Internet user located in France has been raised in several cases. Some partial answers were provided by the Tribunal de Grande Instance de Paris (ordinary court of general jurisdiction for Paris), as discussed in Section IV, "Courts," below.

C. Definition of Personal Data

Personal data are defined as "any information relating to a natural person who can be identified, directly or indirectly, by reference to an identification number or to one or more factors specific to him."[21] The definition is very broad. In addition to data permitting the identification of a person directly (name, photography, sex) or indirectly (date and place of birth, address, email address, social security number, etc.), the term also includes medical and genetic data and all of an individual's biometric characteristics (digital prints, voice, iris, retina, etc.).[22]

There has been some discussion as to whether an IP address constitutes personal data. IP addresses are regarded as personal data by all European data protection authorities.[23] French courts have been divided on the issue, however (see Section IV, "Courts," below).

D. Rights Granted to Data Subjects

The following rights are conferred on data subjects:

Right to Consent

Any data subject must consent to the processing of personal data unless the data controller meets one of the following conditions:

- Compliance with any legal obligation to which the data controller is subject
- Protection of the individual's life
- Performance of a public service mission entrusted to the data controller or the data recipient
- Performance of either a contract to which the data subject is a party or steps taken at the request of the data subject prior to entering into a contract
- Pursuit of the data controller's or the data recipient's legitimate interest, provided this is not incompatible with the interests or the fundamental rights and liberties of the data subject[24]

The 1978 Law does not include a definition of consent. In general, this issue is resolved by looking at what constitutes consent under the Civil Code.[25] A definition of consent has been added to the Post Offices and Electronic Communications Code in relation to direct marketing by electronic means. It is defined as a freely given manifestation of wishes, specific and informed, by which a person accepts that personal data relating to him/her will be used for direct prospecting. This definition is similar to the definition of consent found in Directive 95/46/EC.[26]

Right to Be Informed

A data subject must be informed of the following: identity of the data controller and of his representative; the purposes of the processing for which the data are intended; whether replies to the questions are compulsory or optional; the possible consequences for the individual of the absence of a reply; the recipients or categories of recipients of the data; the rights granted him by Section 2 of Chapter V (right to object, right of access, and right to correct); and, when applicable, the intended transfer of personal data to a State that is not a Member State of the European Union.[27]

Users of electronic communications services such as telephone, fax, e-mail, SMS (Short Message Service) or MMS (Multimedia Messaging Service) must be informed "in a clear and complete manner" of the processing of their data.[28] The 1978 Law also requires that any subscriber or user of an electronic communications service be informed by the data controller before its installation if the controller intends to install a cookie on his/her computer. The subscriber must expressly consent to such installation.[29]

Right to Object

Data subjects may object on legitimate grounds to the processing of their personal data.[30] Legitimate reasons are those reasons related to the particular situation of the individual and having priority over the interest of the data controller. In case of disagreement, the judge generally gives greater weight to the protection of the individual when deciding whether a reason is legitimate.[31]

Data subjects may also object to having their personal data used for advertising or marketing, or disclosed or transferred to any third parties for such purposes. The right to oppose the disclosure of data to third parties must be available at the time the data are collected. The use of automated calling robots, faxes, or e-mails for advertising purposes is prohibited unless prior express consent has been granted by the individual.[32]

Right of Access

A data subject is entitled to interrogate the data controller to obtain the following:

- Confirmation as to whether the personal data relating to him are part of the processing
- Information on the purposes of the processing, the categories of processed personal data, and the recipients or categories of recipients to whom the data are disclosed
- Information on the intended transfer of personal data to a State that is not a Member State of the European Union, if applicable
- Communication, in an accessible form, of the personal data relating to him as well as any available information on the origin of the data
- Information allowing him to learn of and object to the reason for automatic processing, in the case of a decision taken based on automatic processing and producing legal effects in relation to the individual[33]

Any data subject may also obtain a copy of such data in paying a fee or duplication costs against payment of a fee or duplication costs.[34]

Right of Indirect Access

There is also a right of indirect access where the data processing is related to the security of the state, defense, or public security. In this case, the data subject may request that the CNIL check his/her information. The CNIL verifies the relevance and accuracy of the data, and may demand their correction or deletion. If the data controller agrees, the data may be disclosed to the data subject by the CNIL.[35]

Right to Correct and Delete

Any data subject may ask the data controller to correct, complete, update, block, or delete personal data relating to him that are inaccurate, incomplete, equivocal, or obsolete, or whose collection, use, disclosure, or storage is prohibited.[36]

Right to Be Forgotten

Personal data may not be stored beyond the period necessary for the purposes for which they are obtained and processed.[37] On July 12, 2011, for example, the CNIL issued an injunction to cease processing against the association LEXEEK and imposed a €10,000 fine. This association publishes court cases on its Internet site that include the names of the parties. One of the plaintiffs complained to the CNIL that he was refused a position after the potential employer found a twelve-year-old case concerning a minor offense on the website of the association. The CNIL grounded its decision on one of its recommendations on the dissemination of personal data dated November 29, 2001. In this recommendation, the CNIL advised that publishers of legal databases that are freely accessible on the Internet should not include the names of parties or witnesses. The sanction is said to show the firm will of the CNIL to guarantee a true right to be forgotten (*droit à l'oubli*).[38]

E. Obligations of Data Controllers

1. Prior Notifications

Data controllers must notify the CNIL of the processing of personal data except as exempted by law or the CNIL, or where the data controller has appointed a data protection officer (*correspondent à la protection des données personnelles*). The 2004 Law introduced this new institution. This officer is charged with ensuring, in an independent manner, compliance with the obligations set forth in the 1978 Law. Data controllers who appointed such an officer are exempted from the formalities of notification or simplified notification, except where a transfer of personal data to a State that is not a Member State of the European Union is envisaged.[39]

Prior notification is necessary for all processing that is not subject to any other specific regime. For the most common categories of processing of personal data, which are not likely to be a violation of privacy or liberties, only a simplified form of notification is required.[40]

The following three categories of processing do not require prior notifications:

- Processing intended exclusively for public information and open for public consultation or by any person demonstrating a legitimate interest
- Processing carried out by an association or any other not-for-profit religious, philosophical, political, or trade union body only for the data corresponding to the object of that association or body, and concerning their members or individuals who keep regular contact
- Processing for which the data controller has appointed a personal data protection officer, as noted above[41]

2. Authorizations

Collecting and processing personal data that reveal, directly or indirectly, the racial and ethnic origins; the political, philosophical, or religious opinions; or the trade union affiliations of persons, or that concern their health or sexual life, is prohibited unless specifically authorized due to the special purpose of the processing—for example, the processing of personal data for the purpose of medical research or processing necessary for the protection of human life.[42]

The CNIL's authorization is also required in collecting and processing the following data:

- Sensitive data that are to become anonymous in a very short time after being processed
- Genetic data, unless the processing is carried out by physicians or biologists and necessary for preventive medicine, medical diagnosis, or the administration of care or treatment
- Data comprising assessments of the social difficulties of natural persons
- Biometric data necessary for the verification of an individual's identity
- Data relating to offenses, convictions, or security measures, except for those carried out by representatives of justice when necessary to accomplish their task of defending data subjects[43]

The above list is not exhaustive. The CNIL maintains a publicly available registry that lists the automatic processing that satisfies the formalities above, concerning notification, simplified notification, or authorizations. For each processing the list specifies the document containing the decision to create a data processing procedure, the denomination and the purpose of the processing; and the identity and address of the data controller.[44]

3. General Obligations

Data controllers must obtain and process data fairly and lawfully for specified, explicit, and legitimate purposes. They must respect these purposes. Data collected must be adequate, relevant, and not excessive in relation to the purposes for which they are obtained and their processing. Data must be accurate, complete, and, where necessary, updated. Data must be stored in a form that allows the identification of the data subjects for a period no longer than is necessary for the purposes for which they were obtained and processed.[45] Finally, data controllers must preserve data security, avoiding data modification, damage, or access by unauthorized third parties.[46]

F. Protection of Minors

The 1978 Law does not explicitly mention privacy rights of minors. According to its wording it applies to any "natural person," therefore including minors. Only one of its articles specifically mentions minors, under Chapter IX: Processing of Personal Data for the Purpose of Medical Research. It provides that the holders of parental rights for minors are the recipients of the information and exercise the rights provided for in articles 56 (right to object to the lifting of the duty of confidentiality) and 57 (rights of information, access, and correction).

France favors informing parents and children about responsible Internet use. In 2010 the CNIL organized a major communication campaign for minors, and has invested €500,000 in privacy awareness programs for children, parents, and teachers by sending guidelines to schools.[47] It has also created a special website for minors.[48] In addition, the Education Code provides that during civic education classes students must be taught how to develop a critical and reflective approach to the use of online communications. The Code further provides that students must be informed of all their rights under the 1978 Law.[49]

France is also a member of the Safer Internet Program supported by the European Commission.[50] The Safer Internet Program France comprises Internet Sans Crainte, an awareness project; Net Ecoute Famille, a telephone assistance program; and Point de contact, an online service to notify the authorities of illegal websites.[51] Internet Sans Crainte aims both at reaching children and teenagers directly and at addressing their parents and educators. It provides awareness kits to help educators, teachers, and other professionals organize workshops in schools, in educational and leisure centers, and at shows and exhibits.[52]

A recent report published by the National Assembly states that "the protection of minors in the digital universe is particularly difficult to ensure."[53] It cites a 2010 study financed by the Safer Internet Program showing that 40% of minors between the ages of nine and sixteen who use the Internet have been exposed to at least one of the following risks: pornography, harassment, sexual messages, contact with unknown persons, messages containing dangerous information, and the diversion of their personal data.[54] The report further states that the lack of parental supervision over children's use of the Internet is the weak link in the protection of minors and that additional campaigns to sensitize these parents are paramount.[55]

Finally, the report addresses the agreement for the protection of minors signed by seventeen social networking sites including Facebook at the request of the European Union Commission. The report notes that despite this agreement, social sites do not sufficiently check the age of minors who join. The report in particular cites Facebook. It says that although Marc Zuckerberg, president and founder of Facebook has agreed to keep the minimum age to join Facebook at thirteen for the time being, he has not ruled out lowering that age in the future. In addition, the report notes that Facebook has shown as little diligence to protect children as it has in answering questions from the National Assembly.[56]

G. Transfer of Personal Data to Non-EU Member States

Data controllers cannot transfer personal data to a non-EU Member State unless that State provides for a sufficient level of protection of individuals' privacy. The sufficient nature of the protection is assessed by taking account in particular the laws in force in the State; the security measures it applies; the specific characteristics of the processing, such as its purposes and duration; and the nature, origin, and destination of the processed data.[57] The CNIL is required to publish a list of the Member States providing an adequate level of protection established by the EU Commission.[58]

Data controllers, however, may transfer personal data to a non-EU Member State that does not provide an adequate level of protection if the data subject has expressly consented to the data transfer or where the transfer is necessary for any one of the following:

- The protection of the data subject's life
- The protection of the public interest
- To meet obligations ensuring the establishment, exercise, or defense of legal rights
- The consultation of a public register intended for public information and open for public consultation
- The conclusion or performance of a contract between the data controller and the data subject
- The conclusion of a contract, or the performance of a contract that has either been concluded or is to be concluded, in the interest of the data subject between the data controller and a third party[59]

In addition, when filing their prior notification with the CNIL, data controllers must specify whether the processing will result in the transfer of data to a foreign country. In such case, the CNIL verifies that the data transferred will receive a level of protection similar to that provided by French law. The CNIL may request specific guarantees, limit, or prohibit the transfer of information to countries that do not have data protection laws or have not signed the Council of Europe Convention for the Protection of Individuals with regard to Automatic Processing of Personal Data.[60]

Finally, data subjects whose personal data are transferred abroad may be protected by a contract compelling the data recipients to use caution in their use of the data and guaranteeing recourse for data subjects.[61] The European Commission has approved standard contractual provisions to that effect. "Binding corporate rules" are another form of protection. The rules are designed to allow multinational companies to transfer personal data in compliance with the protection principles set forth in Directive 95/46/EC to their affiliates located in countries outside the EU that do not provide an adequate level of protection.[62] Transfers to the United

States are authorized if the receiving company adheres to the Safe Harbor Privacy Principles negotiated between US authorities (the Commerce Department) and the European Commission in 2001.[63]

H. Sanctions

1. Sanctions Imposed by the CNIL

The Select Committee of the CNIL, which comprises six of its members, may, after hearing from all parties, issue a warning to a data controller failing to comply with the obligations set forth in the 1978 Law. Such a warning is regarded as a sanction.[64] The Chairman of the CNIL may also serve a formal notice to comply on said data controller to cease the noncompliance by a given deadline. In the case of an emergency, this deadline may be limited to five days. The Select Committee may impose one of the following sanctions: an injunction to cease processing; the withdrawal of an authorization, if applicable; or a fine.[65]

Where the processing or the use of processed data leads to a violation of the rights listed in article 1 of the 1978 Law (human identity, human rights, privacy, or individual or public liberties), the Select Committee may issue a warning, initiate an emergency procedure in order to stop the processing for a maximum period of three months, or decide to lock up some of the processed personal data for a maximum period of three months.[66]

In the case of a serious and imminent violation of the rights listed above, the CNIL's Chairman, in summary proceedings, may request the competent jurisdiction to order a daily penalty and/or any security measure necessary for the protection of these rights and liberties.[67]

The amount of a fine imposed by the CNIL must be proportional to the severity of the violation committed and to the profits derived from such violation. In the case of a first violation, the fine may not exceed €150,000. In the event of a second violation within five years from the date on which the preceding fine became final, the fine may not exceed €300,000 or, in the case of a legal entity, 5% of its gross revenue for the latest financial year, to a maximum of €300,000.[68] Where the Select Committee issues a fine that is final before a criminal court has definitively ruled on the same or related facts, the criminal court judge may order that the amount of the CNIL fine be deducted from the fine he imposes.[69]

Fines Levied on Google

On March 17, 2011, the CNIL used its enforcement authority to fine Google €100,000 for violating France's data privacy laws.[70] A press release issued by the CNIL stated that for many years Google has been collecting technical data over unsecured Wi-Fi networks and recording personal data (IDs, passwords, login details, and email exchanges revealing information on health and sexual orientation) without the knowledge of the data subjects.[71]

The press release further provided that inspections carried out by the CNIL in late 2009 and early 2010 demonstrated that vehicles (Google Street View cars used for Google Maps services) deployed on the French territory collected and recorded not only photographs but also data transmitted by individuals' wireless Wi-Fi networks without their knowledge. The collection of tens of thousands of Wi-Fi access points via Google cars apparently allowed the company to develop a database of geo-locations that is extremely competitive, and thus to acquire a dominant position in the field of location-based services.[72]

In May 2006 the CNIL requested that Google stop collecting such data and provide a copy of all the data collected on French territory. Google claimed that the data were collected by mistake, that it was seeking assistance in deleting them, and that it had grounded its Street View cars. The CNIL, however, found that Google continued its data collection through its geolocation service Latitude.[73]

2. Criminal Sanctions

The provisions dealing with infringements upon personal rights resulting from data processing contained in the 1978 Law have been incorporated into the Penal Code. Articles 226- 16 through 226-24 define several offenses:

- Collecting automated data without complying with the prerequisite formalities or after receiving an injunction to stop the processing
- Collecting data indicating a person's registration number in the National Register of National Persons unless specifically authorized
- Collecting automated data without taking all the necessary precautions to preserve the security of such data
- Collecting information by fraudulent, unfair, or unlawful means or collecting data concerning a person despite the person's reasonable objections
- Processing data for direct marketing purposes in spite of the person's objection
- Collecting health data without informing the data subject of his/her right of access, correction, and objection, or despite their objection
- Storing data that directly or indirectly discloses the racial origins or the political, philosophic, or religious opinions; trade union membership; or morals principles of a data subject without the explicit agreement of such person
- Storing automated data without the authorization of the CNIL beyond the period originally authorized
- Diverting automated data from its intended use
- Making automated data available to a third person not qualified to receive such data without the consent of the affected person
- Transferring personal data to a State that does not belong to the European Union in violation of measures taken by either the European Union or the CNIL[74]

These offenses are punished by a maximum term of imprisonment of five years and a maximum fine of €300,000, with the exception of making automated data available to a third person not qualified to receive them where such offense is committed by negligence or a lack of prudence. In such cases, the penalty is a maximum term of imprisonment of three years and a fine of €100,000.[75]

3. Civil Sanctions

An individual whose right to privacy is violated may request that a court order such measures to be taken as necessary to end the violation of this right.[76] In addition, the individual may be entitled to damages under article 1382 of the Civil Code, which provides that "[a]ny act whatever of man, which causes damage to another, obliges the one by whose fault it occurred, to compensate it."[77]

I. Retention of Data

Directive 2006/24/EC, known as the Data Retention Directive, requires Member States to compel electronic communications providers to retain traffic and location data for between six months and two years for the purpose of the investigation, detection, and prosecution of serious crime.[78] France transposed Directive 2006/24/EC through several provisions contained in various laws. It added a provision to the Post Offices and Electronic Communication Code providing for the retention of certain types of technical data for a maximum period of one year for research purposes, the detection and prosecution of criminal offenses, and the protection of intellectual property.[79]

Law 2006-64 of January 23, 2006, on the Fight Against Terrorism, specifically empowered police officers to require the communication of certain data from Internet providers without any authorization from the Public Prosecutor.[80] This provision was also incorporated into the Post Offices and Electronic Communications Code.[81] Internet providers may also be required by these police officers to keep the data for one year.[82] The police officers must state the grounds for their requests in writing. These requests are reviewed by a qualified person appointed for three years by the National Commission for the Monitoring of Security Interceptions (Commission nationale de contrôle des interceptions de sécurité). The Commission may verify the officer's requests at any time and notify the Ministry of Interior of any violation of individuals' rights and liberties.[83]

The list of the types of data that must be retained was published in an implementing decree.[84] It includes data that identify the user and his or her terminal equipment; the recipient of the communication; the date, time, and duration of the communication; the additional services used and the suppliers; and, for telephone services, the origin and location of the communication.[85]

Law 2009-669 of June 12, 2009, on Favoring the Dissemination and the Protection of Creation on the Internet, authorizes sworn agents investigating copyright infringements on behalf of the High Authority for the Distribution of Works and the Protection of Rights on the Internet (HADOPI) to request data revealing the identity of an Internet user.[86] These agents may request information from electronic communications providers that are necessary to establish evidence of a copyright infringement including but not limited to the identity, postal address, electronic address, and telephone number of the subscriber.[87]

III. Role of Data Protection Agencies

The CNIL was established by the 1978 Law.[88] Its powers were further increased by the 2004 Law. It is an independent administrative authority. Its budget is allocated from the State budget. Its decisions may be appealed before the administrative courts. The CNIL's primary mission is to inform individuals and data controllers of their rights and obligations and to monitor the observance of the 1978 Law. It does not receive any instructions from any other authorities. Ministers, public authorities, and the heads of private or public enterprises cannot oppose the CNIL's actions and must take steps to facilitate the implementation of its missions.[89]

A. Composition

The CNIL comprises seventeen members: two senators; two members from the National Assembly; two members from the Economic Social and Environmental Council; two members from the Cour de Cassation, France's Supreme Court for civil and criminal matters; two members from the Conseil d'Etat, France's Supreme Court for administrative matters; two members from the Cour des Comptes, France's national audit Court; and five eminent personalities chosen for their knowledge of information technology or questions related to individual liberties, who are appointed by the Cabinet of Ministers (3), the President of the Senate (1), and the President of the National Assembly (1). In addition, the Commission includes the Défenseur des Droits (Civil Rights Ombudsman) or his/her representative, who casts a consultative vote. The CNIL elects its chairman from among its members.[90]

B. Missions and Powers of the CNIL

The CNIL has the following mission and powers:

- To inform all persons or entities concerned of their rights and obligations under the 1978 Law
- To ensure that the processing of personal data is carried out in conformity with the provisions of the 1978 Law
- To establish and publish simplified standards and impose, when necessary, standard regulations bearing on the security of systems
- To receive claims, petitions, and complaints relating to the carrying out of the processing of personal data and inform the initiators of these actions of the decisions taken regarding them
- To respond to requests from public authorities and courts for an opinion and advise individuals and bodies that set up or intend to set up automatic processing of personal data
- To immediately inform the Public Prosecutor, in accordance with article 40 of the Criminal Procedure Code, of offenses of which it has knowledge and eventually present its remarks in criminal proceedings
- To entrust by a special authorization one or several of its members or its General Secretary to undertake or have undertaken by staff members verifications relating to all processing and, if necessary, to obtain copies of all documents or any medium that are useful to its tasks
- To answer requests for access concerning processing that involve state security, defense, or public safety, and public processing in relation to offenses and taxation
- To give an opinion on the conformity with the 1978 Law of draft professional rules, products, and procedures intended to protect data subjects if requested by professional organizations or institutions having mainly data controllers for their members
- To assess the guarantees provided by the professional rules that it has previously recognized to be in conformity with the provisions of the 1978 Law, with respect to the fundamental rights of individuals
- To provide a quality label for products or procedures intended to protect data subjects

- To keep itself informed of developments in information technologies and make public its assessments of the consequences of these developments for the exercise of rights and liberties
- To be consulted on any draft law or decree relating to the protection of data subjects
- To propose legislative or regulatory measures to the government in order to adapt the protection of liberties to developments in computer processes and techniques
- To provide assistance with regard to data protection at the request of other independent administrative authorities
- To contribute, at the request of the Prime Minister, to the preparation and definition of France's position in international negotiations in the field of personal data protection[91]

To perform its mission, the CNIL may act by way of recommendations, guidance, and individual or regulatory decisions.[92] The CNIL also carries out on-site inspections.[93] It intends to carry out about 450 inspections related to personal data protection in 2012.[94] It prepares and presents annually a public report on the performance of its mission to the President of the French Republic, the Prime Minister, and Parliament.[95]

In addition, as mentioned above, the Select Committee of the CNIL, which comprises six members, may issue administrative and pecuniary sanctions ranging from warnings to maximum fines of €300,000 against data controllers who fail to comply with the law.[96]

C. Statistics

The 2010 CNIL activity report shows that it received 4,821 complaints alleging disrespect of the 1978 Law, an increase of 13% compared to 2009. Complaints primarily concerned the following sectors: banking and credit, marketing, the Internet and telecommunications, and labor. The CNIL processed 1,877 requests for indirect access. It conducted 308 inspections, gave three warnings, issued 111 notices to comply, and imposed five financial sanctions. It received notification of 71,410 processing operations by data controllers.[97]

IV. Court Decisions

A. Application of French Law to the Internet

On April 14, 2008, the Tribunal de Grande Instance of Paris addressed the issue of whether French law applies to the Internet where the data controller is not on French territory, but the personal data are posted online by an Internet user located in France. The plaintiff in the case was a user of Google messaging services who challenged Google USA and Google France, claiming that Google Groups archiving of messages published on the Usenet forums was contrary to articles 6 (data protection principles) and 7 (consent) of the 1978 Law. To decide the plaintiff's claims, the court first had to consider whether French law was applicable. It found that the plaintiff did not show that Google USA used for the archiving means, materials, or human beings from the company Google France or any other entity located on French territory other than for transit. As a result, the data contained in the archived message that permitted the direct or indirect identification of the plaintiff could not be regarded as having been processed in France, the court said.[98]

B. IP Addresses

The legal status of IP addresses remains uncertain, as the courts have rendered opposing decisions. In two separate decisions rendered in April and May 2007, the Court of Appeal of Paris ruled that IP addresses that were collected during searches and findings related to acts of Internet-based counterfeiting did not enable, even indirectly, any identification of physical persons, and as a result did not constitute personal data.[99]

These two decisions were strongly criticized and the Article 29 Working Party (a group of European data protection authorities) stated in an opinion dated June 20, 2007, that it considers IP addresses to be personal data. The European Court of Justice followed this opinion in a decision rendered on January 29, 2008, in the *Promusicae* case.[100] This position was also confirmed by article 2 of EU Directive 2006/24/EC of March 15, 2006, on the Retention of Data.[101]

The situation in France, however, remains confused. In a decision dated January 13, 2009, the Cour de Cassation, which could have ruled on the issue, chose to bypass it by focusing instead on the definition of data processing activity.[102] In that case, SACEM, a body representing authors and composers, asked one of its sworn agents to collect evidence of copyright infringement on a peer-to-peer network. After selecting a network, the agent typed the title of a song and searched for all files corresponding to the song. He then selected one of the files and saved information related to that file (IP address, name of the Internet service provider, country of origin, etc.) on a CD-Rom to be used as evidence of infringement. The main issue raised was whether such activity constituted data processing under the 1978 Law and therefore required the prior authorization of the CNIL. Article 9(4) of the 1978 Law authorizes personal data processing relating to offenses, convictions, and security measures by persons listed in articles L321-1 and L331-1 of the Intellectual Property Code, who act on behalf of victims of infringements. Article 25 of the 1978 Law requires that this processing be authorized by the CNIL. The Court found that collecting an IP address manually without using an automatic monitoring device in order to obtain an individual's identity via his Internet service provider falls within the powers of a sworn agent and does not constitute a data processing activity within the meaning of articles 2, 9, and 25 of the 1978 Law. The Court did not address the status of the IP address.[103]

V. Public and Scholarly Opinion

According to a poll taken in October 2008, a few days before the 30th International Conference of Data Protection and Privacy Commissioners held in Strasbourg, France, 71% of French people find privacy protection on the Internet to be insufficient, and 37% of them find it not at all satisfactory. Persons age eighteen to twenty-four who use the Internet on a larger scale are even more concerned, with the percentage of unsatisfied users increasing to 78% among this age group.[104]

During the Conference the Commissioners noted that,

> [a]t present, there is very little protection against copying any kind of personal data from users' profiles (by other network members, or by unauthorized third parties from outside the network) and using them for building personal profiles, or republishing the data elsewhere. It can be very hard, and sometimes even impossible, to thoroughly remove information from the

> Internet once it is published: Even after deletion from the original site (e.g. the social network), copies may be kept by third parties or the social network service providers. Personal data from profiles may also "leak" outside the network when they are indexed by search engines. In addition, some social network service providers make user data available to third parties via application programming interfaces, which are then under the control of these third parties . . . . Among other specific [privacy and security] risks already identified are the increased risks of identity fraud fostered by the wide availability of personal data in user profiles, and by the possible hijacking of profiles by unauthorized third parties.[105]

This lack of protection was fully evidenced by an experiment conducted at the end of 2008 by one of the journalists of the French magazine *Le Tigre*. The journalist was able to recreate a great part of the public and private life of an individual he had never encountered through the sole use of data found on Google. The extent of the information found was such that the CNIL decided to include the journalist's article in its 2008 public report as a warning, without of course naming the individual.[106]

Finally, in a recent interview given to the French newspaper *Le Monde*, Isabelle Falque-Pierrotin, President of the CNIL, reminded citizens of the vital importance of personal data for large Internet companies and social networks and how committed they are to fighting for the continued use of such data. She stated that lobbying against new EU regulations on personal data protection by these groups is fierce, as "personal data are the fuel of the digital world."[107]

VI. Pending Reforms

Following a 2007 Report on Private Life and Digital Memories prepared by the French Senate,[108] a draft law was prepared by a few Senators taking into account some of the report recommendations. The draft law was adopted by the Senate on March 2010.[109] The text, however, has never been reviewed by the National Assembly. If adopted by both chambers, the draft law would classify IP addresses as personal data. In addition, the use of a data protection officer would be mandatory where a public authority or private entity processes personal data and more than fifty persons have direct access to these data.[110]

The draft law seeks to rewrite parts of article 32 of the 1978 Law. This article deals with the information a data controller must provide to the data subject. The new article would first require the data controller to provide, before any processing takes place, "specific, clear and accessible" information regarding the length of storage of personal data and the data subject's ability to exercise his rights of access, correction, or deletion by electronic means where the data controller has an Internet site. Second, it would mandate that the data controller have an Internet site to clearly and permanently post all the mandatory rights listed in article 32I (See *Right to Be Informed*, Section II(D), above, for a list of these rights). Finally, the article would reinforce the data controller's notification obligation regarding cookies and the processing of data not collected directly from the data subject.[111]

The draft law would further clarify the obligation of data controllers to preserve data security and require that the CNIL be notified of security breaches. In addition, it would increase the sanctions power of the CNIL. The maximum fine would be increased to €600,000 instead of €300,000. Through this proposed change, the legislature hopes to encourage the CNIL to show greater firmness. It notes that the Spanish data protection agency imposed fines for a total amount of €22.6 million in 2008 while the CNIL, since its creation to the date of the parliamentary report, had only imposed fines totaling €520,400.[112]

Finally, the proposed measure would strengthen the "right to be forgotten" through several new provisions, while two additional provisions would guarantee better traceability of data transfers and make it easier for data subjects to object to the dissemination of their data by obligating a data controller to clearly and permanently list the data recipients or categories of data recipients on its Internet site, and providing data subjects with the possibility of gaining access to the origin of the personal data. Today only access to the data is provided.[113] The adoption by the EU of the new data protection regulation currently under consideration may, however, render this draft law obsolete.

Nicole Atwill
Senior Foreign Law Specialist
June 2012

GERMANY
ONLINE PRIVACY LAW

Executive Summary

The German Federal Data Protection Act has separate provisions for data processing in the public and private sectors. In addition, Germany has special privacy provisions for electronic information and communication services (telemedia) and yet another set of privacy rules for the providers of services that transmit electronic signals. All these laws apply to some extent to the providers of online services. Through these laws Germany transposed European Union (EU) Directives 95/46 and 2002/58, albeit in a very complex and differentiated manner. Some German experts find that this complexity interferes with the requirement of transparency in that it keeps consumers from being aware of their rights and from exercising them.

In keeping with the Directives, Germany generally prohibits the collection and use of personal data unless the law specifically permits this or the data subject has given his or her informed consent. German law also follows the Directives on issues relating to rights and remedies of data subjects, security requirements, restrictions on location data, minimization of data, and safeguards against transmitting personal data to third countries with lesser standards of protection. The German provisions, however, often call for the balancing of competing interests and the application of the principle of proportionality. These provisions have resulted in an extensive and varied case law.

In Germany, data protection has constitutional dimensions that flow from the guarantees of human dignity and personhood. From these, the Federal Constitutional Court (FCC) crafted the right of informational self-determination that permits the processing of personal data only if authorized by statue or by consent of the data subject. In 2008, the FCC expanded these principles by articulating a constitutional guarantee of the confidentiality and integrity of IT systems. In 2010, the FCC struck down a German law transposition of the EU Data

Retention Directive, for violating the principle of proportionality and the individual's rights of personhood.

Germany has a Federal Data Protection Agency and sixteen state data protection agencies. These often act in concert when making recommendations on how the consumer may navigate safely through the Internet. In addition, German experts often discuss the data protection problems that arise from the widespread collection of data by search engines and social media, and the use of these data to profile the data subject for commercial purposes. Although German law prohibits these practices unless informed consent has been given and although German law applies to any collection of data on German soil, Germany cannot enforce these laws against global players.

I. Legal Framework

Privacy in online services is in part governed by the data protection provisions of the German Telemedia Act (TMA) (§§ 11–16).[1] This Act regulates electronic information and communication services (hereafter telemedia service providers) irrespective of whether their services are gratuitous or fee-based,[2] thus applying to search engines, news groups, chat rooms, and social media.[3] The Federal Data Protection Act (FDPA)[4] also applies to these online services, except where the TMA more specific provisions.[5] In addition, the privacy provisions of the Telecommunications Act (TCA) (§§ 87–116)[6] apply to various technical aspects of telemedia activities.

Germany transposed the European Union (EU) Data Privacy Directive (Directive 95/46)[7] through the TMA as well as the FDPA, making use of the Directive's permission to enact sector-specific legislation.[8] German also made use of the Directive's permissible "margin for maneuvering"[9] by crafting some detailed legal concepts that are not contained in the Directive but adhere to its spirit.[10]

The German legislation also deviates from the wording of the Directive but not its meaning by adhering to pre-existing German terminology and concepts. In particular, the German legislation distinguishes between data collection, processing and use instead of employing the term "data processing" for all these activities, as is done in the Directive.[11] In addition, the German FDPA retained its pre-Directive structure of having separate rules for the public and private sectors, as well as general provisions that apply to both sectors. Of these, only the private sector rules (FDAP §§ 27–38a) and the general provisions (§§ 1–11) apply to telemedia service providers.

Germany transposed the e-privacy Directive (Directive 2002/58)[12] primarily through the Telecommunications Act.[13] Germany had transposed the EU Data Retention Directive[14] in sections 113a and 113b of the Telecommunications Act,[15] but the Federal Constitutional Court voided these provisions as unconstitutional,[16] and German politicians have since then been unable to agree on how to reword these provisions, while the EU Commission initiated proceedings against Germany's tardiness.[17] Germany transposed Directive 2009/136[18] only in part through amendments to the Telecommunications Act.[19] In particular, Parliament could not reach an agreement on the transposition of the all-important "cookie provision"[20] (see below, section VI).

Germany has a long history of data protection. Like the United States, Germany became aware in the late 1960's of the need to protect the privacy of individuals against the data collection capabilities of electronic data processing.[21] In 1970, the German State of Hesse enacted the first Data Protection Act[22] and several German states shortly followed this example.[23] In 1977, Germany enacted the first Data Protection Act at the federal level.[24]

German data protection developed a new dimension in 1983, with the *Census Decision* of the German Federal Constitutional Court (FCC).[25] In this decision, the Court held that the individual has a constitutional right to "informational self-determination." The decision prohibits the handling of personal data unless sp ecific statutory authorization is given or the data subject consents (see below, section IV). In 1990, a new Federal Data Protection Act incorporated these constitutional requirements.

The Act of 1990 is still in effect today, albeit after numerous amendments.[26] Now, as at the time of enactment, the FDPA has aimed at protecting against the abuse of data processing by requiring that governmental data processing be based on specific statutory enabling legislation, while the consent of an individual is generally necessary to permit data processing in the private sector. There is, however, a strong feeling that the complexity of the German legislation is detrimental to its effectiveness.[27]

In addition to the Federal Data Protection Act, the German states (Länder) have data protection acts.[28] These, however, are not very relevant to online privacy, because they regulate the public sector of the states, whereas the regulation of private sector activity is governed primarily by federal law.[29] Some of the states have explicit data protection guarantees in their constitutions, yet these also are of little consequence for online data protection.[30]

II. Current Law

A. General Principles

The privacy provisions of the FDPA address data controllers, that is entities that process (in German parlance, collect, process, and use) personal data.[31] The controllers are required to register with the pertinent state authority, [32]and this also applies to telemedia service providers.[33] Registration is required in particular for controllers who transfer data to others or conduct market research.[34] They must always register even though other controllers can avoid registration if they appoint an internal data protection official.[35]

Telemedia service providers may collect and use personal data only to the extent that the law specifically permits or the data subject has given his consent.[36] Moreover, to the extent that the law permits the collection of data for specified purposes, these data may not be used for other purposes, unless the data subject has consented to other uses.[37] The law recognizes two types of special purpose data: contract data (*Bestandsdaten*) and utilization data (*Nutzungsdaten*) (see below, Personal Data).[38] For all other types of personal data, particularly content data, consent is required in accordance with sections 28 through 30 of the FDPA, a set of stringent provision, particularly with respect to advertisements (see below, Personal Data).

B. Consent

According to section 13 of the TMA, the controller must inform the user of the extent and purpose of the processing of personal data, for any consent to be valid. Consent may be given electronically, provided the data controller ensures that the user of the service declares his consent knowingly and unambiguously, the consent is being recorded, the user may view his consent declaration at any time, and the user may revoke consent at any time with effect for the future.[39] These principles live up to section 4a of the FDPA, which requires consent to be based on the voluntary decision of the data subject. Consent, however, is not always required. Many statutory exceptions allow for the use of data without consent, for various business-related purposes (see below, Personal Data).

C. Transparency

According to TMA section 13(1), the telemedia service provider must inform the user at the beginning of the contractual relationship of the extent and purpose of data collection and use, also on whether the data will be processed outside of the European Union. If the provider intends to use an automated process that will allow the identification of the user, then this information has to be provided when data collection commences, and the user must at any time have access to this instruction.

This provision of the TMA has been interpreted as applying only to contract and utilization data,[40] thus leaving content data under the governance of Section 4(3) of the FDPA. The latter provides that the controller must inform the data subject of the identity of the data controller, the purpose of the collection, processing, and use of the data, and the categories of intended recipients if this is not foreseeable for the data subject. This information must be provided when the data are first collected.[41]

D. Personal Data

The FDAP defines personal data as "individual pieces of information about personal or factual circumstances about an identified or identifiable human being."[42] This definition applies to all the data handled by telemedia service providers irrespective of whether the data are governed by the FDPA or the TMA.[43] Different rules on consent requirements, however, apply to different categories of data.

Contract data (Bestandsdaten), as defined in the TMA, are the data that are required to establish, develop, or change a contractual relationship with a telemedia service provider. Contract data are to be collected sparingly,[44] in order to live up to the principle of data minimization.[45] They may be used only for the intended contractual purpose and must be deleted once they are no longer needed. This use is statutorily permitted. The user's consent, however, is required if the service provider wants to use these for other purposes, such as advertising or market research; a specific agreement from the data subject is required for these uses.[46] The provisions on contract data apply whenever a relationship is established by an online registration. They apply therefore, to Facebook and other social media.[47]

Utilization data are the personal data that a telemedia service provider may collect and use to facilitate use of the service and for accounting purposes. The service provider may use these data to create user profiles for market research and advertising, unless the user objects after having been duly informed. The thus-created profiles must be identified by a pseudonym, and the identity of the user may not be revealed.[48]

Other data, particularly content data, fall under the consent requirements of sections 28 through 30 of the FDPA, if they are collected by online service providers. In their current form, these provisions were introduced through the 2009 reform of the FDPA, and their complexity is legendary.[49] Generally, they allow certain commercial uses of data, including "list-making" and "scoring," albeit under numerous safeguards. Section 29 deals with data collection and storage for a controller's own business purpose and for the purpose of disclosure of the data to third parties, including for the purpose of direct marketing. Such activities are permitted to some extent without the data subject's consent, yet the competing interests must be balanced, and the data subject must be notified of the purpose of the processing.[50]

It has been stated that section 29 of the FDPA is not well-suited to online activities as facilitated by current internet technology that allows the collection of information from websites and the downloading of large quantities of data.[51] Section 29 requires a scrutiny of the permissibility of data processing in each individual case to ascertain circumstances, such as a protection-worthy interest in preventing the data processing, and the public availability of the data. In addition, the law requires random checks of the continued suitability of ongoing operations.

There has been much discussion of whether IP addresses are personal data, and the majority opinion considers them to be always personal data when they are fixed IP addresses that identify a specific computer. If they are movable IP addresses that are assigned by the access provider every time the user logs in, then they are personal data only if the service provider has enough information to actually identify the user, which will usually be the case.[52]

E. Sensitive Data

The FDPA defines sensitive data according to Directive 95/46 as those relating to race, ethnicity, political opinions, religious or philosophical beliefs, or health or sex life.[53] Consent must be expressed specifically in order to permit the collection and use of such data. Moreover, controllers of such data must undergo an examination of their operations as required by Directive 95/46.[54]

F. Profiling

Germany has been averse to the profiling of personally identifiable data subjects since the *Micro Census Decision* of the Federal Constitutional Court in 1969,[55] and the data protection laws guard against profiling in various ways, among them the insistence that data only be used for the purpose for which they have been collected.[56] The TMA, however, allows the creation of profiles with data that have been rendered anonymous (see below, Anonymity). The FDPA also allows the use of some data for market-related purposes. To the extent that they involve profiling, various safeguards, including the informed consent of the data subject, would be necessary.[57] Profiling without the consent of the data subject is at the heart of the German dislike for the "Like" button of Facebook (see below, Data Protection Authorities).

The specter of large-scale profiling through web-crawling and the use of Facebook was raised in June 2012, when it became known that Schufa, a German credit rating agency, was exploring the possibility of enhancing its profiles on the creditworthiness of individuals with these means. German official reaction was largely negative, finding the project offensive if not illegal; even the German IT industry association, Bitkom,[58] suggested that not everything that was doable should be done and worried about consumer confidence in the Internet.[59]

G. Smartphones and Geo Data

Germany transposed article 6 of Directive 2002/58 concerning traffic data in section 96 of the TCA and the Directive's article 9 on other location data in article 98 of the TCA.[60]

Both types of data are highly sensitive, and unless there is consent for further processing, these data may be collected and used only to the extent that they are required. They must be deleted or made anonymous as soon as they are no longer needed. If they are to be used for marketing purposes or for connection to smartphone applications, special forms of consent and notifications are required.[61]

German scholars are of the opinion that programs such as "Facebook Places" violate German law if the mobile phone user logs in. In that case, the location of the user is to be construed as personal data that may be collected and used only if there is consent.[62] There also is established case law that the creation of movement profiles of a person is illegal.[63] Scholars also are of the opinion that the use of radio-frequency identification technology is of questionable legality in view of the potential to create moving profiles and that the current statutory provisions may not provide enough privacy protection.[64]

Google Street View has come under considerable attack in Germany, resulting in the intervention of the data protection agencies and in much litigation. The outcome of this struggle is that Google may take pictures of the street view of houses, but it must blot out identifiable house numbers upon request.[65] In Berlin, the Consumer Protection Ministry decreed that Google could start its picture taking only after the residents had an opportunity to voice their objections. The dwellings and gardens of these citizens had to be rendered totally unrecognizable by Google.[66]

In August 2010, the Federal Council (the Chamber representing the states in the bicameral federal legislature) proposed legislation that would have further restricted the collection of data through photographs by introducing a legally binding right of objection.[67] In December 2010, the Federal Minister for the Interior, together with Bitkom the German industry association for information technology,[68] responded with a counterproposal that recommended self-regulation, as long as certain well-established principles were not violated.[69]

H. Protection of Minors

Germany has no age-specific privacy provisions. Many of the states, however, provide educational programs to make young people aware of the online attacks on privacy. In Hamburg, for instance, the Data Protection Commissioner published a brochure entitled "You Won't Get My Data," that has suggestions on how to include online privacy education in the school curricula.[70] German organizations also participate in the EU-wide initiative "klicksafe."[71] The media authorities of the states also provide and coordinate programs to protect young people from the dangers of the Internet, particularly illegal content.[72]

I. Technical Security

Section 9 of the FDPA requires extensive technical organizational measures to ensure the overall integrity of IT systems that are being used for the processing of personal data,[73] and these requirements live up to article 17 of Directive 95/46. The German provisions, as well as the Directive, call for a proportional interpretation of security requirements, by tailoring the need for security to the risk inherent in specific operations.[74] Additional provisions on technical security are contained in sections 107 and 109 of the Telecommunications Act.

Section 13 of the Telemedia Act requires controllers to install the necessary technical and organizational measures to ensure that:

- the user may terminate the relationship at any time;
- data will be automatically erased or blocked if required by law;
- the use of the service will not become known to third parties;
- data on the use of several telemedia by one user can be accessed separately, except that they can be combined for accounting purposes; and
- data collected under a pseudonym cannot be combined with data personally identifying the user.

In August 2009, Germany introduced a security breach notification requirement that obliges controllers to notify the data subject if data were unlawfully transmitted or otherwise became known to third parties.[75] This requirement was modeled after U.S. law and is intended to increase consumer confidence in automated systems.[76]

According to the German provisions, notification is required only if the security breach threatens to cause serious impairment of the rights or the protection-worthy interests of the data subject.[77] In November 2009, the EU promulgated Directive 2009/136, which requires notification of any type of security breach that led to the destruction, loss, or alteration of data, irrespective of the impairment caused thereby.[78] Germany has not as yet transposed this provision.[79]

J. Anonymity

Rendering data anonymous is a general principle of German data protection law, to be employed whenever feasible so as to minimize the proliferation of data. Data may also be placed under a pseudonym so as to preserve anonymity.[80] These devices allow the data subject to retain control over his data while giving the controller greater possibilities for use and transmittal of the data. When data have become anonymous, they are no longer personal data and can therefore be freely used for market research.[81] They become personal data again if the controller has the possibility of identifying the data subject. It appears that services are available in Germany that facilitate anonymity by allowing the user to communicate over an IP address that differs from his or her own.[82]

Telemedia service providers are required to use pseudonyms for the collection of certain data. For utilization data, the controller must use "pseudonymization" in order to be allowed to create profiles for market research (see above, Personal Data). With regard to contract data, the telemedia service provider must make it possible for the data subject to use the service and pay for it under a pseudonym, and he must also inform the data subject of this option.[83] The law provides, however, that the provider must make "pseudonymization" possible only to the extent that it is technically feasible and can be reasonably expected.[84] This is one of the many "balancing and weighing" clauses that exist in German data protection law.

K. Rights and Remedies of Data Subjects

The privacy rights and remedies of telemedia users are governed to a large extent by the FDPA. The Act imposes duties of notification on the data controller (§§ 4(3) and 33). He must notify the data subject on the types of data that are being collected, the source of the data, the purposes for which data are collected, and to whom they are disclosed.

For the data subject, the Act grants rights of access (§ 34) and rights to effect correction, erasure, and blockage (§ 35). The right to demand erasure[85] often becomes an issue when a user leaves a social medium. Users often waive the right of erasure in standardized terms of contract. It appears that this is currently permissible according to German law.[86] Even if erasure were to be carried out, data are being transmitted to third parties in many different ways in social media, so that erasure often does not fulfill its purpose.[87]

Data subjects may enforce their rights through the judicial remedies provided in civil and commercial law. Injunctive relief as well as damages can be claimed.[88] It appears, however, that damages for pain and suffering are not available for data protection violations in the private sector.[89]

In Germany, the data protection authorities are not necessarily involved in enforcing the rights of individual data subjects. Instead, complaints against domestic controllers must first be lodged with the company's in-house data protection official.[90] Germans believe in self-regulation of the private data processing sector, yet it has been suggested that this German solution is not compatible with EU requirements.[91]

L. Sanctions

Contraventions of the various duties of the TMA are administrative offenses that are punishable with a fine of up to €50,000.[92] This applies to transgressions such as the failure to erase data or to keep them anonymous.[93] Most violations of the FDPA are also administrative offenses. Some are punishable with a fine of up to €50,000, whereas the more serious ones, such as the processing of data without having obtained consent, are punishable with a fine of up to €300,000.[94] Criminal sanctions are available for conduct involving intent to harm others or to make a profit.[95]

M. Cross-Border Application

In keeping with article 4 of Directive 95/46, the law of the seat of the controller applies to data processing occurring in Germany if the controller resides in another Member State of the European Union.[96] German law applies, however, if such an EU-resident controller carries out data processing in Germany through a German subsidiary or establishment. German law also applies for any data processing occurring in Germany that is carried out by a controller who resides outside the European Union.[97]

According to these principles, German law applies to an online search engine or social medium if it places a cookie on a German personal computer.[98] Enforcement of German law, however, can rarely be achieved against foreign controllers.[99]

On the transmittal of data to other countries, Germany also differentiates between recipient countries that are EU or EEA members and third countries.[100] Transfers to the latter generally require assurances that the third country has an EU-compatible standard of data privacy.[101] Transfers to EU/EEA countries are often, but not always, governed by the same provisions of German law that apply domestically.[102]

The issue of applying German law to the collection of German data by controllers in third (non-EU) countries is addressed in the ongoing controversy over whether Facebook qualifies as a EU-domiciled controller because of its corporate address in Ireland.[103] Many German experts are of the opinion that Facebook use in Germany, in particular the use of the "Like" button, is subject to German law and therefore prohibited on the grounds that the data are ultimately transmitted to the United States, which does not have an EU-compatible data protection standard.[104]

N. Data Retention

As mentioned above, Germany has not as yet transposed EU Directive 2006/24, on data retention. If Germany eventually were to comply with this mandate, the German practices and rules on rendering data anonymous might have to be changed (see above, section II(J)).[105]

III. Role of the Data Protection Agencies

Germany has a Federal Data Protection Commissioner and sixteen state data protection authorities, one for each German state. The Federal Commissioner's primary function is the supervision of data processing by the federal government,[106] whereas the state authorities are in charge of overseeing data protection in the public sector of their state on the basis of state law,[107] and data protection in the private sector of their state on the basis of federal law.[108] In a decision of 2010, the European Court of Justice held that the date protection agencies of some of the German states agencies are not independent enough from the state governments;[109] this judgment will lead to institutional reforms in some of the German states.[110]

The state authorities oversee the activities of private data controllers and require them to register with the authority or to appoint an internal data protection official in accordance with federal law.[111] The state authorities also offer assistance to the public,[112] yet complaints against controllers who reside in Germany should at first be brought to the in-house data protection officials (see above, Rights and Remedies). The sate authorities publish biannual reports on their activities.[113] In addition, the state authorities cooperate in the Düsseldorfer Kreis, a periodic conference that publishes resolutions on important data protection issues for the private sector.[114]

In 2009, the Düsseldorfer Kreis recommended standards for the tracking of internet users by search engines, such as through Google Analytics.[115] As a result of these efforts, Google changed its program code through "IP masking," thus collecting the data in an anonymous manner.[116] Nevertheless, Google is still viewed as being in violation of German law for its tracking practices.[117]

In 2011, the Düsseldorfer Kreis published a resolution on data protection in social media. It admonished social media, stating that German law applies to their activities even if they have a subsidiary in another EU member state, and it emphasized that transparency and informed consent are required to make the use of social plug-ins on German personal computers permissible. The resolution, however, adopted a somewhat conciliatory tone by approving of self-regulatory efforts by social media companies.[118]

On the same issue, however, the data protection agency of Schleswig Holstein has taken a more pronounced view, particularly on the "Like" button of Facebook. The agency advised public and private providers of websites that the "Like Buttons" and other social plug-ins violated German law and that German private and public entities should not have a presence on Facebook. In addition, the agency has taken three German enterprises to court for their presence on Facebook. The cases are still pending.[119]

IV. Court Decisions

The Federal Constitutional Court [FCC] shaped German data processing law by subjecting it to the constitutional guarantees of human dignity and free development of one's personality.[120] In 1969, the Court held in the *Micro Census Decision* that it is contrary to human dignity to catalog and register an individual and that there has to be a sphere into which no one can intrude and where the individual can enjoy solitude.[121]

In 1983, the FCC issued its famous *Census Decision* [*Volkszählungsurteil*].[122] According to the Court, the right of informational self-determination derives from the guarantees of personhood and human dignity of the Constitution, and it generally grants the individual the power to decide about the disclosure of his personal data and their use. The Court allows exceptions from this principle only if there is an overriding public interest and if this is explicitly stated in specific statutory provisions. In addition, the constitutional protection requires that data processing activities live up to the principle of proportionality and give the individual procedural remedies and protections. Moreover, data may not be stored indefinitely for undefined future purposes.

In 2008, the FCC issued a decision on online searches by public authorities.[123] The Court created a new constitutional right that guarantees the integrity and confidentiality of IT systems. Consequently, the Court held that online searches by the public authorities require a search warrant. Although the decision addresses the public sector, it may also create duties for the private sector, because the German Constitution is interpreted to the effect that fundamental rights must be observed by the private sector.[124]

In 2010, the FCC referred to the data retention prohibition of the *Census Decision* when it issued a decision on data retention which struck down the German transposition of Directive 2006/24.[125] In addition, the decision of 2010 found that the statutory provisions had violated the secrecy of telecommunications.[126]

The courts of ordinary jurisdiction also have contributed much to the interpretation of data protection law. They are called upon on a daily basis to apply the principle of proportionality and to balance competing interests, such as privacy versus technical feasibility or freedom of expression. There is a flood of cases that limit the right to informational self-determination.

A decision of the Federal Court of Justice (Bundesgerichtshof) of 2009 explains that informational self-determination has to be balanced with other rights, in that case with freedom of speech.[127] A teacher had requested an injunction against an Internet portal that published student evaluations of her performance. The portal had a registration requirement that included naming the school, along with a user name and password. The Court held that providing information on the teacher was permissible, because it was provided to a circle of persons with an interest in the information. The Court also mentioned that individuals have fewer privacy protections in their professional sphere.

In May 2012, the Federal Court of Justice balanced the right to be forgotten with the public's right to know, by rejecting a request from two murderers to enjoin an Austrian Internet portal from retaining an article on them in its online archive.[128] The plaintiffs had been convicted of murder in 1990. The Court first obtained an advisory opinion from the European Court of Justice that confirmed German jurisdiction over the case due to the plaintiff's close connection to Germany. On the merits, the German Court held that under the circumstances of the case, the public's right to know outweighed the interests of the complainants to be shielded from publicity.

V. Public and Scholarly Opinion

Germans are avid users of the Internet and of social networks. Some 75% of the German population uses the Internet; close to one half of them use it on mobile telephones or tablet computers. The use of search engines has become indispensable to many Germans, and Google has an 85% market share in Germany.[129] Some 55% of Germans are active users of social media,[130] with Facebook usership reaching 28% of the population.[131]

Opinions on the need for online privacy protection range from asserting that privacy has become an out-of-date concept[132] to viewing the assault on privacy in online services as a serious problem. Many scholars are of the opinion that developments in technology and user patterns have created a new reality that is not adequately addressed by German law.[133] This is perceived as being particularly true for the numerous applications that are used on smartphones and through which enormous amount of data are processed, often for the purpose of profiling.[134] A recurring theme in this discussion is the compensatory nature of search engine and social media use, the fact that these services are not "free," that there is a consideration to be paid in the form of released information of monetary value.[135]

The German discussion of online privacy is multifaceted; it addresses the constitutional tension between privacy and freedom of information,[136] makes practical suggestions for users and for future technological development, emphasizes education, and recommends law reform. Most writers take a balanced view by recognizing that online services, be they search engines or social media, contribute to the proliferation of knowledge and empower people to express themselves.[137] Moreover, some writers advise against overly strict German regulation of its domestic providers on the grounds that enforcing high standards in Germany will hurt German firms when they are competing with providers in other countries.[138]

On technical developments, Dirk Heckmann, the author and editor of a renowned commentary on Internet law, favors the development of privacy settings by default that would minimize the disclosure of personal data while also offering transparency and assistance.[139] On user behavior, Frank Koch, a practicing attorney, makes several recommendations, including the frequent deletion of cookies while surfing, the frequent change of pseudonyms when using social media, the de-activation of the geo-localization function of smartphones when not needed, frequent reputation management, using of information posted by German data protection authorities on how to better protect privacy, and the use of search engines such as Ixquick[140] that do not collect user data. He believes that these measures would not only protect the user, but also would favor the growth of innovative, small service providers who would be given a better chance if the data collections of the large, oligopolistic providers were less complete.[141]

Phillip Gröschel, a youth protection official for a for social media service provider, emphasizes the need for education, to empower the individual to discern the complexities of the issue.[142] Indra Spieker, a law professor, shares his view that users are not aware of the threats to their privacy; she would favor clearer statutory rules instead of the current practice of balancing and weighing of competing interests.[143] Ultimately, she recognizes the inevitable tension between the right to information and the right to privacy. Legally speaking, she decries the imbalance in power between the network and the user.

A somewhat unconventional idea for law reform comes from Jochem Schneider, an attorney, who would not require informed consent for the processing of all data. He would limit stringent privacy protections to data relating to the home and the intimate sphere of life. He argues that the categorical insistence on a consent requirement for all personal data is responsible for the complexity of German data protection law, which has to create many statutory exceptions. Moreover, he finds that German data protection law, as written, violates the constitutional guarantee of freedom of expression, which therefore has to be inserted into the statutory law through judicial interpretations.[144]

VI. Pending Reform

In June 2011, the German states had introduced draft legislation to transpose the cookie provision of Directive 2009/136, restating article 5(1) of that Directive almost verbatim.[145] However, this draft did not become law, because the federal government is of the opinion that a transposition of the Directive that follows its wording would not be technically feasible without subjecting the user to constant pop-ups.[146] The federal government intends to await a European solution and also favors self-regulation by the telemedia service providers.[147]

Many German experts view the proposed EU Data Protection Regulation[148] favorably. Among them is the German Federal Data Protection Commissioner, who finds that the reform proposal has a chance of improving the current legal situation, in particular vis-à-vis service providers from non-EU member countries. He also hopes that industry interests will not succeed in watering down the proposed standards.[149]

Thilo Weichert, the Data Protection Commissioner of Schleswig-Holstein formulated these expectations as to what the proposed EU Regulation may accomplish as follows:

> Perhaps data transmission to the United States is no longer possible; traffic data can be analyzed only to a limited extent. The user must be better informed, particularly as to his options on the release of data. The collection of data of third persons, as for instance, through address books, must be restricted, if not completely prohibited. Proper consent procedures must be provided for facial recognition. On the granting of information on existing data and their erasure, clear European guidelines exist that Facebook has not observed as yet. Overall, Facebook must considerably improve their standardized terms of contract and consumer protection. You see: there is a multiplicity of demands – technical, organizational, and legal. Facebook must make major efforts.[150]

Some Germans, however, oppose the proposed EU Regulation for violating the EU subsidiarity principle and for potentially lowering German data protection standards, as well as for giving up constitutional sovereignty over the issue.[151]

VII. Concluding Remarks

Germany has invented the right of informational self-determination, and German law appears to be effective in restricting the processing of personal data by the private sector, at least by domestic providers.[152] Germany, however, shows some understanding of commercial interests. This is demonstrated by the allowance of the use of personal data in some situations, for instance when it is possible to render that data anonymous for market research purposes, instead of requiring their deletion. German law also takes a pragmatic approach to imposing data protection requirements by balancing protective requirements with their feasibility. Balancing is also required to reconcile competing fundamental rights, such as freedom of expression, with privacy interests. The courts are frequently called upon to weight these competing interests, and they do not always decide in favor of privacy.

German law, however, suffers from its complexity and from many broad concepts that stand in the way of certainty and predictability. There is also much concern that the existing laws are not adequate to deal with the technical and societal changes that have been brought through globalization, the increased use of search engines, smartphone applications, and social media and the resulting proliferation of personal data that are disclosed by the data subjects themselves. For these reasons, many German lawyers welcome the development of a European Regulation on data protection.

Prepared by Edith Palmer,
Chief,
Foreign, Comparative and International Law Division II
June 2012

ISRAEL
ONLINE PRIVACY LAW

Executive Summary

Online privacy protection in Israel is based on the constitutional right to privacy, on statutory law, and on court rulings. The country's Privacy Protection Law requires a person's informed consent as a precondition for the storage and use of information deriving from, among other means, online communication. The Law also provides a right to request the removal or blockage of information from a database upon the request of the person concerned. Israeli courts have extended the scope of information for which there is a right to privacy under the Law. Violators face criminal, civil, and administrative sanctions. The Israeli Law, Information and Technology Authority regulates different aspects of privacy protection regarding online data, including the registration of databases that collect personal information. The law imposes a requirement of transparency regarding the identity of owners and managers and the type of information they collect and store. Online privacy protection extends to geo data, and in the case of information collected by Google's Street View cars such data is subject to the conditions enumerated in Street View's database registration authorization.

I. Legal Framework

In Israel online privacy protection is based on the constitutional principle guaranteeing privacy as provided in Basic Law: Human Dignity and Liberty;[1] on statutory law, specifically the Privacy Protection Law, 5741-1981;[2] and on court rulings.

Basic Law: Human Dignity and Liberty, as amended, provides as follows:

7. Privacy

a) All persons have the right to privacy and to intimacy.
b) There shall be no entry into the private premises of a person who has not consented thereto.
c) No search shall be conducted on the private premises of a person, nor in the body or personal effects.
d) There shall be no violation of the confidentiality of conversation, or of the writings or records of a person.[3]

The constitutional right to privacy is qualified by a "limitation clause" in section 8 of the Basic Law, which requires that any law that limits the rights set out in the Basic Law, including the protected right to privacy, must "[comport with the] values of the State of Israel, [be] enacted for a proper purpose, and [be enacted] to an extent no greater than is required."[4]

Israel's data protection legislation is governed mainly by the Privacy Protection Law, 5741-1981, as amended (PPL). The PPL was one of the first privacy laws of its kind in the world.[5] Although the PPL contains a special chapter that specifically regulates the protection of privacy in databases, Israeli jurisprudence has extended the general privacy protections provided in the PPL's first chapter to online information as well.

Online privacy protection in Israel is not absolute. Based on the Criminal Procedure (Enforcement Authorities–Telecommunication Data) Law, 5768-2007,[6] the disclosure of otherwise protected online information may be ordered by a court in special cases involving criminal offenses or where it is needed to save or protect a life, investigate or prevent offenses, or contribute to the indictment of offenders or to lawful confiscation of property.

In discussing online privacy protection under Israeli law it is important to recognize that the Israeli legal system adheres to *stare decisis*. Supreme Court decisions on the scope and application of privacy protection with regard to online data bind all other courts and form an integral part of the applicable law. A discussion of relevant decisions by Israel's Supreme Court is provided in Section IV of this report.

II. Current Statutory and Regulatory Law

A. Collection, Storage and Use of Personal Data by Online Media or Services

The collection, storage, and use of certain types of personal data by online media or services, including smartphones, are prohibited unless such activities are based on the informed consent of the data subject and under conditions enumerated by law.

Based on the PPL general part contained in Chapter A, the infringement of a person's privacy without his informed consent is prohibited whether or not it results in the collection of personal information.[7] The following is a summary of actions listed in the PPL general part that may constitute an infringement of privacy:

1. Spying or trailing a person in a manner likely to harass him,[8] or any other harassment
2. Listening in, where prohibited under any law
3. Photographing a person while he is in the private domain
4. Publishing a person's photograph under such circumstances that publication is likely to humiliate him or subject him to contempt
5. Publishing a photograph of an injured person taken at the time of the injury or soon thereafter in a way that allows him to be identified and under circumstances that may cause embarrassment, except for a photograph taken instantly that does not deviate from what is reasonable under the circumstances[9]
6. Publication of the photograph of a deceased person in a way that allows that person to be identified without the deceased's prior permission, permission of relatives listed by law, or the passage of fifteen years since his death
7. Copying or using, without permission from the addressee or writer, the contents of a letter or any other writing, including digitally transmitted information that is not intended for publication, unless the writing is of historical value or fifteen years have passed since the time of the writing
8. Using a person's name, title, picture, or voice for profit
9. Infringing a duty of secrecy laid down by law or by express or implicit agreement with respect to a person's private affairs
10. Using or passing on information about a person's private affairs for a purpose other than that for which it was given
11. Publication of a matter relating to a person's personal affairs, including his sexual history, his health status, or his behavior in the private domain[10]

Chapter B of the PPL specifically addresses protection of privacy in databases. It defines protected "information" as "data on the personality, personal status, intimate affairs, state of health, economic position, vocational qualifications, opinions and beliefs of a person."[11]

Israeli courts have extended the scope of privacy protection that is applicable to online databases by subjecting them to the application of the PPL general part contained in Chapter A, discussed above.[12] Additionally, in the absence of a definition of the term "private affairs" in either chapter, the types of data that enjoy privacy protection based on inclusion under this category have been continuously added by the Israeli courts and jurisprudence.

B. The Requirement of Informed Consent and the Right to Object

The PPL requires the following details to accompany any request for information that is intended for "keeping and use thereof in a data base":

1. whether that person is under a legal duty to deliver that information or whether its delivery depends on his volition and consent;
2. the purpose for which the information is requested;
3. to whom the information is to be delivered and the purpose of such delivery.[13]

Additional provisions apply specifically to "direct mail." This type of communication is defined by the PPL as any direct contact, including online communication, with a person that is based on his affiliation with a population group that was determined on the basis of one or more characteristics of persons whose names are included in a database.[14]

Any request for information from direct mail requires the placing of a clear and prominent notice containing the following details:

1. Identification of the request as direct mail
2. Notice of the right to be erased from a database that is being used for the collection of information by direct mail, and contact information gathered for that purpose
3. The identity and the address of the database owner and the sources from which he retrieved the information[15]

Under the PPL any person may request to have information about him originating from direct mail and found in a database removed, or access to the information temporarily or permanently blocked with regard to a person or category of persons. The database owner must honor the request and inform the requester in writing of the owner's action. In the event the database owner fails to so inform the requester within thirty days from the date of the request the requester may file his request in court.[16]

C. The Scope of Personal Data That Enjoys Privacy Protection

An interpretation of the term "private affairs" for the purpose of privacy protection, as listed in the first part of the PPL, is included in the Attorney General's Directives Regarding Transfer of Information from Telephone Companies to Bodies with Investigation Authority. This interpretation, as reflected in the Directives, is based on leading decisions of the Supreme Court. For the purpose of online privacy protection, the Directives provide that the term "private affairs" "should be interpreted in a dynamic way, according to what is acceptable at a specific time, place and society, in a way that will reflect the reasonable expectations of the public concerned."[17]

The Directives further recognize that details such as a subscriber's bank account and credit card number that are provided by a subscriber to a telecommunications company for the purpose of receipt of services qualify as a person's "private affairs." Furthermore, in the absence of the subscriber's consent such details should not be used or transferred by the telecommunications company for purposes other than those for which they were initially provided.[18]

The Directives similarly recognize that the right to privacy extends to information on a person's telecommunications record, including

> telephone numbers from and to whom conversations were made, the time of the dialing or receipt of the conversation and its duration. These details, possessed by the telephone companies, are not delivered to them by the subscriber, but are collected through technology that enables the provision of service to the subscriber. These details are undoubtedly "a person's private affairs," and also constitute sensitive information as defined in section 7 of the Privacy Protection Law, because they may point to the persons with whom he is in touch, the frequency of the contact, the types of services that he consumes and many additional details that may be deduced from the data over time.[19]

The list provided by the Directives is not an exhaustive list. For additional types of online data regarding private affairs that enjoy privacy protection, see Section IV of this report, titled "Court Decisions."

D. Regulation of Data Activity

The PPL regulates the management, possession, and use of databases. A database is defined as a collection of data stored by magnetic or optical means and designated for digital processing, excluding a collection for personal use (not for business purposes), and a collection that includes only names, addresses, and communications data, the existence of which by itself does not affect the privacy of the persons whose names it includes, as long as the owner or a corporation under his control does not have an additional collection.[20]

According to the PPL, the management and possession of a database generally requires registration with the registrar of databases, who is appointed by the government. A database must be registered if it contains information that has not already been published or made available based on legal authority[21] and fulfills one of the following conditions:[22]

1. Contains information regarding over 10,000 persons
2. Contains sensitive information (defined as relating to a person's character, intimate affairs, health or economic status, views and beliefs[23])
3. Contains information regarding persons that was obtained without their consent
4. Belongs to local governmental or other bodies fulfilling public duties by law or by a decree issued by the Minister of Justice under conditions enumerated by the law
5. Is utilized for direct mail services based on a person's affiliation with a population group designated in accordance with one or more characteristics of persons whose names are included in the database[24]

E. Transparency of Data

The PPL authorizes the government to appoint a registrar of databases. The registrar must keep a register that includes information regarding the identity of the owners and possessors of databases and the purpose for which the databases were established. The register must also include information regarding the types of information the database is intended to store; details regarding the transfer of data outside of Israel's borders; and any routine retrieval of data from governmental, local, and other bodies fulfilling public duties by law.[25]

The register will be open for full public inspection. However, specific information regarding databases maintained by a defense agency, including the types of data included in such databases, its transfer outside of state borders, and its receipt on a permanent basis from public bodies without the consent of the data subject, is not available to the public.[26]

The PPL recognizes the right of every person to inspect any information about him kept in a database.[27] However, a database owner may refuse to provide information relating to a person's medical or mental state to that person if he believes that it would endanger his physical or mental health. Instead, the information will be delivered to a physician or to a psychologist on the requester's behalf.[28]

The legal right to view information regarding a person's private affairs does not apply to databases managed by Israel's Police, the Intelligence Branch of the General Staff and the Military Police of the Israel Defense Forces, the General Security Police, Israel Secret Intelligence Service (the Mossad),[29] and the Authority for Protection of Witnesses.[30] The legal right to view information regarding a person's private affairs similarly does not apply to the database of Israel's Prisons Authority or Tax Authority.[31]

Exceptions to the legal right to view information regarding a person's private affairs further include situations where the State's security, foreign relations, or legislative provisions require nondisclosure of information about a person; where the Minister of Justice, after consultation with the Ministers of Defense or Foreign Affairs, determines that the data should not be disclosed based on requirements of state security or foreign relations; and where the information concerns law enforcement, criminal investigations, or special data collected at the Ministry of Justice regarding money laundering.[32]

F. Users Anonymity

The law regarding the preservation of anonymity of users is based on court rulings and is discussed under Section IV of this report, titled "Court Decisions."

G. Limits on Geo Data

On August 10, 2011, Israel's data protection authority, the Israeli Law Information and Technology Authority (ILITA), authorized Google to operate its Street View cars in public areas in Israel and to include the photos collected by cars in Google Maps.[33] According to ILITA, considering the type of "data collected, the scope of the footage, the attribution of the exact geographical location of photos taken, and the advancements in facial and plate automatic identification technologies . . . the collection of photographs recorded by Google is a 'database'" under the PPL.[34] The registration of the Google Street View database was authorized by the registrar of databases subject to conditions that were designed to safeguard the rights of the Israeli public, "especially in this case where Google is based outside of Israel's jurisdiction."[35] The authorization to register the Street View database is subject to the following terms:

a) **Civil Jurisdiction** – Google Inc., the service provider based in the USA, will appoint Google Israel as an authorized recipient of court papers in Israel on its behalf . . . ; this appointment will allow Israeli citizens to file civil litigation against Google with regards to the services' [sic] operated in Israel, despite the fact that the company is based outside Israel's jurisdiction and that the database will be held outside of it as well.

b) **Administrative and Criminal Jurisdiction** – Google has agreed to abstain from claims regarding ILITA's administrative or criminal powers by the law regarding its operation of Google Street View in Israel, despite the fact it is based outside Israel's jurisdiction.

c) **Requests for blurring** – Google Street View's website which provides photos taken in Israel, will offer the public an effective and efficient online mechanism to request that further images, license plates and homes will be blurred after the photo is made public, in cases where the automatic blurring applied to photos before making them public malfunctioned or was inadequate.

d) **Transparency** – Google will provide the public online and in newspapers with information about the service, the right to request further blurring and general information about the planned photography route. Also, the Google Street View cars will be clearly marked in order to enable the public to recognize them easily.

e) **Privacy by Design** – Google has agreed to operate the service while applying principles of Privacy by Design and to apply the strictest of standards regarding the collection and processing of photographs.[36]

H. Protection of Minors

Israeli law does not currently contain any specific regulation of harmful content on the Internet. Instead, online activities are subject to laws that regulate telecommunications, advertisements, and computers in general. The following legal provisions may apply to protect minors from Internet-related offenses:

- The Prevention of Sexual Harassment Law, 5758-1998, prohibits harassment through the use of a computer, computer software, or data, and subjects convicted offenders to three to five years' imprisonment;[37]
- The Penal Law subjects persons who publish, display, organize, or produce obscene materials to three years' imprisonment; those who publish obscene advertisements depicting an image of a minor, including by Photoshop or by a drawing of a minor, to five years' imprisonment; those who use the body of a minor for such purposes to seven years' imprisonment, and those who committed any of the above while being parents or guardians of the minor to ten years' imprisonment.[38] The Law defines "advertisement" as including dissemination by a computer.[39]

In December 2010 ILITA published a draft proposal for Ethical and Behavioral Rules for Database Owners who Collect Information on Minors.[40] Information regarding these rules is contained in Section VI, "Pending Reforms," below.

I. Rights and Remedies for Users

1. Civil and Criminal Remedies

A violation of the right to privacy constitutes a civil wrong.[41] If committed intentionally and with malice, it may, under certain circumstances, also constitute a criminal offense punishable by five years' imprisonment.[42] In addition to a criminal penalty, the court may impose a fine on the convicted person in an amount not exceeding 50,000 New Israeli Shekels (about US$13,049), or double this amount in cases where an intent to harm is proved. These fines may be imposed by the court even without proof that actual injury was incurred by the victim.[43]

The PPL lists possible defenses in both civil and criminal trials involving violations of privacy, including among others the defendant's lack of knowledge or ability to know of the potential harm to a person's privacy, perpetration of the violation in the regular course of the defendant's job, and the justifiable need to disclose information for reasons of public interest.[44]

2. Strict Liability Provisions

The PPL further establishes offenses that result in one year of imprisonment if the accused is convicted, without the need to prove negligence or criminal intent. Such offenses include the management or use of data from an unregistered database and the provision of misleading information in an attempt to obtain private information from a database.[45]

3. Administrative Injunctions

In addition to any other remedy, the PPL authorizes the court to order any of the following in any civil or criminal trial for violation of the right to privacy:

- Prohibition or confiscation of harmful materials
- Payment of costs associated with publication of the verdict by the defendant
- Delivery of the harmful materials to the injured party
- Destruction of or prohibition on the use of information received unlawfully[46]

J. Cross-Border Application

Although the PPL does not specifically address its cross-border application, in the absence of any contrary provision Israeli victims could presumably use the PPL to sue online services that operate internationally over harm incurred in Israel. Similarly, under Israeli criminal law offenses committed either fully or partially in Israel are subject to the jurisdiction of Israeli courts.[47] Offenses committed by online services operating internationally may, therefore, be subject to Israeli jurisdiction.

As discussed above, the registration authorization of the Google Street View database by Israel's Registrar of Databases on August 10, 2011, expressly subjects its operations to civil, criminal, and administrative jurisdiction in Israeli.[48]

III. Role of Data Protection Agencies

The Israeli Law, Information and Technology Authority (ILITA), was established as Israel's data protection authority by the Ministry of Justice of Israel in September 2006. The Ministry of Justice website describes ILITA's mission as the reinforcement of personal data protection, the regulation of the use of electronic signatures, and the increase of the enforcement of privacy and IT-related offenses. "ILITA also acts as a central knowledge-base within the Government for technology-related legislation and large governmental IT projects, such as eGovernment."[49]

According to the Ministry of Justice website, ILITA as a data protection regulator constitutes a merger of the following three preexisting regulatory functions:

- The Database Registrar which according to Protection of Privacy Act, 5761-1981 is responsible for data protection regulation and enforcement.
- The Credit Data Services Registrar which according to Credit Data Services Act, 5782-2002 is responsible for the licensing and oversight of credit data bureaus.
- The Certification Authorities Registrar which according to Electronic Signature Act, 5781-2001 is responsible for the registration and supervision of electronic signature certification authorities.[50]

In accordance with the above laws, ILITA's mandate and regulatory authority apply to both the private and public sectors, and include the following powers:

- Inspections at [sic] data controllers and license holders, including powers of search and seizure
- Complaint handling
- Investigation of criminal offences
- Imposition of administrative fines
- Licensing of credit data services and certification authorities
- Registration of databases that include personal information
- Setting guidelines and standard codes of practice for data controllers and license holders
- Raising public awareness to [sic] the right to the data protection among both data controllers and data subjects[51]

According to its website, ILITA also represents Israel in the international data protection arena and promotes international cooperation. Specifically, ILITA

- acts as delegate of the Israeli government to the Committee on Information, Communications and Computer Policy and the Working Party on Information Security and Privacy of the Organisation for Economic Co-operation and Development,
- handles Israel's application to the EU for recognition under Article 25(6) of Directive 95/46/EC[52] as offering an "adequate level of protection" for personal data, and
- conducts a twinning data protection program funded by the EC in collaboration with the Agencia Española de Protección de Datos (AEPD, the Spanish Agency for Data Protection).[53]

IV. Court Decisions

The Supreme Court has contributed extensively to the development of Israel's online privacy law. The following is a brief summary of landmark decisions on online data protection.

A. Constitutional Protection of the Right to Privacy

As discussed earlier in this report, Basic Law: Human Dignity and Liberty, as amended,[54] expressly recognizes the right to privacy, subject to the conditions enumerated in its limitation clause. Accordingly, any law that limits the right to privacy must itself "[comport with the] values of the State of Israel, [be] enacted for a proper purpose, and [be enacted] to an extent no greater than is required" (hereafter the "triple test").[55]

A decision rendered by the Supreme Court prior to the enactment of the Basic Law interpreted the legality of statutory and regulatory provisions authorizing a violation of privacy in a manner consistent to that set out in the Basic Law and its limitation clause. The case concerned a petition submitted by the Association for Human Rights in Israel to prohibit the State from transferring data from the Ministry of Interior to private sector financial bodies. The respondents argued that the transfer to public bodies was authorized by the PPL and that the transfer of data to banks was "anchored in laws that require banks to identify their clients."[56]

The Court recognized that the transfer of information to public bodies was authorized under the conditions enumerated by the PPL and regulations issued in accordance with this law. The Court held, however, that the legal basis for the transfer lacked specificity and had a disproportionate effect on personal privacy, and therefore failed the triple test of the limitation clause.[57] The court further held that appropriate legislation that would improve privacy protection safeguards had to be put in place before the transfer of data from the Ministry of Interior's database to banks could resume.[58]

B. The Scope of Application of the Right to Online Privacy

In a 1990 decision regarding a bank's request for release of information regarding vehicle owners that was stored in the database of the Vehicle Registration Authority, the Supreme Court held that

> the term "information" apparently refers only to data concerning an individual person (Section 7 of the [PPL]). Yet I do not believe it should be interpreted so narrowly as to exclude data such as those concerning automobile license plates discussed herein. The term "information" must be interpreted in line with the legislative intent of the [PPL]. It should include data that can be derived from a database which is not indexed according to individual names. In other words . . . if financial data concerning an individual can be derived from a database that is not indexed on a personal basis, it should be regarded as "information" under Section 7 of the [PPL].[59]

In a subsequent leading decision rendered in 1994 the Supreme Court added the following details to those included in the definition of "information" protected under Chapter 2 of the PPL: "any information relating to a person's private life, including his name, address, telephone number, place of work, identity of his friends, and his relationship with his wife and a spouse and with other members of his family, etc."[60]

A person's telecommunication record has similarly been viewed as part of his "private affairs" that should be protected from disclosure. In a leading 2007 decision the Supreme Court confirmed that penetration into the computer of a cellular phone company for the purpose of surveying a life partner's telecommunications record constituted, among other things, a violation of his right to privacy because the information was related to his private affairs.[61]

C. Anonymity of Internet Protocol (IP) Addresses

In a 2010 decision regarding slanderous messages in comments on a blog, the Supreme Court rejected a request to disclose the IP addresses of the slanderers. The Court held that "to a large extent anonymity makes the Internet what it is, and without it freedom in the virtual world will be lacking."[62]

V. Public and Scholarly Opinion

In his analysis on the legal framework of data protection in Israel, Ian Bourne, the Head of Data Protection Projects, Information Commissioner's Office, UK commented as follows:

> Respect for personal privacy is a well established part of Israel's culture. Its roots go back to the founding of the state. Israel has a population that is certainly not afraid to take action when it feels its privacy rights are being infringed. There is certainly no prospect of ILITA's workload diminishing in the immediate future.[63]

Israeli scholars have repeatedly cautioned that technical developments, particularly the abilities to cross-reference information among various databases and compile profiles of certain groups in society, pose a threat to the constitutional right to privacy. At the end of the day, one scholar has proposed, a public debate on the right to privacy is an attempt to determine the quality of society's public, political, and individual well-being.[64]

VI. Pending Reforms

A. Protection of Personal Information in the Workplace

A draft guide on protecting personal information in workplace environments was recently published by ILITA with a June 17, 2012, deadline for receipt of public comments.[65] Once formally released, the guide is intended to serve as a basis for ILITA's enforcement activities in workplace environments.[66]

The guide recognizes that modern technologies enable employers to collect personal information regarding employees from a variety of technical systems, such as office computers, email, the Internet, smartphones, and iPads that are provided to employees by their employers.[67] It therefore proposes the adoption of the following principles to guide employers in this regard:

1. An ongoing review of the data collected by the employer throughout the employment term and the purposes of data collection
2. Mapping the data stored by the employer, the purpose of its use, and identification of those who have accessed it
3. Maintaining adequate information security rules, procedures, and mechanisms to prevent leaks or misuse by authorized users
4. Providing ongoing, appropriate guidance to relevant personnel
5. Maintaining close supervision on outsourcing services
6. Setting an explicit and clear policy that covers the permitted use of information technologies and the employer's ability to monitor such use[68]

Israeli lawyers specializing in computer law have noted that although some of the provisions contained in the proposed guide are already implemented by many employers in Israel, employers who have not yet implemented them "will need to allocate additional attention and resources to meet the guide's requirements."[69]

B. Protection of Minors

In December 2010 ILITA published a draft proposal for Ethical and Behavioral Rules for Databases Owners Who Collect Information on Minors.[70] According to the Knesset Center for Research and Information, the proposed Rules express ILITA's view regarding the interpretation of privacy laws that should guide enforcement in cases involving minors.[71]

Among the proposed rules are a general duty to protect the privacy of minors and minimize their vulnerability for harm, and prohibitions on the misuse of a minor's weaknesses, collection of indecent information, collection of any information regarding a minor under fourteen, and collection of sensitive information regarding a minor under eighteen in the absence of parental consent.

The proposed Rules will further require the provision of clear information to parents and minors regarding the use of the requested information, as well as the adoption of a privacy policy by suppliers who collect information regarding minors. In addition, the proposed rules prohibit the publication of information that enables the identification of a child younger than fourteen years of age.[72]

Ruth Levush
Senior Foreign Law Specialist
June 2012

ITALY
ONLINE PRIVACY LAW

Executive Summary

The right to privacy, which encompasses the right to the protection of the individual's personal data, was first recognized by the Italian courts in the 1970s, and was then acknowledged by the legislature. In 2003, the Personal Data Protection Code, which implements EU Directives on data protection and on privacy and electronic communications, was adopted.

The Code governs all types of data processing, including online data processing. The main purpose of the Code is the general prohibition of the collection, storage, and use of personal data, unless the data subject has given his or her prior informed consent. Transparency is ensured by the adoption of codes of conduct and professional practice by service providers, and by the general duty of providing adequate information to data subjects. Security is guaranteed through the imposition of the "minimum safety measures" standard. In addition to the right to be informed, data subjects are entitled to several other rights, including the right to object to the processing of the data concerning them or to obtain the updating, correction, integration, or erasure of such data. Spamming is prohibited unless the subscriber or user has given his or her consent.

A supervisory authority is tasked with verifying compliance of data processing with laws and regulations, responding to data subjects' complaints, and blocking unlawful or unfair data processing operations. Administrative, nonjudicial, or judicial remedies to protect rights of data subjects are foreseen.

Presently, no proposals for reforming the current legislation have been presented.

I. Legal Framework

The Italian Constitution contains no express guarantee of the right to privacy.[1] The jurisprudential debate over its existence began in the 1950s, but it was only in 1973 that the Constitutional Court[2] expressly acknowledged privacy as a right,[3] followed by the Court of Cassation two years later.[4]

Initially, the right to privacy protected a person's private life and domicile; over time, as technology evolved, it was extended to protect the ability of individuals to determine what sort of information about themselves is collected and how that information is used.[5]

The first law dealing specifically with the issue of data protection was enacted in 1996,[6] in order to implement EU Directive 95/46 on Data Protection.[7] This act was then repealed and replaced in 2003 by the Codice in Materia di Protezione dei Dati Personali (Personal Data Protection Code, hereafter referred to as the Code),[8] which implements both EU Directive 95/46 on Data Protection and Directive 2002/58 on Privacy and Electronic Communications.[9] The Code expressly recognizes the existence of a right to personal data protection.[10]

As of this writing, no specific laws or regulations regulate location data or smartphone applications.

II. Current Law

The Personal Data Protection Code governs all kinds of data processing, including online data processing.[11] The provisions of Title X are, however, dedicated specifically to some aspects of the processing of personal data in connection with electronic communications.

The definition of electronic communications is given in the introductory part of the Code, where it is stated that this expression "shall mean any information exchanged or conveyed between a finite number of parties by means of a publicly available electronic communications service."[12]

A. Subject Matter and Scope of Application

The provisions of the Code apply to providers of electronic communications services, subscribers, and users. While no definition is given for providers, the Code specifies that a subscriber "shall mean any natural or legal person, body, or association who or which is party to a contract with the provider of publicly available electronic communications services for the supply of such services, or is otherwise the recipient of such services by means of prepaid cards."[13] A user, on the other hand, is "a natural person using a publicly available electronic communications service for private or business purposes, without necessarily being a subscriber to such service."[14] The distinction between subscriber and user extends the protection offered by the Code to those who occasionally use an electronic communications service without having signed a contract with the service provider (e.g., those using their friend's computer or a hotel guest using a hotel Internet connection).[15]

As to the scope of application, the Code applies to the "processing of personal data, including data held abroad, where the processing is performed by any entity established either in the State's territory or in a place that is under the State's sovereignty."[16] It also applies when the processing "is performed by an entity established in the territory of a country outside the European Union, where said entity makes use in connection with the processing of equipment, whether electronic or otherwise, situated in the State's territory, unless such equipment is used only for purposes of transit through the territory of the European Union."[17]

B. Data Processing

Title X of the Code begins with a general prohibition against using "an electronic communications network to gain access to information stored in the terminal equipment of a subscriber or user, to store information or monitor operations performed by a user."[18] In fact, terminals are considered to be an integral part of the private sphere of the individual, and are thus protected by the right to privacy.[19]

The general prohibition on collection, storage, and use of personal data is subject to only one exception: for specific, legitimate purposes, the service provider may store information in order to transmit a communication or provide a specific service as requested by a subscriber or user; however, such technical storage cannot last longer than is strictly necessary and "the subscriber or user must give his or her consent based on prior information, whereby the purposes and duration of the processing shall be referred to in detail, clearly and accurately."[20]

Location data, which indicate the geographic position of the terminal equipment of a user,[21] may only be processed when they are made anonymous;[22] otherwise, it is necessary for the data subject to give his or her prior consent, which may be withdrawn at any time. In both cases, the data may be processed "to the extent and for the duration necessary for the provision of a value-added service."[23]

Traffic data, which are those data necessary for the "purpose of the conveyance of a communication on an electronic communications network or for the billing thereof,"[24] must be either erased or made anonymous when they are no longer necessary for the purpose of transmitting the electronic communication.[25]

C. Data Retention

The Code stipulates that service providers should retain traffic data for two years "with a view to detecting and suppressing criminal offenses."[26] Within that term, the data may be acquired from the provider "by means of a reasoned order of the judicial authority at the request of either the public prosecutor, defense counsel, the person under investigation, the injured party, or any other private party."[27] The Ministry of the Interior as well as the police may request the service provider to "keep and protect traffic data" for up to ninety more days for "purposes of investigation and suppression of crimes."[28] Nonetheless, data processing "shall be carried out by complying with the measures and precautions to safeguard data subjects."[29]

D. Transparency

In order to ensure transparency, the Code provides that the supervisory authority, the Garante per la Protezione dei Dati Personali (Data Protection Authority, discussed in Section III of this report), "shall encourage the adoption of a code of conduct and professional practice applying to the processing of personal data" by service providers, in order to "ensure and streamline adequate information and awareness by users of public and private electronic communications networks as to the categories of personal data processed and the mechanisms for such processing—in particular, by providing information notices online using simple means and in an interactive manner."[30]

Even in the absence of such a code of conduct, the subscriber or user is protected by the general provision of article 12, according to which the service provider must preliminarily inform the data subject,

> either orally or in writing, as to the purposes and modalities of the data processing; the obligatory or voluntary nature of providing the requested data; the consequences if he or she fails to reply; the entities or category of entities to whom or which the data may be communicated, and the scope of dissemination of said data; his or her rights; the identification data concerning the data controller; and, where designated, the data controller's representative in the State's territory and the data processor.[31]

E. Security

In order to ensure "security of its services and integrity of traffic data, location data, and electronic communications against any form of unauthorized utilization or access," the service provider shall take "all suitable technical and organizational measures that are adequate in light of the existing risk."[32] Moreover, in case of a particular risk of a breach of network security, the provider shall inform subscribers and users of said risk and the possible remedies.[33]

According to the Code, the minimum security measures that a service provider may adopt include

a) computerized authentication;
b) implementation of authentication credentials management procedures;
c) use of an authorization system;
d) regular update of the specifications concerning scope of the processing operations that may be performed by the individual entities in charge of managing and/or maintaining electronic means;
e) protection of electronic means and data against unlawful data processing operations, unauthorized access, and specific computer programs;
f) implementation of procedures for safekeeping backup copies and restoring data and system availability;
g) keeping an up-to-date security policy document;
h) implementation of encryption techniques or identification codes for specific processing operations performed by health-care bodies in respect of data disclosing health and sex life.[34]

F. Data Subjects' Rights

The Code provides that data subjects "have the right to obtain confirmation as to whether or not personal data concerning [them] exists."[35] They also have the right to be informed of the source of the personal data, the purposes and methods of the processing, the identification data concerning data controller and data processors, and the entities to whom the personal data may be communicated.[36] Once they have been so informed, data subjects have the right to object, in whole or in part, to the processing,[37] and also to obtain updating, correction or integration, erasure, anonymization, or blocking of such data.[38] All these rights may be exercised simply by making a request to the data controller or processor without formalities, and the processor must reply without delay.[39]

G. Spamming

The Code regulates the practice of spamming, stating that the use of automated emails without human intervention "for the purposes of direct marketing or sending advertising materials, or else for carrying out market surveys or interactive business communications, shall only be allowed with the subscriber's consent."[40]

H. Minors

No specific provisions exist in the Code or elsewhere as to the specific issue of online privacy for minors. The general rules of the Code therefore apply.

I. Remedies

If a provision of the Code is violated, data subjects may choose among three kinds of remedies to protect their rights: administrative,[41] nonjudicial,[42] and judicial.[43]

In the case of administrative remedies, the data subject may lodge a claim of infringement with the national data protection authority, the Garante. No specific formalities are required. The claim must contain as many details as possible.[44] As long as the claim is not found to be manifestly groundless, the Garante may take different actions:[45] the data controller may be asked to block the processing of their own initiative, or an order may be issued for the data controller to take such measures as are necessary or appropriate to bring the processing into line with the provisions in force.[46] If the service provider fails to comply or if there is an actual risk of a considerable prejudice to one or more of the data subjects, the Garante may also block or prohibit the processing. The same will happen if such processing is in conflict with a substantial public interest.

Nonjudicial remedies are also offered by the Garante. If data subjects have not yet brought an action before a judicial authority, they may protect their rights by filing a complaint with the Garante[47] (once such a complaint is lodged, data subjects cannot change their minds and seek a judicial remedy).[48] The Garante gathers the necessary information relevant to the complaint and, if it is well-founded, may order the data controller to abstain from the unlawful conduct, and may also specify the remedies to enforce the data subject's rights and set a term for their implementation.[49] If no decision is rendered within sixty days of the date on which the complaint was lodged, the complaint must be regarded as dismissed.[50] The decision or tacit dismissal of the Garante may be challenged before the judicial authorities.[51]

Finally, the data subject may choose to file a lawsuit at the Civil Court, and the petition may be granted or dismissed, in whole or in part. The court may also order the necessary measures; provide for damages, if claimed; and award legal costs to the losing party.[52] Appeal against the judgment is not possible; however, it may be challenged before the Court of Cassation.[53]

J. Sanctions

Violations of the Code are punishable with sanctions that, according to the nature of the violation, may be either administrative or criminal, and are specific to each violation.[54] For instance, in the case of no or inadequate information provided to data subjects, the service provider may be punished with a fine of between three thousand and eighteen thousand euro (about US$3,700 to $22,255); the amount may be increased up to three times if it is found to be ineffective on account of the offender's economic status.[55] Another example is unlawful data processing, which may be punished, if harm is caused, with imprisonment of up to twenty-four months.[56] Finally, failure to adopt security measures may be punished either with detention for up to two years or with a fine of up to fifty thousand euro (about US$61,820).[57]

III. Role of Data Protection Agencies

The Garante per la Protezione dei Dati Personali (Data Protection Authority) was instituted by Law 675/96 in order to ensure lawful data processing and the respect of people's fundamental rights.[58] It is an independent and autonomous collegiate body composed of four members, two of whom are elected by the Chamber of Deputies and two by the Senate from among "persons ensuring independence and with proven experience in the field of law or computer science."[59] The elected members hold office for four years, and the appointment may be renewed only once.[60] Under penalty of losing office, they cannot carry out professional or advisory activities, manage or be employed by public or private entities, or hold elective offices.[61]

The tasks of the Garante are described in article 154 of the Code and include the following:

- Verifying whether data processing operations are carried out in compliance with laws and regulations
- Receiving reports and complaints
- Ordering data controllers or processors to adopt such measures as are necessary or appropriate for the processing, to comply with the provisions in force
- Prohibiting unlawful or unfair data processing operations, in whole or in part, or blocking such processing operations
- Drawing the attention of the Parliament and government to the advisability of legislation
- Issuing opinions whenever required
- Raising public awareness of the legislation governing personal data processing and its relevant purposes, as well as of data security measures

IV. Court Decisions

As discussed in the first section of this report, the right to privacy was first recognized by the courts. After World War II, the courts were forced to take affirmative steps toward the protection of a person's private life in order to answer the challenges of technological evolution, as the legislature did not want to intervene.

From the 1950s until the first half of the 1970s, there was a clear contrast between the decisions of the Tribunals of First Instance and those of the Appellate Courts: the former recognized the right to privacy, while the latter refused to acknowledge it.[62] An example of this contrast can be found in the well-known *Caruso* case.[63] Caruso was a famous opera singer; after his death, his heirs asked the Tribunal of Rome to protect his private life by barring the disclosure of certain indiscretions that would have harmed his privacy and memory.[64] The Tribunal rendered an innovative decision, recognizing the existence of a right to privacy, which implied the prohibition of intruding into someone's private sphere.[65] Nonetheless, the Court of Appeals[66] and then the Court of Cassation[67] reversed the decision rendered by the Tribunal, stating that the simple desire for privacy alone could not be protected by the law.[68]

It was only in 1975 that the Court of Cassation finally acknowledged the existence of the right to privacy, stating that "a general right to privacy is deemed to exist in our legal system, a right protecting strictly personal and domestic situations [from disclosure] if not justified by preeminent public interests."[69] This case opened the way for a series of decisions confirming the right to privacy. There were no landmark cases; rather, the courts, with their intense activity, built a path that, decision after decision, led to the adoption of Law 95/46, followed by the Personal Data Protection Code. After these laws were enacted, there was a sudden slowdown in the jurisprudential activity; as of this writing, no decision has yet been rendered with regard to online data protection.

V. Public and Scholarly Opinion

The Personal Data Code has been well received both by the public and by legal scholars. According to Sabina Kirschen, a scholar of civil law, "the undeniable complexity of the subject . . . has forced the legislature to intervene and transform the multitude of existing rules into an organic law," which "represents an important accomplishment in the history of Italian privacy law, as well as a foundation on which to build its future."[70]

Another civil law scholar, Silvia Melchionna, praised the ability of the Code to finally "simplify the interpretation of the provisions about personal data protection."[71]

The provisions of the Code that deal with electronic communications have been particularly popular, principally because of the "comprehensive protection it gives to consumers . . . by specifying the duties of service providers and giving value to the rights of users," according to an Italian jurist and former member of the Garante, Giuseppe Santaniello.[72]

VI. Pending Reforms

As of this writing, no proposals have been presented to reform the current legislation concerning online privacy.

Prepared by Laura Andriulli
Law Library Intern under the supervision of Nicole Atwill
Senior Foreign Law Specialist
June 2012

JAPAN
ONLINE PRIVACY LAW

Executive Summary

Online privacy in Japan is primarily governed by a general law, the Act on Protection of Personal Information (APPI), rather than a specialized law on online privacy. The APPI applies to business operators that hold the personal information of 5,000 or more individuals. Japan has other personal information protection laws that apply to the government and public organizations.

The APPI does not provide the details of personal information protection, but establishes basic rules. It requires all business operators handling personal information to specify the purpose for which personal information is utilized. Data subjects can request disclosure of their personal information that the business operators hold.

The APPI did not create a data protection agency and does not provide the government with strong enforcement powers. The legislature thought self-regulation by businesses would be appropriate. Businesses may form an Authorized Personal Information Protection Organization that issues personal information protection guidelines and mediates disputes.

I. Legal Framework

There are three main laws related to the protection of personal information in Japan: □ the Act on the Protection of Personal Information (APPI),[1]

- the Act on the Protection of Personal Information Held by Administrative Organs,[2] and
- the Act on the Protection of Personal Information Held by Independent Administrative Agencies, etc.[3]

The APPI outlines basic data protection policies. These are not limited to online data protection. Those businesses that are subject to the APPI must specify the purpose of personal information collection. The APPI requires businesses to prevent the unauthorized disclosure, loss, or destruction of personal data. It limits transfers of data to third parties unless the data subject consents. The other two laws apply to government agencies and independent administrative agencies, as the titles suggest.

The government has established the Basic Policy on the Protection of Personal Information,[4] as required by the APPI.[5] The Basic Policy sets out the basic direction and actions to be taken by the State, local public bodies, independent administrative agencies, and entities handling personal information. Also, based on the APPI, ministries have issued guidelines on the protection of personal information.[6] As of 2007, thirty-five guidelines had been issued. The Quality of Life Policy Bureau then called for uniformity in the guidelines.[7] In 2008, a number of government agencies met and decided to modify the guidelines to make them more uniform[8] in accordance with the Cabinet Office's directive.[9] As of July 2010, there were forty guidelines and they are more uniform than before.[10]

II. Current Law

The APPI applies to any business in Japan that holds personal data.[11] Businesses that hold the personal data of less than 5,000 individuals are excluded.[12] In addition, the press, academic institutions, religious organizations, and political organizations are excluded, though they must try to take "necessary and appropriate measures for controlling the security of personal data, and the necessary measures for the processing of complaints about the handling of personal information."[13] The term "personal information" means information about a living individual that identifies the specific individual by name, date of birth, or other description contained in such information, including such information as will allow easy reference to other information and will thereby enable the identification of the specific individual.[14]

A. Purpose of Utilization

The APPI requires all businesses handling personal information to specify the purpose for which personal information is utilized as much as possible. 15 Upon acquiring personal information, a business handling such information must promptly notify the data subject of the purpose of its utilization or publicly announce the purpose of utilization of personal information.[16] A business must obtain consent from data subjects before using the information for any other purpose than the one originally stated.[17] However, when the handling of personal information is based on laws and regulations or is necessary for the protection of the life, body, or property of an individual and it is difficult to obtain the consent of the data subject, as well as in other specified cases, prior consent may not be necessary.[18] A business handling personal information cannot change the purpose of utilization to the point where the new purpose of utilization is not duly related to the old one.[19] A business operator cannot acquire personal information by deception or other wrongful means.[20]

B. Data Security

A business handling personal information must take necessary and proper measures for the prevention of leakage, loss, or damage, and for other security control of the personal data.[21] Two specific measures are prescribed in the law. One is supervision over the employee who handles personal data. A business operator must exercise necessary and appropriate supervision over the employee who handles personal data to ensure the security control of the personal data.[22] The other is supervision over the trustee who handles personal data for the business. When a business operator handling personal information entrusts an individual or a business operator with the handling of personal data in whole or in part, it must exercise necessary and appropriate supervision over the trustee to ensure the security control of the entrusted personal data.[23]

Ministry Guidelines provide more details on security measures. For example, the Guidelines on the Act on Protection of Personal Information in the Areas of Economy and Industry list examples of four types of measures: organizational measures, employee management, physical management, and technical measures. [24] As computer and network security measures, it recommends control over data access, such as the number of people who can access data at the same time, and blocking any access outside of business hours. It recommends that passwords have expiration dates and that IDs are suspended after someone has tried to log in with the wrong password for a certain number of times. It also recommends keeping firewall and antivirus software up to date.[25]

C. Disclosure

With respect to retained personal data, a business operator handling personal information must make the following matters easily available for data subjects:

- The name of the business operator handling personal information
- The purpose of utilization of all retained personal data
- Procedures for requesting corrections and disclosure, and filing complaints[26]
- Contact information for the entity that accepts complaints, including contact information for the Authorized Personal Information Protection Organization to which the business operator belongs, if any[27]

When a data subject requests that a business operator handling personal information disclose retained personal data that may lead to the identification of the person, the business operator must disclose the retained personal data without delay. Such disclosure includes notifying the data subject that the business operator has no such retained personal data that may lead to his/her identification.[28] However, the business operator may keep all or part of the retained personal data undisclosed in those cases where disclosure

- is likely to harm the life, body, property, or other rights or interests of the data subject or a third party;
- is likely to seriously impede the proper execution of the business of the business operator handling personal information; or
- violates other laws and regulations.[29]

When a business operator has decided not to disclose all or part of such retained personal data, the business operator must notify the data subject of that decision and the underlying reason without delay.[30]

D. Transfer to Third Party

A business operator handling personal information must not provide personal data to a third party without the prior consent of the data subject, except where the transfer is

- based on laws and regulations;
- necessary for the protection of the life, body, or property of an individual and it is difficult to obtain the consent of the data subject;
- especially necessary for improving public health or promoting the sound growth of children and it is difficult to obtain the consent of the data subject; or
- necessary for the affairs, prescribed by laws and regulations, conducted by a state organ, local government, or person who is authorized to conduct such affairs by these entities, where obtaining the consent of the person is likely to impede execution of the affairs.[31]

E. Complaints and Remedies – Business Operator

The APPI states that a business operator handling personal information must endeavor to appropriately and promptly process complaints about the handling of personal information,[32] and recommends that such business operators establish a system for this processing.[33]

When a data subject requests that a business operator handling personal information correct, add, or delete such retained personal data as may lead to the identification of the person on the ground that the retained personal data is contrary to the facts, the business operator must make a necessary investigation without delay.[34] Based on the results of the investigation, the business operator must correct, add, or delete the retained personal data. There may be other laws and regulations that establish special procedures for such correction, addition, or deletion. In such cases, the business operator follows the established procedures.[35] The business operator must promptly notify the requester of its decision and the actions taken, including the content of the correction, addition, or deletion, if performed, or the reason for refusing to modify or delete the data.[36]

When a data subject finds that a business operator who handles personal information is using the retained personal data in a manner that may lead to the identification of the person beyond the stated purpose for the utilization of the data, or learns that the data was acquired by deception or other wrongful means, he or she may request that the business operator discontinue using or erase such retained personal data.[37] When the business operator finds that the request is well-founded, it must either discontinue using or erase the retained personal data concerned without delay, to the extent necessary for redressing the violation.[38] Also, when a data subject finds that a business operator is providing a third party with retained personal data that may lead to the identification of the person without having obtained the prior consent of the person, he or she may request that the business operator discontinue doing so.[39] If the business operator finds that the request is well-founded, it must discontinue providing the retained personal data to a third party without delay. However, in cases where it would cost a large amount of money or would otherwise be difficult to discontinue using or erase the retained personal data, the business operator may take alternative measures as long as those measures can protect the rights and interests of the person.[40] The business operator must promptly notify the data subject of its decision and, when the request is declined, the reason for refusing to act.[41]

A business operator may establish procedures for receiving requests[42] and collect a reasonable amount of fees to disclose retained personal information.[43]

F. Complaints and Remedies – Authorized Personal Information Protection Organization

Because many business organizations issued guidelines on personal information protection and regulated their members before the enactment of the APPI,[44] the APPI followed a self-regulation model. Business operators typically form a juridical person, or an association or foundation, in order to conduct the following business for the purpose of ensuring the proper handling of personal information:

- Processing complaints about the handling of personal information
- Providing information for business operators to ensure the proper handling of personal information

- Any other business necessary for ensuring the proper handling of personal information by target entities[45]

Such a juridical person, or an association or foundation, may apply for such an authorization with a competent minister.[46] The competent minister examines whether the applicant has sufficient knowledge, abilities, and financial backing and has established a business execution method necessary for properly and soundly processing complaints. If the applicant conducts any other business, the minister also considers whether that other business would impede the applicant's fairness in terms of the proper handling of personal information.[47]

An Authorized Personal Information Protection Organization must issue personal information protection guidelines concerning the specification of the purpose of utilization, security control measures, procedures for complying with individuals' requests, and other matters.[48] For example, regarding the Internet business, the Internet Association Japan issued Personal Information Guidelines on Electronic Network Management in 1994, and updated this document after the APPI was enacted.[49]

A data subject may file a complaint about the handling of personal information by a business operator with an Authorized Personal Information Protection Organization if the business operator is a member of the Organization. When an Authorized Personal Information Protection Organization receives such a complaint, the Organization must give the data subject necessary advice and investigate the circumstances pertaining to the complaint. The Organization also forwards the complaint to the business operator and requests that the operator resolve the complaint promptly. [50] Where an Authorized Personal Information Protection Organization finds it necessary for assessing the complaint, the Organization may request that the business operator provide explanations or submit relevant materials.[51]

It seems, however, that the ability of an Authorized Personal Information Protection Organization to resolve disputes between data subjects and business operators handling personal information is limited. In a 2008 court case where a data subject and a business operator disagreed on the proper handling of personal information, a district court held that the Authorized Personal Information Protection Organization did not have to continue mediating the dispute after the Organization had relayed the parties' opinions and came to the point where both parties firmly disagreed with each other.[52]

G. Complaints – Local Governments

The APPI obligates local governments to mediate the processing of complaints and take other necessary measures in order to ensure that any complaint arising between a business operator and a person regarding the handling of personal information will be handled appropriately and promptly. 53 Local governments have established a section to receive complaints on the handling of personal information and to advise people who consult with them.[54]

H. Complaints – National Consumer Affairs Center

The National Consumer Affairs Center also receives complaints, advises data subjects, and/or mediates disputes between the business operator handling personal information and the data subject.[55]

I. Judicial Enforcement

The APPI does not have a provision for an injunction or civil damages when a business operator does not respond to or refuses a data subject's request. One district court has held that a data subject cannot use a lawsuit to force a business operator handling personal information to disclose his/her information because a data subject must follow the procedures for information disclosure between a business operator and a data subject provided by the APPI.[56] As explained in section IV, below, this decision has been criticized.[57]

J. Administrative Sanctions

See section III, below.

K. Criminal Sanctions

Though it is not specifically designed to protect online privacy, Japan does have a law to punish unauthorized access to computers. The Act on the Prohibition of Unauthorized Computer Access punishes a person who accesses a computer by breaking access control measures, such as using the authorized person's identification and password without authorization or by creating a security hole. These acts may be punished by imprisonment of not more than one year or a fine of not more than 500,000 yen (about US$6,200).[58] In a 2005 case a person accessed a website without authorization through a security hole and copied the personal information of 1,200 users of the website. He was found guilty and sentenced to eight months' imprisonment, but the sentence was suspended.[59]

L. Cross Border Application

The APPI applies to business operators doing business in Japan.[60]

M. PrivacyMark

The Japan Information Processing Development Corporation (JIPDEC) established the "PrivacyMark" system in 1998 upon instruction from the Ministry of International Trade and Industry (currently the Ministry of Economy, Trade and Industry, METI).[61] This system assesses whether a business operator handling personal information has taken appropriate measures to protect personal information and grants those who meet certain standards the right to display the PrivacyMark label in the course of their business activities.[62] The system provides incentives for business operators to gain social credibility. A PrivacyMark conformity assessment body evaluates the business operator's compliance with all relevant laws and regulations. 63 The system is in compliance with Japan Industrial Standards (Personal Information Protection Management System – Requirements, JIS Q15001 (2006)). 64 In accordance with the PrivacyMark agreement, a business operator who obtains the right to use the mark must report any incidents in which data subjects' personal information was leaked. JIPDEC reviews the incidents and may cancel the grant of the right to use the PrivacyMark.[65]

N. Smartphones

There is no specific regulation on data collection by smartphone applications. As long as the business operator collects the personal information of 5,000 or more people, the APPI applies.

The Ministry of Internal Affairs and Communications (MIC) initiated the Smart Phone and Cloud Security Research Society in October 2011. The Society recently released a draft report on smartphone and cloud security, as explained in section VI of this report.

O. Protection of Minors

Although protection of minors from harmful content on the Internet has been discussed in the government,[66] no regulation has yet been issued that addresses the topic.

III. Role of Competent Ministers

Japan has no data protection agency. Instead, the government ministers who have jurisdiction over the business of the business operator handling personal information (the "competent ministers") oversee the handling of such information.[67] Business operators handling personal information related to employment management may have an additional competent minister: the Minister of Health, Labor and Welfare. In the case of the employment management of mariners, the Minister of Land, Infrastructure, Transport and Tourism is the additional competent minister.[68] The APPI states that competent ministers must maintain close contact and cooperate with each other.[69]

The competent minister may ask a business operator to report on the handling of personal information[70] and give its advice.[71] When a business operator handling personal information neglects its legal obligations (by using personal information beyond the scope necessary for the achievement of the purpose of utilization, not taking necessary and proper security measures, etc.), the competent Minister may recommend that the business operator cease the violation(s) and take other necessary corrective measures. [72] If a business operator handling personal information does not take the recommended measures without justifiable grounds after it has received the recommendation, and when the competent minister finds that a serious infringement of the rights and interests of individuals is imminent, the competent minister may order the business operator to take the measures that the minister recommends.[73]

In certain cases, a competent minister can skip the recommendation and immediately issue an order. Where the violation by a business operator handling personal information concerns the actions listed below, and the competent minister finds that urgent action is necessary as there is a serious infringement of the rights and interests of individuals, the competent minister may order the business operator to cease the violation and take other necessary measures to rectify the violation.[74] These violations are:

- Handling personal information beyond the scope necessary for the achievement of the purpose of utilization without obtaining the prior consent of the person[75]
- Acquiring personal information by deception or other wrongful means[76]
- Failing to take necessary and proper measures for the prevention of leakage, loss, or damage, and for other security control of the personal data[77]
- Failing to exercise necessary and appropriate supervision over an employee who handles personal data for the security control of the personal data[78]
- Failing to exercise necessary and appropriate supervision over the trustee of personal data for the security control of the entrusted personal data[79]

- Providing personal data to a third party without obtaining the prior consent of the data subject[80]

Though the legal basis of the notice was not clearly specified, just before Google's new privacy policy took effect on March 1, 2012, the MIC and METI issued a notice to Google Japan, emphasizing the importance of following the APPI and the Telecommunications Business Act.[81]

For an Authorized Personal Information Protection Organization, a competent minister is the minister that has granted the permission or approval of the organization or the minister who has jurisdiction over the business conducted by the member entities of the Authorized Personal Information Protection Organizations.[82] The competent minister may have an Authorized Personal Information Protection Organization make a report on the authorized businesses[83] and may order the organization to improve the method of conducting its authorized businesses, to amend its personal information protection guidelines, or to take any other necessary measures.[84] A competent minister may rescind its authorization when an Authorized Personal Information Protection Organization violates the APPI.[85]

If a business operator or an Authorized Personal Information Protection Organization did not make a report or submitted a false report after a competent minister's request, it is subject to a fine of not more than 300,000 yen (about US$3,750).[86] When a business operator or an Authorized Personal Information Protection Organization violates a competent minister's order, it is subject to a term of imprisonment of not more than six months or a fine of not more than 300,000 yen.[87]

Though Japan has no data protection agency, there is a coordinating body. When the APPI was enacted, the Quality of Life Policy Bureau of the Cabinet Office was designated as a coordinating body for the government agencies and given the task of promoting the protection of personal information.[88] When the Consumer Affairs Agency was established in 2009, these responsibilities were transferred to the Consumer Affairs Agency.[89] Based on article 53 of the APPI, all government agencies must submit an annual report on implementation of the APPI to the Consumer Affairs Agency. The Consumer Affairs Agency then issues an annual government report on implementation of the APPI.[90] The website of the Consumer Affairs Agency provides various educational materials for consumers and business operators handling personal information.[91]

IV. Court Decisions

A. APPI Cases

Several court cases have involved claims based on the APPI,[92] but most of them are irrelevant to online privacy issues. One of the few relevant cases involved the question of whether a data subject could use a judicial procedure to obtain his/her personal information from a business operator handling that information. The Tokyo District Court denied the data subject's request based on the following grounds:

- The APPI provides various measures to solve disputes outside of the judicial process. If the disclosure of personal information could be enforced directly by litigation, provisions of the APPI might be ignored and lose their importance, which was not intended.

- Article 25, paragraph 1 of the APPI obligates business operators to disclose personal information. It does not state that data subjects have rights to obtain their personal information.[93]

The District Court's decision has been criticized. For example, the Federation of Japan Bar Associations stated that the reasons the Tokyo District Court gave for its decision did not support the denial of the right of data subjects. Rather, the legislative history and the government materials that explained the APPI implied that the right would be enforceable by lawsuits.[94]

B. Privacy and the Right to Control One's Own Information

Though there is a no legal provision that explicitly protects the right to privacy, the right has been recognized by the courts. The first decision in which a court recognized the privacy right based on article 13 of the Constitution[95] was issued by the Tokyo District Court in 1964.[96] The first Supreme Court decision recognizing the right to privacy was rendered in 1969.[97] Article 13 of the Constitution states that

> [a]ll of the people shall be respected as individuals. The right to life, liberty, and the pursuit of happiness shall, to the extent that it does not interfere with the public welfare, be the supreme consideration in legislation and in other governmental affairs.

In a 1969 Supreme Court case, a police officer took photos of street demonstrators on the front lines of a march who were suspected of violating the conditions that the local government imposed when it issued a permit for the demonstration. The photos were submitted to the court as one piece of the evidence. The defendant claimed that taking the photos was illegal because it violated his portrait right. The Court stated that individuals have the right not to have their photos taken without consent. However, it also stated that this right can be restricted when it interferes with public welfare. When a police officer takes photos of suspected criminals and crime scenes in an appropriate way in a given circumstance, it does not violate someone's right to his portrait, the court said.[98]

Recently, the Supreme Court issued a decision on personal information databases and privacy, citing its 1969 decision. Japan has maintained the resident registry, a personal information database, since 1951.[99] Municipalities have maintained the basic resident registries that record the name, date of birth, sex, address, name of the head of the household, starting date of the residency, etc.[100] The government amended the Basic Resident Registry Law in 1999[101] in order to connect some of the information in the resident registries online between the national and local government agencies (Jūki Net) and make many national and local government resident services and other procedures effective.[102] The government launched Jūki Net in 2003 and linked residency registries of local governments by compiling citizens' names, birth dates, sex, and addresses, and assigning an eleven-digit code to each person.[103]

At least seventeen citizen groups filed lawsuits against local governments, claiming that Jūki Net violates the right to privacy protected under article 13 of the Constitution.[104] Most courts dismissed the citizen groups' claims, but the Kanazawa District Court[105] and the Osaka

High Court[106] held that Jūki Net was unconstitutional. In particular, the Osaka High Court stated that the individual's interest in determining how to deal with information concerning his/her private matters (the right to control one's own information) is guaranteed by article 13 of the Constitution, as the right is included in the right to privacy. The court said that information concerning a person's name, birth date, address, sex, and resident number is not in and of itself confidential information, but liberty in private lives can still be threatened if it is used against the data subjects' will. Therefore, this information is subject to legal protection and subject to the right to protect one's own information. The court also found a risk of misuse of personal information in the Jūki Net system.[107]

However, the Supreme Court reversed the Osaka High Court decision, stating that an individual's name, birth date, address and sex, and resident number are not confidential; there is no significant system risk of leaking the information; and misuse by people handling the information is prohibited by administrative and criminal sanctions. Therefore, the government's acts to manage and utilize Jūki Net did not violate the citizens' liberty in private life protected under article 13 of the Constitution because it did not constitute the disclosure of personal information to a third party or make such information public without good reason.[108] The Supreme Court did not mention the right to control one's own information.

V. Public and Scholarly Opinion

According to a public opinion poll concerning personal information protection conducted by the Cabinet Office in 2006, about 70% of Japanese people are anxious about how their personal information is handled, such as the unauthorized distribution of their personal information.[109]

The Japan Federation of Bar Associations (JFBA) adopted a resolution demanding the protection of privacy in advanced information/communication networks in 2010. In the resolution, the JFBA recommended legislation to protect the right to control personal information. More specifically, it recommended a system whereby a data subject would be notified before his/her information was collected of the purpose and methods of collection. It also recommended that the government regulate the collection of data even if the data does not specify the identity of the data subject (and therefore is not subject to the APPI), such as behavioral targeting advertising.[110]

VI. Government Research and Discussions

The government started to examine the possible introduction of a citizen identification system in September 2010. In February 2012, the Cabinet submitted a bill on the Act on Use of Numbers to Identify Individuals in Administrative Procedures.[111] This law would be a special law supplementing the APPI and laws on personal information protection for information held by the government and public entities, and would establish some exceptions for the provisions of the personal information protection laws.[112]

The Consumer Commission under the jurisdiction of the Cabinet Office is monitoring implementation of the APPI, and the MIC is monitoring issues relating to information communication technology. They continue to examine new situations and new technologies.

The Consumer Commission established the Personal Information Protection Special Research Subcommittee in December 2009. The Subcommittee researches and discusses matters on the proper handling of personal information and reviews the Basic Policy on Personal Information Protection.[113] The Subcommittee submitted a report to the Consumer Committee in July 2011.[114] In that report, the Subcommittee recommended discussion of an independent organization to enforce personal information protection based on the discussion of the citizen identification system.[115] Such an organization would be established for the citizen number system when the Act on Use of Numbers to Identify Individuals in Administrative Procedures is enacted.[116] In the report, the Subcommittee also recommends, among other things,

- discussions on expanding the scope of business operators handling personal information that are subject to the APPI (currently, only business operators dealing with the personal information of 5,000 or more people are covered);
- promotion of technical measures to prevent accidents, such as encryption; and
- clear provisions on the data subject's right to obtain, correct, and seek to stop the use of personal information.[117]

In April 2009, the MIC established the Study Group on Consumer Issues with ICT Services in order to examine new issues that arise from the introduction of new services and new technologies in the field of communications.[118] The Study Group has researched various matters from time to time. One of the topics included the "lifelog" monitoring service. The Japanese use lifelog as a log of an individual's life built up over time, including website browsing histories, purchasing and payment histories on e-commerce sites, and location information obtained from mobile devices' global positioning system (GPS) data.[119]

The Study Group released a report, *An Examination of Lifelog-Monitoring Services*, in May 2010.[120] The report looked at behavioral advertising and location-based personalized assistance services. The report stated that "[p]roviders of behavioral advertising and similar applications are generally not thought to be business operators handling personal information, as legally defined, because the information they handle is, itself, not personal information."[121] However, that information typically required for behavioral advertising [122] "can become personally identifiable when retained information permits the identification of a specific individual through simple reference to other information."[123] In such cases, the APPI applies to the business operator.[124] In addition, the report states "lifelog-monitoring services, depending on their circumstances, can violate privacy rights or provoke consumer concerns."[125] The report calls on business operators to take reasonable steps to preserve privacy, so that they can limit the likelihood of infringing upon privacy rights.[126]

The report rejects the suggestion that "administrative bodies draw up guidelines and procedures on the practices (of lifelog monitoring services) businesses should follow" because "lifelog-monitoring services are in their infancy and it is not wise to place excessive burdens on businesses that will hamper their growth." 127 Instead, the Study Group recommends "encourag[ing] businesses to draft their own self-regulatory guidelines" in reference to the following six consumer-centric principles established by the Study Group:[128]

A. Publicity, promotion, and education activities;
B. Assurance of transparency;
C. Assurance of opportunities for consumer participation;
D. Assurance of data collection by appropriate means;
E. Assurance of adequate security controls; and
F. Assurance of frameworks to address complaints and inquiries.[129]

The report further examines "behavioral advertising using deep packet inspection (DPI) technology."[130] DPI is "an advertising modality in which an Internet service provider (ISP) intercepts and inspects packets passing over its networks to predict customers' preferences and interests—information that is then used to deliver targeted advertisements to customers."[131] DPI "usually refers to the technology that parses the headers and payloads of packets passing over a network and screens them for certain communication characteristics and behaviors."[132] In addition to the APPI and privacy violations, the breach of communication confidentiality matters "because DPI-based behavioral advertising involves ISPs inspecting packets passing over their networks." 133 The report concludes that DPI-based behavioral advertising violates the confidentiality of communications without consumer consent. 134 The report states that "businesses engaged in DPI-based behavioral advertising should make their service mechanisms and operations sufficiently transparent to consumers"[135] and also recommends that businesses "[p]rovide consumers with opportunities to easily opt out."[136]

After the report was released, the Japan Internet Advertising Association (JIAA) amended its Behavioral Advertising Guidelines in June 2010.[137] The amendment was also influenced by the Self-Regulatory Principles for Online Behavioral Advertising in the United States.[138] The 2010 amendment added articles concerning transparency and an opt-out option, among other things.[139]

The MIC initiated the Smart Phone and Cloud Security Research Society in October 2011.[140] The Research Society released its draft final report on smartphone and cloud security on April 26, 2012, and solicited public comments.[141] The final report was released on June 29, 2012. [142] MIC also launched the Working Group on the User Information Sent Through Smartphone in January 2012 to examine current conditions and consider policies necessary for the handling of smartphone user information.[143] The Working Group released its Interim Report in April 2012.[144] The Interim Report examined current conditions and a selected agenda: how to deal with user information and how to inform users.[145] The issue of protection of minors was included in the agenda. At the same time that it released the Interim Report, the Working Group issued the Smartphone Privacy Guide in order to inform users of the privacy risks of smartphones and how to deal with smartphones to protect their privacy.[146] The Working Group released its final draft report on June 29, 2012, and is now soliciting public comments.[147]

Sayuri Umeda
Senior Foreign Law Specialist
June 2012

NETHERLANDS[*]
ONLINE PRIVACY LAW

The Netherlands has a high percentage of general Internet, social network site, and smartphone users. The Dutch Constitution contains a provision on the protection of privacy of personal data. The Personal Data Protection Act broadly governs the protection of personal data; online privacy is addressed in particular by the Telecommunications Act, which was recently amended to incorporate privacy provisions deemed by some commentators to be stricter than those of the EU. The Netherlands has incorporated key European Union directives on privacy, such as the Directive on Personal Data, the Data Retention Directive, and the Privacy and Electronic Communications Directive, into its national law.

The processing of any personal data in the Netherlands requires the data subject's unambiguous consent; certain types of personal data, such as that concerning a person's religion may not be processed, however. Internet service providers have an obligation to protect the privacy of users and subscribers. The Dutch Data Protection Authority is a key agency involved in the protection of personal data, but two other agencies play a role in supervising telecommunications service providers and the telecom market. Among possible future changes in the Dutch legal framework of online privacy is the adoption of a constitutional amendment on the protection of digital rights.

According to statistics published by the Organisation for Economic Cooperation and Development (OECD), in 2010 nearly 91% of Dutch households had access to the Internet. The Netherlands ranked third among thirty-five OECD Member States (including the European Union as a whole) surveyed, after Korea and Iceland.[1] Nearly 80% of households in the Netherlands had access to broadband as of that year, placing the country sixth among forty-one jurisdictions surveyed for this feature.[2] As of December 2011, there were over fifteen million Internet users in the country, almost 90% of the population.[3] In terms of frequency of Internet visits, the Netherlands ranked highest among European countries, with 78.2 visits per visitor in a study conducted for the month of September 2010.[4] In 2011, 53% of Internet users reported being active on social networking sites like the Dutch network Hyves, Facebook, and Twitter in the previous three months, with 88% of those users under the age of twenty-five.[5] Reportedly, the Internet penetration in the Netherlands of two key global social networking sites, Twitter and LinkedIn, is the highest worldwide.[6]

I. Legal Framework

The Constitution of the Kingdom of the Netherlands provides for the protection of privacy in article 10, which states as follows:

1. Everyone shall have the right to respect for his privacy, without prejudice to restrictions laid down by or pursuant to Act of Parliament.
2. Rules to protect privacy shall be laid down by Act of Parliament in connection with the recording and dissemination of personal data.

3. Rules concerning the rights of persons to be informed of data recorded concerning them and of the use that is made thereof, and to have such data corrected shall be laid down by Act of Parliament.[7]

The Constitution also provides for the inviolability of the person[8] and the home[9] and protects against the violation of the privacy of correspondence and of the telephone and telegraph, except as otherwise provided by acts of Parliament.[10]

The Telecommunications Act[11] is of major importance in the governance of online privacy in the Netherlands. In order to implement revised EU electronic communications, privacy, and telecom directives,[12] on June 22, 2011, the House of Representatives (Tweede Kamer) of the Dutch Parliament (States-General, or Staten-Generaal) adopted ten proposed amendments to the Telecommunications Act, rejecting only an eleventh proposed revision concerning Internet access as a universal service.[13] The Senate (Eerste Kamer) adopted the proposed changes on May 8, 2012, including new provisions on online privacy.[14] Of related significance are the Telecommunications Data Retention Act (*Wet bewaarplicht telecommunicatiegegevens*) of August 28, 2009,[15] and the Media Act (*Mediawet*) of December 29, 2008.[16]

Another key item of legislation governing the recording and use of personal data in the Netherlands is the Personal Data Protection Act (*Wet bescherming persoonsgegevens*) (PDPA), which came into force on September 1, 2001.[17] This Act covers "every use—'processing'—of personal data, from the collection of these data up to and including the destruction of personal data."[18] The PDPA, together with the PDPA Exemption Decree (*Vrijstellingsbesluit*) of May 7, 2011, transpose in the Netherlands the Data Protection Directive of the European Union.[19] In connection with the PDPA, the Ministry of Security and Justice has also published Guidelines for Personal Data Processors.[20] There are also codes of conduct that might apply to the handling of personal data on the Internet. For example, in 2008 the Dutch government and the private sector adopted a non-legally binding Notice-and-Take-Down Code for handling reports of unlawful Internet content.[21]

II. Current Law

A. Scope of Application

The Telecommunications Act covers electronic communications networks, electronic communications services, public electronic communications services, and public electronic communications networks.[22]

The PDPA applies to "the fully or partly automated processing of personal data, and the non-automated processing of personal data entered in a file or intended to be entered therein,"[23] with a file being "any structured set of personal data."[24] The Act is not applicable to the processing of personal data that is "for exclusively journalist, artistic or literary purposes,"[25] except as otherwise provided in the Act and/or under conditions set forth under certain provisions of the Act. The PDPA applies to personal data processing carried out by responsible parties established in the Netherlands, as well as by or for responsible parties not established in the European Union that use "automated or non-automated means situated in the Netherlands, unless these means are used only for forwarding personal data."[26] Such non-

EU responsible parties are prohibited from processing personal data unless they designate a person or body in the Netherlands to act on their behalf.[27]

B. Prohibition on Processing without Consent

Processing of personal data is permissible only under certain conditions. Most important, perhaps, is that the data subject's unambiguous consent (*ondubbelzinnige toestemming*) is required.[28] It is also allowed where the processing is necessary for, among other purposes,

- the performance of a contract to which the data subject is party, or for actions to be carried out at the request of the data subject and which are necessary for the conclusion of a contract;
- compliance with a legal obligation to which the responsible party is subject;
- protection of a vital interest of the data subject; or
- upholding the legitimate interests of the responsible party or of a third party to whom the data are supplied, except where the data subject's interests or fundamental rights and freedoms, in particular the right to protection of individual privacy, prevail.[29]

The PDPA prohibits, except as otherwise provided in the Act, the processing of personal data "concerning a person's religion or philosophy of life, race, political persuasion, health and sexual life, or personal data concerning trade union membership." The ban also applies to personal data related to criminal behavior or to prohibited unlawful or objectionable conduct.[30]

In addition, the PDPA provides protection of data transferred to third countries, i.e., countries outside the EU. Personal data subject to or intended for processing after such a transfer will only be transferred if the third country guarantees an adequate level of protection, without prejudice to the PDPA's provisions.[31] By way of derogation from this provision, personal data can be transferred if that country is party to the May 2, 1992, Oporto Agreement on the European Economic Area (Netherlands Treaty Series (TRACTATENBLAD) 1992, No. 132)), unless a decision of the European Commission or the Council of the European Union results in such transfer being limited or forbidden.[32] An assessment of the adequacy of the level of protection given the personal data is to take into account the circumstances affecting the transfer operation or the category of data transfer operations, and in particular the type of data, the purpose or purposes and the duration of the planned processing, the applicable legal provisions in the third country concerned, and so on.[33]

The above provisions regarding third-party transfers notwithstanding, transfers to a third country that does not provide guarantees for an adequate level of protection can take place if certain conditions apply. For example, it may occur if the data subjects have unambiguously consented to it, if the transfer is necessary for the performance of a contract between the data subjects and the responsible parties or in order to protect a vital interest of the data subjects, or if the transfer is made on the basis of a model contract as referred to in article 26(4) of EU Directive 95/46/EG on the processing of personal data and the free movement of such data.[34] Moreover, notwithstanding this provision, the Minister of Security and Justice, after consulting the Dutch Data Protection Authority (DPA), may issue a permit for personal data transfer or category of transfer to a third country that does not provide the adequate level of guarantees, but the permit must have attached to it "the more detailed rules required to protect the individual privacy and fundamental rights and freedoms of persons and to guarantee implementation of the associated rights."[35]

C. Safeguards and Transparency Obligations of Providers

The Telecommunications Act prescribes a general obligation for providers of public telecommunications networks and services to "ensure the protection of the personal data and the protection of the privacy of subscribers to and users of its network or services."[36] To that end, such providers must "take appropriate technical and organization measures to ensure the safety and protection of the networks and services they provide," at a level proportionate to the risks involved, while taking into account the state of technology and the costs involved.[37]

The Telecommunications Act provides for a general level of transparency in connection with data subjects, stipulating that network and service providers are to ensure that subscribers are informed of (a) special risks of breach of the security or protection of the network or service provided, and (b) any means, other than the technical and organizational measures referred to above (i.e., under article 11.3(1)) that the provider concerned must take in order to counter such risks, as well as an estimate of the likely expense involved.[38]

D. Limits on the Creation of Personal Profiles

Building up a personal profile with data on surfing behavior through the use of tracking cookies, such as Google Analytics cookies, is in violation of privacy laws. 39 The Telecommunications Act makes the PDPA applicable to the use of all tracking cookies, through the introduction of "the legal presumption that the use (placing and reading the file on the device of an end user) of a tracking cookie constitutes processing of personal data."[40] This therefore also means that the consumer's "unambiguous consent" is required in order for cookies to be placed.[41] Additionally, it will result in a shift of the burden of proof from the DPA to the party that places the tracking cookie, to prove that its cookie does not process personal data.[42] Thus, if an online company does not specifically request unambiguous consent to use tracking cookies, it must prove that its cookies are not handling personal data, and failure to do so may result in its activities being deemed unlawful by supervisory authorities and made subject to fines.[43]

The new provision on tracking cookies, article 11.7a, which has been called the *Cookiewet* (Cookie Act) created heated public debate because it is stricter than the relevant EU Directives 2009/136/EC 44 (Privacy and Electronic Communications Directive) and 2009/140/EC[45] (Better Regulation Directive).[46] According to the Dutch government, however, the sole purpose of the legal presumption is to facilitate the DPA's enforcement capabilities, and it does not materially change the applicability of the PDPA to tracking cookies.[47] The legal presumption article of the Act might not be enforced until December 31, 2012, if a motion to that effect is adopted by the Dutch Senate. The motion of Member of Parliament C.S. Franken calls upon the government to actively support the EU development of a "Do Not Track" standard and to facilitate dialogue between the supervisors, the advertising industry, and consumers to achieve maximum clarity about the scope of the provision and, if necessary, lay down detailed rules for it; these are the reasons behind seeking a delay in the enforcement of article 11.7a.[48]

Article 11.7a of the Telecommunications Act states in item 1:

Without prejudice to the Personal Data Protection Act, anyone who by means of electronic communications networks wishes to obtain access to data stored in a user's peripherals or who wishes to store data in the user's peripherals shall:

a) provide the user clear and complete information in accordance with the PDPA, and in any case, concerning the purposes for which one wishes to obtain access to the relevant data or for which one wishes to store data, and
b) obtain the consent of the user for the relevant action.

E. Smartphone Applications Data Collection

In 2011, mobile Internet usage in the Netherlands "skyrocketed."[49] According to a European Parliament study of the Internet and citizens' privacy, moreover, "De Randstad, the industrial and service agglomeration encompassing the four largest cities of the Netherlands, is the third-largest site of intense mobile traffic in the world."[50] Although as of this writing no specific legal provisions were found governing smartphone applications and data collection, it would appear that data collection by smartphone apps would fall under article 11.7a of the Telecommunications Act, in particular. Smartphones might also be covered under the definition of "terminal equipment" (*randapparaten*) in article 1.1 of the Act:

> [Terminal equipment is] equipment intended for connection to a public telecommunications network in such a way that it: can be connected directly to network termination points, or can be used for interaction with a public telecommunications network via direct or indirect connection to network termination points for the purpose of the transmission, processing or reception of data.[51]

E. Limits on Geodata

Article 11.5a of the Telecommunications Act deals specifically with location data. It stipulates that the processing of such data, with the exception of traffic data related to subscribers or users of a public electronic communications network or service, is permitted only if the data is made anonymous or if the given subscriber or user has given consent to the processing for the purpose of the supply of a value-added service.[52] The processing of location data for this purpose is permissible only to the extent and for the duration that is necessary for the supply of the service in question.[53]

Before obtaining the consent of the subscriber or user, the supplier of the value-added service to the subscriber or user must provide the following information: (1) the type of location data that will be processed, (2) the purposes for which the location data is processed, (3) the duration of the processing, and (4) whether the data will be provided to a third party for the purpose of supplying a value-added service.[54] A subscriber or user can revoke at any time the consent for the processing of the data concerning him.[55]

G. Protection of Minors

The PDPA stipulates that if the data subjects are minors under sixteen years of age, or if they are persons under guardianship on whose behalf a mentorship has been instituted, instead of the data subject's consent, that of a legal representative is required.[56] The PDPA further provides that "the data subjects or their legal representative may withdraw consent at any time."[57]

Under article 37(3) of the PDPA, such legal representatives also have the authority to make requests in regard to whether the personal data of the persons they represent are being processed (and related matters), and upon being informed about that data, to request that the responsible party correct, supplement, delete, or block it (except in the case of public registers set up by law) if the data "is factually inaccurate, incomplete or irrelevant to the purpose or purposes of the processing, or is being processed in any other way which infringes a legal provision."[58] The information requested will be provided to the legal representative.[59]

H. Technical and Organizational Security Measures to Protect Data

The PDPA requires the implementation of measures to protect personal data. It states that "[t]he responsible party must implement appropriate technical and organizational measures to secure personal data against loss or against any form of unlawful processing."[60] Such measures are to "guarantee an appropriate level of security, taking into account the state of the art and the costs of implementation" as well as "the risks associated with the processing and the nature of the data to be protected," while seeking to prevent "unnecessary collection and further procession of personal data."[61] The agreement governing processing of personal data made between a responsible party and a processor must set down in written form, or the equivalent, the security measures, for purposes of maintaining proof.[62]

If a responsible party has personal data processed for it, it must ensure "that the processor provides adequate guarantees concerning the technical and organizational security measures for the processing to be carried out," and that such measures are complied with.[63] The responsible party must also make sure that the processor complies with the above-stated technical, organizational, and security obligations incumbent upon the responsible party.[64] This duty of the responsible party notwithstanding, if the processor is established in another EU Member State, the responsible party must ensure that the processor complies with the laws of that Member State.[65]

I. User Anonymity

Under the Telecommunications Act, network and service providers are to delete or anonymize traffic data processed and stored by them relating to subscribers or users once this traffic data is no longer needed for the purpose of the transmission of communications, without prejudice to certain other provisions of the Act.[66] For example, a service provider may process traffic data to the extent and duration necessary for: (a) market research or sales activity relating to electronic communications services, or (b) the supply of value-added services, provided that the subscriber or user to whom the traffic data relates has given his consent, and the subscriber or the user may at any time revoke the consent given for such processing.[67]

J. Data Protection Agencies

The Dutch Data Protection Authority (DPA) (*College Bescherming Persoonsgegevens*) administers personal data protection-related matters in the Netherlands by authority of the PDPA. The Radiocommunications Agency Netherlands (*Agentschap Telecom*) (RCA) supervises the obligations of Internet access and telecom providers. The Independent Post and Telecommunications Authority (*Onafhankelijke Post en Telecommunicatie Autoriteit*, OPTA) is oriented toward promoting investment in the communications sector while protecting consumer interests. Some features and functions of these agencies will be discussed in more detail below.

K. Rights of and Remedies for Users

Under article 35 of the PDPA, data subjects have the right, "freely and at reasonable intervals," to request the responsible party to inform them as to whether personal data related to them are being processed. The responsible party must inform data subjects in writing within four weeks as to whether such data are being processed.[68] Data subjects may also request responsible parties to provide information on the logic that underlies the automated processing of data concerning them (*de logica die ten grondslag ligt aan de geautomatiseerde verwerking van hem betreffende gegevens*).[69]

Users also have the right to request changes in the data. Article 36 of the PDPA prescribes that persons informed of their personal data in accordance with the above provision "may request the responsible party to correct, supplement, delete or block the said data in the event that it is factually inaccurate, incomplete or irrelevant to the purpose or purposes of the processing, or is being processed in any other way which infringes a legal provision."[70]

1. Decisions Taken by Administrative Bodies Regarding Requests for Information

Certain decisions taken in response to requests concerning the processing of personal data fall under the rubric of administrative decisions. These include decisions made in response to requests having to do, for example, with the provision of information on data processing that is exempt from the notification requirement;[71] with whether or not a data subject's personal data is being processed or with the underlying logic of the data processing of such data);[72] with requests for correction, supplements, etc.;[73] and with the provision of information on the parties to whom information has been provided.[74]

2. Court Petitions

For decisions other than those made by administrative bodies, the PDPA allows suits for injunctive relief and damages. Thus, the party concerned can submit a written petition requesting the district court to order the responsible party to grant or reject a request having to do with the matters stated in the preceding paragraph, or to recognize or reject an objection of the kind indicated above.[75] The petition must be submitted within six weeks of receipt of the reply from the responsible party; where the responsible party has not replied within the time limit to the party concerned's request for information, etc., the petition must be submitted within six weeks of the expiry of that time limit.[76] According to the PDPA, the court will find in favor of the request "where it is ruled to be well-founded," but before issuing a ruling, it will when necessary give the parties concerned an opportunity to present their views.[77] The section on penalty payments (*dwangsom*) of the Code of Civil Procedure applies.[78] The court may also request the parties and others to provide it with written information; the responsible party and the party concerned are required to comply with such requests.[79]

The party concerned may also apply to the DPA to mediate or to give an opinion in the dispute with the responsible party, provided the application is made within the lawful time limits.[80]

3. Right to Fair Compensation

Persons who have suffered harm as a result of acts concerning them that infringe the provisions of the PDPA have the right to fair compensation for harm not constituting property damage.[81] Responsible parties are liable for the damage or harm resulting from noncompliance with those provisions, and processors are liable for the damage or harm incurred insofar as it resulted from their operations.[82] If they can prove that the harm cannot be attributed to them, the responsible parties or the processors may be exempted in whole or in part from liability.[83]

When responsible parties or processors act in contravention of the PDPA and another party suffers or may suffer damage as a result, the court may, on the petition of the injured party, impose a ban on such conduct and order them to take measures to remedy the consequences of the conduct.[84] However, legal persons cannot base a petition on the processing of personal data if the persons affected by the processing object.[85]

L. Administrative and Criminal Sanctions

The DPA has the authority to apply administrative sanctions, including constraint measures and administrative fines, pursuant to obligations laid down in the PDPA. [86] In particular, the DPA may impose an administrative fine not to exceed €4,500 (about US$5,626) in respect of the violation "of, by, or under" articles 27 (on notification of the DPA before processing of personal data commences), 28 (on the particulars to be included in the notification, etc.), or 79(1) (on the time limit of bringing into conformity with the Act the processing already taking place before the Act's entry into force).[87] A DPA decision imposing an administrative fine will be inoperative until the deadline for making objections has expired or, if an objection has been made, until a decision has been rendered on the objection.[88] (For criminal offenses, see immediately below).

M. Cross-border Application

Responsible parties who contravene the provisions laid down by or under the three articles cited in the paragraph immediately above, or articles 4(3) (the prohibition against processing of personal data by responsible parties not established in the EU unless they designate a person or body in the Netherlands to act on their behalf) or 78(2) of the PDPA, will be subject to a fine of the third category.[89] Article 78(2) prescribes that, pursuant to a decision of the European Commission or the Council of the European Union, the Dutch Minister of Security and Justice will lay down a ministerial ruling or decision to the effect that (a) the transfer to a third country (i.e., a country outside the EU) is prohibited, or (b) a permit issued under the PDPA for personal data transfer or a category of transfers to a third country that has not provided guarantees for an adequate level of protection is withdrawn or modified. Responsible parties that deliberately commit offenses under these various articles will be punished with a prison sentence of up to six months or a fourth-category fine.[90]

N. Data Retention

The Netherlands has transposed the EU Data Retention Directive[91] into its national law through the adoption of the 2009 Telecommunications Data Retention Act (TDRA) amending the Telecommunications Act and the Act on Economic Offenses. [92] Authorities in the Netherlands allow data retention for the purpose of investigation and prosecution of serious offenses (e.g., terrorism) for which custody may be imposed under the Dutch Code of Criminal Procedure.[93] The investigating police officer, by order of a prosecutor or an investigating judge, is the competent authority that has access to retained data.[94] The retention period for all types of retained data is one year.[95] The TDRA provides for observation by operators of the four data security principles covered by the Directive, i.e., that the retained data shall be (1) of the same quality and subject to the same security and protection as network data; (2) subject to appropriate measures to protect the data against unlawful destruction, loss, etc.; (3) subject to appropriate measures to ensure authorized access only; and (4) destroyed at the end of the period of retention, with certain exceptions.[96]

Recently, the Dutch Independent Post and Telecommunications Authority (OPTA) stated, after receiving an "unspecified complaint," that some hotels that provide free Wi-Fi to guests must register as ISPs, which would thereby make them "subject to the E.U.'s stringent rules on data retention." [97] The Telecommunications Act requires ISPs to be registered, for purposes of monitoring crime and terrorism.[98] Thus far, there has been no comment on the legality of the OPTA's move, "which has raised questions about whether small hotels have the resources to comply" with the EU Directive.[99]

III. Role of Data Protection Agencies

The Dutch Data Protection Authority is the main agency generally in charge of personal data processing. The Radiocommunications Agency Netherlands (*Agentschap Telecom*) (RCA) supervises the obligations of Internet access and telecom providers. The Independent Post and Telecommunications Authority (OPTA) "is an independent administrative body and works closely with its fellow international regulators. Three of its departments act to promote competition and protect consumers."[100]

A. DPA

The Dutch Data Protection Authority (DPA) began operations in September 2001, with the entry into force of the PDPA, under which it was established, and succeeding the previous agency in charge of data protection.[101] The DPA, which is covered under articles 51–61 of the PDPA, is headed by a Chairman and two Commissioners; special members may also be appointed, with an effort made "to reflect the various sectors of society."[102] The Chairman is appointed by royal decree, on the proposal of the Minister for Security and Justice, for a six-year, renewable term; the two Commissioners and special members are similarly appointed, for four-year renewable terms.[103] The Chairman directs the work of the DPA and its secretariat.[104] The support staff comprises about seventy employees, serving in one of four major divisions: the supervisory departments (subdivided into private sector, public sector, and international sections), the Legal Affairs Department, the Communication Department, and Operational Management Department.[105]

The PDPA provides that responsible parties or the organizations with which they are affiliated may appoint their own data protection officer (*de functionaris voor de gegevensbescherming*), who are to register with the DPA.[106] For example, police officials, under the Police Data Act, are to appoint a chief privacy officer (*privacyfunctionaris*) to oversee the processing of police data; that officer reports to the chief privacy officer of the DPA.[107] Among other tasks, the DPA oversees the legal processing of personal data and monitors such processing done in the Netherlands in accordance with the law of another EU Member State;[108] makes recommendations on relevant legislative proposals; enforces implementation of the law by imposing fines, using administrative coercion, or detecting criminal offenses against the PDPA; [109] tests codes of conduct for the handling of personal data by various sectors of society;[110] handles the notification and preliminary examination procedures connected with the processing of personal data;[111] mediates disputes over the exercise of rights related to personal data protection;[112] handles requests on how to interpret the privacy legislation;[113] advises the Minister of Security and Justice on the granting of permits for transfer of personal data when a third country lacks an adequate level of protection;[114] and provides an annual report on its activities.[115] The DPA also has the power to grant exemptions from the prohibition against the processing of sensitive data.[116] The extent to which the DPA focuses on online service providers in carrying out its functions is unclear.

B. RCA

The RCA is a specialized body under the Ministry of Economic Affairs, Agriculture and Innovation. Its three main tasks are "to obtain, allocate and protect frequency space," and its day-to-day work "covers the entire field of wireless and wired communication."[117] A protocol specifies the nature of cooperation between the DPA and the RCA.[118]

C. OPTA

The Independent Post and Telecommunications Authority of the Netherlands (OPTA) was established in the Netherlands on August 1, 1997. Its duties and scope of authority are laid down in the Independent Post and Telecommunications Authority Act (*OPTA wet*), the Postal Act (*Postwet*), and the Telecommunications Act. [119] Among its functions are stimulating investment in fiber optic networks, securing Internet safety, promoting competition in the communications sector, and protecting consumers. 120 Because OPTA is an independent government agency, the Minister of Economic Affairs does not directly control its decisions, but the Minister does appoint the members of the OPTA commission and approve OPTA's budget and its continued existence. Moreover, under the Independent Post and Telecommunications Authority Act, the Minister is required to evaluate OPTA every year.[121]

IV. Administrative Decisions and Court Cases

A. DPA Investigations

1. TomTom N.V.

In late December 2011, the DPA issued a report on its official investigation of the processing of geolocation data by TomTom N.V.[122] TomTom collects personal data worldwide through its "TomTom" devices that have a screen and built-in GPS sensor to use in planning road routes; the route planner is also available as a smartphone (iPhone) application.[123] The investigation was launched based on media reports that appeared in late April 2011 alleging that TomTom had "provided geolocation data from users of TomTom devices to third parties," particularly to the police "but also directly to commercial parties such as Eindhoven Airport."[124] At issue was whether TomTom processed personal data as defined under article 1, introduction and (a), of the PDPA; whether TomTom had grounds for processing personal data as referred to in article 8 of the Act on unambiguous user consent; and whether TomTom had provided personal data to third parties, and if so, whether that additional processing was consistent with the purpose for which the personal data was acquired, as required by article 9 of the Act.[125]

The report noted that TomTom does not request separate consent for collecting and processing realtime geolocation data before its service is used on online devices and a smartphone application. As a result, "[t]he data subject only sees a general reference to the TomTom privacy statement if he creates an account, that is at the moment that he links the device to the TomTom servers via his (own) computer connection," but the DPA "has decided on several occasions that consent for the processing of personal data cannot be obtained via general terms and conditions."[126] Because there was no "unambiguous consent for the processing of *historical* and *realtime* geolocation data on current *offline* and *online* devices and the smartphone application,"[127] the report concluded, TomTom was acting in contravention of article 8. On the issue of further processing of personal data in connection with article 9 of the PDPA, the report found that "TomTom provides historical journey data only in aggregated form to third parties" and in that form the data cannot be "reasonably directly or indirectly traced to natural persons, either by TomTom or another party, and so this is not personal data as defined under the PDPA and the PDPA does not apply to the provision of such data.[128]

2. Google Penalty Order

The DPA imposed a penalty order on Google on March 23, 2011, after an investigation indicated that the company had used its Street View vehicles to collect data on more than 3.6 million Wi-Fi routers in the Netherlands, both secured and unsecured, during the period March 4, 2008, to May 6, 2010, and had also calculated a geolocation for each router. Such acts constituted a violation of the PDPA. According to a DPA press release, "MAC [media access control] addresses combined with a calculated geolocation constitute personal data in this context, because the data can provide information about the owner of the WiFi router in question."[129]

Subsequently, the DPA verified Google's compliance with all the requirements of the order, one of which was to offer an opt-out option enabling people to object to the processing of data on their WiFi routers. Beginning in mid-November 2011, "Google has offered users the option to add '_nomap' to the network name of their WiFi router to stipulate their refusal to let Google process their information"; in the DPA's view, "Google now provides those involved with a free and effective opt-out possibility."[130] Google also indicated that it was destroying all data collected in the Netherlands by means of the Street View vehicles and would be implementing that step globally.[131] The DPA further determined that Google had complied with the requirements to irreversibly delete network names (SSIDs) and to report its data processing to the DPA.[132]

3. 2005 Court Case

The Supreme Court of the Netherlands issued a decision on November 25, 2005, in a dispute between the ISP Lycos and Pessers, a stamp seller via e-Bay. A Lycos-hosted website entitled "Stop the fraud" called Pessers a swindler. The attempt by Pessers to contact the holder of the website failed. Pessers contacted Lycos and requested that the website be removed and its holder's name and address revealed, but Lycos refused to provide the information. Pessers' argument before the court was "that Lycos should reveal the identity of the holder of the website and that Lycos' refusal to do so could be considered unlawful."[133] On the basis of the EU's E-Commerce Directive,[134] the Dutch Court of Appeal held that it is not justifiable for an ISP to remove "information that cannot be considered to be manifestly unlawful," but that the request to reveal the website holder's identity "should be judged independently of the ISP's liability" based on that Directive, and that, in some circumstances refusal to reveal the website holder's identity "might constitute an unlawful act."[135] The Court of Appeal decided, therefore, "that an ISP, such as Lycos, should provide the name and address of the holder of the website," on the basis of four circumstances enumerated in the ruling, e.g., the possibility that it "can to a reasonable extent be assumed" that "the information, in itself, may be unlawful and harmful towards the third party," and "[t]he third party has a concrete interest in obtaining the name and address of the website holder."136

The Supreme Court upheld the Court of Appeal decision, ruling in part that

1. the Lycos argument that a third party can obtain a website holder's name and address only "when it is obvious to the ISP that a certain act is manifestly unlawful" or when a case that the criminal authorities are willing to prosecute is involved "would lead to a situation in which the group of persons able to obtain the name and address of a holder of a website would be fairly small";[137] and
2. the circumstances set forth by the Court of Appeal "do not automatically lead to the conclusion that an ISP must reveal" a website holder's identity, even though its "conclusion that Lycos should provide the name and address of the holder of the website could be justified." Nevertheless, "[t]he balancing of interests might lead to a different result in other circumstances."[138]

The legal documents cited by the court decision include the Dutch Civil Code, the EU e-Commerce Directive, the PDPA, and the European Convention on Human Rights.[139]

V. Public and Scholarly Opinion

Before the amendment of the Telecommunications Law to conform to the EU directive on online privacy, "website developers and publishers . . . warned that such a move would not only be a drag on their operations but would also cause troubles for users as they will have to deal with more pop-up windows."[140] Moreover, ISPs cautioned that the new measures might force them to move some of their operations outside the Netherlands.[141]

Dutch lawyers have reported that in the Netherlands, as in other countries, the incautious use of social media has created an increase in lawsuits. A Dutch cyclist who was receiving disability benefits had to repay part of the benefits when his messages on the Hyves social network website about his grueling cycling trip across the French Alps were spotted and reported to the authorities. According to a Dutch labor law attorney, the authorities are allowed to use the social network sources "because they are in the public domain," and "[u]nless the employee's account is password protected, the employer has the right to read what the employee says. However, this does not negate freedom of speech."[142] An Internet lawyer sees the issue differently, arguing that insurance companies that search the Facebook pages of their clients violate privacy laws, and that while the DPA "has ruled that information published on the Internet is in the public domain, . . . Facebook is not the same thing as a blog, where things are intentionally published."[143]

According to the Dutch legal scholar Colin Prins, certain recent developments in online technology trigger various concerns about privacy. These developments include the popularity of tailored and individualized services using numerous personal data and "ubiquitous computing" (whereby "numerous systems scan our environment for data and serve us with particular information, based on certain notions about what is appropriate for us as unique individual persons given the particulars of daily life and context").[144] These developments, in his view, may profoundly affect relationships between individuals, organizations, and/or communities, and of particular concern is the issue of user identification, which

> raises privacy problems as well as concerns with respect to inclusion and exclusion. Personalisation may be a threat to a user's privacy because it provides companies and organisations with a powerful instrument to know in detail what an individual wants, who he is, whether his conduct or behaviour shows certain symptoms, and so forth. Also, personalisation may be disturbing because it facilitates the selected provision to specific users only and may thus diminish certain preferences, differences and values.[145]

Prins therefore believes that the debate on how to deal with the above-mentioned developments should not be limited to a discussion on how to protect individual data, but should encompass the impact on people's identity. He further notes:

> A key feature of personalisation is that individuals are given new ways to present and profile themselves . . . in certain roles or "identities". They act as a certain type of citizen, consumer, patient, voter, etc. As a result, the growing importance of the context-specific concept of online identity raises challenging new questions with regards to the role and status of identity and identification.[146]

He calls for redirection of the debate towards "how individuals are typified . . . and who has the instruments and power to do so," and for privacy protection in present-day society to "cover the capability to know and to control how our identities are constructed."[147]

VI. Recent Developments and Future Reforms

A. Constitutional Amendment Proposed to Protect Digital Rights

In July 2009, the government had appointed a new state commission to draft a bill to amend the Constitution, "*inter alia* in order to improve the accessibility of the Constitution and to adapt constitutional rights and freedoms to the digital age."[148] In February 2012, the Senate indicated that it wanted more changes in the Constitution than the government intends, but less than the state commission proposed in November 2010.[149] In regard to the issue adapting the Constitution to the digital age, it was noted that article 13 of the Constitution on the privacy of correspondence and of the telephone and telegraph offers "no or insufficient protection to new means of communication in the digital age."[150]

The Dutch Christian-Democratic Party (*Nederlandse christendemocratische partij*) (CDP) proposed, instead of the wording on amending article 13 put forward by government, that a new paragraph 3 be added, to read: "All other means of communication are inviolable, except in cases determined by law or by or with the authorization of those designated for that purpose by law."[151] Senator Swagerman of the People's Party for Freedom and Democracy (*Volkspartij voor Vrijheid en Democratie*, or VVD) wished to add protection of both confidential communication and the confidentiality of the communication itself, and asked whether the government was planning to introduce a notification requirement, to the effect that anyone whose right to confidentiality will be limited be informed of that restriction as soon as possible.[152]

A report on the adjustment of article 13 of the Constitution appeared on the Dutch House of Representatives website on May 23, 2012. Among other views put forward, the report suggested that it was not sufficient to revise article 13 alone, and that articles 7 through 10 of the Constitution should also be amended in order to meet the needs of the digitial age.[153] According to a House news item about the report, the government is preparing a bill on the revision of article 13, to be drafted by the Minister of the Interior and Kingdom Relations before the 2012 summer legislative recess. The final bill must be adopted by the House, reconsidered by the new House after the elections, and adopted on the second ballot by a two-thirds majority.[154]

B. Deep Packet Inspection

In 2011, questions arose over the use of Deep Packet Inspection (DPI), software ISPs deploy to scan all the data packets—packages of information sent and received online by users, the labels on which Internet routers read to "determine what they are, who they're from, and where they're going"—that pass through its network.[155] After the contents have been scanned (and sometimes logged), they are blocked or routed to the appropriate destination.[156] In May 2011, the Dutch telecom provider KPN revealed that it had used DPI to track the use of certain applications such as Whatsapp ("a free alternative to text messaging") and Skype ("a free alternative for voice telephony and chat").[157] This gave rise to concerns about potential invasion of privacy and possible contravention of the net neutrality principle (due to prioritizing of certain modes of Internet traffic). As a result, telecom regulator OPTA launched an investigation into providers' possible infringement "of specific articles of Dutch telecommunication law relating to personal data and privacy protection (secrecy of correspondence), security measures and delivery guarantees."[158] The OPTA concluded a month later that, while there were grounds for concern, more specific research was necessary, and so it turned the investigation over to the DPA.[159]

C. Hotline for Reporting Online Privacy-Related Incidents

On April 6, 2012, it was announced that OPTA and RCA have established a hotline for reporting by ISPs of privacy-related incidents and malfunctions, so that all breaches of protection of personal data must be reported to OPTA.[160]

D. Merger of OPTA and Other Agencies into New Consumer Authority

The OPTA itself will be undergoing a change. By January 1, 2013, three regulators—the OPTA, the Netherlands Consumer Authority, and the Netherlands Competition Authority—are to be merged into one new authority, the Netherlands Authority for Consumers and Markets (ACM). This is the name stipulated in a bill on the establishment of the new agency, "the proposal for which is currently at [the] advisory stage."[161] Two separate bills will be considered in order to achieve consolidation of the three current authorities. The bill on the ACM's establishment will ensure the independent position of the new authority. Moreover,

> [t]he new authority will be run by a board, consisting of three members, and governing in a spirit of collegiality. It will focus on three main themes: consumer protection, industry-specific regulation, and competition oversight. Governance anchored in collegiality will safeguard the coherence between these three themes. The [second,] substantive bill will simplify procedures, and streamline powers.[162]

Prepared by Wendy Zeldin
Senior Legal Research Analyst
June 2012

PORTUGAL
ONLINE PRIVACY LAW

Executive Summary

Constitutional principles guarantee the protection of personal data in Portugal. In 1991, the country issued its first law regulating the use and control of personal data and creating a regulatory agency.

European Union Directives 95/46/EC, 97/66/EC, 2000/31/CE, and 2002/58/EC have since been transposed to the country's domestic legal system, requiring an update of the law according to European Union standards. To this effect, the country enacted Law No. 67 of October 26, 1998, to regulate the protection of personal data; Law No. 69 of October 28, 1998, to regulate the protection of personal data and the protection of privacy in the telecommunications sector; Decree-Law No. 7 of January 7, 2004, to address aspects of electronic commerce in the internal market and processing of personal data; and Law No. 41 of August 18, 2004, which revoked Law No. 69, and now regulates the processing of personal data and the protection of privacy in the electronic communications sector.

It appears that reforms of the laws dealing with the protection of personal data and addressing the new technological developments that make use of such data will only be implemented after the European Commission issues a new directive in this regard.

I. Legal Framework

In Portugal, the protection of personal data used in connection with information technology is a fundamental right guaranteed by the Constitution of 1976.[1] However, it was only on April 29, 1991, that the country adopted its first law (Law No. 10) regulating the use and control of personal data and creating a regulatory agency on the subject.[2]

In 1995, the European Union issued Directive 95/46/EC on the protection of individuals with regard to the processing of personal data and on the free movement of such data,[3] and imposed a period of three years from its entry into force for the Member States to transpose it to their national rules.[4]

During Portugal's Constitutional Review of 1997, article 35 of the Constitution was amended to enable an adequate transposition of Directive No. 95/46/EC into Portugal's Constitutional Charter.[5] Subsequently, Law No. 67 of October 26, 1998, was enacted as the new law on protection of personal data, which transposed Directive No. 95/46/EC into Portugal's domestic legislation and revoked Law No. 10 of April 29, 1991.[6]

On October 28, 1998, Law No. 69 was issued to regulate the protection of personal data and the protection of privacy in the telecommunications sector, transposing Directive 97/66/EC into Portugal's domestic legal system.[7] On August 18, 2004, Law No. 41 was enacted to regulate the protection of personal data in the electronic communications sector.[8] Law No. 41 revoked Law No. 69 and transposed Directive 2002/58/EC on Privacy and Electronic Communications into Portugal's domestic legislation.[9]

II. Current Law

A. Constitutional Principle

The Constitution determines that the law must establish effective guarantees against the acquisition and abusive use, or use that is contrary to human dignity, of information concerning individuals and families.[10] According to article 35 of the Constitution,

1. All citizens have the right to access any computerized data relating to them; to require its correction and update; and to be informed of the use for which the data is intended, according to the law.
2. The law determines the concept of personal data as well as the conditions applicable to automatic processing, connection, transmission, and use thereof, and must guarantee its protection by means of an independent administrative entity.
3. Computerized storage may not be used for information concerning a person's ideological or political convictions, a person's political party or trade union affiliations, religious beliefs, private life, or ethnic origin, except where there is express consent from the data subject, authorization is provided for under the law with guarantees of nondiscrimination, or in the case of data for statistical purposes that do not identify individuals.
4. Access to personal data of third parties is prohibited, excluding exceptional cases specified by law.
5. It is prohibited to give citizens a national number.
6. Everyone is guaranteed free access to public information networks, and the law defines the regulations applicable to the transnational data flows and the adequate forms of protection for personal data and for data that should be safeguarded in the national interest.

7. Personal data kept on manual files must receive the same protection provided for in article 35 of the Constitution, in accordance with the law.[11]

B. Personal Data Protection

Personal data in Portugal is protected by Law No. 67 of October 26, 1998,[12] supplemented by Law No. 41 of August 18, 2004.[13]

1. Law No. 67 of October 26, 1998

According to article 6 of Law No. 67/98, personal data may be processed only if the data subject has unambiguously given his consent or if processing is necessary for

a) execution of a contract or contracts to which the data subject is a party or in order to take steps at the request of the data subject prior to entering into a contract or a declaration of his will to negotiate;
b) compliance with a legal obligation to which the controller is subject;
c) protection of the vital interests of the data subject if the latter is physically or legally incapable of giving his consent;
d) performance of a task carried out in the public interest or in the exercise of official authority vested in the controller or in a third party to whom the data are disclosed; [or]
e) pursuing the legitimate interests of the controller or the third party to whom the data are disclosed, except where such interests are overridden by interests of fundamental rights, freedoms, and guarantees of the data subject.[14]

2. Definitions

Law No. 67/98 defines "personal data" (*dados pessoais*) as information of any type, irrespective of the type of media involved, including sound and image, relating to an identified or identifiable natural person (the "data subject").[15] An "identifiable person" is a person who can be identified, directly or indirectly, in particular by reference to an identification number or to one or more elements specific to his physical, physiological, mental, economic, cultural, or social identity.[16]

The "processing of personal data" (*tratamento de dados pessoais*) is defined as any operation or set of operations performed upon personal data, whether entirely or partially by automatic means, such as collection, recording, organization, storage, adaptation or alteration, retrieval, consultation, use, disclosure by transmission, dissemination or otherwise making available, with "comparison or interconnection" as well as its blocking, erasure, or destruction.[17]

"Controller" (*responsável pelo tratamento*) is defined as the natural or legal person, public authority, agency, or any other body that alone or jointly with others determines the purposes and means of the processing of personal data; where the purposes and means of processing are determined by laws or regulations, the controller must be designated in the Act establishing its organization and functioning, or in the statutes of the legal or statutory body competent to process the personal data concerned.[18]

"Consent of the data subject" (*consentimento do titular de dados*) is defined as any free, specific, and informed expression of intent under which the data subject accepts the processing of his personal data.[19]

3. Law No. 41 of August 18, 2004

Law No. 41 of August 18, 2004, applies to the processing of personal data in the context of networks and electronic communication services available to the public, specifying and supplementing the provisions of Law No. 67/98.[20]

4. Transparency

The processing of personal data needs to be done transparently and with strict respect for the private life, as well as for fundamental rights, freedoms, and guarantees.[21]

5. Sensitive Data

The processing of personal data referring to philosophical or political beliefs, political party or union membership, religious faith, private life, and racial or ethnic origin, as well as the processing of data concerning a person's health or sex life, including genetic data, is prohibited under article 7(1) of Law No. 67/98.[22]

Article 7(2) of the Law determines that the processing of the data mentioned in article 7(1) is allowed if permission is provided by law or authorized, in specific situations, by the National Commission of Data Protection (*Comissão Nacional de Protecção de Dados – CNPD*).[23]

The processing of the data referred to in article 7(1) of Law No. 67/98 must also be permitted when one of the following conditions applies:[24]

a) when it is necessary to protect the vital interests of the data subject or of another person where the data subject is physically or legally incapable of giving his consent;
b) [when processing is done] with the consent of the data subject by a foundation, association or nonprofit entity with a political, philosophical, religious or union character, within their legitimate activities, provided that the treatment concerns only members of these bodies or people who have regular contacts connected to their purposes, and the data are not disclosed to third parties without consent of the data subject;
c) when it relates to data that are manifestly made public by the data subject, provided his consent for their processing can be clearly inferred from his declarations;
d) when it is necessary for the declaration, exercise or defense of a right concerning a legal dispute and it is exclusively carried out for that purpose.

The processing of data relating to a person's health and sex life, including genetic data, is permitted if it is necessary for the purposes of preventive medicine, medical diagnosis, provision of care or treatment, or management of health-care services, provided that those data are processed by a health professional bound by professional secrecy or by another person also subject to an equivalent obligation of secrecy, the CNPD is notified under article 27 of Law No. 67/98, and suitable safeguards are provided.[25]

Pursuant to article 12 of Law No. 67/98, the data subject has the right

a) except where otherwise provided by law, and at least in the cases referred to in articles 6(d) and 6(e) of Law No. 67/98, to object at any time, on compelling legitimate grounds relating to his particular situation, to the processing of data relating to him, and where there is a justified objection, the processing of data performed by the controller may no longer involve those data;

b) to object, on request and free of charge, to the processing of personal data relating to him which the controller anticipates being processed for the purposes of direct marketing or any other form of research, or to be informed before personal data are disclosed for the first time to third parties for the purposes of direct marketing or for use on behalf of third parties, and to be expressly offered the right to object, free of charge, to such disclosure or uses.[26]

Laws No. 67/98 and 41/2004 are silent regarding data collection by smartphone applications and specific protections of minors. Neither law includes an age threshold for registering on social networking sites.

6. Personal Profiles

According to article 5(1) of Law No. 67/98, personal data must be

a) processed lawfully and with respect for the principle of good faith;
b) collected for specified, explicit, and legitimate purposes and not further processed in a way incompatible with those purposes;
c) adequate, relevant, and not excessive in relation to the purposes for which they are collected and further processed;
d) accurate and, where necessary, updated, and with adequate measures taken to ensure that data that are inaccurate or incomplete are erased or corrected, taking into account the purposes for which they were collected or for which they will be further processed; [and]
e) kept in a way that permits identification of their subjects for no longer than is necessary for the purposes for which they were collected or for which they are further processed.[27]

The storing of data for historical, statistical, or scientific purposes for periods longer than specified in article 5(1)(e) of Law No. 67/98, which determines that personal data must be kept in a way that permits identification of their subjects for no longer than is necessary for the purposes for which they were collected or for which they are further processed, may be authorized by the CNPD at the request of the controller in the case of a legitimate interest.[28] The controller is charged with the duty to observe and comply with the provisions of article 5 of Law No. 67/98.[29]

7. Location Data

In cases where location data (*dados de localização*) are processed in addition to traffic data (*dados de tráfego*) relating to subscribers or users of public communication networks or electronic communication services available to the public, the processing of these data is allowed only if they are made anonymous.[30]

The recording, processing, and transmission of location data for/to organizations with legal authority to receive emergency calls for the purpose of responding to such calls are allowed, however.[31] The processing of location data is also permitted to the extent and for the time required for the rendering of value-added services, provided that prior consent of the subscribers or users is obtained.[32]

Companies that provide electronic communications services accessible to the public must inform the users or subscribers, prior to obtaining their consent, of the type of location data that will be processed, the duration and purposes of the processing, and the possible transmission of data to third parties for the purpose of providing value-added services.[33] Companies that provide electronic communications services accessible to the public must ensure that subscribers and users have the option, through simple and free means,[34] ithdrawing consentpreviouslygiven for the processingof location datareferred toarticle 7 of Law No. 41/2004 at any time,of wthe in[35] and temporarily refusing the processing of such data for each network connection or for each transmission of a communication.[36]

The processing of location data must be limited to workers and employees of companies that offer network or electronic communication services accessible to the public or third parties providing value-added service, and must be restricted to what is necessary for such activity.[37]

According to Law No. 41/2004, "electronic communication" means any information exchanged or conveyed between a finite number of parties by means of an electronic communication service available to the public.[38] "Traffic data" is defined as any data processed for the purpose of sending a communication over an electronic communication network or for the billing thereof.[39] "Location data" means any data processed in an electronic communication network indicating the geographic position of the terminal equipment of a subscriber or any user of an electronic communication service available to the public.[40]

8. Security Measures to Protect Data

The controller must implement appropriate technical and organizational measures to protect personal data against accidental or unlawful destruction, accidental loss, alteration, or unauthorized disclosure or access, in particular where the processing involves the transmission of data over a network, and against all other unlawful forms of processing. These measures must ensure, given the expertise and the cost of their implementation, a level of security appropriate to the risk that the processing presents and the nature of the data to be protected.[41]

Companies that offer networks and companies providing electronic communication services must work together towards the adoption of technical and organizational measures to ensure effective security of their services and, if necessary, the security of the network itself.[42] In case of a particular risk of a breach of network security, companies that provide electronic communication services to the public must inform the subscribers of such risk, as well as of possible solutions to prevent it and the likely cost of such measures, free of charge.[43]

Companies that offer networks or electronic communication services must ensure the inviolability of communications and related traffic data through public communication networks and electronic communication services available to the public.[44]

9. Anonymity

With regard to the possibility of remaining anonymous while using online services, it appears that Law No. 41/2004 only covers telephone communications. Article 9(1) determines that when caller identification is offered, the companies that provide electronic communication services to the public must ensure that subscribers who make the calls and have the option, through simple and free means, to prevent the caller's identification from being revealed on each call to other users.[45] Companies that offer networks or electronic communication services to the public are required to make available to the public, and especially to subscribers, transparent and updated information on the possibilities outlined in article 9 of Law No. 41/2004.[46]

10. Data Protection Agency

The National Commission of Data Protection (*Comissão Nacional de Protecção de Dados – CNPD*) is the agency is charge of controlling and inspecting the enforcement of laws and regulations on the protection of personal data.[47]

11. User's Rights and Remedies

When personal data is collected directly from the data subject, the controller or his representative must provide, unless it is already known by that person, notification of the existence of and the conditions for accessing and correcting such data, as necessary taking into account the specific circumstances of data collection to ensure that the person is provided with fair processing of the data.[48]

In the case of collection of data on open networks, the data subject must be informed, unless the person is already aware, that his personal data can travel on the network without security, and of the risk of that data being seen and used by unauthorized third parties.[49]

The data subject has the right to obtain from the controller, freely and without constraint, at reasonable intervals and without excessive delay or expense, the correction, erasure, or blocking of data whose processing does not comply with the provisions of Law No. 67/98, in particular because of the incomplete or inaccurate nature of the data.[50] The controller must also provide notification to third parties to whom the data have been disclosed of any correction, erasure, or blocking carried out in compliance with article 11(1)(d) of Law No. 67/98, unless this proves impossible.[51] Article 12 of Law No. 67/98 defines the situations where the data subject has the right to object to the processing of data relating to him.

Without prejudice to the right to submit a complaint to the CNPD, any person may resort to administrative or judicial measures to ensure compliance with the legal provisions on protection of personal data.[52] Any person who has suffered damage as a result of an unlawful processing of data or of any other acts incompatible with legal provisions in the area of personal data protection is entitled to receive compensation from the controller for the damage suffered.[53]

12. Criminal and Administrative Sanctions

Violations of the privacy provisions discussed above may result in fines and/or imprisonment.

Articles 35 to 45 of Law No. 67/98 and article 14 of Law No. 41/2004 establish the offenses (*contra-ordenações*)[54] that are punishable by a fine and the respective amount of such fines. For example, entities that fail to appoint a representative in accordance with article 4(5) of Law No. 67/98 or comply with the obligations established in articles 5, 10–13, 15, 16, and 31(3) of that Law are punishable by a minimum fine of 100000$00 (one hundred thousand *escudos*) (about US$626.00) and maximum of 1000000$00 (one million *escudos*) (about US$6,260.00).[55] The fine amount is doubled when the obligations contained in articles 6, 7, 8, 9, 19, and 20 of Law No. 67/98 are not fulfilled.[56]

The president of the CNPD is responsible for the application of the fines provided for in Law No. 67/98, subject to prior deliberation by the Commission.[57] Once approved by the president and after being discussed by the CNPD, the fine is enforceable if it is not challenged within the statutory period.[58]

Articles 43 to 49 of Law No. 67/98 list crimes that are punishable by up to two years in prison and the payment of a fine. Examples include noncompliance with obligations relating to data protection,[59] unauthorized access to personal data,[60] falsification or destruction of personal data, [61] and breach of secrecy.[62]

13. Cross-border Application

On January 7, 2004, Portugal issued Decree-Law No. 7, which transposed EU Directive No. 2000/31/EC on Electronic Commerce.[63] According to Decree-Law No. 7, the courts and other authorities including entities with a supervisory capacity may restrict the circulation of a specific service "information society service" from another Member State of the European Union if it seriously injures or threatens, inter alia, tuman dignity or the public order including the protection of minors and the incitement to hatred based on race, sex, religion, or nationality, for reasons including the prevention or repression of crimes or social offenses.[64]

"Information society service" is defined as any service provided at a distance by electronic means for remuneration, or at a minimum within the context of an economic activity, following an individual request by the recipient.[65]

The restrictive measures taken under Decree-Law No. 7 must be preceded by a request to the Member State where the service provider is located asking that it put an end to the situation.[66] If the Member State does not act upon the request, or the measures taken are deemed inappropriate, notification to the CNPD and the Member State of the intention to take restrictive measures is required. 67 The notification provisions are without prejudice to judicial proceedings, including preliminary proceedings and acts carried out under a criminal investigation or concerning a violation of public order (*ilícito de mera ordenação social*).[68] The measures taken must be proportionate to the purposes of the safeguard.[69]

14. Retention of Data

On July 17, 2008, Law No. 32 was issued to regulate the storage and transmission of traffic data and location data relative to natural persons and legal entities, as well as the related data necessary to identify the subscriber or registered user, for purposes of investigation, detection, and prosecution of serious crimes by the competent authorities.[70] Law No. 32 transposed Directive 2006/24/EC[71] into Portugal's domestic legal system.

According to Law No. 32, the retention of data revealing the content of communications is prohibited, without prejudice to the provisions of Law No. 41/2004 and criminal procedure law on the interception and recording of communications.[72]

The storage and transmission of data must be made exclusively in connection with the investigation, detection, and prosecution of serious crimes by the competent authorities.[73] The transmission of data to the competent authorities can only be authorized by a written order issued by a judge, in accordance with article 9 of Law No. 32/2008.[74] The files for the retention of data under Law No. 32/2008 must be separated from any other files used for other purposes.[75] The data subject cannot oppose their storage and transmission.[76]

III. Role of Data Protection Agencies

The National Commission of Data Protection (*Comissão Nacional de Protecção de Dados – CNPD*) was created by Law No. 10 of April 29, 1991.[77] The Commission was initially charged with generic responsibility for controlling the automated processing of personal data, with strict respect for human rights and the fundamental freedoms and guarantees provided by the Constitution and the law.[78]

With the revocation of Law No. 10/91 by Law No. 67/98,[79] the CNPD was established as the national authority charged with the power to supervise and monitor compliance with laws and regulations in the area of personal data protection, with strict respect for the human rights and fundamental freedoms and guarantees provided by the Constitution and the law.[80]

The CNPD has the power to investigate, inquire about, and access data that has been processed and to collect all the information necessary to carry out its supervisory duties;[81] order the blocking, erasure, or destruction of data, and prohibit, temporarily or permanently, the processing of personal data, even if included in open networks of data transmission from servers situated within Portuguese territory;[82] and issue opinions prior to the processing of personal data to ensure the publication of such data in a manner that complies with the law.[83]

In the event of repeated breaches of legal provisions regarding personal data, the CNPD can warn or publicly censure the controller, as well as raise the matter before the Assembly of the Republic, the government or other bodies or authorities, in accordance with their respective powers.[84] The CNPD has jurisdiction to intervene in proceedings for violations of Law No. 67/98 and must report to the Public Prosecutor's Office (*Ministério Público*) criminal offenses that it gains knowledge of in the exercise of its functions, as well as take necessary and urgent precautionary measures to secure the evidence.[85]

The CNPD must be consulted on any legal provisions, or legal instruments being prepared in communitarian or international institutions, relating to the processing of personal data.[86] The Commission is responsible in particular for ensuring the right of access to information and the exercise of the right to correct and update such information;[87] acting on an application made by any person or by an association representing that person concerning the protection of the person's rights and freedoms with regard to the processing of personal data, and informing the person of the outcome;[88] carrying out the request of any person to check the lawfulness of data processing where such processing is subject to restrictions on access or information, and informing the person of the completion of the verification;[89] assessing claims, complaints, and petitions from individuals;[90] and promoting the dissemination and clarification of rights relating to data protection and periodically publicizing its activities including the publication of an annual report.[91] It is not clear, however, whether the CNPD has been focusing on online service providers in carrying out these functions or in the protection of personal data as a whole.

IV. Administrative Decisions

In 2010, the CNPD prohibited Google from gathering images in Portugal for Google's Street View service because CNPD believed that the service did not guarantee the anonymity of people and vehicles, and that such service qualified as the processing of personal data.[92] Google asserted that the service was legal because it did not expose people's faces or the license plates of vehicles due to the fact that before being made available to the public, such features of the images were blurred, making then unidentifiable.[93]

CNPD's spokeswoman, Clara Guerra, explained that Google was supposed to provide CNPD with additional technical information regarding the feasibility of guaranteeing anonymity in images, which did not occur.[94] As a consequence, CNPD notified Google that the service was prohibited in Portugal because it did not meet the legal conditions regarding the protection of personal data.[95] Further research on the subject did not reveal whether Google's service, Street View, has resumed its activities in Portugal.

V. Public and Scholarly Opinion

Since 2011 the CNPD has made available a survey that allows Internet users to verify their level of vulnerability to identity theft, both online and offline, in an effort to call people's attention to the risks of not properly protecting their personal information.[96] The survey is a multiple choice quiz that concerns eleven daily situations in which a person may be subject to identity theft.[97] At the end of the test, a score is given for each topic covered, and an overall assessment of the degree of exposure to identity theft is provided.[98] Along with the survey, CNPD also released the guide *Read and Learn*, which contains advice for safer behavior, so that data such as one's name, address, and bank account numbers, among others, do not fall into the wrong hands.[99] According to CNPD's spokeswoman Clara Guerra, the purpose of these initiatives is to alert and sensitize people to the need for the protection of personal data.[100] The results of the survey are not available to the public; therefore it is not possible to assess how members of the public feel about online data protection.

Information regarding egregious cases of violations or questionable practices is scarce and, as such, it is not possible to evaluate whether there has been an impact strong enough to shape the public opinion regarding such practices. Research on the subject failed to identify any evaluations prepared by Portuguese scholars concerning the existing laws or comments on a balance between commercial interests of the service providers and the privacy interest of the users. Discussions of such issues are currently underway in the European Union.[101]

VI. Pending Reforms

Recently, the European Commission proposed a comprehensive reform of the EU's 1995 data protection rules to strengthen online privacy rights and boost Europe's digital economy.[102] According to the European Commission,

> [t]echnological progress and globalisation have profoundly changed the way our data is collected, accessed and used. In addition, the 27 EU Member States have implemented the

> 1995 rules differently, resulting in divergences in enforcement. A single law will do away with the current fragmentation and costly administrative burdens, leading to savings for businesses of around €2.3 billion a year. The initiative will help reinforce consumer confidence in online services, providing a much needed boost to growth, jobs and innovation in Europe.[103]

Existing Portuguese laws related to the protection of personal data were issued to transpose earlier European Union directives into the country's domestic legal system. Reforms in this regard will apparently be implemented only after the European Commission issues a new directive.

Prepared by Eduardo Soares
Senior Foreign Law Specialist
June 2012

SPAIN
ONLINE PRIVACY LAW

Executive Summary

Among the EU countries, Spain has some of the strictest legislation on personal data protection. It has transposed all of the EU Directives related to this matter. Spanish law has even been successfully challenged before the European Court of Justice (ECJ) for imposing additional requirements in its domestic legislation regarding the release of personal data without the consent of the data subject. Spain's data protection agency has been very active and responsive to citizens' complaints and imposes heavy fines on violators of data protection laws.

Spain has recently been engaged in "right to be forgotten" litigation with Google. Although Google obtained a positive ruling from a Spanish court on jurisdictional grounds, the court did not address the right to be forgotten. That issue went to the ECJ for an advisory opinion, which will be binding on all EU Member countries when issued.

I. Legal Framework

The 1978 Spanish Constitution[1] provides for the protection of personal and family privacy,[2] stating that the law must set limitations on the use of information technology in order to guarantee the honor as well as the personal and family privacy of individuals and the full exercise of their rights.[3] This provision constitutes the framework and basis for Spanish legislation on data protection, which in 1978 was a novel concept unlikely to be found in a constitutional norm.[4]

In 1999, Spain enacted an Organic Law on the Protection of Personal Data (Ley Orgánica de protección de datos de carácter personal, LOPDP)[5] to transpose the European Union (EU) Data Privacy Directive (Directive 95/46).[6] The LOPDP governs personal and family privacy, and guarantees and protects fundamental rights and freedoms with respect to the processing of personal information.[7] In 2007, Spain enacted an implementing regulation to the LOPDP that also serves to transpose Directive 95/46: the Regulation on the Development of the Organic Law on the Protection of Data (Reglamento de desarollo del la Ley Orgánica 15/1999, de protección de datos de carácter personal, RLOPDP),[8] which aims to bring more legal certainty to the data protection regime, particularly on issues that over the years have proven to be in need of further regulatory implementation.[9]

In 2007, Spain enacted Law 25/2007 on the Retention of Data Generated or Processed in Connection with Electronic or Public Communications Networks,[10] to transpose European Directive 2006/24/EC, on Telecommunications Data Retention.[11] On March 30, 2012, Spain transposed Directive 2002/58/CE (the E-Privacy Directive) as amended by Directive 2009/136,[12] when it passed Royal Decree 13/2012,[13] introducing the European regulation of "cookies" into domestic law, as discussed further in section II(B) of this report.

II. Current Law

A. Scope of Application

The LOPDP applies to personal data stored in a physical medium susceptible of being processed and the use of such data in the public or private sectors.[14] This law applies as long as

- the data controller carries out his activities in Spain;
- the person responsible for the data processing is not located in Spain but is subject to Spanish law under international rules; or
- the person is not established in the EU but is using processing means located in Spain, unless such means are used only for transit.[15]

The LOPDP includes provisions for setting up a national data protection agency, the Agencia Española de Protección de Datos (AEPD), whose functions are discussed in section III, as the enforcement agency with the authority to hear complaints on personal data protection matters and to impose sanctions.[16]

Protected personal data are defined in both the LOPDP[17] and the RLOPDP[18] as any information presented in any alphanumeric, graphic, photographic, acoustic, or any other format related to identified or identifiable individuals.[19] Files in private ownership containing personal data may be created when it is necessary to carry out the legitimate business and purpose of the person or entity owning them, provided the safeguards required under the LOPDP are met.[20]

The following types of data are excluded from protection:

- Data created or kept by an individual for personal use related to his or her private or family life
- Data related to classified material, which is subject to special data protection legislation
- Data related to investigations of terrorism and organized crime.[21]

B. Right to Consent

The processing of data and their transfer to third parties are allowed only with the prior consent of the data subject,[22] except under certain statutorily described circumstances that include the following:

- authorization by a regulation with the force of law, or under EU law, and in particular
  - in pursuit of the legitimate interest of the data controller or the recipient, as long as the interest or fundamental rights and liberties of the data subject are not affected; or
  - when the processing or transfer of data is necessary for the data controller to comply with his or her legal obligations;[23]
- collection to carry out public administration duties under regulations having the force of law or EU legislation;
- collection by the data controller in compliance with a contract or pre-contract, or in the course of a business, employment, or administrative relationship to which the data subject is a party and for which the collection of data is needed;[24]
- processing for the benefit of the data subject's life or health;
- required transfer for the development, performance, or control of a legal relationship;
- transfer intended for the ombudsman, the Office of the Public Prosecutor, judges, courts, or the Spanish Court of Audits, or to the Autonomous Communities authorities with similar functions to that of the ombudsman or the Spanish Court of Audit; or
- transfer between public administration entities, as long as (a) data is processed for historical, statistical, or scientific purposes; (b) personal data has been collected or obtained by one public administration entity to be provided to another; or (c) the communication of personal data is done in fulfillment of identical powers or powers related to the same matters.[25]

In addition, the public administration may only transfer data collected from publicly available sources to private data controller's files when such a transfer is allowed by a regulation having the force of law.[26]

Royal Decree 13/2012[27] regulates the use of "cookies," defined as devices or features that allow for web browsing while also allowing access to the private information of the user. Data hidden in cookies is exchanged among web users' hard drives and website servers. The Decree aims to ensure that users are safeguarded with proper information and appropriate tools to protect their privacy.[28] The Decree amends Law 34/2002 on Services of the Information Society and E-commerce,[29] providing that the service provider has two ways of obtaining the required consent from the user in order to use cookies: (1) through an opt-in consent that must be released after the user has been given adequate information about the cookies; or (2) through a preset consent in the browser's settings or any other application.[30] This Spanish transposition of Directive 2009/136 is stricter than the Directive itself, in that it requires express consent by the user.[31]

C. Right to Consult the General Data Protection Register

Individuals have the right to access the General Data Protection Register (see below, section III) free of charge to verify the records of their personal data, the purpose for which they were collected and stored, and the identity of the controller.[32]

D. Right to Challenge Data Processing

Data subjects have the right to not be bound by a decision with legal consequences for them, or which significantly affects them, and which is solely based on data processed to assess certain aspects of the person's personality.[33]

A data subject may challenge any administrative and private decision based on an assessment of his behavior if such an assessment is based only on personal data that includes a definition of the person's personality or characteristics.[34] In this case, the data subject has the right to obtain information about the criteria used by the data controller in processing the personal data in question.[35]

E. Right of Access

A data subject has the right to obtain, free of charge, information about how his personal data that is subject to processing was obtained, as well as how such data has been and will be used or communicated to others.[36]

F. Right to Correct and Erase

If the personal data is inaccurate or incomplete, or has been processed in violation of the LOPDP, the data subject has the right to have it corrected or erased by the data controller within ten days of the request.[37]

Erased data will be blocked and kept only at the discretion of the public administration entities, judges, and courts, for the purpose of establishing possible liabilities deriving from processing, while the statute of limitations for such liability is still running. After this period expires the data must be deleted.[38]

G. Right to Seek Redress and Damages

In the case of violations of the LOPDP, data subjects are entitled to file complaints with the AEPD[39] and to seek compensation for damages.[40]

H. Notifications

Data controllers must report to the AEPD the creation of personal data files,[41] the name of the controller, the purpose of the file, the type of data included, security measures taken, and any domestic or international transfers intended to be performed (see also below, section III).[42]

The first transfer of data must be reported to the data subject, indicating the purpose of the transfer and the name of the recipient (with a few exceptions listed under article 11 of the LODPD).[43]

Personal data contained in a "promotional census"[44] or in publicly accessible sources, such as the lists of members of professional associations whose files are open to the public, public registries, telephone directories, newspapers, official gazettes, and the media, should be limited to the information necessary to meet the needs for which the list was created. The inclusion of additional data by the entities responsible for managing these sources requires the consent of the data subject, which may be revoked at any time.[45]

Data subjects are entitled to require the entity responsible for keeping such lists to note in the list, free of charge, that their data is not to be used for advertising or market research purposes.[46] Data subjects also have the right to have their personal data removed from the promotional census list, free of charge, by the entity responsible for keeping such data.[47]

I. Sensitive Personal Data

Under the Spanish Constitution, no one may be required to reveal his or her ideology, religion, or beliefs.[48] Therefore, individuals must be notified of their right to refuse to provide such information when requested.[49]

Personal data that include a person's ideology, trade union membership, religion, and beliefs may be processed only with the written consent of the data subject. Exceptions to this principle are member data files kept by political parties, trade unions, churches, religious institutions or communities, and associations, foundations, and other nonprofit organizations with a political, philosophical, religious, or trade union purpose. However, the transmittal of such data always requires the data subject's prior consent.[50] Files created with the sole purpose of storing personal data revealing ideology, trade union membership, religion, beliefs, racial or ethnic origin, or sex life are forbidden.[51]

Personal data that include information on racial origin, health, or sex life may only be collected, processed, and transferred when a law so requires on public interest grounds, or with the specific consent of the data subject.[52] This data may also be processed if it is necessary for preventive or diagnostic medical needs, medical care or treatment, or management of health-care services, and only if such data are processed by a health-care professional bound by professional secrecy or any other person also subject to an equivalent obligation of secrecy,[53] or if the processing of the data is needed to protect the vital interests of the data subject (or another person, if the data subject is physically or legally incapable of giving his consent).[54]

Personal data on criminal or administrative offenses may be included in files of public administration entities only under the conditions established under their regulations.[55]

J. Protection of Minors

Until the passage of the RLOPDP in 2007, there was no specific reference to the protection of the personal data of minors in Spanish law.[56] The RLOPDP now requires the consent of parents or legal representatives in order to process the personal data of minors under the age of fourteen.[57] The personal data of minors older than fourteen may be processed with the minor's consent, except when the law specifically requires the parent's or legal representative's assistance in providing such data.[58]

The RLOPDP prohibits the gathering of information about parents or any other family members through the minor.[59]

When dealing with the processing of data on minors, the information addressed to them should be provided in a simple and easy language.[60] It is the data controller's responsibility to verify the minor's age and the authenticity of the consent given by the parent, guardian, or legal representative.[61]

The law requires social media and other online services to provide an efficient technology to securely identify the age of the users. However, the reality is that these systems are not yet generally available and minors are constantly at risk of having their consent obtained in violation of the law.[62]

K. Data Retention

With regard to data retention, Law 25/2007 on the Retention of Data Generated or Processed in Connection with Electronic or Public Communications Networks,[63] transposes European Directive 2006/24, on Telecommunications Data Retention.[64] The new law regulates the retention of data related to electronic communications and public communications networks in order to detect, investigate, and prosecute serious crimes.[65] Law 25/2007 lists the types of data that must be kept in order to identify both ends of the communication and the date and time, duration, and type of service and equipment to be used; the law requires the retention of these utilization data but not the retention of content data (those disclosing the content of the communication).[66] The data must be retained for a period of twelve months, which may be reduced or adjusted according to the type of data involved.[67] The Law also sets restrictions as to the competent authorities to whom the data may be transferred. These authorities are members of the security forces, customs authority agents, and National Center of Intelligence staff who perform judicial police duties.[68]

Law 25/2007 has generated opposition from different groups, such as European Digital Rights (EDRI)[69] and XS4ALL,[70] who filed a complaint, maintaining that the retention of data on national security grounds often violates basic human rights such as the privacy of individuals.[71]

L. Data Security

The data controller and the data processor are required to adopt technical and organizational measures needed for the security of personal data and to prevent its alteration, loss, or unauthorized processing or access, considering the state of the art, the nature of the data stored, and the risks to which they are exposed.[72]

Personal data may not be recorded in files that do not meet the security safeguards required by the regulations.[73] Security measure regulations are covered in detail in Title VIII of the RLOPDP.[74]

M. Infractions

Data controllers and processors are subject to penalties that vary depending on the type of infraction.[75] Article 44 of the LOPDP classifies the infractions. It may be translated as follows:

Article 44. Types of Infractions

1. The infractions are classified as minor, serious, and very serious.
2. Minor infractions are:

a) Failure to respond, for formal reasons, to a data subject's request for rectification or cancellation of personal data subject to processing.
b) Failure to provide information as requested by the Spanish Agency for Data Protection [AEPD] in the exercise of its legally assigned functions, concerning non-substantive aspects of data protection.

c) Failure to request the entry of a file of personal data in the General Data Protection Register, unless this constitutes a serious infraction.
d) Commencing the collection of personal data of data subjects without providing them the required information as specified in article 5 of the present law.
e) Failure to fulfill the secrecy requirements as established in article 10 of the present law , unless this constitutes a serious infraction.[76]

3. Serious infractions are:

a) Creation of public-ownership files, or initiation of the gathering of personal data for [the creation of] such files—without the proper authorization [having been]published in the Boletin Oficial del Estado or an equivalent official gazette.
b) Creation of private-ownership files, or initiation of the gathering of personal data for such files, for purposes different from those that constitute the legitimate objective of the enterprise or entity [involved].
c) Collection of personal data without obtaining the specific consent of the data subjects, when such consent is required.
d) Use or processing of personal data in violation of the LOPDP and implementing regulations when this does not constitute a very serious infraction.
e) Impeding or obstructing the exercise of the rights of access and objection of data subjects, and refusing to provide requested information.
f) Maintaining inexact personal data or failing to effectuate the correction or deletion of such data from the files that are legally required when the rights of persons who are protected by the present law (LOPDP) are affected.
g) Violation of the duty to maintain secrecy of the personal data introduced into files that contain data related to the perpetration of administrative or criminal offenses, the Public Treasury, financial services, provision of "patrimonial solvency" [financial solvency] and credit services, as well as other files that contain a collection of personal data that would be sufficient to "obtain an evaluation" [form a profile] of the personality of the individual.
h) Keeping files, premises, programs, or hardware containing personal data without the required security measures as statutorily prescribed.
i) Failure to provide the AEPD with the notifications required by this Law or its implementing provisions as well as failure to notify this agency in a timely manner of the number of documents and information that it should receive or that it should require for the se purposes.
j) Obstructing inspections.
k) Failure to enter a file of personal data in the General Register of Protected Data [GDP Register] upon the Director of the AEPD's request.
l) Failure to provide information required under articles 5, 28, and 29 of this Law, when the data has been obtained from a person other than the data subject.[77]

4. Very serious infractions are:

a) Fraudulent or misleading collection of data.
b) Unauthorized communication or transfers of personal data,

c) Collection and processing personal data referred to in article 7(2) without the express consent of the data subject; collection and processing of the data referred to in article 7(3) without statutory authorization or express consent of the data subject or violation of the prohibition contained in article 7(4) when it is required under the law, or obtaining and processing data in violation of the LOPDP.
d) Failure to stop the illegitimate use of processing of personal data operations when required to do so by the Director of the AEPD or by those with rights of access thereto.
e) Transfer of personal data, either temporarily or permanently, of data that were the object of processing or had been collected in order to submit them to processing to countries with no comparable level of data protection safeguards without the authorization of the Director of the AEPD.
f) Illegitimate [Improper] handling of personal data or with disregard [contempt] of the principles and guarantees that are applicable, when acting in this manner results in the impediment or an attempt against the exercise of fundamental rights.
g) Breach of the duty of secrecy regarding personal data referred to in article 7(2) and (3) as well as data collected for police use without the data subject's consent.
h) Systematically preventing or failing to comply with the exercise of the rights of access, correction, erasure , or objection.
i) Systematic failure to comply with the duty to make the required notification of the entry of personal data in a file.[78]

N. Penalties

Violations of the LOPDP are punished with fines that are adjusted on a regular basis.[79] Minor infractions are punished with a fine of €601–60,101 (about US$750–75,800), serious infractions with a fine of €60,000–300,000 (about US$75,700–378,500), and very serious infractions with a fine of €300,000–600,000 (about US$378,500–757,000).[80]

Penalties are applied according to the nature of the right that has been affected, the volume of the processing operations carried out, the profits obtained, the intentional nature of the offense, the repetition of the offense or recidivism of the offender, the damage caused to the data subjects and to third parties, and any other consideration relevant to determining the degree of illegality and culpability of the specific wrongdoing.[81]

The Director of the AEPD may also require data controllers to end the use or illegal transfer of data, in cases of very serious infractions. If the violation persists, the AEPD may, through a reasoned decision, block the files in order to restore the rights of the data subjects.[82]

In addition to the administrative fines that may be imposed under the LOPDP, the 1995 Criminal Code also addresses crimes dealing with violations of privacy involving the processing of personal data, such as

- collecting personal data in violation of someone's privacy by illegally intercepting electronic communications, messages, files, or other communication signals;
- the unauthorized misappropriation, use, or alteration of confidential information or personal data kept in electronic files, whether public or private, to the detriment of the data subject or a third person; and
- transferring illegally obtained personal data.[83]

These offenses are punished with terms of imprisonment ranging from one to five years and a fine.[84]

Aggravated sanctions of up to seven years imprisonment apply in the following cases:

- Transfers of data illegally obtained by the personal data controller or data processor;
- The collection and transfer of personal data revealing the data subject's ideology, religion, beliefs, health, racial origin, or sexual orientation, or if the victim is a minor or disabled; or
- The above-mentioned illegal data transfers and collection when done for profit[85]

O. Civil Liability

Data subjects who suffer damage to their property or rights as a consequence of violations of the LOPDP by the data controller or processor have the right to compensation.[86] Compensation is governed by the Civil Code,[87] which provides that the person who, by action or omission, causes damage to others by fault or negligence is liable for the damage.[88]

III. Spain's Data Protection Agency

The Agencia Española de Protección de Datos (AEPD) was created under the LOPDP[89] as an independent administrative agency with a budget provided in the general national budget[90] to oversee compliance with personal data protection laws.

The AEPD's functions are as follows:

- Enforcement of data protection legislation
- Issuance of authorizations required by law
- Issuance of instructions for processing operations to comply with the standards of the LOPDP
- Consideration of applications and complaints from the data subjects
- Provision of information on the rights related to personal data processing
- Ensuring controllers' compliance with the LOPDP and, when applicable, ordering termination of processing or deleting the files that have been processed in violation of the LOPDP
- Imposing administrative sanctions under the LOPDP
- Providing information on the draft regulations implementing the LOPDP
- Gathering information and assistance from the data controllers deemed necessary for the fulfillment of its duties
- Informing the public about the existence of personal data files
- Publication of an annual report for the Ministry of Justice
- Monitoring and issuing authorizations for international movements of data
- Ensuring compliance with the collection of statistical data and issuing instructions and advisory opinions on the security conditions of the files set up for statistical purposes[91]

In addition, the AEPD maintains a General Data Protection Register. It records data files maintained by the public and private sectors, required authorizations, and sectoral best practice agreements.[92] These records must be kept up-to-date.[93]

The AEPD provides direct assistance in response to citizens' questions or concerns about their rights. According to statistics it recently released, there has been an increase in the number of requests for protection, including requests to enforce the right to cancel and the right to access.[94] In 2007, investigations initiated based on complaints filed by individuals or upon the initiative of the Director of the AEPD increased by 7% to a total of 1,263 compared to the previous year.[95] Inspections conducted were mostly related to telecommunications companies and financial institutions, with an increase of over 400% over previous years.[96] In 2007, the AEPD imposed 399 sanctions with a total of €19.6 million (about US$24.65 million) in fines.[97]

IV. Court Decisions

A. Right to Be Forgotten

The so-called "right to be forgotten" is an issue that has been the subject of an increasing number of complaints and lawsuits in Spain. On February 23, 2012, a civil lower court of Amposta, Tarragona, dismissed a claim against Google Spain by Alfacs Vacances SL concerning the right to be forgotten, which sought to prevent Google from displaying images of burned bodies from an accident that had occurred in the late 1970s.[98]

Alfacs Vacances SL is a Spanish company that operates a campground in Tarragona. In 1978, the campground was hit by a deadly gas explosion; more than two hundred people died and others were seriously wounded by a tanker truck loaded with flammable liquid that went up in flames on the highway just in front of the campground.[99] The owners of the campground had no responsibility for or connection with the accident. However, in spite of the fact that the explosion occurred more than thirty years ago and that Alfacs was acquitted of any liability, the photos from the accident continued to show up near the top of the first page of Google Search results for the Alfacs campground (Alfaques, in Spanish), including disturbing photos of burned corpses.[100]

In June 2011, Alfacs filed suit against Google Spain SL, Google's Spanish subsidiary, requesting damages and an immediate halt to the way in which Google displayed search results, claiming that it was damaging Alfacs's business reputation and discouraging new clients.[101] Because the company actually operating the search engine is Google Inc., and Google Spain SL's activity is restricted to marketing and advertising services, Google Spain alleged a lack of standing to be sued. The judge accepted this contention and dismissed the case for lack of standing. However, because Google Spain won on jurisdictional grounds, the court decision did not address the substantive underlying issue of the right to be forgotten, which is of paramount importance not only for Spain but for all EU countries.[102]

In March 2012, the Audiencia Nacional (High Court) of Spain filed a request with the European Court of Justice (ECJ) for clarification on the jurisdictional issue involving privacy complaints against Google and all other search engines.[103] Google maintains that privacy complaints should be filed in California, the location of its headquarters, and that its activities are therefore out of reach of the Spanish data protection law. However, the Spanish court's position is that the protection of a fundamental right may not depend on the place where the search engine operator has chosen to locate its technology processing operations.[104] The matter is still pending before the ECJ.[105]

The AEPD used the same reasoning when it examined the complaint of an individual whose name appears on the Internet linked to a judicial decision ordering the seizure of his property for debts he owed to Social Security. In 2009, he unsuccessfully requested the newspaper *La Vanguardia*, where the information was published, as well as Google to remove his personal information, because the debt problem was resolved long ago and the information had no current relevance whatsoever.[106]

In response to the AEPD's call for removal, *La Vanguardia* responded that the information was provided upon the request of the Ministry of Labor and therefore they were legally required to keep it. The AEPD agreed with the newspaper. Google also refused to remove the information, stating that it is only subject to US law and that Google Spain is not involved in data processing but only in the sale of advertising on its Spanish webpage.[107]

The ECJ will render an opinion as to whether EU legislation may be applied to Google in this case, depending on whether search engines, when indexing information, are in fact processing personal data and whether or not data protection includes the right to be forgotten.[108] The response to the Spanish request on this issue will be applicable to all Member States of the EU and will certainly be considered in the context of discussions underway since January 2012 by the European Commission (EC) on draft legislation amending privacy protections in the EU to include the right to be forgotten.[109]

B. Processing Data Without Consent: Legitimate Interest Requirement

On February 8, 2012, Spain's Tribunal Supremo (TS) ruled on a case[110] in which various provisions of article 10 of the RLOPDP were challenged by the Federation of Electronic Commerce and Direct Marketing (Federación de Comercio Electrónico y Marketing Directo, FECEMD) and ADigital, because the data protection requirements of the Spanish regulation go beyond the EU data protection standards set out by article 7.f of EU Directive 95/46/.[111] The Spanish regulation requires that in order to process personal data without the data subject's consent when such processing is necessary to pursue a legitimate interest of the data controller or of another person or persons to whom the data is disclosed, it is necessary not only to prove that the fundamental rights and freedoms of the data subject are protected, but also that the data should be available in a public source.[112]

The TS requested a preliminary ruling from the ECJ, which conclusively stated that article 7.f of Directive 95/46/EC precludes national legislation from establishing requirements for the processing of personal data without consent that go beyond those provided by EU legislation. The ECJ also expressly stated that article 7.f is directly applicable in EU Member States.[113] Based on the ECJ ruling, the TS declared article 10.2.b of the RLOPDP void. This article had listed the appearance of the data in a public source as an exception to the consent requirement for data processing (see above, sections II(B) and IV).[114]

V. Public and Scholarly Opinion

Although Spain is considered to have some of the strictest data protection legislation in Europe,[115] there are still many issues that remain unresolved. There is growing public concern about the right to be forgotten and the right to delete an Internet data trail, an issue that will soon be addressed at the EU level in order to formulate a common position.[116] The number of complaints by Spaniards about the treatment of their personal data online has increased by 75% per year, according to the Director of the AEPD.[117]

One of the main complaints by data controllers concerns the lack of a common approach taken among the national systems regarding the concept of consent, ranging from written consent to implied consent. This situation is especially troublesome in Internet data transfers in a cross-border environment. The lack of harmonization is one of the main recurring issues raised by private companies, because of the additional administrative costs incurred from the application of different rules.[118]

The protection of personal data is currently a hot topic in Spain. Although more awareness and information is needed, at least in Spain, the society at large is aware of the risks and issues involving the processing of their personal data.[119] A September 2009 poll released by the Center of Sociological Studies in Spain reveals a high level of distrust by Spaniards in the security of their personal data on the Internet.[120] According to the Director of the AEPD, the results of this poll and the recent increase in the number of claims and consultations with the AEPD show an increasing awareness of citizens about the value of their personal information and their rights.[121]

With regard to the trust that people have in the level of data security, 56.6% believe that security and privacy on the Internet is deficient, worse than data security offered by utility companies, banks, and businesses.[122] In addition, more than 70% of people believe that using the Internet facilitates intrusions into people's privacy. Social media, texting, and chats are services most distrusted by people when it comes to the safety of their personal information.[123] More than 65% of Spaniards acknowledge that they never read the privacy policies of the websites they visit because they are unintelligible and not user friendly.[124]

This data suggests that there is an urgent need for online service providers to improve the level of security and privacy of users. To this end, the AEPD has been working with the major data processing companies and social media services to make sure that they adjust their business rules and procedures according to the standards set by data protection legislation.[125]

VI. Pending Reforms

Spain is currently awaiting the advisory opinion of the ECJ to clarify the scope of the right to be forgotten.[126] At the same time, the EU has been drafting stricter rules on data privacy, putting greater responsibility on companies such as Facebook to protect users' information and threatening those who violate the rules with heavy fines, of up to 2% of the company's yearly income. Once these rules are adopted, companies that are already processing data in Spain will not experience a great deal of change, because many of the new EU rules have already been in force in Spain under the LOPDP and RLOPDP.[127]

The EU proposal, which will become EU legislation in 2013 if approved by all EU Members and the European Parliament, aims to address new technologies that were developed after the current data protection legislation was adopted, in order to better protect consumers' personal data and privacy.[128]

Prepared by Graciela Rodriguez-Ferrand, Senior Foreign Law Specialist
June 2012

SWEDEN
ONLINE PRIVACY LAW

Executive Summary

Sweden was the first country to enact a comprehensive statute regulating privacy online. Swedish legislation focuses primarily on protecting integrity and regulating the use of personal data by the government or private users without consent, rather than on private companies to which the individual has provided personal information. Even if consent is given for the use of personal information this consent may be revoked at any time. Unsolicited advertisements are permissible provided that the recipient has not expressly stated that he or she does not want this form of advertisement.

I. Legal Framework

Sweden was the first country in the world to enact a comprehensive statute to protect the privacy of personal data on computers when it adopted the Data Act in 1973.[1]

Certain personal freedoms, including the right to protection of personal data, are also found in the Swedish Constitution. The Swedish Constitution consists of four parts, Regeringsformen (RF) (Instrument of Government), Tryckfrihetsförordningen (TF) (Freedom of the Press Act), Yttrandefrihetslagen (YGL) (Freedom of Expression Act), and Sucessionsordningen (SO) (Act of Succession). Following changes to the RF in 2010, which entered into force on January 1, 2011, chapter 2, article 6 now states that every individual is protected from the public against intrusions in his or her personal integrity, if such an intrusion takes place without the approval of the individual and consists of surveillance or monitoring of the individual.[2] Prior to these amendments, it was expressly stated in the Constitution that "every citizen shall be protected to the extent specified in law, against any violation of personal integrity resulting from the registration of personal information by automatic data processing."[3] However, when revising the Constitution, the government found this regulation superfluous since it did not provide any right beyond what was already provided by statute.[4] The regulation was interpreted to mean only that the legislature had to keep any form of personal right regarding the private integrity for automatic data processing as part of current law.[5] The Article was removed because such protection can be found in the Personuppgiftslag [Personal Data Act] (PUL).[6]

As a general rule, the same protection applies to both Swedish citizens and foreigners, pursuant to RF chapter 2, section 25.

Subsequent to the 1973 enactment of the Data Act, Sweden joined the EU in 1995 and become bound by its legislation, including Directive 95/46 and Directive 2002/58. Directive 95/46 was transposed by amending the PUL in 1998. The PUL is the general legislation for protection of personal information such as personal identification numbers, health records, and the like. By amending the Personal Data Act to more clearly include personal data online, the parliament also decided to replace the Data Act that was then in place. The new legislation was quickly found to be inadequate by the parliament, as it was too restrictive on private individuals with private blogs, and upon motions from several parliament members an investigation was initiated in 1999.[7] These efforts included lobbying for a new EU Directive.[8]

Sweden has transposed the EU Directive 2002/58 in two pieces of legislation. The main piece of legislation is the lag om elektronisk kommunikation (SFS 2003:389) (Electronic Communications Act), which entered into force in 2003. In addition the Swedish legislature has amended the PUL to make it conform with Directive 2002/58. The Electronic Communications Act is *lex specialis* to the PUL, which means that where there is a conflict, the Electronic Communications Act should apply, but where the Electronic Communications Act is inapplicable, the more general terms of the PUL govern.[9]

An important distinction exists between privacy laws and the Swedish approach of protecting the personal integrity of its citizens.[10] Swedish privacy legislation focuses on the use by others of personal and sensitive information online, and not on the individual's right to privacy when he or she acts online, i.e., the right to be anonymous online.[11]

II. Current Law

When Sweden implemented the first EU Directive (95/46), almost all use of personal data became a violation, including what in current legislation is referred to as harmless information.

It was sufficient that someone (with great effort) could find out the identity of a person mentioned in an online publication (i.e., blogpost, public chatroom, newsletter, webpage, etc.). One example is that Carl Bildt (now the foreign minister of Sweden) reported his own newsletter's violations to the Data Inspection Board because he named people without their express consent.[12] Today the legislation allows for the use of common knowledge information, and permits private citizens to disclose information about others if it is not considered sensitive in nature.[13]

A. Personal Data Act (PUL)

The general principle for publication and use of any personal data is that the user must first obtain the express consent from the person mentioned.[14] However, there are certain situations where such consent is not required. Consent is not required when processing information is necessary to fulfill an agreement between the data subject and the publisher, to complete an undertaking the data subject requested, to fulfill a legal requirement, to ensure that vital interests of the data subject shall be protected; to fulfill the public interest, or to complete a government action. It is also not required when a recognized interest of the publisher of the information outweighs the interest of the data subject in protection against personal integrity violations.[15] Certain sensitive information may not be published unless it falls within an explicit exception, i.e., consent or publication by the data subject, necessity, use by non-profit organizations in their internal operations only, use by health providers, or use for research and statistical purposes only.[16]

Consent

Consent to any use of personal data that requires express consent may be revoked at any time.[17] However, if use is expressly permitted despite lack of consent, the data subject cannot demand that the information be withdrawn.[18]

Unsolicited Advertisement

If the person whose information is being registered has, in writing, asked to be excluded from any direct advertisement, his or her information may not be used for that purpose.[19] Conversely, if no such objection has been filed, it is permissible to use personal data for personally directed (targeted) advertisements.

The Data Inspection Board, Sweden's enforcement agency for privacy rights, has attempted to specify when unsolicited advertisements are permissible without the express consent of the recipient.[20] Unsolicited advertisement is also governed by Marknadsföringslagen (the Marketing Act)[21] and through self-regulation by the Swedish advertising industry, whose trade association, SWEDMA, has published guidelines on the use of personal data in direct marketing.

Protection of Minors

The protection of minors is not specifically mentioned in the PUL. However, the Data Inspection Board has found that the use of personal information of children under the age of 13 requires consent from the parent of the child.[22] It is thus not sufficient that a child under 13 consents to the treatment of his or her personal information.

Security Measures

Section 31 of the PUL states that

> [a] person or corporation that harbors personal information must take appropriate technical and organizational precautions to protect the personal data which is processed. These measures shall ensure a security level that is appropriate considering:

a) The technical measures available
b) The cost of the measures
c) The specific risks involved in the processing of the personal data.

In addition section 31 provides that the individual or corporation supplying a data subject's personal information has the responsibility to ensure that the processor of the personal information treats the information in a satisfactory manner.

B. Electronic Communications Act (LEK)

The Electronic Communications Act is mostly concerned with access to the Internet via Internet providers, fair use, competition and pricing.[23] However, chapter 6 deals with traffic information and integrity protection.[24] It includes provisions concerning security measures, information requirements and storage of traffic information.

LEK chapter 6, section 3 requires that a service provider that processes personal data ensure that such data is protected.[25] The level of technical and organizational security is required to be proportional to the risk to the personal data.[26]

Traffic information or information regarding a user may not be kept longer than necessary to provide access to the service.[27] As soon as it is no longer needed all identification information should be stripped.[28] Information required to be kept under data retention provisions in crime prevention legislation may be kept longer.[29] Information may not be monitored by the service provider.[30] The service provider must inform the user what traffic information it retains, for what purpose and for what period of time.[31]

Limits on Geographical Data

Chapter 6, section 9 of the Electronic Communications Act (LEK) provides that only geographical data that is necessary for the function of an agreed service or otherwise specifically consented to by the user may be used by the service provider. The information may not be stored by the service provider longer than is necessary to provide the service to the user.[32] This regulation is primarily focused on GPS functions.

Safeguards against Data Collection by Smartphone Applications

The same provisions regarding personal data collection apply to smartphone applications, i.e., they must comply with the PUL and the LEK.

C. Cookies

One of the new provisions that came into force with implementation of EU Directive 2002/58 was a requirement to inform users and receive their permission for the use of cookies on a website. Cookies are used to transfer information between the website and the user, allowing for a more efficient use of the website. LEK chapter 6, section 18 provides that no information may be stored or withdrawn from a user's computer without his or her express consent. This means that all Swedish websites must provide information regarding the use of cookies, its purposes, and the duration cookies are saved on the user's computer.[33] This specific provision entered into force on July 1, 2011, and has been heavily debated. It has been argued that to ask whether the user accepts cookies requires a website to save a cookie on the user's computer, possibly resulting in the website breaking the law by attempting to follow it.[34]

D. Data Protection Agencies

There are two main data protection agencies in Sweden. The government delegates the division of responsibility among the two agencies. The statutory mandates for the enforcement agencies are found in the relevant legislation, i.e., the Electronic Communications Act (chapter 1, section 3) and the Personal Data Act (PUL sections 20, 21, 35, 36 and 50). For more detail please see section III below.

E. Remedies & Sanctions

Personal Data Act

PUL section 48 regulates when and how an injured party may obtain monetary damages from a company or person that has used and published personal information in a manner inconsistent with the PUL.[35] To receive compensation there must have been damage to the data subject and a violation of his or her personal integrity.[36] The amount of damages can be reduced if the respondent can show that the violation was not his or her fault.[37] The data subject also has a right to demand that the respondents cease using the personal information.

The PUL provides for a variety of sanctions ranging from a fine to two years imprisonment, depending on the severity of the crime.[38] These crimes include providing false information to the enforcement agency, misusing personal information, transferring personal information to a third country, and failure to report automatic processing of personal data. The provisions of the PUL that are sanctioned are listed in section 49; the sole sanction for any provision not mentioned in PUL section 49 is damages in accordance with PUL section 48. In cases of minor violations of the provisions in PUL section 49, no sanctions are awarded.[39]

Electronic Communications Act

LEK chapter 6, section 2 provides that the same sanctions for personal information violations apply under the LEK as under the PUL.[40]

F. International Jurisdiction

The PUL and the LEK only apply to companies that are based or established in Sweden. However, the general criminal jurisdiction is broader. In accordance with the territorial principle of Penal Code chapter 2, section 1, crimes that are conducted in or can be presumed to be conducted in Sweden shall be governed in accordance with Swedish law. Even if the crime is conducted abroad, it shall be governed by Swedish law when it is carried out by a Swedish citizen or resident. However, Swedish legislation does not hold Internet service providers responsible for violations on websites, but rather holds the person publishing the personal information responsible.

III. Role of Data Protection Agencies

As noted above, Sweden has separate data protection agencies that ensure the implementation and enforcement of the LEK and compliance with the PUL. The main agencies are Datainspektionen, which is responsible for compliance with the PUL, and Post- och telestyrelsen (PTS), which is responsible for compliance with the LEK.[41]

A. Datainspektionen (Data Inspection Board)

The Datainspektionen (Data Inspection Board) was first established in 1973 pursuant to the Data Act. It is an independent government agency which both issues permits and oversees the enforcement of relevant provisions.[42] As the regulation of personal data has changed, so has the authority of the Data Inspection Board, and following 2001 this authority has expanded.[43] Its overarching mandate is to "protect the individual's privacy in the information society without unnecessarily preventing or complicating the use of new technology."[44] The Board oversees compliance with four large pieces of legislation, the PUL, the Debt Recovery Act[45] the Credit Information Act[46] and the Patient Data Act.[47] Of these, only the PUL is covered in this report.

In addition, the Data Inspection Board also issues general guidance that is not binding on the user but that suggests means to comply with the binding regulations of the PUL.[48] The Data Inspection Board has also issued its own regulations.[49] In order to ensure the enforcement of the PUL the Board monitors compliance and issues administrative sanctions. This includes both responding to complaints and conducting its own investigations.[50]

The legislative history of amendments to the PUL from 2006 also provides that the Data Inspection Board should provide guidance on what constitutes a violation of the personal integrity of a person (i.e., if a publication violates a person's integrity and thus violates PUL section 13).[51]

The Data Inspection Board may not by itself demand that information that violates the PUL be erased but may request an administrative court to issue a decision that such information be removed.[52] The Agency may, however, when it cannot determine whether a use is legal or not, require that the information holder only retain and store the information and issue an injunction coupled with damages if the information is transmitted by the information holder.[53]

B. Post- och telestyrelsen (Swedish Post and Telecom Authority)

Post- och telestyrelsen (PTS) (the Swedish Post and Telecom Authority) was established in 1992 and is a government agency guarding electronic communication and mail in Sweden. It has four overreaching goals: working for long-term consumer benefit, long-term sustainable competition, an effective use of resources, and safe communication.[54]

PTS assists data subjects in the pursuit of their rights by making sure market participants follow the integrity rules under the LEK. PTS does this by processing complaints, conducting inspections, and monitoring to ensure compliance with determined requirements.[55]

Most of the decisions by the PTS have concerned free competition among Internet providers, pricing, and Internet access, rather than Internet security or Internet privacy.[56]

C. Enforcement Agencies' Relationship with Facebook and Google

The Data Inspection Board does not have jurisdiction over Facebook and Google, as the PUL only extends to private companies based in Sweden. However, the Data Inspection Board does have indirect jurisdiction over content on Facebook and Google insofar as Swedish companies or municipalities provide them with information that is covered by the PUL. That is, the Swedish Data Inspection Board does not regulate these services directly but regulates their users. For example, the Data Inspection Board has undertaken enforcement efforts against Swedish municipalities that use Google's cloud server to store personal data. In these efforts the Data Inspection Board has found that these municipalities have violated their responsibilities to data subjects. To legally use cloud services the municipalities must establish *personuppgiftsbiträdesavtal* (data collector agreements) not only with Google but also with all of its subsidiaries that may use and store personal data in order to guarantee that the information is stored securely and in accordance with the PUL.[57] PTS has also joined the Norwegian data inspection board in a letter addressing several questions to Facebook including what they do with the information they obtain and how long they store personal data information.[58] Facebook has responded to these questions in a letter.[59] It is unclear at present how the Data Inspection Board intends to respond.[60]

Swedish legislation is much less concerned with its citizens' voluntary use and submission of their own personal data online. It is sufficient that the Internet user is given the option not to use the service, which is why cookies are heavily regulated. A user must consent to the use of cookies either each time it visits a homepage or from a site provider indefinitely under the precondition that this consent may at any time be revoked (see section II, above.)

IV. Court Decisions

Because the enforcement of data protection is placed with two governmental agencies, the Data Inspection Board and the PTS, a number of authoritative decisions have been decided by these agencies, but not by the courts. Following the implementation of the 2002/58 Directive there have been very few court decisions, but some agency decisions, that address the permissible use of personal data online.

Bodil Case

As a case involving the Swedish implementation of the EU Directive 95/46, the *Bodil* case[61] is noteworthy in that it made its way to the European Court of Justice. However, because the applicable Swedish law has been amended following the decision, it is of less importance today.

In *Bodil*, a communion teacher, for the benefit of her students, published some information about her co-workers on her church's web page. She wrote the presentations herself, but made it appear that they had been written by the coworkers themselves in the first person. Among the information published was information regarding the health of a janitor who was on sick leave with a sprained ankle. The district court found that the teacher had violated the PUL, (1) for not having applied for a permit with the Data Inspection Board before publishing the information, (2) for processing sensitive personal information (i.e. the sprained ankle) without prior approval, and (3) for transferring personal information to third countries (because it was published online).

The case was appealed to the court of appeals. The court of appeals posed seven questions to the European Court of Justice concerning the interpretation of European law on data privacy. While the European Court of Justice found that no data had been transferred to a third country (which triggers certain requirements under the EU Directive) simply because it had been published online, it also stated that it was up to the national courts to make certain that a correct balance was achieved in the case between rights and obligations of the community. (Bodil published the information in Swedish, on a Swedish site using a Swedish Internet connection.) Once the case was finally decided by the court of appeals, it found that, while the teacher had published personal data online without authorization, and thus breached the PUL, the infringements were petty offenses which should not be subject to any sanction.

Ramsbro Case

PUL section 7 provides for the use of personal data for freedom of the press purposes without having to follow the otherwise stringent PUL provisions. In the *Ramsbro* case,[62] the Supreme Court of Sweden was faced with defining the press freedom exception. The court ruled that the exception permitted publication of information that was of interest for the public, intended to be used to initiate or continue a public debate, and the like, even if it was done in a manner that violated the personal integrity of the person mentioned. However, it said that information that is purely private does not normally have such a journalistic purpose and is of little interest to the public at large.

Lundsberg Case

The Supreme Court ruled in the 2005 *Lundsberg* case[63] that publication by a school principal of an employee's medical condition on the school's website was a violation of PUL section 13 that resulted in a fine for the principal.[64]

Katrineholm Municipality Decision

The Data Inspection Board had occasion to rule on legal use of social media by government agencies in the *Katrineholm* municipality decision.[65] The municipality of Katrineholm was found to be responsible for the processing of personal information found on the municipality's Facebook page, on its blog page and on its Twitter account. The Data Inspection Board found that the municipality's legal responsibility for personal information found on Facebook and on the blog did include both personal information published by the municipality as well as personal information posted by the users. On the municipality Twitter account, the responsibility of the municipality only extended to the personal information the municipality itself had published due to its lack of control over other person's Twitter accounts.

Reco.se Decision

In a matter concerning Reco.se,[66] a website where the visitor can leave comments and grade companies, the Data Inspection Board in 2010 found that the company was responsible for ensuring all the information posted on the website by visitors complied with legal requirements. The company provided the service and had every opportunity to remove, edit, alter or block personal information data. Thus, both the individual publisher and the company which provided the forum had a responsibility to make sure that the comments were consistent with PUL.

Hitta.se Decision

In the *Hitta.se* case,[67] the Data Inspection Board received several complaints from the public over a Swedish service (Hitta.se) which was similar to Google maps (a website that displays pictures of apartment buildings and landmarks, but not individual houses), requesting a response to whether it is illegal to display pictures of buildings that also include the registration numbers of cars outside buildings and individual persons. The Data Inspection Board found that it was not illegal under PUL as the service provider had a publication certificate and because they were covered by the Press Freedom exception in PUL section 7. The Data Inspection Board therefore ruled it had no means of regulating how the personal data was used on the website.

Jurisdictional Cases Decided by the Data Inspection Board

In accordance with EU law, as implemented by Sweden, jurisdiction over PUL violators requires that the person or organization is established in Sweden with "an effective and real operation with the help of a stable structure."[68] The legislation in itself gives no further definition. The Data Inspection Board has ruled that an organization will be found to be established in Sweden for purposes of its jurisdiction when the website is in Swedish, the domain name suffix is .se, the audience is Swedish speaking Internet users, and the personal information pertains to Swedish nationals.[69] The Data Inspection Board has found that it is not a precondition that the responsible parties for the website are based in Sweden for these conditions to apply.[70] On the contrary, even when a Swedish citizen publishes information on foreign sites he or she may be held responsible in accordance with PUL.[71]

Relationship between Enforcement of IPR Infringements and Protecting Integrity

In a recent decision, *Bonnier Audio AB and Others v. Perfect Communication Sweden AB* (C461/10),[72] the European Court of Justice found that it was possible for Member States to demand that Internet service providers disclose personal data to identify intellectual property infringements.[73] The European Court of Justice left the determination whether a disclosure was necessary in this specific case to the Swedish courts.[74]

V. Public and Scholarly Opinion

Public opinion (and outrage) in regard to Internet protection has focused mainly on wiretapping legislation known as the FRA Law that expands the government's power to combat crime on the Internet by surveillance of personal data and electronic communication.[75] Although not part of this report, these changes have overshadowed discussion of Google and Facebook's use of information that they have obtained from their users.

The implementation of the first EU Directive 95/46, as mentioned in section II above, was heavily criticized for being inefficient. Today's criticism has focused mostly on the expansion of the government's power of surveillance and the general lack of regulation of private companies' use of information that they have obtained by consent from their users.

Swedish public opinion reflects that legislation in Sweden has focused more on the protection of personal integrity (i.e. information about individuals) and less on the right to privacy. Swedish legislators have also focused more on the relationship between government and citizens than the relationship between citizens and private companies. The government-citizen relationship continues to be more controversial to the general public than the relationship between consumer and sellers. This is particularly the case as Sweden's enforcement agencies have recently stepped up their enforcement of intellectual property infringements. This in turn has led to a growing number of Swedes using anonymous services that hide their true identity.[76] The increase in the use of these services may be related to a desire to protect one's privacy online, regardless of whether such use is lawful or not.

VI. Pending Reforms

A. Implementation of the Data Retention Directive

Sweden decided in 2011 to postpone its implementation of the EU Data Retention Directive (Directive 2006/24), despite threats of impending fines.[77] The proposed legislation received sharp criticism not only prior to but also after the most recent proposal won majority in the parliament.[78] The current version of the bill proposes additional surveillance powers to be expanded to the Säkerhetspolisen (Swedish Security Service) and Rikskriminalpolisen

(National Bureau of Investigations).[79] The government finally won support for its bill in the Swedish parliament in May 2012.[80]

B. Secret Surveillance Measures

On June 28, 2012, the Justice Department suggested that secret surveillance measures that have temporarily been available be made permanent.[81] This would allow police to use wiretapping and camera surveillance more often than under previous legislation.[82]

C. Integrity Committee

In 2011 the government and the opposition agreed on the creation of a commission to investigate how and when personal integrity is violated online.[83] The proposed details on the Integrity Committee can be accessed on the Government website.[84]

On June 25, 2012, Morgan Johansson, member of the Social Democrats (the leading oppositional party) wrote an op-ed in the daily paper Svenska Dagbladet (SVD) calling for additional scrutiny of the use of personal information by private companies such as Google and Facebook.[85]

Prepared by Elin Hofverberg,
Foreign Law Consultant,
under the supervision of Edith Palmer,
Chief,
Foreign, Comparative and International
Law Division II
June 2012

UNITED KINGDOM
ONLINE PRIVACY LAW

Executive Summary

Data protection legislation in the UK is primarily based upon Directives from the European Union. It aims to protect the rights of individuals to ensure that their personal information remains private and secure. It provides individuals with a number of rights, including a right to access information and correct any errors. The Information Commissioner has an active role in educating the public and organizations about the data protection legislation, assisting data subjects in enforcing their rights, and imposing sanctions and enforcement actions against those who breach the legislation. The Information Commissioner's role as enforcer has been strengthened, with increased penalties available for cases of egregious breaches of the laws.

I. Legal Framework

The United Kingdom does not have a written constitution that enshrines a right to privacy for individuals and there is no common law that provides for a general right to privacy. The UK has, however, incorporated the European Convention on Human Rights into its national law, which provides for a limited right of respect towards an individual's privacy and family life.[1] The primary legislation in the UK that regulates the holding of an individual's personal data by companies, and consequently has an impact on information concerning the private lives of individuals, is the Data Protection Act 1998 (DPA).[2] The Information Commissioner has stated that the aim of the DPA is "to strike a balance between the rights of individuals and the sometimes competing interests of those with legitimate reasons for using personal information."[3]

A. Data Protection Act 1998

The DPA was enacted and implemented to meet the requirements of the European Union's Data Protection Directive 95/46/EC. Although the DPA implements the Data Protection Directive, which refers expressly to privacy, the DPA does not mention the word privacy in any of its provisions.[4]

The DPA regulates the processing of personal information of individuals. It is broad and applies to obtaining, holding, using or disclosing this personal information.[5] Following implementation of the DPA, the Deputy Data Protection Registrar noted that

> if the 1998 Act satisfies the Directive, then it serves to protect the rights of individuals to privacy, as at least in respect of the processing of personal data . . . . I do not assert that data protection legislation is comprehensive privacy legislation protecting every aspect of that right, but I do ask how it can be doubted that, as a matter of law, data protection is a form of privacy protection.[6]

While the DPA is a relatively recent piece of legislation largely based on the requirements of the European Union Directive, its origin can be seen in the 1960s, and the Younger Committee on Privacy. This Committee was established amid growing concern over the amount of personal data held by organizations to which individuals had no right of access. The terms of reference of the Committee was to "consider whether legislation is needed to give further protection to the individual citizen and to commercial and industrial interests against intrusion into privacy by private persons and organisations and companies."[7] While the committee did not see a need for the legislation at the time, it did formulate ten principles for good data management. These principles have continued to be in use since their formation and have been the staple of data protection legislation in the UK.

Schedule 1 of the DPA contains eight principles that regulate how personal data should be handled, which are "based on the premise of compliance with principles of good data management."[8] These principles apply to both online and offline data and require that

- Personal data shall be processed fairly[9] and lawfully and, in particular, shall not be processed unless
    - At least one of the conditions in Schedule 2 is met, and

  - In the case of sensitive personal data, at least one of the conditions in Schedule 3 is also met.
- Personal data shall be obtained only for one or more specified and lawful purposes, and shall not be further processed in any manner incompatible with that purpose or those purposes.
- Personal data shall be adequate, relevant and not excessive in relation to the purpose or purposes for which they are processed.
- Personal data shall be accurate and, where necessary, kept up to date.
- Personal data processed for any purpose or purposes shall not be kept for longer than is necessary for that purpose or those purposes.
- Personal data shall be processed in accordance with the rights of data subjects under this Act.
- Appropriate technical and organisational measures shall be taken against unauthorised or unlawful processing of personal data and against accidental loss or destruction of, or damage to, personal data.
- Personal data shall not be transferred to a country or territory outside the European Economic Area unless that country or territory ensures an adequate level of protection for the rights and freedoms of data subjects in relation to the processing of personal data.[10]

"Personal data" is defined as data that "relate to a living individual who can be identified—(a) from those data, or (b) from those data and other information which is in the possession of, or is likely to come into the possession of, the data controller."[11] In the leading case on the interpretation of "personal data," the Court of Appeal interpreted the term narrowly. It considered the fact that data may be associated with an individual's name was not sufficient to make it personal. Two additional factors are required: that the information should be "biographical in a significant sense,"[12] and that the data should not include a merely incidental reference to the data subject. The information must affect the data subject's "privacy, whether in his person or family life, business or professional capacity."[13]

The DPA applies to individuals and entities that are established in the UK and that process data in the context of the establishment.[14] The law regards those that are ordinarily resident in the UK as established in the country. There are a number of means under which various entities are or may be ordinarily resident in the UK. Corporate bodies are considered to be ordinarily resident and thus established in the UK if they are incorporated under UK law. Partnerships and other unincorporated associations are treated as being established in the UK if they are either formed under UK law or maintain a regular practice, office branch, or agency through which they conduct activities in the UK.[15] A "branch" in this instance refers to the "term used in Community law for an organizational sub-division of a company which has some degree of both identity and independence."[16]

II. Current Law

A. The Collection, Storage, and Use of Personal Data by Online Media or Services

While the DPA accords data subjects certain rights over their personal data, these rights do not absolutely prohibit a company from collecting data about them. The collection, storage, and use of personal data by online media or services is permitted, within the constraints of the DPA. The Information Commissioner has noted that it is bad practice to require a name and email from someone simply to allow them to view a website.[17] Further information obtained about data subjects through online services, particularly through cookies, is regulated through the Privacy and Electronic Communications (EC Directive) Regulations 2003, as amended, which implemented European Directives 2002/58/EC[18] and 2009/136/EC[19] into the national law of the UK.[20] This regulation provides that

> 6.—(1) Subject to paragraph (4), a person shall not use an electronic communications network to store information, or to gain access to information stored, in the terminal equipment of a subscriber or user unless the requirements of paragraph (2) are met.
>
> (2) The requirements are that the subscriber or user of that terminal equipment—
>
> (a) is provided with clear and comprehensive information about the purposes of the storage of, or access to, that information; and
>
> (b) is given the opportunity to refuse the storage of or access to that information.[21]

B. Other Means of Regulating Data Activity

The DPA regulates the collection, storage, and use of personal data by both offline and online media or services. Data subjects' rights include a right of access to personal data held about them, the right to have this information corrected if it is wrong, and the right to stop personal data from being used for the purposes of direct marketing.[22]

C. Retention of Data

The laws governing the retention of data by Internet Service Providers (ISPs) are contained in the Data Protection Act 1998;[23] the Privacy and Electronic Communications (EC Directive) Regulations 2003;[24] and the Anti-terrorism, Crime and Security Act 2001,[25] along with its Code of Practice.[26]

The retention of data by ISPs for the purpose of national security was initially governed by the Anti-terrorism, Crime and Security Act 2001. This Act required the Secretary of State to establish what was initially a voluntary Code of Practice in relation to the retention of communications data that was approved by Houses of Parliament prior to coming into force.[27] The Act required that the Code of Practice contain any provisions necessary for the purposes of safeguarding national security, preventing or detecting crime, or prosecuting offenders.[28] As the Code was voluntary, a breach of any of its provisions did not lead to criminal or civil sanctions; however, if the Secretary of State felt that the voluntary Code of Practice was ineffective, he had authority to impose mandatory retention orders on ISPs, although these required the approval of both Houses of Parliament.[29]

The Data Retention (EC Directive) Regulations 2009[30] replaced this voluntary regime and imposed a statutory requirement on public communications providers to retain data that is necessary to trace and identify the source, destination, type, date, time, and duration of a communication for all types of communications (fixed telephone lines, mobile phones, and Internet communications). For cell phones, communications providers must also retain data necessary to identify the user's communications equipment and the data required to identify the location of the equipment. For communications conducted via the Internet, the communications provider must also retain information relating to the user's communication equipment.[31]

1. Types of Data to Be Retained

A Code of Practice issued under the DPA provides that if a business has personal information that it does not use, that information should no longer be collected and any existing data should be deleted.[32] The Information Commissioner recommends that if data can be stored without identifying information, then this should be done. For example, it recommends that the last eight numbers of an IP address be removed, or the last identifying numbers of a postal code.[33] Data subjects have a right under the DPA to request that any personal information held on them be deleted. The Information Commissioner recommends that this occur unless there are other legal obligations to retain the data.[34]

2. Amount of Time Data Must Be Retained

The Data Retention (EC Directive) Regulations 2009[35] sets forth specific requirements for the retention of communications data with regard to both landline telephones, mobile telephones, and Internet access, and email or Internet phones. This regulation moved the UK away from a voluntary regime of communications data retention to a mandatory system. The intention was that creating certainty by retaining this data for a set period of time would enable law enforcement to build stronger cases and prevent serious offenses before they occur.[36] This regulation provides that the communications data associated with these forms should be retained for a period of twelve months.[37]

3. The Cost of Retention

The Data Retention (EC Directive) Regulations 2009 provides that the Secretary of State may reimburse public communications providers for any costs incurred in complying with the requirements of the Regulations.[38]

D. Transparency

One of the primary purposes of the DPA is to make sure that data subjects are aware of how information collected about them will be used.[39] This information should be contained in the sites' privacy notice. The Code states that this notice should "[have] sufficient prominence for people to access it easily. It should be written in a way that the people who access your service are likely to understand. It should use font sizes and colours that make the text easy to read."[40]

As noted above, the Privacy and Electronic Communications Regulations 2003 provide that

> (1) Subject to [the exceptions noted below], a person shall not use an electronic communications network to store information, or to gain access to information stored, in the terminal equipment of a subscriber or user unless the requirements of paragraph (2) are met.
>
> (2) The requirements are that the subscriber or user of that terminal equipment—
>
> (a) is provided with clear and comprehensive information about the purposes of the storage of, or access to, that information; and
>
> (b) is given the opportunity to refuse the storage of or access to that information.[41]

While the statute is drafted broadly, this provision predominantly applies to the use of cookies for online users. The data subject must be made aware that the cookies are there and of what the cookies are doing, and must provide consent for the cookies to be placed on his/her computer.[42] There are two exceptions to this rule for situations where the cookie is "(a) for the sole purpose of carrying out or facilitating the transmission of a communication over an electronic communications network; or (b) where such storage or access is strictly necessary for the provision of an information society service requested by the subscriber or user."[43]

The DPA provides that data subjects may, by written notice, require the data controller to stop, or not begin, to process their personal data if it will or is likely to cause unwarranted substantial damage or substantial distress to the data subject or another person.[44]

E. Special Safeguards for Personal Data

When questioned about companies' policies concerning harvesting and retaining personal data from users, the ICO stated that one of the Data Protection requirements is that UK companies must be "open and up front" with any users about how, and for what purposes, their personal data will be used.[45]

F. Safeguards against Data Collection by Smartphone Applications

There is no current law specific to smartphones. The collection of data by smartphone applications is subject to the same data protection requirements as other online services.

G. Limits on Geo Data

Geo data (known as "location data" in the UK) may only be processed if the subscriber or user cannot be identified from the data.[46] If the service provider has the data subject's consent, it may process geo data "where it is necessary to provide a value-added service."[47] There is no prescribed form as to how the consent should be obtained;[48] however, the data subject must have information on "(a) the types of location data that will be processed; (b) the purposes and duration of the processing of those data; and (c) whether the data will be transmitted to a third party for the purpose of providing the value-added service."[49]

The ICO provides guidance that the data subject "should be given enough clear information for them to have a broad appreciation of how the data is going to be used and the consequences of consenting to such use."[50] Once the data subject has provided consent, he or she has the opportunity to withdraw it at any point in time.[51]

H. Protection of Minors and Facebook

The Department for Education supports the UK's Council for Child Internet Safety (UKCCIS), a voluntary organization that works to protect children from online risks, such as cyberbullying, accessing harmful or inappropriate information (e.g., suicide information or pro-anorexia sites), sexual predators, and scams.[52] The UKCCIS promotes Internet safety for children through both education and industry guidelines. The education element includes a behavioral code entitled "click clever click safe." This code "encourage[s] children to keep personal information safe; avoid opening links and emails from unknown senders; and tell someone they trust if they encounter anything online that upsets them."[53]

The use of social media among children has exploded: 43% of nine- to twelve-year-olds across the UK have a profile on a social networking site. One in three has a Facebook account, despite the minimum age set by the company to join being thirteen. One quarter of these nine- to twelve-year-olds do not use privacy restrictions on their Facebook profile, and one-fifth of these publicly display their address and/or phone number. A study into the use of social media by children has noted that "[m]any providers try to restrict their users to 13-year-olds and above but we can see that this is not effective. Especially younger children are less likely to use privacy options and to understand the safety features that are available."[54] During a conference on children and the UK media in 2012, Facebook informed delegates that they were "unable to prevent children under 13 setting up Facebook accounts, despite this being against government policy."[55]

Many schools across the UK have issued guidance notes on how to address online bullying conducted through Facebook. The guidance particularly focuses on those under the age of thirteen. The main measure taken is that the site is routinely blocked by filters at schools. In cases where bullying arises through Facebook outside of school and spills over into school hours, the general policy is to contact Facebook to request the removal of these accounts if the children involved are under the age of thirteen.[56]

I. Technical and Organizational Security Measures

Principle seven of the DPA requires that

> [a]ppropriate technical and organisational measures shall be taken against unauthorised or unlawful processing of personal data and against accidental loss or destruction of, or damage to, personal data.[57]

Guidance on the level of security to be taken is provided in the DPA, but is rather general:

> Having regard to the state of technological development and the cost of implementing any measures, the measures [taken] must ensure a level of security appropriate to—(a) the harm that might result from such unauthorised or unlawful processing or accidental loss, destruction or damage as are mentioned in the seventh principle, and (b) the nature of the data to be protected.[58]

These requirements apply, even if the processing of data is outsourced.[59] The ICO currently expects the minimum standard of adequate security to be encryption.[60]

J. User Anonymity

The DPA does not require online services to allow users to remain anonymous. The Privacy and Electronic Communications (EC Directive) Regulations 2003 provides that users should have the opportunity to refuse to use cookies, to help enable them to remain anonymous; however, "it does not specify whose wishes should take precedence if they are different."[61]

K. Data Protection Agencies

The Agency responsible for overseeing the implementation of the Data Protection Act in the UK is the Information Commissioner's Office (the ICO). The functions of the ICO include monitoring practices of the online media and service providers, imposing sanctions, educating the public as well as assisting data subjects enforcing their rights provided for under the DPA.[62] Further information about the ICO is provided below.

L. Rights and Remedies for Users

The DPA provides data subjects with seven rights under its provisions:

1. The right to subject access (discussed below)
2. The right to prevent processing
3. The right to prevent processing for direct marketing
4. Rights in relation to automated decision making
5. The right to compensation
6. The right to rectification, blocking, erasure and destruction
7. The right to ask the Commissioner to assess whether the Act has been contravened[63]

If requested by a data subject who feels that his/her personal information has not been processed in accordance with the provisions of the DPA, the ICO may make an assessment of compliance. If this assessment determines that the DPA has been breached, the ICO may serve an enforcement notice on the data controller.[64]

M. Subject Access

Pursuant to section 7 of the DPA, a data subject in the UK has a right of access to personal data, and data controllers must respond within forty days of receiving the data subject's request for such access.[65] When accessing data, the DPA allows the data controller to impose a fee, typically £10 (approximately US$15), on the data subject requesting the access. However, the Code of Practice provides that it is good practice not to impose this fee if the data controller does not incur any additional costs.[66]

The right provided by section 7 is not unfettered. As stated by the court, it is "not an automatic key to any information, readily accessible or not, of matters in which [the data subject] may be named or involved."[67]

Section 7 of the DPA provides that the data subject may be informed whether any personal data that he/she is the subject of is being processed by or on behalf of the data collector. If the data controller holds personal data relating to the data subject, the data controller is required to provide the data subject with

> (i) the personal data of which that individual is the data subject, (ii) the purposes for which they are being or are to be processed, and (iii) the recipients or classes of recipients to whom they are or may be disclosed.[68]

The data controller must also provide the data subject with the source of this data and, if the data is processed automatically for the purposes of evaluating matters relating to the data subject (i.e., the subject's creditworthiness), the data controller must inform the data subject of "the logic involved in that decision-taking."[69]

There are some exemptions to providing information in response to a subject access request. If providing a copy of the data involves a disproportionate effort, the data controller is exempt from the requirements contained in section 7.[70] If the information that the data controller holds also relates to an identifiable third party, the data controller is under no obligation to disclose the information unless the third party consents, or it is "reasonable in all the circumstances to comply with the request without the consent of the other individual."[71]

Cases interpreting this section have ruled that it simply provides the data subject with a right to know whether his/her personal data is being processed, the purposes for this, and to whom this data is being disclosed.[72] While there is a statutory right for the data subject to receive "information constituting any personal data of which that individual is the data subject,"[73] the case law provides that this right is not "coterminous with a right to disclosure of documents."[74] The duty of data controllers to conduct searches for the personal data of the data subject has also been considered before the court. For this issue, the court found that certain data controllers could receive voluminous requests that imposed a large burden. As a result, the court held that the duty of the data controller is to make a "reasonable and proportionate search" in response to a subject access request.[75] This judgment has been criticized with regard to the "reasonable and proportionate" search limit; however, one commentator has noted that while this judgment narrowed down the responsibilities of the data controller it would be "illogical for proportionality to only apply to the supply of a copy of the data, when the real difficulty and expense is in locating, retrieving and collating the information in the first place."[76]

The DPA contains a number of exemptions to the types of personal data that may be requested.[77] These exemptions generally mirror those contained in the Data Protection Directive, such as information to be used for the purposes of the prevention or detection of crime, national security, crime prevention, or journalism. The DPA does contain some additional exemptions that are specific to it. These include data relating to the preparation of confidential references, the armed forces, Crown employment, negotiations, corporate finance, examination scripts, management forecasts, a legal professional privilege, or self-incrimination.[78]

If a data controller refuses to comply with a subject access request, the applicant may make a complaint to the Information Commissioner, or apply to the Court for an order to compel the controller to disclose the information. Under the DPA, if the court is satisfied that the data controller has not met its obligations under the Act, it can order the data controller to comply with the request.[79]

N. Right to Prevent Processing

In accordance with the Data Protection Directive, the DPA includes the right to prevent the processing of data that is likely to cause damage or distress, that will be used for the purposes of direct marketing, or in relation to automated decision making.[80] In the case of *Roberson v. Wakefield Metropolitan District Council*, a data subject wished to have his name withheld from the electoral register, as the information on the register was sold for direct marketing purposes. The electoral registration officer refused to comply with the request, noting that electors were required to complete certain forms and be listed on the register in order to be able to lawfully vote. The court found for the complainant and held that "the legal rules concerning representation of the people must be construed in a manner which is Directive compliant and consistent with the Data Protection Act 1998."[81] As a result of this judgment, the electoral register is now in two parts, one that allows data subjects to opt out of direct marketing, and a second register that is open.

To exert the right to prevent the processing of data in these circumstances the data subject must apply to court and, in certain cases, may be able to obtain compensation. In cases where the information is inaccurate, the court has the power to order the correction, blocking, erasure, or destruction of the relevant data.[82]

O. Sanctions

The ICO has stated that its "aim is to ensure organisations comply with the law."[83] If an organization fails, or refuses to comply voluntarily with the DPA, the ICO has a range of both criminal and administrative sanctions at its disposal. These sanctions have been strengthened over the past few years. For example, in 2008, through the Criminal Justice and Immigration Act,[84] the Information Commissioner was provided with the authority to serve a monetary penalty notice on data controllers in certain circumstances.

The sanctions available to the ICO include the following:

- **Information notice:** this requires organisations to provide the Information Commissioner with specified information within a certain time period.
- **Undertaking:** this commits an organisation to a particular course of action in order to improve its compliance.
- **Enforcement notice:**[85] this compels an organisation to take the action specified in the notice to bring about compliance with the Regulations. For example, a notice may be served to compel an organisation to start gaining consent for cookies. Failure to comply with an enforcement notice can be a criminal offence.
- **Monetary penalty notice:** a monetary penalty notic e requires an organisation to pay a monetary penalty of an amount determined by the ICO, up to a maximum of £500,000. This power can be used in the most serious of cases.[86]

Under revised regulations, public electronic communications service providers must notify the ICO if a personal data breach occurs. A personal data breach is defined as

> a breach of security leading the accidental or unlawful destruction, loss, alteration, unauthorised disclosure of, or access to, personal data transmitted, stored or otherwise processed in connection with the provisions of a public electronic communications service.[87]

Under the Privacy and Electronic Communications (EC Directive) Regulations, if a service provider fails to notify the Information Commissioner of a breach of security the ICO has the authority to issue a fixed monetary penalty of £1,000 (approximately US$1,600).[88] In cases of serious contraventions of the Privacy and Electronic Communications Regulation that are deliberate, or where the person responsible for preventing the contravention fails to take reasonable steps to prevent it, and where the breach is likely to cause substantial damage or distress, the ICO has the authority to impose a higher civil monetary penalty. This penalty may be a fine of up to £500,000 (approximately US$700,000).[89]

P. Criminal Offenses

While breaching the data protection principles alone is not a criminal offense, it may give rise to claims for compensation from data subjects that have suffered damage and distress, or the imposition of a financial penalty from the ICO. There are a number of criminal offenses contained within the DPA. The ICO has the authority to bring criminal proceedings in relation to these offenses. The offenses are generally strict liability regulatory offenses. The most important offenses with regard to data subjects involve obtaining personal data without authorization.[90] These offenses relate to knowingly or recklessly obtaining, disclosing, or procuring disclosure, where there is a risk that the DPA would be contravened. This contravention requires the offending party to have failed to take reasonable steps to prevent the contravention, with this breach being likely to cause substantial damage or distress to the party whose data has been compromised.[91] If a person to whom the DPA applies knowingly or recklessly discloses or obtains personal data, he or she is guilty of an offense and subject to a fine. The court can also order the forfeiture, destruction, or erasure of any information that appears to have been used in the commission of an offense under the DPA.[92]

Criminal offenses created by the DPA include

- unlawfully obtaining, disclosing, or procuring the disclosure of personal data;
- selling, or offering to sell, personal data which has been unlawfully obtained;
- processing personal data without notifying the Information Commissioner (and other offences related to notification);
- failing to comply with an enforcement notice or an information notice, or knowingly or recklessly making a fals e statement in compliance with an information notice;
- obstructing, or failing to give reasonable assistance in, the execution of a search warrant;
- requiring someone, for example during the recruitment process, to exercise their subject access rights to supply certain information (such as records of their criminal convictions), which the person wanting it would not otherwise be entitled to. This offence, known a s "enforced subject access", is not yet in force; and
- the unlawful disclosure of certain information by the Information Commissioner, his staff or agents.[93]

Individuals that are in management roles within a corporation or company may be personally guilty of an offense as well as the corporate body if "the offence was committed with their consent or connivance; or the offence is attributable to neglect on their part."[94]

As noted above, actions for offenses under the DPA are typically brought by the Information Commissioner. If the case is heard in the magistrates' court a fine of up to £5,000 (approximately US$7,000) may be imposed. This rises to an unlimited amount if the case is tried on indictment and heard by the Crown Court.[95]

Q. Application of the Data Protection Act to Transborder Data Flows

The Eighth Data Protection Principle prohibits the transfer of personal data outside of the European Economic Area (EEA) ("transborder data flow"), unless the recipient country either has an adequate level of personal data protection or the transfer falls within an exception or derogation. Specifically, the DPA provides that

> [p]ersonal data shall not be transferred to a country or territory outside the European Economic Area unless that country or territory ensures an adequate level of protection for the rights and freedoms of data subjects in relation to the processing of personal data.[96]

In order to lawfully transfer personal data outside of the EEA in compliance with the DPA to a company in a country that does not have laws considered to be adequate, it must meet one of the exemptions or derogations contained in the DPA.[97]

The derogations to the DPA that permit the transfer of personal data to third countries considered to have inadequate levels of protection arise where the

- data subject has provided his/her consent for the transfer;
- transfer is necessary for the performance or conclusion of a contract between the data subject and data controller that is entered to at the request or is in the interests of the data subject;
- transfer is necessary for reasons of substantial public interest;
- transfer is necessary for the purpose of, or in connection with, any legal proceedings; or is necessary to obtain legal advice or for defending legal rights;
- transfer is necessary to protect the vital interests of the data subject;
- transfer is of part of personal data on a public register and all conditions regarding the register are complied with; or
- transfer is made on terms that are of a kind approved by the Commissioner ensuring that data subjects have adequate safeguards, rights, and freedoms.[98]

If any of these derogations are met, personal data that falls within the scope of the DPA may be lawfully transferred outside of the EEA.

III. Role of Data Protection Agencies

The UK's Information Commissioner's Office (ICO) was established as the "independent authority . . . to uphold information rights in the public interest . . . and data privacy for individuals."[99] The ICO received its name in 2001, when it replaced the Data Protection Commissioner, as the office was given the additional responsibility of handling issues under the Freedom of Information Act.[100] The original office of Data Protection Registrar was established in 1984 in response to the enactment of the Data Protection Act 1984.[101]

The ICO is responsible for promoting good practice and observance of the DPA by data controllers, producing codes of practice, reporting to Parliament on the operation of the DPA, and providing assistance to data subjects who are bringing proceedings under some provisions of the DPA.[104]

A. Functions of the ICO

1. Monitoring Observance of the Law

The ICO monitors the observance of the DPA and, where necessary, implements enforcement measures against those who breach it.[105] The ICO launched a Personal Information Online Code of Practice in 2012,[106] made under section 51 of the Data Protection Act. This Code details how the Act "applies to the collection and use of personal data online [and] provides good practice advice for organisations that do business or provide services online."[107] The Code is the Information Commissioner's interpretation of "what the DPA requires when personal data is collected and used online."[108] The Code aims to fill the gap created by the requirements of the DPA, which the ICO notes "provides no guidance on the practical measures that could be taken to comply with them."[109] The Code does not apply to the collection of anonymized or statistical data.[110]

2. Enforcement

The ICO has an enforcement role and is responsible for ensuring that the provisions of the DPA are followed by any data controller, whether online or offline. The ICO has a number of both civil and criminal enforcement measures available to it. These are discussed in Part II, above, under the subheading "Sanctions."

Concerns have been raised over the duplicity of roles the ICO has, and the potential for conflicts of interest. The original rationale behind the multiple roles was the "need for the best use of resources, together with consistency of approach."[111] Commentators have noted that the enforcement function of the ICO is "arguably of central importance, with other duties, such as dissemination of information, being ancillary to this."[112]

The ICO has been behind several amendments to the DPA. For example, it had a role in the introduction of additional financial penalties under the DPA.[113]

IV. Public and Scholarly Opinion

Data protection laws and subject access rights are commonly known across the UK, with the Data Protection Act consistently being the most requested piece of legislation from the UK government's online legislative database.[114] It appears that the public is becoming increasingly aware of their rights under the DPA. The ICO has noted an increase in the number of complaints over the past few years from data subjects who believe that their privacy has been breached. Since being authorized to administer financial penalties, the ICO has issued over twenty-one penalty notices totaling £2 million (approximately US$3.4 million) in fines.[115]

V. Pending Reforms

The ICO is actively working with the EU on a new Data Protection Directive that aims to be "technology neutral."[116] In terms of the retention of data for the purposes of preventing crime, a new draft Communications Data Bill was recently introduced in Parliament that would update the Regulation of Investigatory Powers Act. It requires UK ISPs to retain data of a much wider range than is currently required, extending to social networking sites, webmail, and gaming site information.[117]

Prepared by Clare Feikert-Ahalt
Foreign Law Specialist
June 2012

End Notes for Australia

[1] Privacy Act 1988 (Cth), http://www.comlaw.gov.au/Details/C2012C00271/. Other federal laws that are relevant to the protection of individuals' privacy online include the Telecommunications Act 1997, Telecommunications (Interception and Access) Act 1979, the SPAM Act 2003, and the Cyber Crime Act 2000. For general information on federal laws containing provisions relating to the protection of privacy, *see* AUSTRALIAN

LAW REFORM COMMISSION (ALRC), FOR YOUR INFORMATION: AUSTRALIAN PRIVACY LAW AND PRACTICE [ALRC REPORT 108], paras. 2.2–2.9 (Aug. 12, 2008, *last modified* Sept. 1, 2010), http://www.alrc.gov.au/publications/ 2.%20 Privacy%20Regulation%20in%20Australia/federal-regulation-privacy, full report *available at* http://www.alrc.gov.au/publications/report-108. *See also* Office of the Privacy Commissioner, Private Sector Information Sheet 26, Interaction Between the Privacy Act and the Spam Act (Aug. 2008), http://www.privacy .gov.au/materials/types/infosheets/view/6559. Australian states and territories also have privacy laws that apply primarily to public sector entities, although some also have laws relating to information collected by private healthcare providers. For general information on state privacy laws, *see* ALRC REPORT 108, paras. 2.10–2.88, http://www .alrc.gov.au/publications/2.%20Privacy%20Regulation%20in%20Australia/state-and-territory-regulation-privacy.

[2] *See* Graham Greenleaf, *Australia*, at 2 & 7, in European Commission Directorate-General Justice, Freedom and Security, Comparative Study on Different Approaches to New Privacy Challenges, in Particular in the Light of Technological Developments (Douwe Korff ed., May 2010), http://ec.europa.eu/justice/policies/privacy/docs/ studies/new_privacy_challenges/final_report_country_report_B2_australia.pdf.

[3] Privacy Act 1988 (Cth) s 6. For a discussion of this definition, *see* ALRC REPORT 108, *supra* note 1, paras. 6.2–6.6, http://www.alrc.gov.au/publications/6.%20The%20Privacy%20Act%3A%20Some%20Important %20Definitions/what-%E2%80%98personal-information%E2%80%99.

[4] Privacy Act 1988 (Cth) s 6. For a discussion of this term, *see* ALRC REPORT 108, *supra* note 1, paras. 6.88–6.122, http://www.alrc.gov.au/publications/6.%20The%20Privacy%20Act%3A%20Some%20Important%20 Definitions/sensitive-information.

[5] Privacy Act 1988 (Cth) s 6C(1). Registered political parties and public sector agencies or authorities are also excluded from the definition of organizations, with different provisions applying to such entities. There is also an exemption for private individuals acting in a nonbusiness capacity (s 7B(1)), and obligations in the legislation relating to the protection of personal information do not apply to processes carried out by a person solely for the purposes of, or in connection with, his or her "personal, family or household affairs" (s 16E).

[6] Id. s 6D(1).

[7] *Id.* s 6D(4)(c)–(d).

[8] *Id.* s 6E. *See also Register of Businesses That Have Opted into Privacy Act Coverage*, OFFICE OF THE AUSTRALIAN INFORMATION COMMISSIONER (OAIC), http://oaic.gov.au/privacy-portal/resources_ privacy/optinregister.html (last visited June 5, 2012).

[9] Privacy Act 1988 (Cth) s 16A; *see also* s 13A(1)(b), which states that "an act or practice of an organisation is an interference of privacy if . . . the act or practice breaches a National Privacy Principle in relation to the personal information that relates to the individual." To the extent that an approved privacy code is in effect in relation to the particular organization, the code will apply in place of the NPPs.

[10] *See* Greenleaf, *supra* note 2, at 6. *See also* OECD GUIDELINES ON THE PROTECTION OF PRIVACY AND TRANSBORDER FLOWS OF PERSONAL DATA (1980), http://www.oecd.org/document/18/0,3746,en_ 2649_34223_ 1815186_1_1_1_1,00.html.

[11] House of Representatives, Privacy Amendment (Private Sector) Bill 2000: Explanatory Memorandum 1, http://parlinfo.aph.gov.au/parlInfo/download/legislation/ems/r1049_ems_aebd4d72-266b-44ca-a5b0-dabb68c 2405a/upload_pdf/30758%5B1%5D.pdf;fileType=application%2Fpdf.

[12] Privacy Act 1988 (Cth) pt IIIAA.

[13] The Privacy Commissioner is the federal regulator for privacy in Australia. There are also state-level commissioners responsible for enforcing the privacy laws of those states.

[14] *See* Privacy Act 1988 (Cth) s 16A; *see also* s 13A(1)(a), which states that "an act or practice of an organisation is an interference of privacy if . . . the act or practice breaches an approved privacy code that binds the organisation in relation to personal information that relates to the individual."

[15] *Privacy Codes Register*, OAIC, http://www.privacy.gov.au/business/codes/register (last visited Apr. 30, 2012).

[16] *Id.* The draft Internet Industry Privacy Code of Practice is available on the website of the Internet Industry Association (IAA), http://www.iia.net.au/index.php/section-blog/68/127-supporting-documents.html. Information relating to the draft code can also be found *in IAA Privacy Virtual Taskforce*, IIA, http://www.iia.net .au/index.php/component/content/36.html?task=category&sectionid=4 (last visited June 11, 2012).

[17] Privacy Amendment (Private Sector) Act 2000 (Cth), http://www.comlaw.gov.au/Details/C2004A00748.

[18] Privacy Amendment (Private Sector) Bill 2000: Explanatory Memorandum, *supra* note 11, at 1.

[19] Directive 95/46/EC, of the European Parliament and of the Council of 24 October 1995 on the Protection of Individuals with Regard to the Processing of Personal Data and on the Free Movement of Such Data, 1995 O.J. (L 281) 31, http://eur-lex.europa.eu/LexUriServ/LexUriServ.do?uri=CELEX:31995L0046:en:HTML.

[20] Privacy Amendment (Private Sector) Bill 2000: Explanatory Memorandum, *supra* note 11, at 14.

[21] Examples of technologies that may be used to collect, store, and transmit information about individuals in the online environment include developments relating to Internet search engines, cookies, social networking sites, cloud computing, smartphones and application software (apps), location detection technology, and Voice over Internet Protocol. *See Protecting Your Privacy on the Internet*, OAIC, http://www.privacy.gov.au/topics/technologies/privacy (last visited June 4, 2012).

[22] Information relating to this inquiry, including copies of submissions and the committee's final report, are available on the committee's website: *Senate Standing Committees on Environment and Communications: The Adequacy of Protections for the Privacy of Australians Online*, PARLIAMENT OF AUSTRALIA, http://www.aph.gov .au/Parliamentary_Business/Committees/Senate_Committees?url=ec_ctte/online_privacy /index.htm (last visited June 4, 2012).

[23] ALRC REPORT 108, *supra* note 1.

[24] *See Privacy Act Snapshot*, OAIC, http://www.privacy.gov.au/aboutprivacy/snapshot (last visited June 4, 2012).

[25] Privacy Amendment (Private Sector) Bill 2000: Explanatory Memorandum, *supra* note 11, at 9.

[26] The Senate, Environment and Communications References Committee, The Adequacy of Protections for the Privacy of Australians Online [Senate Committee Report] 21–22 (April 2011), http://www.aph.gov.au/Parliamentary_Business/Committees/Senate_Committees?url=ec_ctte/online_privacy/report/report.pdf.

[27] Privacy Act 1988 (Cth), sch 3 cl 1.2.

[28] *Id.* sch 3 cl 1.3.

[29] *Id.* sch 3 cl 3.

[30] *Id.* sch 3 cl 4.2.

[31] Senate Committee Report, *supra* note 26, at 37.

[32] *See Privacy Fact Sheet 4 – Online Behavioural Advertising: Know Your Options*, OAIC, http://www.oaic.gov.au/publications/privacy_fact_sheets/privacy_fact_sheet_advert_know_options.html.

[33] Senate Committee Report, *supra* note 26, at 41.

[34] *Id.*

[35] *See, e.g.*, Australian Association of National Advertisers (AANA), AANA Code of Ethics (Jan. 1, 2012), http://www.aana.com.au/data/Documents/Codes/AANACodeofEthics_1Jan2012.pdf; *and* AANA et al., AUSTRALIAN BEST PRACTICE GUIDELINES FOR ONLINE BEHAVIOURAL ADVERTISING (Mar. 2011), http://s3.amazon aws.com/admaweb-production/assets/342/Australian_Best_Practice_Guideline_FINAL_FINAL_original.PDF.

[36] Senate Committee Report, *supra* note 26, at 44.

[37] *Id.* at 45.

[38] ALRC REPORT 108, *supra* note 1, para. 68.1, http://www.alrc.gov.au/publications/68.%20Decision%20Making%20by%20and%20for%20Individuals%20Under%20the%20Age%20of%2018/introduction.

[39] OFFICE OF THE FEDERAL PRIVACY COMMISSIONER, GUIDELINES TO THE NATIONAL PRIVACY PRINCIPLES 21 (Sept. 2001), http://www.privacy.gov.au/materials/types/download/8774/6582.

[40] Senate Committee Report, *supra* note 26, at 18.

[41] ALRC REPORT 108, *supra* note 1, paras. 67.51–67.83, http://www.alrc.gov.au/publications/67.%20Children%2C%20Young%20People%20and%20%20Attitudes%20to%20Privacy/online-social-networking.

[42] *Id.*, paras. 68.102–68.126, http://www.alrc.gov.au/publications/68.%20Decision%20 Making%20by%20and%20for%20Individuals%20Under%20the%20Age%20of%2018/alrc%E2%80%99s-view.

[43] *Id.*, paras. 69.7–69.40, http://www.alrc.gov.au/publications/69.%20Particular%20Privacy%20 Issues%20Affecting%20Children%20and%20Young%20People/online-consumers-and-.

[44] *See Cybersecurity*, DEPARTMENT OF BROADBAND, COMMUNICATIONS AND THE DIGITAL ECONOMY, http://www.dbcde.gov.au/online_safety_and_security/Cyber_Security (last modified Apr. 11, 2012); *and Cyber Security*, ATTORNEY-GENERAL'S DEPARTMENT, http://www.ag.gov.au/Cybersecurity/Pages/default.aspx (last visited June 4, 2012).

[45] *See Connecting with Confidence: Optimising Australia's Digital Future,* AUSTRALIAN GOVERNMENT, http://cyberwhitepaper.dpmc.gov.au/ (last visited June 4, 2012); *and The Cyber White Paper: Connecting with Confidence*, DEPARTMENT OF THE PRIME MINISTER AND CABINET, http://www.dpmc.gov.au/national_security/cyber_ white_paper_factsheet.cfm (last updated June 3, 2011).

[46] Press Release, Australian Human Rights Commission, Privacy Rights Exists [sic] in a Virtual World (Apr. 23, 2012), http://www.hreoc.gov.au/about/media/news/2012/37_12.html.

[47] ALRC REPORT 108, *supra* note 1, para. 19.3, http://www.alrc.gov.au/publications/19.%20Consent/ background.

[48] Privacy Act 1988 (Cth) s 6.

[49] GUIDELINES TO THE NATIONAL PRIVACY PRINCIPLES, *supra* note 39, at 22.

[50] Senate Committee Report, *supra* note 26, at 30.
[51] *Id.* at 31.
[52] *Id.* at 31–32.
[53] Privacy Amendment (Private Sector) Bill 2000: Explanatory Memorandum, *supra* note 11, at 129.
[54] GUIDELINES TO THE NATIONAL PRIVACY PRINCIPLES, *supra* note 39, at 30.
[55] ALRC REPORT 108, *supra* note 1, para. 20.2, http://www.alrc.gov.au/publications/20.%20Anonymity%20and%20Pseudonymity/introduction.
[56] GUIDELINES TO THE NATIONAL PRIVACY PRINCIPLES, *supra* note 39, at 57.
[57] *Id.* at 44.
[58] *Id.* at 44–45.
[59] Privacy Act 1988 (Cth) s 36(1).
[60] *Id.* s 40(1A).
[61] *Id.* s 41(1).
[62] *Id.* s 41(2).
[63] *Id.* s 36(2)–(2A).
[64] *See* Senate Committee Report, *supra* note 26, at 8.
[65] *See Functions of the Australian Human Rights Commission*, AUSTRALIAN HUMAN RIGHTS COMMISSION, http://www.hreoc.gov.au/about/functions/index.html (last visited June 4, 2012).
[66] Graham Greenleaf & Katrine Evans, *Privacy Enforcement Strengthens in Australia & New Zealand* UNSWLRS 4 (2012), *available at* http://www.austlii.edu.au/au/journals/UNSWLRS/2012/4.html (referring to *Rummery and Federal Privacy Commissioner and Anor* AATA 1221 (Nov. 22, 2004), *available at* http://www.austlii.edu.au/au/cases/cth/AATA/2004/1221.html).
[67] ALRC REPORT 108, *supra* note 1, para. 50.19, http://www.alrc.gov.au/publications/50.%20Enforcing%20the%20Privacy%20Act/enforcing-determinations.
[68] *Id.*, paras. 46.47–46.59, http://www.alrc.gov.au/publications/46.%20Structure%20of%20the%20 Office%20of%20the%20Privacy%20Commissioner/accountability-mechanisms. *See also* Greenleaf, *supra* note 2, at 30–31.
[69] ALRC REPORT 108, *supra* note 1, para. 59.163, http://www.alrc.gov.au/publications/59.%20Access%20and%20Correction,%20Complaint%20Handling%20and%20Penalties/penalties.
[70] Graham Greenleaf, *Major Changes in Asia Pacific Data Privacy Laws: 2011 Survey*, UNSWLRS 3 (2012), *available at* http://www.austlii.edu.au/au/journals/UNSWLRS/2012/3.html.
[71] ALRC REPORT 108, *supra* note 1, paras. 74.1–74.6, 74.16–69, http://www.alrc.gov.au/publications/74.%20Protecting%20a%20Right%20to%20Personal%20Privacy%20/introduction *and* http://www.alrc.gov.au/publications/74.%20Protecting%20a%20Right%20to%20Personal%20Privacy%20/right-personal-privacy% E2%80%94developments-austral.
[72] Greenleaf, *supra* note 2, at 13.
[73] Privacy Amendment (Private Sector) Bill 2000: Explanatory Memorandum, *supra* note 11, at 56.
[74] GUIDELINES TO THE NATIONAL PRIVACY PRINCIPLES, *supra* note 39, at 58.
[75] Senate Committee Report, *supra* note 26, at 45.
[76] *Id.* at 46.
[77] *See, e.g.*, Ben Grubb, *Inside Australia's Data Retention Proposal*, ZDNET (June 16, 2010), http://www.zdnet.com.au/inside-australias-data-retention-proposal-339303862.htm; *and* Ben Grubb, *Govt Wants ISPs to Record Browsing History,* ZDNET (June 11, 2010), http://www.zdnet.com.au/govt-wants-isps-to-recordbrowsing-history-339303785.htm.
[78] Telecommunications (Interception and Access) Act 1979 (Cth), http://www.comlaw.gov.au/Details/C2012C00381.
[79] Senate Committee Report, *supra* note 26, at 58. *See also* OAIC, Information Sheet (Private Sector) 7, Unlawful Activity and Law Enforcement (2001), http://www.privacy.gov.au/materials/types/infosheets/view/6566.
[80] Senate Committee Report, *supra* note 26, at 54.
[81] *Id.* at 68–69. *See also* John Hilvert, *Senate Committee Warning on ISP Data Retention*, SC MAGAZINE (Apr. 8, 2011), http://www.scmagazine.com.au/News/253746,senate-committee-warning-on-isp-data-retention.aspx.
[82] Cybercrime Legislation Amendment Bill 2011 (Cth), http://www.comlaw.gov.au/Details/C2011B00116; *and Cybercrime Legislation Amendment Bill 2011*, PARLIAMENT OF AUSTRALIA, http://www.aph.gov.au/Parliamentary_Business/Bills_Legislation/Bills_Search_Results/Result?bId=r4575 (last visited June 4, 2012).
[83] Parliament of Australia, Bills Digest No. 31 2011-12, http://www.aph.gov.au/Parliamentary_Business/Bills_Legislation/bd/bd1112a/12bd031.
[84] House of Representatives, Cybercrime Legislation Amendment Bill 2011: Explanatory Memorandum, http://parlinfo.aph.gov.au/parlInfo/download/legislation/ems/r4575_ems_ecca7d37-7fb2-4218-9837-

da3ab80f531e/ upload_pdf/357071.pdf;fileType=application%2Fpdf#search=%22legislation/ems/r4575_ems_ecca7d37-7fb2-4218- 9837-da3ab80f531e%22.

[85] Josh Taylor, *Roxon Goes Public on Data Retention*, ZDNET (May 4, 2012), http://www.zdnet.com.au/ roxon-goes-public-on-data-retention-339337213.htm.

[86] Attorney-General's Department, Briefing to the Attorney-General on Online Privacy Inquiry – Response Recommendation 9 (Sept. 22, 2011), http://www.ag.gov.au/Freedomofinformation/Documents/12353405DOC %20%20R%20-%20Data%20Retention.pdf; *and Documents Concerning the Current Status of Data Retention Scheme Considerations*, ATTORNEY-GENERAL'S DEPARTMENT (May 21, 2012), http://www.ag.gov.au /Freedom ofinformation/Pages/DocumentsreleasedunderFOI/Documents-concerning-the-current-status-of-data-retentionscheme-considerations.aspx.

[87] Darren Pauli, *Govt Wants Public Vote on Data Retention*, ITNEWS (May 4, 2012), http://www.itnews .com.au/News/299402,govt-wants-public-vote-on-data-retention.aspx; Luke Hopewell, *Data-Retention Inquiry Hits Speed Bump*, ZDNET (May 17, 2012), http://www.zdnet.com.au/data-retention-inquiry-hits-speed-bump-339338 105.htm; *and* Stephanie McDonald, *Ozlog: Government Pushes Ahead with Data Retention Plans*, COMPUTERWORLD (May 28, 2012), http://www.computerworld.com.au/article/425847/ozlog_ government_pushes _ahead_data_retention_plans/.

[88] Renai LeMay, *Data Retention Proposal Still Hazy, Even Within Govt*, DELIMITER (May 31, 2012), http://delimiter.com.au/2012/05/31/data-retention-proposal-still-hazy-even-within-govt/.

[89] ALRC REPORT 108, *supra* note 1, para. 45.8, http://www.alrc.gov.au/publications/45.%20Overview %3A%20Office%20of%20the%20Privacy%20Commissioner%20/facilitating-compliance-privacy-act.

[90] *See id.*, para. 46.10, http://www.alrc.gov.au/publications/46.%20Structure%20of%20the%20 Office%20of% 20the%20Privacy%20Commissioner/structure-functions-and-powers. The functions of the Office of the Privacy Commissioner were integrated into the Office of the Australian Information Commissioner in 2010. *See Privacy Complaints*, OAIC, http://oaic.gov.au/privacy-portal/complaints_privacy.html (last visited June 4, 2012).

[91] ALRC REPORT 108, *supra* note 1, para. 45.12, http://www.alrc.gov.au/publications/45.%20Overview %3A%20Office%20of%20the%20Privacy%20Commissioner%20/powers-opc.

[92] Privacy Act 1988 (Cth) s 27.

[93] *Id.* s 40(2).

[94] ALRC REPORT 108, *supra* note 1, para. 45.23, http://www.alrc.gov.au/publications/45.%20Overview %3A%20Office%20of%20the%20Privacy%20Commissioner%20/enforcing-privacy-act. For completed own motion investigations, *see Investigation Reports—Privacy*, OAIC, http://oaic.gov.au/publications/reports. html# omi_reports (last visited June 4, 2012).

[95] *Public Interest Determinations*, OAIC, http://www.privacy.gov.au/law/act/pid (last visited June 30, 2012).

[96] Privacy Act 1988 (Cth), ss 29(a)–(b). *See also* ALRC REPORT 108, *supra* note 1, paras. 46.36–46.46, http://www.alrc.gov.au/publications/46.%20Structure%20of%20the%20Office%20of%20the%20Privacy%20 Comm issioner/manner-exercise-powers.

[97] For discussion about developments relating to the tort of invasion of privacy in Australia, *see* Des Butler, *A Tort of Invasion of Privacy in Australia?*, 29(2) MELB. U.L. REV. 339 (2005), http://www.austlii.edu.au/cgi-bin/sinodisp/au/journals/MULR/2005/11.html; Peter D. Applegarth, *The Tort of Privacy Invasion in Australia After Jane Doe*, QLD. J. SCHOL. 9 (2009), http://www.austlii.edu.au/au/journals/QldJSchol/2009/9.html; *and* Penelope Watson, *Remedies for Novel Torts: Invasion of Privacy*, 1 J. AUST. LTA 391 (2008), http://www.austlii.edu.au/au/ journals/JlALawTA/2008/35.html.

[98] The Privacy Commissioner has commissioned surveys on community attitudes to privacy every few years, with the most recent being completed in 2007. The next survey is expected to be conducted this year. *See Community Attitudes*, OAIC, http://www.privacy.gov.au/aboutprivacy/attitudes (last visited June 5, 2012).

[99] *See, e.g.*, Press Release, Timothy Pilgrim, Australian Privacy Commissioner, OAIC, Investigation into Sony Data Breach (May 4, 2011), http://www.oaic.gov.au/news/statements/statement_investigation_into_Sony_ data_breach.html; Press Release, Office of the Privacy Commissioner (NSW), Privacy Commissioner Concerned about Continued Database Security Breaches (Oct. 18, 2011), http://www.ipc.nsw. gov.au/lawlink/privacynsw /ll_pnsw.nsf/vwFiles/privacy_media_release_firststatesuper_191011.pdf/$file /privacy_media_release_firststatesuper _191011.pdf; *and* OAIC, VODAFONE HUTCHISON AUSTRALIA: OWN MOTION INVESTIGATION REPORT (Feb. 16, 2011), http://www.oaic.gov.au/publications /reports/Report-Investigation-Vodafone_Hutchison_Australia OMI.html.

[100] *Data Breach Notification: A Guide to Handling Personal Information Security Breaches*, OAIC (Apr. 2012), http://www.oaic.gov.au/publications/guidelines/privacy_guidance/data_breach_notification_guide_april 2012.html.

[101] CENTRE FOR INTERNET SAFETY, PRIVACY AND THE INTERNET: AUSTRALIAN ATTITUDES TOWARDS PRIVACY IN THE ONLINE ENVIRONMENT (Apr. 2012), http://www.canberra.edu.au/cis /storage/Australian% 20Attitutdes%20Towards%20Privacy%20Online.pdf. *See also Australians Demand Online Data Breach Notification: UC Survey Reveals*, UNIVERSITY OF CANBERRA MEDIA, http://www.canberra.edu.au/mediacentre/2012/may/australians-demand-online-data-breach-notification-uc-survey-reveals (last updated May 1, 2012); *and* Supratim Adhikari, *Internet Users Seek Mandatory Data Breach Guidelines: Survey*, TECHNOLOGY SPECTATOR (May 1, 2012), http://technologyspectator.com.au/security/data-security/internet-users-seek-mandatory-data-breachguidelines-survey.

[102] *Id.*; *and* ALRC REPORT 108, *supra* note 1, paras. 51.73–51.109, http://www.alrc.gov.au/publications/ 51.%20Data%20Breach%20Notification/alrc%E2%80%99s-view.

[103] *See* Bruce Arnold, *Care Don't Share: What Medvet Breach Says About Australian Privacy Laws*, THE CONVERSATION (Aug. 8, 2011), http://theconversation.edu.au/care-dont-share-what-medvet-breach-says-aboutaustralian-privacy-laws-2594; *and* Greenleaf, *supra* note 2, at 32–33.

[104] Press Release, OAIC, Privacy—It's All About You (Apr. 27, 2012), http://www.oaic.gov.au/news/ media_releases/media_release_120427jaw2012.html.

[105] Sharon Nye, *Internet Privacy—Regulating Cookies and Web Bugs*, PRIVACY L. & POL. R. 26 (2002), http://www.austlii.edu.au/au/journals/PLPR/2002/26.html.

[106] *The Personal Information Project*, UNIVERSITY OF QUEENSLAND, CENTRE FOR CRITICAL AND CULTURAL STUDIES, http://www.cccs.uq.edu.au/personal-information-project (last visited June 8, 2012).

[107] *Id.*

[108] Press Release, University of Queensland, Centre for Critical and Cultural Studies, Australians Concerned for Online Privacy (Mar. 16, 2012), http://cccs.uq.edu.au/project-news.

[109] Dan Svantesson, *Protecting Privacy on the "Borderless" Internet—Some Thoughts on Extraterritoriality and Transborder Data Flow*, 19(1) BOND L. REV. 168 (2007), http://www.austlii.edu.au/au/ journals/BondLawRw/2007/7.html.

[110] *Id.* at 181–83.

[111] OFFICE OF THE PRIVACY COMMISSIONER, COMMUNITY ATTITUDES TO PRIVACY 2007 at 36 (Aug. 2007), http://www.privacy.gov.au/materials/types/download/8820/6616.

[112] Australian Government, Enhancing National Privacy Protection: First Stage Response to the Australian Law Reform Commission Report 108 (Oct. 2009), http://www.dpmc.gov.au/privacy/alrc_docs/stage1_aus_govt_ response.pdf. The government has not yet responded to the Senate committee's report regarding the adequacy of the current privacy framework for protecting the information of Australians online.

[113] Information relating to this inquiry, including submissions received and the final two-part report, is available on the Parliament of Australia's website, *Exposure Drafts of Australian Privacy Amendment Legislation*, http://www.aph.gov.au/Parliamentary_Business/Committees/Senate_Committees?url=fapa_ctte/priv_exp_draf ts/ind ex.htm (last visited June 8, 2012).

[114] *Privacy Amendment (Enhancing Privacy Protection) Bill 2012*, PARLIAMENT OF AUSTRALIA, http://www.aph.gov.au/Parliamentary_Business/Bills_Legislation/Bills_Search_Results/Result?bId=r4813 (last visited June 4, 2012); *AGD Privacy Act Amendments*, ATTORNEY-GENERAL'S DEPARTMENT, http://www.ag.gov .au/Privacy/Pages/AGD-Privacy-Act-Amendments.aspx (last modified May 25, 2012); *Privacy Reforms*, ATTORNEY-GENERAL'S DEPARTMENT, http://www.ag.gov.au/Privacy/Pages/Privacy-Reforms.aspx (last modified Mar. 16, 2012); *and* Press Release, Nicola Roxon, Minister for Emergency Management, Attorney-General for Australia, Privacy Reform Laws Introduced into Parliament (May 23, 2012), http://www.attorneygeneral.gov.au/Media-releases/Pages/2012/Second%20Quarter/23-May-2012---Privacy-reformlaws-introduced-into-Parliament.aspx.

[115] Privacy Amendment (Enhancing Privacy Protection) Bill 2012, Second Reading: Nicole Roxon (May 23, 2012), http://parlinfo.aph.gov.au/parlInfo/search/display/display.w3p;query=Id%3A%22chamber%2 Fhansardr%2Fa097ab46-bef0-4ed3-b3f0-27f3b075e04e%2F0013%22.

[116] House of Representatives, Privacy Amendment (Enhancing Privacy Protection) Bill 2012: Explanatory Memorandum, http://parlinfo.aph.gov.au/parlInfo/download/legislation/ems/r4813_ems_00948d06-092b-447e9191-5706fdfa0728/upload_pdf/368711.pdf;fileType=application%2Fpdf.

[117] *Id.* at 1–2, 52–53.

[118] *Id.* at 60–61.

[119] *Id.* at 4.
[120] *Id.* at 81.
[121] APEC PRIVACY FRAMEWORK (2005), http://www.apec.org/Groups/Committee-on-Trade-andInvestment /~/media/Files/Groups/ECSG/05 ecsg privacyframewk.ashx.
[122] *Id.* at 70, 83.
[123] *Id.* at 73–74.
[124] *Id.* at 54, 74–76.
[125] *Id.* at 5.
[126] Privacy Amendment (Enhancing Privacy Protection) Bill 2012, Second Reading, *supra* note 115. An enforceable undertaking is a type of enforcement action that may be used instead of a court action or as part of a settlement. The ALRC explains that an enforceable undertaking is "essentially a promise enforceable in court. A breach of the undertaking is not contempt of court but, once the court has ordered the person to comply, a breach of that order is contempt." ALRC Report 108, *supra* note 1, para. 50.53, http://www.alrc.gov.au/publications/50.%20Enforcing%20the%20Privacy%20Act/other-enforcement-mechanisms-following-non-compliance.
[127] Privacy Amendment (Enhancing Privacy Protection) Bill 2012: Explanatory Memorandum, *supra* note 116, at 5, 49.
[128] Privacy Amendment (Enhancing Privacy Protection) Bill 2012, Second Reading, *supra* note 115.
[129] *Inquiry into the Privacy Amendment (Enhancing Privacy Protection) Bill 2012*, PARLIAMENT OF AUSTRALIA, HOUSE STANDING COMMITTEE ON SOCIAL POLICY AND LEGAL AFFAIRS, http://www.aph.gov.au/ Parliamentary_Business/Committees/House_of_Representatives_Committees?url=spla/bill%20privacy/index. htm (last visited June 4, 2012).
[130] Department of the Prime Minister and Cabinet, Issues Paper: A Commonwealth Statutory Cause of Action for Serious Invasion of Privacy (Sept. 2011), http://www.dpmc.gov.au/privacy/causeofaction/docs /issues%20paper_cth_stat_cause_action_serious_invasion_privacy.pdf; *and A Commonwealth Statutory Cause of Action for Serious Invasion of Privacy*, Department of the Prime Minister and Cabinet, http://www.dpmc.gov.au/ privacy/causeofaction/ (last updated Nov. 1, 2011).
[131] The submissions are being progressively published online *at A Commonwealth Statutory Cause of Action for Serious Invasion of Privacy*, ATTORNEY-GENERAL'S DEPARTMENT, http://www.ag.gov.au /Consultations reformsandreviews/Pages/ACommonwealthStatutoryCauseofActionforSeriousInvasionof Privacy.aspx (last modified June 12, 2011).

End Notes for Canada

[1] Canadian Charter of Rights and Freedoms, Part I of the Constitution Act, 1982, *being* Schedule B to the Canada Act, 1982, c. 11 (U.K.), http://laws-lois.justice.gc.ca/eng/charter/.
[2] *Id.* § 7.
[3] *Id.* § 8.
[4] R. v. Dyment, [1988] 2 S.C.R. 417, http://scc.lexum.org/en/1988/1988scr2-417/1988scr2-417.html.
[5] Privacy Act, R.S.C. 1985, c. P-21, http://laws-lois.justice.gc.ca/eng/acts/P-21/index.html.
[6] *Canada: Data Protection*, PRIVIREAL (PRIVACY IN RESEARCH ETHICS & LAW), http://www.privireal .org/content/dp/canada.php (last modified Nov. 29, 2005).
[7] Personal Information Protection and Electronic Documents Act [PIPEDA], S.C. 2000, c. 5, http://laws-lois.justice.gc.ca/eng/acts/P-8.6/index.html.
[8] *Id.*, preamble.
[9] Tina Piper, *Personal Information Protection and Electronic Documents Act: A Lost Opportunity to Democratize Canada's Technological Society*, 23 DALHOUSIE L.J. 253 (2000).
[10] Council Directive 95/46/EC, of the European Parliament and of the Council of 24 October 1995 on the Protection of Individuals with Regard to the Processing of Personal Data and on the Free Movement of Such Data, art. 25(6), 1995 O.J. (L 281) 31, http://eur-lex.europa.eu/LexUriServ/LexUriServ.do?uri=CELEX:31995 L0046:EN:HTML.
[11] *Id.*

[12] Juliana M. Spaeth, Mark J. Plotkin, & Sandra C. Sheets, *Privacy, Eh!: The Impact of Canada's Personal Information Protection and Electronic Documents Act on Transnational Business*, 4 VAND. J. ENT. L. & PRAC. 28, 30 (2002).

[13] Commission Decision 2002/2/EC, of 20 December 2001 Pursuant to Directive 95/46/EC of the European Parliament and of the Council on the Adequate Protection of Personal Data Provided by the Canadian Personal Information Protection and Electronic Documents Act, http://eur-lex.europa.eu/LexUriServ/LexUriServ.do ?uri=CELEX:32002D0002:EN:NOT.

[14] Personal Information Protection Act, S.B.C. 2003, c. 63, http://www.bclaws.ca/EPLibraries/bclaws_ new/document/ID/freeside/00_03063_01.

[15] Personal Information Protection Act, S.A. 2003, c. P-6.5, http://www.qp.alberta.ca/574.cfm?page =P06P5.cfm&legjype=Acts&isbncln=9780779748938&display=html.

[16] An Act Respecting the Protection of Personal Information in the Private Sector, R.S.Q., c. P-39.1, http:// www2.publicationsduquebec.gouv.qc.ca/dynamicSearch/telecharge.php?type=2&file=/P_39_1/P39_1_A.html.

[17] Health Information Act, R.S.A. 2000, c. H-5, *available at* http://www.canlii.org/en/ab/laws/stat/rsa-2000- c-h-5/latest/rsa-2000-c-h-5.html.

[18] Health Information Protection Act, S.S. 1999, c. H-0.021, *available at* http://www.canlii.org/en/sk/laws/ stat/ss-1999-c-h-0.021/latest/ss-1999-c-h-0.021.html.

[19] Personal Health Information Act, C.C.S.M., c. P33.5, http://web2.gov.mb.ca/laws/statutes/ccsm/p033-5e.php.

[20] Personal Health Information Protection Act, 2004, S.O. 2004, c. 3, Schedule A, http://www.e-laws.gov.on.ca/html/statutes/english/elaws_statutes_04p03_e.htm.

[21] Personal Health Information Privacy and Access Act, S.N.B. 2009, c. P-7.05, *available at* http://www.canlii.org/en/nb/laws/stat/snb-2009-c-p-7.05/latest/snb-2009-c-p-7.05.html.

[22] Megan Evans, *A Primer on the Personal Information Protection and Electronic Documents Act ("PIPEDA") for Pharmaceutical and Medical Device/Technology Companies That Conduct Business in Canada*, LONGWOODS.COM (2003), http://www.longwoods.com/content/16404.

[23] PIPEDA § 2(1), S.C. 2000, c. 5, http://laws-lois.justice.gc.ca/eng/acts/P-8.6/index.html.

[24] *Electronic Commerce in Canada: Frequently Asked Questions*, INDUSTRY CANADA, http://www.ic.gc.ca/eic/site/ecic-ceac.nsf/eng/gv00466.html#question2 (last modified July 20, 2009).

[25] *Id.*

[26] Canadian Standards Association, Model Code for the Protection of Personal Information, http://www.csa.ca/cm/ca/en/privacy-code/publications/view-privacy-code (last visited on June 28, 2012).

[27] Spaeth, Plotkin, & Sheets, *supra* note 12, at 33.

[28] INDUSTRY CANADA, *supra* note 24.

[29] PIPEDA, Sch. 1, cl. 4.3, S.C. 2000, c. 5, http://laws-lois.justice.gc.ca/eng/acts/P-8.6/index.html.

[30] *Id.* cl. 4.3.2.

[31] *Id.* cl. 4.3.1.

[32] *Id.* cl. 4.3.4, 4.3.6.

[33] *Id.* cl. 4.3.6.

[34] *Id.*

[35] *Id.*

[36] *Id.* cl. 4.3.7.

[37] *See id.* § 7(1) for collection of personal information without knowledge or consent, § 7(2) for use without knowledge or consent, § 7(3) for disclosure without knowledge or consent, and § 7(4) for use without consent and disclosure without consent. *See also* Sch. 1, cl. 4.3, which states, "In certain circumstances personal information can be collected, used, or disclosed without the knowledge and consent of the individual. For example, legal, medical, or security reasons may make it impossible or impractical to seek consent. When information is being collected for the detection and prevention of fraud or for law enforcement, seeking the consent of the individual might defeat the purpose of collecting the information. Seeking consent may be impossible or inappropriate when the individual is a minor, seriously ill, or mentally incapacitated. In addition, organizations that do not have a direct relationship with the individual may not always be able to seek consent. For example, seeking consent may be impractical for a charity or a direct-marketing firm that wishes to acquire a mailing list from another organization. In such cases, the organization providing the list would be expected to obtain consent before disclosing personal information."

[38] *Id.* cl. 4.8.

[39] *Id.* cl. 4.8.1.

[40] *Id.*

[41] *Id.*

[42] *Id.* cl. 4.8.2.
[43] *Id.* cl. 4.8.3.
[44] *Id.*
[45] *Id.* cl. 4.2.
[46] *Id.* cl. 4.2.1.
[47] *Id.* cl. 4.2.4.
[48] *Id.* cl. 4.2.3.
[49] *Id.* cl. 4.7.
[50] *Id.* cl. 4.7.1.
[51] *Id.* cl. 4.7.2.
[52] *Id.* cl. 4.7.5.
[53] *Id.* cl. 4.7.3.
[54] *Id.* cl. 4.7.4.
[55] *Id.* cl. 4.5.2.
[56] *Id.* cl. 4.5.3.
[57] *Id.*
[58] OFFICE OF THE PRIVACY COMMISSIONER OF CANADA, REPORT ON THE 2010 OFFICE OF THE PRIVACY COMMISSIONER OF CANADA'S CONSULTATIONS ON ONLINE TRACKING, PROFILING AND TARGETING, AND CLOUD COMPUTING (May 2011), http://www.priv.gc.ca/resource/consultations/report_201105_e.asp.
[59] Kristy Kirkup, *Privacy Watchdog Pushes Penalties for Non-compliant Social Media Sites*, THE OBSERVER (May 29, 2012), http://www.theobserver.ca/2012/05/29/privacy-watchdog-pushes-penalties-for-noncompliant-social-media-sites.
[60] *Id.*
[61] *Privacy Commissioner: Facebook Shows Improvement in Some Areas, But Should Be More Proactive on Privacy When Introducing New [Features]*, BLOOMBERG (Apr. 4, 2012), http://www.bloomberg.com/apps/news?pid=conewsstory&tkr=FB:US&sid=aG.rfEf5lcvU.
[62] *Id.*
[63] *Preliminary Letter of Findings: Complaints Under the Personal Information Protection and Electronic Documents Act (the Act)*, OFFICE OF THE PRIVACY COMMISSIONER OF CANADA, http://www.priv.gc.ca/media/nrc/2010/let_101019_e.asp?cnn=yes (last modified Oct. 19, 2010).
[64] News Release, Office of the Privacy Commissioner of Canada, Letter to Google Inc. Chief Executive Officer (April 19, 2010), http://www.priv.gc.ca/media/nr-c/2010/let_100420_e.asp.
[65] *Id.*
[66] REPORT ON THE 2010 OFFICE OF THE PRIVACY COMMISSIONER OF CANADA'S CONSULTATIONS ON ONLINE TRACKING, PROFILING AND TARGETING, AND CLOUD COMPUTING, *supra* note 58, at 7.
[67] Valerie Steeves, *It's Not Child's Play: The Online Invasion of Children's Privacy*, 3 UNIV. OTT. L. & TECH. J. 169, 181 (2006), http://www.uoltj.ca/articles/vol3.1/2006.3.1.uoltj.Steeves.169-188.pdf.
[68] *Government of Canada Moves to Enhance Privacy of Individuals During Commercial Transactions*, INDUSTRY CANADA (Sept. 29, 2011), http://www.ic.gc.ca/eic/site/ic1.nsf/eng/06802.html.
[69] Ameena Sultan, *PIPEDA: Privacy and Consent Legislation*, WHALEY ESTATE LITIGATION (Feb. 15, 2011), http://whaleyestatelitigation.com/blog/2011/02/pipeda-privacy-and-consent-legislation/.
[70] Lisa R. Lifshitz, Chris Oates, & Rene Bissonnette, *Government Introduces Amendments to PIPEDA*, GOWLINGS 1, http://www.gowlings.com/knowledgeCentre/publicationPDFs/Government-Introduces-Amendmentsto-PIPEDA.pdf (last visited June 12, 2012).
[71] Matt Hartley, *Privacy Commissioner Lays Out New Rules for Online Advertising*, FINANCIAL POST (Dec. 6, 2011), http://business.financialpost.com/2011/12/06/privacy-commissioner-lays-out-new-rules-for-online-advertising/.
[72] PIPEDA § 16(c).
[73] An Act to Promote the Efficiency and Adaptability of the Canadian Economy by Regulating Certain Activities That Discourage Reliance on Electronic Means of Carrying Out Commercial Activities, and to Amend the Canadian Radio-Television and Telecommunications Commission Act, the Competition Act, the Personal Information Protection and Electronic Documents Act and the Telecommunications Act, S.C. 2010, C. 23, http://Laws-Lois.Justice.Gc.Ca/Eng/Acts/E-1.6/Page-1.Html.
[74] *About the Office of the Privacy Commissioner*, OFFICE OF THE PRIVACY COMMISSIONER OF CANADA, http://www.priv.gc.ca/au-ans/index_e.asp (last modified July 19, 2010).

[75] PIPEDA § 11(1), S.C. 2000, c. 5, http://laws-lois.justice.gc.ca/eng/acts/P-8.6/index.html.
[76] *Id.* § 11(2).
[77] *Id.* § 12(1).
[78] *Id.* § 12(4).
[79] *Id.* § 12.2(1).
[80] *Id.* §§ 13(1), 13(3).
[81] *Id.* § 14(1).
[82] *Id.* § 16.
[83] Kirkup, *supra* note 60.
[84] Nammo v. TransUnion of Canada, [2010] F.C. 1284, http://decisions.fct-cf.gc.ca/en/2010/2010fc1284/2010fc1284.html.
[85] *PIPEDA Case Law Update: Federal Court Issues a Landmark Decision on Damages*, ACCESS PRIVACY (Feb. 1, 2011), http://www.accessprivacy.com/News/View/2113.
[86] OFFICE OF THE PRIVACY COMMISSIONER OF CANADA, LEADING BY EXAMPLE: KEY DEVELOPMENTS IN THE FIRST SEVEN YEARS OF THE PERSONAL INFORMATION PROTECTION AND ELECTRONIC DOCUMENTS ACT (PIPEDA), 14 (2008), http://publications.gc.ca/collections/collection_2008/privcom/IP54-6-2008E.pdf.
[87] Lawson v. Accusearch, [2007] F.C. 125, *available at* http://www.canlii.org/en/ca/fct/doc/2007/2007fc125/2007fc125.html.
[88] OFFICE OF THE PRIVACY COMMISSIONER OF CANADA, *supra* note 74, at 14.
[89] State Farm Mutual Automobile Insurance Company v. Privacy Commissioner of Canada, [2010] F.C. 736, *available at* http://www.canlii.org/en/ca/fct/doc/2010/2010fc736/2010fc736.html. *See also* Charles S. Morgan, *Federal Court Rules on Scope of "Commercial Activity" under PIPEDA*, MCCARTHY TÉTRAULT LLP (Nov. 11, 2010), http://www.mccarthy.ca/article_detail.aspx?id=5170. This article notes that "many had hoped that this decision would resolve the issue of the constitutionality of *PIPEDA* as regards its application to the intra-provincial activities of provincially regulated entities. As the court declined to determine this question, the status quo has been maintained in this respect, at least for now."
[90] *Recent Court Activity: State Farm v. Privacy Commissioner and AG of Can.*, OFFICE OF THE PRIVACY COMMISSIONER OF CANADA, http://www.priv.gc.ca/leg_c/court_p_03_e.asp (last modified July 12, 2010).
[91] Jeremy Warner, *The Right to Oblivion: Data Retention from Canada to Europe in Three Backward Steps*, 2 U. OTTAWA L. & TECH. J. 75, 92 (2005), http://www.uoltj.ca/articles/vol2.1/2005.2.1.uoltj.Warner.75-104.pdf.
[92] *See* Meagan Fitzpatrick, *Social Media Websites Ignoring Privacy Laws, Watchdog Says*, CBC NEWS (May 29, 2012), http://www.cbc.ca/news/politics/story/2012/05/29/pol-social-media-privacy.html.
[93] Micheal Fekete & Patricia Wilson, *PIPEDA: A Clearly Canadian Approach to Privacy Protection*, PRIVACY REG. 4, 7 (Spring 2004), http://www.wiggin.com/files/Privacy%20Regulation%20Langer-Spring2004.pdf.
[94] Piper, *supra* note 9, at 1.
[95] AVNER LEVIN & MARY JO NICHOLSON, *Privacy Law in the United States, the EU and Canada: The Allure of the Middle Ground*, 2 OTTAWA L. & TECH. J. 357, 381 (2005).
[96] Piper, *supra* note 9, at 10.
[97] *Id.*
[98] *Id.*
[99] *Id.*
[100] *Id.*
[101] *Id.*
[102] HOUSE OF COMMONS STANDING COMMITTEE ON HUMAN RIGHTS AND THE STATUS OF PERSONS WITH DISABILITIES, PRIVACY: WHERE DO WE DRAW THE LINE? 6 (Apr. 1997), http://www.priv.gc.ca/information/02_06 03d e.pdf.
[103] *Id.* at 7.
[104] PRIVACY COMMISSIONER OF CANADA, 2011 CANADIANS AND PRIVACY SURVEY: FINAL REPORT (Mar. 31, 2011), http://www.priv.gc.ca/information/por-rop/2011/por_2011_01_e.asp.
[105] *Id.*
[106] *Id.*
[107] *Id.*
[108] An Act to amend the Personal Information Protection and Electronic Documents Act, Bill C-12, 41st Parl., 1st Sess. (Can. 2011), *available at* http://www.parl.gc.ca/HousePublications/Publication.aspx?Docid=5144601&file=4.

[109] Lifshitz, Oates, & Bissonnette, *supra* note 70.
[110] *Id.*
[111] *Id.*
[112] *Id.*

End Notes for France

[1] Loi 78-17 du 6 janvier 1978 relative à l'informatique, aux fichiers et aux libertés (version consolidée au 27 août 2011) [Law 78-17 of January 6, 1978, on Information Technologies, Data Files and Civil Liberties (consolidated version as of Aug. 27, 2011)], LEGIFRANCE, http://legifrance.gouv.fr/affichTexte.do?cidTexte= JORFTEXT000000886460&fastPos=1&fastReqId=411489546&categorieLien=cid& oldAction= rechTexte, unofficial English version available on the CNIL website, *at* http://www.cnil.fr/fileadmin /documents/en/Act78- 17VA.pdf.
[2] *Id.* art. 1.
[3] CELINE CASTETS-RENARD, DROIT DE L'INTERNET § 26 (Ed. Montchrestien, 2009).
[4] Directive 95/46/EC of the European Parliament and of the Council of October 24,1995, on the Protection of Individuals with regard to the Processing of Personal Data and on the Free Movement of Such Data, 1995 O.J. (L 281) 31, http://eur-lex.europa.eu/LexUriServ/LexUriServ.do?uri=CELEX:31995L0046:EN:PDF.
[5] Loi 2004-801 du 6 août 2004 relative à la protection des personnes physiques à l'égard des traitements de données à caractère personnel et modifiant la loi n° 78-17 du 6 janvier 1978 relative à l'informatique, aux fichiers et aux libertés [Law 2004-801 of August 6, 2004, on protection of natural persons with respect to the processing of personal data and amending Law 78-17 of January 6, 1978, on Information Technologies, Data Files and Civil Liberties], LEGIFRANCE, http://legifrance.gouv.fr/affichTexte.do;jsessionid=46284B 7113DCD 877F7481BE 7C32348A2.tpdjo10v_1?cidTexte=JORFTEXT000000441676&categorieLien=id.
[6] Directive 2002/58/EC of the European Parliament and of the Council of 12 July 2002 Concerning the Processing of Personal Data and the Protection of Privacy in the Electronic Communications Sector, 2002 O.J. (L 201) 37, http://eur-lex.europa.eu/LexUriServ/LexUriServ.do?uri=CELEX:32002L0058:EN:PDF.
[7] Décret 2007-451 du 25 mars 2007 modifiant le décret 2005-1309 du 20 octobre 2005 pris pour l'application de la loi 78-17 du 6 janvier 1978 relative à l'informatique, aux fichiers et aux libertés, modifiée par la loi 2004-801 du 6 août 2004 [Decree 2007-451 amending decree 2005-1309 of October 20, 2005, implementing law 78-17 on Information Technologies, Data Files and Civil Liberties], LEGIFRANCE, http://legifrance.gouv.fr/ affichTexte.do;jsessionid=17C1695456DDEE360E99261A83CC2812.tpdjo02v_3?cidTexte=JORFTEXT0000 0082 4352&categorieLien=id.
[8] Loi 2009-526 du 12 mai 2009 de simplification et de clarification du droit et d'allègement des procédures [Law 2009-526 on the simplification and clarification of the law and procedures], LEGIFRANCE, http://legifrance .gouv.fr/affichTexte.do;jsessionid=FB83D8D1AA5FB46FCB0F1DC8228DA4DF.tpdjo10v_1?cidTexte=JOR FTEX T000020604162&categorieLien=id.
[9] Loi organique 2010-704 du 28 juin 2010 relative au Conseil économique, social et environnemental [Organic Law 2010-704 of June 28, 2010, relating to the Economic, Social and Environmental Council], LEGIFRANCE, http://legifrance.gouv.fr/affichTexte.do?cidTexte=JORFTEXT000022402454&fastPos=2& fastReqId=1815216044&categorieLien=id&oldAction=rechTexte.
[10] Loi 2011-334 du 29 mars 2011 relative au Défenseur des droits [Law 2011-334 of March 29, 2011 relating to the Defender of Rights], LEGIFRANCE, http://legifrance.gouv.fr/affichTexte.do?cidTexte=JORFTEXT 000023781252&fastPos=2&fastReqId=1285209417&categorieLien=id&oldAction=rechTexte.
[11] Ordonnance 2011-1012 du 24 août 2011 relative aux communications électroniques [Ordinance 2011- 1012 of August 24, 2011, on Electronic Communications], LEGIFRANCE, http://legifrance.gouv.fr/affich Texte.do?cidTexte=JORFTEXT000024502658&fastPos=2&fastReqId=1947455443&categorieLien=id&oldA ction =rechTexte.
[12] Décret 85-1203 du 15 novembre 1985 portant publication de la convention pour la protection des personnes à l'égard du traitement automatisé des données à caractère personnel, faite à Strasbourg le 28/01/1981 [Decree 85-1203 of November 15, 1985, publishing the Convention for the Protection of Individuals with regard to Automatic Processing of Personal Data signed in Strasbourg on January 1981], LEGIFRANCE, http://legifrance.gouv. fr/jopdf/common/jo pdf.jsp?numJO=0&dateJO=19851120&numTexte=&page Debut=13436&pageFin.

[13] *Internet-Téléphonie, Que dit la CNIL sur ...* [*Internet-Telephone, What the CNIL is Saying ...*], CNIL, http://www.cnil.fr/dossiers/internet-telecoms/ (last visited May 30, 2012) (scroll to *Que dit la CNIL sur...*).

[14] *See Smartphone and Privacy: Best Friends Forever?*, CNIL (Jan. 3, 2012), http://www.cnil.fr/ english/news-and-events/news/article/smartphone-and-privacy-best-friends-forever/.

[15] *Id.*

[16] *Ce que le "Paquet Télécom" change pour les cookies* [*What the Telecom Package Changes for Cookies*], CNIL (Apr. 26, 2012), http://www.cnil.fr/en-savoir-plus/fiches-pratiques/fiche/article/ce-que-le-paquettelecom-change-pour-les-cookies/.

[17] Loi 78-17 du 6 janvier 1978, *supra* note 1, art. 2.

[18] *Id.* (all translations in this report are by the author).

[19] *Id.* art. 5.

[20] *Id.*

[24] Loi 78-17 du 6 janvier 1978, *supra* note 1, art. 7.

[25] Douwe Korff, *France*, *in* EUROPEAN COMMISSION, DIRECTORATE GENERAL JUSTICE, FREEDOM AND SECURITY [DG JFS], COMPARATIVE STUDY ON DIFFERENT APPROACHES TO NEW PRIVACY CHALLENGES, IN PARTICULAR IN THE LIGHT OF TECHNOLOGICAL DEVELOPMENTS: COUNTRY STUDIES 4 (May 2010), http://ec.europa.eu/justice/policies/privacy/docs /studies/new_privacy_challenges/final_report_country_report_A3_fr ance.pdf.

[26] CODE DES POSTES ET DES COMMUNICATIONS ÉLECTRONIQUES art. L.34-5, LEGIFRANCE, http://legifrance. gouv.fr/affichCode.do?cidTexte=LEGITEXT000006070987&dateTexte=20120525.

[27] Loi 78-17 du 6 janvier 1978, *supra* note 1, art. 32 I.

[28] *Id.* art. 32 II.

[29] *Id. See also*, *What the Telecoms Package Changes for Cookies*, CNIL (Dec. 20, 2011), http://www.cnil. fr/english/news-and-events/news/article/what-the-telecoms-package-changes-for-cookies/.

[30] Loi 78-17 du 6 janvier 1978, *supra* note 1, art. 38.

[31] CASTETS-RENARD, *supra* note 3, § 108.

[32] *Id.*

[33] Loi 78-17 du 6 janvier 1978, *supra* note 1, art. 39.

[34] *Id.*

[35] *Id.* art. 41.

[36] *Id.* art. 40.

[37] *Id.* art. 6.

[38] *Droit à l'oubli sur Internet: injonction de cesser le traitement et amende de 10,000 euros pour LEXEEK* [*The Right to be Forgotten on the Internet: Injunction to Cease Processing and a €10,000 Fine for LEXEEK*], CNIL (Oct. 10, 2011), http://www.cnil.fr/nc/la-cnil/actu-cnil/article/article/droit-a-loubli-sur-internet-injonction-de-cesserle-traitement-et-amende-de-10000-euros-pour/.

[39] Loi 78-17 du 6 janvier 1978, *supra* note 1, art. 29(III)(1).

[40] *Id.* arts. 23, 24.

[41] *Id.*

[42] *Id.* art. 25.

[43] *Id.* arts. 8, 25.

[44] *Id.* art. 31.

[45] *Id.* art. 6.

[46] *Id.* art. 34.

[47] CNIL, 31E RAPPORT D'ACTIVITE 2010 at 10, http://www.cnil.fr/fileadmin/documents/La_CNIL/ publications/CNIL_rapport_annuel_%202010.pdf.

[48] CNIL, ESPACE JEUNES, http://www.jeunes.cnil.fr/ (last visited May 28, 2012).

[49] CODE DE L'ÉDUCATION art. L.312-15, LEGIFRANCE, http://legifrance.gouv.fr/affichCode.do? cidTexte=LEGITEXT000006071191&dateTexte=20120525.

[50] *Safer Internet Programme: Empowering and Protecting Children Online*, EUROPEAN COMMISSION, INFORMATION SOCIETY, http://ec.europa.eu/information_society/activities/sip/index_en.htm (last visited May 28, 2012).

[51] INTERNET SANS CRAINTE, http://www.internetsanscrainte.fr/le-projet/safer-internet-program (last visited May 28, 2012).

[52] *Id.*

[53] ASSEMBLÉE NATIONALE, RAPPORT D'INFORMATION 3560 SUR LES DROITS DE L'INDIVIDU DANS LA RÉVOLUTION NUMÉRIQUE 209 (2011), http://www.assemblee-nationale.fr/13/pdf/rap-info/i3560.pdf.

[54] *Id.* at 211, 212.

[55] *Id.* at 224–229.

[56] *Id.* at 234.

[57] Loi 78-17 du 6 janvier 1978, *supra* note 1, art. 68.

[58] *Id.* art. 31.

[59] *Id.* art. 69.

[60] CASTETS-RENARD, *supra* note 3, § 197.

[61] *Id.* § 199.

[62] *Id.*

[63] *Le transfert des données à l'étranger* [*The Transfer of Personal Data to Other States*], CNIL, http://www.cnil.fr/vos-responsabilites/le-transfert-de-donnees-a-letranger/ (last visited on May 29, 2012).

[64] Loi 78-17 du 6 janvier 1978, *supra* note 1, arts. 45, 46.

[65] *Id.*

[66] *Id.*

[67] *Id.*

[68] *Id.* art. 47.

[69] *Id.*

[70] CNIL, Délibération N° 2011-035 de la formation restreinte prononçant une sanction pécuniaire à l'encontre de la société GOOGLE Inc. [Deliberation N°2011-035 of the Select Committee Imposing a Fine Against Google], http://www.cnil.fr/fileadmin/documents/La_CNIL/actualite/D2011-035.pdf.

[71] *Google Street View: CNIL Pronounces a Fine of 100,000 Euros*, CNIL (Mar. 21, 2011), http://www.cnil.fr/english/news-and-events/news/article/google-street-view-cnil-pronounces-a-fine-of-100000-euros/.

[72] *Id.*

[73] *Id.*

[74] CODE PÉNAL arts. 226-6 to 226-24, LEGIFRANCE, http://legifrance.gouv.fr/affichCode.do;jsessionid=0241B929941F92D05D0AD6A5AD8C9547.tpdjo13v_1?cidTexte=LEGITEXT000006070719&dateTexte=20120515.

[75] *Id.*

[76] CODE CIVIL art. 9, LEGIFRANCE, http://legifrance.gouv.fr/affichCode.do?cidTexte=LEGITEXT000006070721&dateTexte=20120525.

[77] *Id.* art. 1382.

[78] Directive 2006/24/EC on the Retention of Data Generated or Processed in Connection with the Provision of Publicly Available Electronic Communications Services or of Public Communications Networks, 2006 O.J. (L 105) 54, http://eur-lex.europa.eu/LexUriServ/LexUriServ.do?uri=CELEX:32006L0024:EN:PDF.

[79] CODE DES POSTES ET DES COMMUNICATIONS ÉLECTRONIQUES arts L.34-1(II), L.34-1(III), LEGIFRANCE, http://legifrance.gouv.fr/affichCode.do?cidTexte=LEGITEXT000006070987&dateTexte=20120525.

[80] Loi 2006-64 du 23 janvier 2006 relative à la lutte contre le terrorisme et portant dispositions diverses relatives à la sécurité et aux contrôles frontaliers [Law 2006-64 on Combating Terrorism and on Various Provisions Concerning Security and Borders Controls] art. 7, LEGIFRANCE, http://legifrance.gouv.fr/affichTexte.do?cidTexte=JORFTEXT000000454124&fastPos=1&fastReqId=937565431&categorieLien=id&oldAction=rechTexte.

[81] CODE DES POSTES ET DES COMMUNICATIONS ÉLECTRONIQUES art L.34-1-1.

[82] *Id.* [83] *Id.*

[84] Décret 2006-358 du 24 mars 2006 relatif à la conservation des données des communications électroniques [Decree 2006-358 of March 24, 2006, on the Retention of Telecommunication Data], LEGIFRANCE, http://legifrance.gouv.fr/affichTexte.do?cidTexte=JORFTEXT000000637071&fastPos=2&fastReqId=1762290333 &categorieLien=id&oldAction=rechTexte.

[85] *Id.* art. 1.

[86] Loi 2009-669 du 12 juin 2009 favorisant la diffusion et la protection de la création sur internet [Law 2009-669 of June 12, 2009, on Favoring the Dissemination and the Protection of Creation on the Internet] art. 5, LEGIFRANCE, http://legifrance.gouv.fr/affichTexte.do?cidTexte=JORFTEXT000020735432&fastPos=2&fastReqId=1456457676 &categorieLien=id&oldAction=rechTexte.

[87] *Id.*
[88] Loi 78-17 du 6 janvier 1978, *supra* note 1, art. 11.
[89] CNIL, LA CNIL EN BREF 2, 3 (2011), http://www.cnil.fr/fileadmin/documents/Guides_pratiques/CNIL_EN_BREF-VFVD.pdf.
[90] Loi 78-17 du 6 janvier 1978, *supra* note 1, art. 13.
[91] *Id.* arts. 11, 12.
[92] *Id.* art. 11.
[93] *Id.* art. 44.
[94] *Quel programme des contrôles pour 2012* [*What is the Program of On-site Inspections for 2012*], CNIL (Apr. 19, 2012), http://www.cnil.fr/la-cnil/actualite/article/article/quel-programme-des-controles-pour-2012/.
[95] Loi 78-17 du 6 janvier 1978, *supra* note 1, art. 11.
[96] *Id.* art. 49.
[97] CNIL, 31E RAPPORT D'ACTIVITE 2010 at 13, http://www.cnil.fr/fileadmin/documents/La_CNIL/publications/CNIL_rapport_annuel_%202010.pdf.
[98] CASTETS-RENARD, *supra* note 3, § 101.
[99] CNIL, *supra* note 23.
[100] Case C-275/06 Productores de Música de Espãna (Promisicae) v. Telefónica de Espãna SAU, 2008 E.C.R. I-271, http://curia.europa.eu/juris/document/document.jsf;jsessionid=9ea7d0f130d5ddebd4124ad947878958e2b45700f2cb.e34KaxiLc3eQc40LaxqMbN4Oa3aQe0?text=&docid=70107&pageIndex=0&doclang=EN&mode=doc&dir=&occ=first&part=1&cid=2187029.
[101] Directive 2006/24/EC of the European Parliament and of the Council of 15 March 2006 on the Retention of Data Generated or Processed in Connection with the Provision of Publicly Available Electronic Communications Services or of Public Communications Networks and Amending Directive 2002/58/EC, 2006 O.J. (L 105) 54, http://eur-lex.europa.eu/LexUriServ/LexUriServ.do?uri=CELEX:32006L0024:EN:PDF.
[102] Cour de Cassation [Cass.] crim., Arrêt 3530 du 16 juin 2009 (n° 08-88.560), http://www.courdecassation.fr/jurisprudence_2/chambre_criminelle_578/3530_16_15171.html.
[103] *Id.*
[104] *71% des Français jugent la protection de la vie privée sur Internet insuffisante* [*71% of French People Find the Protection of Private Life Insufficient on Internet*], CNIL (Oct. 13, 2008), http://www.cnil.fr/la-cnil/actualite/article/article/71-des-francais-jugent-la-protection-de-la-vie-privee-sur-internet-insuffisante/.
[105] SENAT, RAPPORT DU SENAT 441 (2008–2009), LA VIE PRIVEE A L'HEURE DES MEMOIRES NUMERIQUES. POUR UNE CONFIANCE RENFORCEE ENTRE CITOYENS ET SOCIETE DE L'INFORMATION [PRIVATE LIFE AND DIGITAL MEMORIES. FOR A REINFORCED CONFIDENCE BETWEEN CITIZENS AND THE TECHNOLOGY SOCIETY] 34, 35, http://www.senat.fr/rap/r08-441/r08-4411.pdf.
[106] *Portrait Marc L. paru dans le volume 28 du Tigre (novembre-decembre 2008)* [*Portrait of Marc L. Published in Volume 28 of the Tigre (November-December)*], *in* CNIL, 29E RAPPORT D'ACTIVITÉ 2008 at 123, http://www.cnil.fr/fileadmin/documents/La_CNIL/publications/CNIL-29erapport_2008.pdf.
[107] Laure Bélot, *Les données privées sont le carburant du numérique* [*Private Data is Digital Fuel*], LEMONDE.FR (May 21, 2012), http://www.lemonde.fr/vous/article/2012/05/21/les-donnees-privees-sont-lecarburant-du-numerique_1704823_3238.html (last visited 05/29/2012).
[108] SENAT, RAPPORT DU SENAT 441, *supra* note 105.
[109] Proposition de loi visant à mieux garantir le droit à la vie privée à l'heure du numérique [Draft Law to Better Guarantee the Right to Privacy in the Digital Age] No. 93, Sénat Session Ordinaire de 2009–2010, http://www.senat.fr/leg/ppl09-093.html.
[110] *Id.* art. 3.
[111] *Id.* art. 6.
[112] *Id.* art. 12.
[113] *Id.* art. 8.

End Notes for Germany

[1] Telemediengesetz [TMG] [Telemedia Act], Feb. 26, 2007, BUNDESGESETZBLATT [BGBL.] I at 179, *as last amended by* Gesetz, May 31, 2010, BGBL. I at 692, §§ 11–16, http://www.gesetze-im-internet.de/tmg/index.html.

[2] TMG § 1.

[3] DIRK HECKMANN, INTERNETRECHT Ch. 1.1 60–65 (3rd ed. 2011, updated through June 15, 2012), *available at* http://www.juris.de (by subscription).

[4] Bundesdatenschutzgesetz [BDSG] [Federal Data Protection Act], repromulgated Jan. 14, 2003, BGBL. I at 66, *as last amended by* Gesetz, Aug. 14, 2009, BGBL. I at 2814, http://www.gesetze-im-internet.de/bdsg_1990/ index.html.

[5] TMG § 12(2).

[6] Telekommunikationsgesetz [TKG] [Telecommunications Act], June 22, 2004, BGBL. I at. 1190, *as last amended by* Gesetz, May 3, 2012, BGBL. I at 958, §§ 91–107, http://www.gesetze-im-internet.de/tkg_2004/ index.html.

[7] Directive 95/46/EC, of the European Parliament and of the Council of 24 October 1995 on the Protection of Individuals with Regard to the Processing of Personal Data and on the Free Movement of Such Data, 1995 O.J. (L 281) 31, http://eur-lex.europa.eu/LexUriServ/LexUriServ.do?uri=CELEX:31995L0046:en:HTML.

[8] *Id.*, recital 68.

[9] *Id.*, recital 9.

[10] For instance by differentiating between contract data and utilization data. TMG §§ 14 & 15. *See also* Kerstin Tscherpe *in* KOMMENTAR ZUM BDSG 1103 (Jürgen Taeger & Detlev Gabel, eds. 2010).

[11] Directive 95/46 art. 3 (1).

[12] Directive 2002/58/EC of the European Parliament and of the Council of 12 July 2002 Concerning the Processing of Personal Data and the Protection of Privacy in the Electronic Communications Sector, 2002 O.J. (L 201) 37, http://eur-lex.europa.eu/LexUriServ/LexUriServ.do?uri=CELEX:32002L0058:EN:PDF.

[13] TKG §§ 87–116.

[14] Directive 2006/24/EC on the Retention of Data Generated or Processed in Connection with the Provision of Publicly Available Electronic Communications Services or of Public Communications Networks, 2006 O.J. (L 105) 54, http://eur-lex.europa.eu/LexUriServ/LexUriServ.do?uri=CELEX:32006L0024:EN:PDF.

[15] TKG, *as amended by* Gesetz, Dec. 21, 2007, BGBL. I at 3198.

[16] Bundesverfassungsgericht [BVerfG], Mar. 2, 2010, 125 ENTSCHEIDUNGEN DES BUNDESVERF ASSUNGSGERICHTS [BVERFGE] 260.

[17] *Brüssel verklagt Deutschland auf 300,000 Euro täglich,* FRANKFURTER ALLGEMEINE ZEITUNG [FAZ], June 1, 2012, at 1.

[18] Directive 2009/136/EC on Universal Service and User's Rights Relating to Electronic Communications Networks and Services, 2009 O.J. (L 377) 11, http://eur-lex.europa.eu/LexUriServ/LexUriServ.do?uri=OJ:L:2009: 337:0011:0036:EN:PDF.

[19] TKG-Änderungsgesetz, May 3, 2012, BGBL I at 958; *see also* Bernd Holznagel, *Das neue TKG: Im Mittelpunkt steht der Verbraucher*, NEUE JURISTISCHE WOCHENSCHRIFT [NJW] 1622 (2012).

[20] Directive 2009/136 art. 5(1).

[21] For the U.S., *see* ARTHUR MILLER, THE ASSAULT ON PRIVACY 225 (1971); for Germany, *see* Jürgen Taeger & Berndt Schmidt, *in* KOMMENTAR, *supra* note 10, at 3.

[22] Datenschutzgesetz [Data Protection Act], Oct. 7, 1970, HESSISCHES GESETZ-UND VERORDNUNGSBLATT I at 625.

[23] Taeger & Schmidt, in KOMMENTAR, *supra* note 10, at 4.

[24] Gesetz zum Missbrauch personenbezogener Daten bei der Datenverarbeitung [Act Concerning the Abuse of Data in Data Processing], Jan. 27, 1977, BGBL I at 201.

[25] Bundesverfassungsgericht [BVerfG], Dec. 15, 1983, 65 Entscheidungen des Bundesverfassungsgerichts [BVerfGE] 1. For a summary in English, *see* DONALD P. KOMMERS, THE CONSTITUTIONAL JURISPRUDENCE OF THE FEDERAL REPUBLIC OF GERMANY 299 (1997).

[26] In 2001, the BDSG was amended to transpose Directive 95/46; in 2009, a major amendment introduced provisions on "scoring" and "rating." *See* Taeger & Schmidt *in* KOMMENTAR, *supra* note 10, at 6.

[27] Thomas Hoeren, Ein Lob für Frau Reding, – der neue Entwurf zur allgemeinen Europäischen Datenschutzverordnung [Praise for Ms. Reding – the New Draft on the General European Data Protection Regulation], BETRIEBS-BERATER [BB] Die erste Seite 2012, no. 8.

[28] Douwe Korff, *Germany*, *in* European Commission, Directorate General Justice, Freedom and Security [DG JFS], Comparative Study on Different Approaches to New Privacy Challenges, in Particular in the Light of Technological Developments: Country Studies A.4 (May 2010), http://ec.europa.eu/justice/policies/privacy/docs/studies/new_privacy_challenges/final_report_country_report_A4_germany.pdf.

[29] BDSG § 29.

[30] HECKMANN, *supra* note 3, at ch. 9 31.

[31] BDSG § 1.

[32] BDSG § 38.

[33] HECKMANN, *supra* note 3, at ch. 9, ¶ 85.

[34] BDSG § 4d.

[35] BDSG § 38.

[36] TMG § 12(1).

[37] TMG § 12(2).

[38] TMG § 14.

[39] TMG § 13(2).

[40] HECKMANN, *supra* note 3, ch. 9, 194.

[41] BDSG § 4(3).

[42] BDSG § 3(1).

[43] HECKMANN, *supra* note 3, ch. 9, 118.

[44] GERALD SPINDLER & FABIAN SCHUSTER, RECHT DER ELEKTRONISCHEN MEDIEN 1554 (2nd ed. 2011).

[45] BDSG § 3a.

[46] HECKMANN, *supra* note 3, ch. 9, 316.

[47] *Id.* 303–05.

[48] TMG § 15.

[49] Jochen Schneider, *Hemmnis für einen modernen Datenschutz: Das Verbotsprinzip* [*Impediment for Modern Data Protection: The Prohibition Principle*], ANWALTSBLATT [ANWBL] 233 n.2 (2011).

[50] See Korff, *supra* note 28, at 20.

[51] Wolfgang Däubler et al., Bundesdatenschutzgesetz 497 (2010).

[52] Benedikt Buchner, *in* KOMMENTAR, *supra* note 10, at 74.

[53] BDSG § 3(9); Directive 95/46 art. 8.

[54] Directive 965/46, art. 20; BDSG § 4d(5).

[55] BVerfG, July 16, 1969, 27 BverfGE 19.

[56] Taeger & Schmidt, *in* KOMMENTAR, *supra* note 10, at 14.

[57] BDSG §§ 28–30.

[58] *Federal Association for Information Technology, Telecommunications, and New Media*, BITKOM (2012), http://www.bitkom.org/en/.

[59] *Schufa will Internet für Personenprofile auswerten* [*Schufa Wants to Exploit the Internet for Personal Profiling*], FAZ 9 (June 8, 2012).

[60] BERLINER KOMMENTAR ZUM TELEKOMMUNIKATIONSGESETZ 2325 (Franz, Säcker ed., 2nd ed. 2009).

[61] TKG §§ 96 & 98.

[62] HECKMANN, *supra* note 3, ch. 9, 492.

[63] Thilo Weichert, *Datenschutz und Meinungsfreiheit* [*Data Protection and Freedom of Opinion*], ANWBL. 252, 254 (2011).

[64] Til Pörksen, *Der Einsatz von RFID Chips für Location Based Services* [*The Use of Radio Frequency Identification Technology for Location-Based Services*], ANWZERT ITR 4/2009, http://www.juris.de (by subscription).

[65] Kammergericht Berlin [Berlin Appellate Court] Mar. 15, 2011, Docket No. 10 W 127/10, http://www.juris.de (by subscription).

[66] Ole Reissman, *W-Lan-Mitschnitte - Google gesteht Datenpanne bei Street View* [*Wi-Fi Data Collection, Google Admits Street View Data Mistake*], SPIEGELONLINE (May 15, 2010), http://www.spiegel.de/netzwelt/netzpolitik/w-lan-mitschnitte-google-gesteht-datenpanne-bei-street-view-a-694885.html.

[67] Weichert, *supra* note 63.

[68] Bitkom, *supra* note 58.

[69] Bundesministerium des Inneren, *Bundesinnenminister stellt Gesetzentwurf zur "roten Linie" vor und nimmt Datenschutz-Kodex in Empfang* [*Federal Minister of the Interior Presents Draft Law on "Red Line" and*

Accepts Data Protection Codex], BUNDESMINISTERIUM DES INNERN (Dec. 1, 2010), http://www.bmi.bund.de/Shared Docs/Kurzmeldungen/ DE/2010/11/Daten schutzkodex RoteLinie.html.

[70] DIE HAMBURGISCHE BEAUFTRAGTE FÜR DATENSCHUTZ UND INFORMATIONSFREIHEIT, MEINE DATEN KRIEGT IHR NICHT, http://www.datenschutz-hamburg.de/uploads/media/Broschuere_ Meine_Daten_kriegt_ ihr_nicht.pdf (last visited July 8, 2012).

[71] *Die EU-Initiative Klicksafe*, KLICKSAFE.DE, http://www.klicksafe.de/ueber-klicksafe/dieinitiative/projektinfo/ (last visited June 25, 2012).

[72] Jugendschutzgesetz, July 23, 2002, BGBL., I at 2739, *as amended.*

[73] These requirements are further specified in BDSG, Anlage 1 zu § 9 [App. 1 to § 9].

[74] Jyn Schultze-Melling, *in* KOMMENTAR, *supra* note 10, at 390–94.

[75] TMG § 15a & BDSG § 42a.

[76] HECKMANN, *supra* note 3, ch. 9, 420.

[77] Legislative intent required notification for tangible detriments such as disclosure of banking information as well as social detriments such as identity fraud. *See* HECKMANN, *supra* note 3, ch. 9, 426.

[78] Directive 2009/136 arts. 2(1), 2(4).

[79] Flemming Moos, *in* KOMMENTAR *supra* note 10, at 1139.

[80] BDSG § 3a.

[81] For the telemedia sector, *see* SPINDLER & SCHUSTER, *supra* note 44, at 1551.

[82] *Id.*

[83] TMG § 13(6).

[84] *Id.*

[85] BDSG § 35(2).

[86] HECKMANN, *supra* note 3, ch. 9, 504–506.

[87] *Id.*

[88] Korff, *supra* note 28, at 46. Tort liability arises in particular from a failure to notify of security breaches. *See supra* notes 75–77 and accompanying text. *See also* HECKMANN, *supra* note 3, ch. 9, 433.

[89] Schneider, *supra* note 49, at 237. Damages for pain and suffering are available for public sector violations. *See* BDSG, § 8.

[90] Korff , *supra* note 28, at 47.

[91] *Id.*

[92] TMG § 16.

[93] Moos, *supra* note 79, at 1137.

[94] BDSG § 43.

[95] *Id.* § 44.

[96] *Id.* § 1(5). Germany also applies this principle to controllers residing in one of the European Economic Area Countries (Iceland, Liechtenstein, and Norway); *see* also Korff, *supra* note 28, at 9.

[97] BDSG § 1(5). These rules also apply to data that are governed by the privacy provisions of the TMG. *See* Moos, *supra* note 79, at 1059.

[98] Alexander Dix, Datenschutzkontrolle im Internet – unmöglich? [Data Protection Control on the Internet – Impossible?], Lecture at a 2008 Summer Academy on Internet Privacy (Sept. 1, 2008), http://www.datenschutzberlin.de/attachments/518/Sommerakademie_2008. pdf?1221566444.

[99] Philippe Gröschel, *Bedrohen soziale Netzwerke den Datenschutz?* [*Do Social Media Threaten Data Protection?*], ANWBL. 276 (2011).

[100] BDSG § 4b(1).

[101] There are, however, many exceptions. *See* Detlev Gabel, *in* KOMMENTAR, *supra* note 10, at 165.

[102] *Id.*

[103] Press Release, Unabhängiges Landeszentrum für Datenschutz Schleswig-Holstein, ULD zum FacebookAudit des irischen Datenschutzbeauftragten: Erkenntnisse stützen weiteres Vorgehen des ULD [Independent Data Protection Office for Schleswig-Holstein [ULD] on the Facebook Audit of the Irish Data Protection Commissioner: Findings Support Further ULD Action] (Dec. 22, 2011), https://www.datenschutzzentrum.de /presse/20111222- facebook-irland.htm.

[104] HECKMANN, *supra* note 3, ch. 9, 539.

[105] *Id.*, ch. 9, 270–274.

[106] BDSG §§ 22–26.

[107] *Über uns*, LANDESBEAUFTRAGTER FÜR DATENSCHUTZ UND INFORMATIONSFREIHEIT NORD RHEINWESTFALEN, https://www.ldi.nrw.de/mainmenu_Ueberuns/index.php (last visited June 27, 2012).

[108] BDSG § 38–38a.

[109] Judgment of the ECJ, Grand Chamber, Mar. 9, 2010, European Commission v. Federal Republic of Germany, Case C-518/07, http://curia.europa.eu/juris/liste.jsf?language=en&num=C-518/07.

[110] DER BAYERISCHE LANDESBEAUFTRAGTE FÜR DEN DATENSCHUTZ INFORMIERT 17 (2009/2010), http://www.datenschutz-bayern.de/tbs/tb24/tb24.pdf.

[111] BDSG § 4d–4e.

[112] Landesbeauftragter für Datenschutz, *supra* note 107.

[113] BDSG § 38(1).

[114] These Resolutions are available on the webpages of the state data protection authorities, as, for instance, that of the state of Hesse, http://www.datenschutz.hessen.de/beschluesse.htm (click on Beschlüsse des Düsseldorfer Kreises) (last visited July 13, 2012).

[115] As described in HECKMANN, *supra* note 3, ch. 9, 547. The resolution appears to be no longer available online.

[116] *Id.*

[117] *Id.* 548.

[118] Beschluss des Düsseldorfer Kreises vom 8. Dezember 2011, *Datenschutz in sozialen Netzwerken, [Data Protection in Social Media]*, http://www.bfdi.bund.de/SharedDocs/Publikationen/Entschliessungssammlung/DuesseldorferKreis/08122011DSInSozialenNetzwerken.html?nn=409242.

[119] Interview by Michael Hahnfeld with Thilo Weichert, Datenschutzbeauftragter des Landes Schleswig Holstein, *Facebook hat ein Problem* [*Facebook has a Problem*], FAZ 33 (May 18, 2012).

[120] Grundgesetz für die Bundesrepublik Deutschland [GG] [Basic Law] May 23, 1949, BGBL. 1, arts. 1(1), 2(1).

[121] BVerfG, July 16, 1969, BVerfGE 27, 1; for a summary, *see* EVELIEN BROUWER, DIGITAL BORDERS AND REAL RIGHTS 417 (2008).

[122] BVerfG, Dec. 15, 1983, *supra* note 25.

[123] BVerfG, Feb. 27, 2008, 120 BVERFGE 274.

[124] BRUNO SCHMIDT-BLEIBTREU ET AL., GRUNDGESETZ 103 (12th ed. 2010).

[125] BVerfG, *supra* note 16.

[126] Grundgesetz für die Bundesrepublik Deutschland, [Basic Law], May 23, 1949, BGBL. 1, art. 10, *as amended.*

[127] Bundesgerichtshof [BGH], June 23, 2009, Docket No. VI ZR 196/08, http://juris.bundesgerichtshof. de/cgi-bin/rechtsprechung/document.py?Gericht=bgh&Art=en&sid=e299e63452248193f28e4ef4031e7ae7&nr=48601&pos=16&anz=23.

[128] BGH, May 8, 2012, Docket No. VI ZR 217/08., http://juris.bundesgerichtshof.de/cgibin/rechtsprechung/document.py?Gericht=bgh&Art=pm&Datum=2012&Sort=3&anz=59&pos=0&nr=60505&linked=urt&Blank=1&file=dokument.pdf.

[129] *Suchmaschinen-Optimierung leicht gemacht* [*Search Engine Optimization Made Easy]*, http://suchmaschinenoptimierung.michaelsattler.de/suchmaschinen.html (last visited July 13, 2012).

[130] Marion Müller, *Mediennutzung in Deutschland*, DIE AKTIENGESELLSCHAFT R 161 (2012).

[131] *Planet der Freundschaft* [*Planet of Friendship*], DER SPIEGEL 133 (May 7, 2012).

[132] *Post Privacy Debatte: Ist Privatsphäre noch zeitgemäss?*, STERN.DE (Mar. 24, 2011), http://www.stern.de/digital/online/post-privacy-debatte-ist-privatsphaere-noch-zeitgemaess-1667312.html.

[133] Gröschel, *supra* note 99; Indra Spiecker, *Kommunikation als Herausforderung: Neue Wege für Datenschutz* [*Communication as a Challenge: New Paths for Data Protection*], ANWBL 256 (2011); Schneider, *supra* note 49.

[134] HECKMANN, *supra* note 3, ch. 9, 68–72.

[135] Reinhard Müller, *Verschwimmende Grenzen – Altes Recht und neue Medien: Brauchen wir eine neue Ordnung?* [*Blurred Borders – Old Law and New Media: Do We Need a New Order?*], FAZ 10 (June 11, 2012).

[136] Thorsten Feldmann, *Datenschutz und Meinungsfreiheit: Regulierung ohne BDSG* [*Data Protection and Freedom of Opinion: Regulation Without FDPA*], ANWBL 250 (2011); Thilo Weichert, *Datenschutz und Meinungsfreiheit: Regulierung im BDSG* [*Data Protection and Freedom of Opinion: Regulation in FDPA*], ANWBL 253 (2011); Spiecker, *supra* note 133.

[137] Gröschel, *supra* note 99; Spiecker, *supra* note 133.

[138] Dix, *supra* note 98.

[139] HECKMANN *supra* note 3, ch. 9, 73.

[140] Ixquick, https://ixquick.com/deu/company-background.html, known in the U.S. as Startpage, http://www.startpage.com (both last visited July 13, 2012).

[141] Frank Koch, *Schutz der Persönlichkeit im Internet: spezifische Gefährdungen* [*Protection of Personhood in the Internet:Specific Dangers*], DER IT RECHTSBERATER 158 (2011).

[142] Gröschel, *supra* note 99.

[143] Spiecker, *supra* note 133.

[144] Schneider, *supra* note 49.

[145] Bundesrat Drucksache 156/11, June 17, 2011.

[146] Christopher Brosch, *Die Umsetzung der Cookie-Richtlinie* [*The Transposition of the Cookie Directive*], AnwZert ITR 16/2011, Anm. 2, http://www.juris.de (by subscription).

[147] *Id.*

[148] Proposal for a Regulation of the European Parliament and of the Council on the Protection of Individuals with Regard to the Processing of Personal Data and on the Free Movement of Such Data (General Data Protection Regulation), COM (2012) 11 final (Jan. 15, 2012), http://eur-lex.europa.eu/LexUriServ/LexUriServ.do?uri=COM:2012:0011:FIN:EN:PDF.

[149] Bundsebeauftragter für den Datenschutz und die Informationsfreiheit, *Europäischer Startschuss für die Datenschutzreform* [*European Starting Shot for Data Protection Reform*], (May 7, 2012), http://www.bfdi.bund.de/ DE/Oeffentlichkeitsarbeit/RedenUndInterviews/2012/DuDGastbeitrag 2012.html?nn=408922.

[150] Interview with Thilo Weichert, *supra* note 119 (translation by author).

[151] *Verfassungs- und Europa Ausschuss, Widerstand gegen die geplante EU Datenschutzverordnung* [*Bavarian Parliament, Opposition to the Planned EU Data Protection Regulation*], BAYERISCHER LANDTAG (Mar. 1, 2012), http://www.bayern.landtag.de/cps/rde/xchg/landtag/x/-/www1/7538_8746.htm.

[152] *UK Ranks 21st in Europe for Privacy Protection*, INFORMATION AGE (Jan. 24, 2012), http://www.information-age.com/channels/security-and-continuity/news/1687058/uk-ranks-21st-in-europe-forprivacy-protection-.thtml.

End Notes for Israel

[1] Basic Law: Human Dignity and Liberty, SEFER HAHUKIM [SH] No. 1391, 5752 (Mar. 25, 1992), *as amended*, http://www.knesset.gov.il/laws/special/eng/basic3_eng.htm. Israel does not have a written constitution contained in one document. Based on the 1951 Harari Knesset (Israel's Parliament) Resolution, Israel's Basic Laws were intended to form chapters in its future constitution. *See* "The Harari Proposal," *in The Constitution*, THE KNESSET, http://www.knesset.gov.il/description/eng/eng_mimshal_hoka.htm#4 (last visited May 16, 2012). Basic Law: Human Dignity and Liberty as well as Basic Law: Freedom of Occupation, both enacted in 1992, however, contain provisions that have been interpreted by the Supreme Court as providing the Court with the authority to repeal statutory legislation that conflicts with the Laws' provisions.

[2] The Privacy Protection Law, 5741-1981, 35 LAWS OF THE STATE OF ISRAEL [LSI] 136 (5741-1980/81), *as amended*, up-to-date version *available at* NEVO LEGAL DATABASE, http://www.nevo.co.il (in Hebrew; by subscription).

[3] Basic Law: Human Dignity and Liberty § 7, SH No. 1391, 5752 (Mar. 25, 1992), *as amended.*

[4] *Id.* § 8.

[5] Michael Birnhack & Niva Elkin-Koren, *Does Law Matter Online? Empirical Evidence on Privacy Law Compliance*, 17 MICH. TELECOMM. TECH. L. REV. 337, 351 (2011), http://www.mttlr.org/volseventeen/birnhack &elkin-koren.pdf.

[6] Criminal Procedure (Enforcement Authorities–Telecommunication Data) Law, 5768-2007, SH No. 2122 p. 72.

[7] The Privacy Protection Law § 1.

[8] Note that references to "him" or "he" throughout this report are intended to be gender equal.

[9] Protection of Privacy Law (Amendment No. 11) 5771-2011, http://www.knesset.gov.il/privatelaw/data/18/3/358_3_3.rtf; *see* Ruth Levush, *Israel: Prohibition on Publishing Photos of Injured or Deceased*, GLOBAL LEGAL MONITOR (Apr. 22, 2011), http://www.loc.gov/lawweb/servlet/lloc_news?disp3_l205402640_text.

[10] The Privacy Protection Law §§ 2, 2A.

[11] *Id.* § 7.

[12] In a leading decision on interpretation of the authorities of the Registrar of Databases under the PPL, the Supreme Court determined that the Registrar's authority to enforce the PPL enables him to check, at the time of registration, the legality of the collection, storage, and use of online data also under Chapter A, which deals with collection of data without consent, thereby applying Chapter A requirements to databases that are specifically regulated under Chapter B of the PPL. CA 439/88 Database Registrar v. Ventura, 48(3) PD 808, 821 (1994).

[13] The Privacy Protection Law § 11.

[14] *Id.* § 17C.
[15] *Id.* § 17F.
[16] *Id.*
[17] Attorney General's Directives Regarding Transfer of Information from Telephone Companies to Bodies with Investigation Authority 2 (Feb. 16, 2003, revised May 16, 2007), MINISTRY OF JUSTICE, http://www.justice.gov.il/NR/rdonlyres/AEA86927-F41F-4CA2-BAC4-4E0A6EE1042A/0/42101.pdf (in Hebrew; translation by author).
[18] *Id.*
[19] *Id.* at 6 (translation by author).
[20] The Privacy Protection Law § 7.
[21] *Id.* § 8(d).
[22] *Id.* § 8(c).
[23] *Id.* § 7.
[24] *Id.* §§ 8(c), 17C.
[25] *Id.* §§ 9, 12, 23.
[26] *Id.* §§ 12, 9.
[27] *Id.* § 13(a).
[28] *Id.* § 13(c).
[29] For information on the Mossad's objectives *see* ISRAEL SECRET INTELLIGENCE SERVICE WEBSITE, http://www.mossad.gov.il/Eng/AboutUs.aspx (last visited May 7, 2012).
[30] The Privacy Protection Law §§ 13(e)(1), 19(c).
[31] *Id.* § 13(e)(1a, 3).
[32] *Id.* § 13(e)(3–6).
[33] *See* Letter from Yoram HaCohen, Registrar of Databases, to Attorney Doron Avni, Representative of Google in Israel, Approving a Request for Registration of Street View Data Database (Aug. 10, 2011), *available at* http://www.justice.gov.il/NR/rdonlyres/59E17B6B-DD61-4834-BA32-65FFF247C501/29525/streetview.pdf (in Hebrew). ILITA's role and authority are discussed in more detail in Section III, "Role of Data Protection Agencies," below.
[34] *ILITA Authorized Google to Operate Street View in Israel*, MINISTRY OF JUSTICE, ILITA, http://www.justice.gov. il/MOJEng/ILITA/News/googlestreetview.htm (last visited May 11, 2012).
[35] *Id.*
[36] *Id.*
[37] Prevention of Sexual Harassment Law, 5758-1998, SH 5758 No. 1661 p. 166 (1998), *as amended.*
[38] Penal Law, 5737-1977, §§ 214, 368A, LSI SPECIAL VOLUME, *as amended* (hereinafter Penal Law).
[39] *Id.* § 34W.
[40] ILITA, Request for Comments: Ethical and Behavioral Rules for Database Owners Who Collect Information on Minors (Dec. 2010), http://www.justice.gov.il/NR/rdonlyres/92556C61-AD16-4602-870F182902AC9ABA/24159/minorsdataposition.pdf.
[41] The Privacy Protection Law § 4.
[42] *Id.* § 5.
[43] *Id.* § 29A.
[44] *Id.* § 18.
[45] *Id.* § 31A.
[46] *Id.* § 29.
[47] *See* Penal Law § 7.
[48] *ILITA Authorized Google to Operate Street View in Israel*, *supra* note 34.
[49] *About ILITA*, MINISTRY OF JUSTICE, ILITA, http://www.justice.gov.il/PrivacyGenerations/about_ilita.htm (last visited May 8, 2012).
[50] *Id.*
[51] *Id.*
[52] In its January 31, 2011, decision pursuant to Directive 95/46/EC of the European Parliament and of the Council on the adequate protection of personal data by the State of Israel with regard to automated processing of personal data, the European Commission held that "[f]or the purposes of Article 25(2) of Directive 95/46/EC, the State of Israel is considered as providing an adequate level of protection for personal data transferred from the European Union in relation to automated international transfers of personal data from the European Union or, where they are not automated, they are subject to further automated processing in the State of Israel."

Commission Decision of 31 January 2011, 2011 OFFICIAL JOURNAL OF THE EUROPEAN UNION (L 27) 39, http://eurlex.europa.eu/LexUriServ/LexUriServ.do?uri=OJ:L:2011:027:0039:0042:EN:PDF (2011/61/EU).

[53] *Id.*

[54] Basic Law: Human Dignity and Liberty § 7, SH No. 1391, 5752 (Mar. 25, 1992), *as amended.*

[55] *Id.* § 8.

[56] HC 8070/98 Association for Human Rights in Israel v. Minister of Interior, 58(4) Piske Din [PD] [Decisions of the Supreme Court] 842 (2004).

[57] *Id.*

[58] *Id.* at 855.

[59] CA 86/89 State of Israel v. Bank HaPoalim, 24(2) PD 726, 731, para. 10 (5750/51-1990), *as translated by* IAN BOURNE, A GUIDE TO DATA PROTECTION IN ISRAEL 9 (Twinning Project IS/2007/ENPAP/JH/019, Jan. 2010), http://www.justice.gov.il/NR/rdonlyres/C7DE27A2-4CC2-4C5E-9047-C86CC70BD50B/18333 /Aguide todataprotectioninIsrael1.pdf. Note that Bourne translates the cited law's name as the "Protection of Privacy Act" (PPA) rather than as the "Privacy Protection Law" (PPL).

[60] CA 439/88 Database Registrar v. Ventura, 48(3) PD 808, 821 (1994).

[61] CA 9893/06 Laufer v. State of Israel (Dec. 31, 2007), NEVO LEGAL DATABASE (by subscription).

[62] Request for CA 4447/07 Mor v. Barak ITC, para. 16 (Mar. 25, 2010), NEVO LEGAL DATABASE (by subscription; translation by author).

[63] BOURNE, *supra* note 59, at 20.

[64] MICHAEL BIRENHAKAND, THE RIGHT TO PRIVACY BETWEEN LAW AND TECHNOLOGY 474 (2011).

[65] ILITA, MINISTRY OF JUSTICE, PROTECTION OF INFORMATION AT THE WORKPLACE, http://www.justice.gov.il/NR/rdonlyres/C9073FCB-3E0E-4791-99E1-131FF731FF09/34744/employerguide.pdf (in Hebrew; last visited May 8, 2012).

[66] *Id.* at 3, para. 1.

[67] *Id.* para. 2.

[68] ILITA, MINISTRY OF JUSTICE, *supra* note 65, at 3–4.

[69] *Id.*

[70] Request for Comments: Ethical and Behavioral Rules, *supra* note 40.

[71] KNESSET INFORMATION AND RESEARCH CENTER, CHILDREN IN SOCIAL MEDIA ON THE INTERNET 19 (May 23, 2011), http://www.knesset.gov.il/mmm/data/pdf/m02856.pdf.

[72] Request for Comments: Ethical and Behavioral Rules, *supra* note 40.

End Notes for Italy

[1] GIUSEPPE CASSANO, DIRITTO DELLE NUOVE TECNOLOGIE INFORMATICHE E DELL'INTERNET [NEW INFORMATION TECHNOLOGY AND INTERNET LAW] 128 (Ipsoa, 2002).

[2] Corte di Cassazione [Cass.] 12 aprile 1973, n. 38, Corte Costituzionale [Corte Cost.], 1973, I, 354.

[3] CASSANO, *supra* note 1, at 130.

[4] Cass. 27 maggio 1975, n. 2129, Giurisprudenza Italiana [Giur. it.], 1976, I, 1, 970.

[5] ROCCO PANETTA, LIBERA CIRCOLAZIONE E PROTEZIONE DEI DATI PERSONALI [FREEDOM OF MOVEMENT AND PERSONAL DATA PROTECTION] 6 (Giuffrè, 2006).

[6] Legge 31 dicembre 1996, n. 675, GAZETTA UFFICIALE DELLA REPUBBLICA ITALIANA [G.U.] 8 gennaio 1997, n. 5.

[7] Directive 95/46/EC, of the European Parliament and of the Council of 24 October 1995 on the Protection of Individuals with Regard to the Processing of Personal Data and on the Free Movement of Such Data, 1995 O.J. (L 281) 31, http://eur-lex.europa.eu/LexUriServ/LexUriServ.do?uri=CELEX:31995L0046:en:HTML.

[8] Decreto Legislativo [D. Lgs.] n. 196 del 30 giugno 2003, G.U. 29 luglio 2003, n. 174.

[9] Directive 2002/58/EC of the European Parliament and of the Council of 12 July 2002 Concerning the Processing of Personal Data and the Protection of Privacy in the Electronic Communications Sector, 2002 O.J. (L 201) 37, http://eur-lex.europa.eu/LexUriServ/LexUriServ.do?uri=CELEX:32002L0058:en:HTML.

[10] Art. 1 Codice in Materia di Protezione dei Dati Personali [C.m.p.], http://www.garanteprivacy.it/garante/doc.jsp?ID=1311248.

[11] Art. 2 C.m.p.

[12] Art. 4.2 C.m.p. (all Code translations by author).
[13] *Id.*
[14] *Id.*
[15] PANETTA, *supra* note 5, at 1563.
[16] Art. 5 C.m.p.
[17] *Id.*
[18] Art. 122 C.m.p.
[19] PANETTA, *supra* note 5, at 1564.
[20] Art. 122 C.m.p.
[21] Art. 4 C.m.p.
[22] Art. 126 C.m.p.
[23] *Id.*
[24] Art. 4 C.m.p.
[25] Art. 123 C.m.p.
[26] Art. 132.1 C.m.p., as amended by D. Lgs. 30 maggio 2008, n. 109, G.U. 18 giugno 2008, n. 141, implementing Directive 2006/24/EC.
[27] Art. 132.3 C.m.p.
[28] Art. 132.4 C.m.p.
[29] Art. 132.5 C.m.p.
[30] Art. 133 C.m.p.
[31] Art. 13 C.m.p.
[32] Art. 32 C.m.p.
[33] *Id.*
[34] Art. 34 C.m.p. (footnotes dropped).
[35] Art. 8 C.m.p.
[36] *Id.*
[37] *Id.*
[38] *Id.*
[39] *Id.*
[40] Art. 130 C.m.p.
[41] Arts. 142–144 C.m.p.
[42] Arts. 145–151 C.m.p.
[43] Art. 152 C.m.p.
[44] Art. 142 C.m.p.
[45] Art. 143 C.m.p.
[46] *Id.*
[47] Art. 145 C.m.p.
[48] *Id.*
[49] Art. 150 C.m.p.
[50] *Id.*
[51] Art. 151 C.m.p.
[52] Art. 152 C.m.p.
[53] *Id.*
[54] Arts. 161–172 C.m.p.
[55] Art. 161 C.m.p.
[56] Art. 167 C.m.p.
[57] Art. 169 C.m.p.
[58] *See Compiti del Garante* [*The Tasks of the Data Protection Authority*], GARANTE PER LA PROTEZIONE DEI DATI PERSONALI, http://www.garanteprivacy.it/garante/doc.jsp?ID=34737 (last updated Dec. 9, 2009).
[59] Art. 153 C.m.p.
[60] *Id.*
[61] *Id.*
[62] TOMMASO AMEDEO AULETTA, RISERVATEZZA E TUTELA DELLA PERSONALITÀ [PRIVACY AND PROTECTION OF THE PERSONALITY] 68 (Giuffrè, 1978).
[63] Tribunale Ordinario di Roma 14 settembre 1953, Foro it., 1954, I, 115.
[64] CASSANO, *supra* note 1, at 129.
[65] *Id.*

[66] Corte d'Appellodi Roma 17 maggio 1955, Foro it., 1956, I, 793.
[67] Cass. 22 dicembre 1956, n. 4487, Foro it., 1957, I, 5.
[68] CASSANO, *supra* note 1, at 129.
[69] Cass. 27 maggio 1975, n. 2129, Diritto d'autore [Dir. aut.], 1975, 367–78, *as cited in* PANETTA, *supra* note 5, at 161 (translation by author).
[70] Sabina Kirschen, *Il Codice della Privacy, fra Tradizione ed Innovazione* [*The Privacy Code, Between Tradition and Innovation*], *in* PANETTA, *supra* note 5, at 7 (translation by author).
[71] SILVIA MELCHIONNA, IL CODICE DEL TRATTAMENTO DEI DATI PERSONALI [THE DATA PROTECTION CODE] 68 (Giappichelli, 2007) (translation by author).
[72] GIUSEPPE SANTANIELLO, LA PROTEZIONE DEI DATI PERSONALI [PROTECTION OF PERSONAL DATA] 1 (Cedam, 2005) (translation by author).

End Notes for Japan

[1] Kojin jōhō no hogo ni kansuru hōritsu [Act on the Protection of Personal Information (APPI)], Act No. 57 of 2003 (May 30, 2003), *last amended by* Act No. 49 of 2009 (June 5, 2009). The English translation of selected laws are available on Japanese Law Translation, which is managed by the Ministry of Justice, *at* http://www.japaneselawtranslation.go.jp/ (last visited June 25, 2012); the English translation of the unamended version of the APPI is *available at* http://www.japaneselawtranslation.go.jp/law/detail_main?re=02&vm=&id=130.
[2] Gyōsei kikan no hoyū suru kojin jōhō no hogo ni kansuru hōritsu [Act on the Protection of Personal Information Held by Administrative Organs], Act No. 58 of 2003 (May 30, 2003), *last amended by* Act No. 102 of 2005 (Oct. 21, 2005).
[3] Dokuritsu gyōsei hōjin tō no hoyū suru kojin jōhō no hogo ni kansuru hōritsu [Act on the Protection of Personal Information Held by Independent Administrative Agencies], Act No. 59 of 2003 (May 30, 2003), *last amended by* Act No. 94 of 2011 (Aug. 10, 2011).
[4] Kojin jōhō no hogo ni kansuru kihon hōshin [Basic Policy on the Protection of Personal Information], Cabinet Decision (Apr. 2, 2004), *last amended by* Cabinet Decision (Sept. 1, 2009), http://www.caa.go.jp/seikatsu/kojin/kakugi2009.pdf, 2008 English version *available at* http://www.caa.go.jp/seikatsu/kojin/foreign/basicpolicy-tentver.pdf.
[5] APPI art. 7.
[6] *Id.* arts. 6–8. Article 8 states that "the State shall provide information, [and] formulate guidelines to ensure the appropriate and effective implementation of measures to be taken by entities and others . . . ."
[7] Quality of Life Policy Bureau of the Cabinet Office, Kojin jōhō hogo ni kansuru torimatome (iken) [Summary Regarding Personal Information Protection (Opinion)] 9–11 (June 29, 2007), http://www.caa.go.jp/seikatsu/shingikai/kojin/20th/torimatome.pdf.
[8] Kojin jōhō no hogo ni kansuru gaidorain no kyōtsūka ni tsuite [Regarding Uniformity of Guidelines on Personal Information Protection], Consumer Affairs Agency, http://www.caa.go.jp/seikatsu/kojin/ gaidorainkentou2.html (last visited June 5, 2012).
[9] Gaidorain no kyotsuka no kangaekata ni tsuite [Regarding the Concepts of Making Guidelines More Uniform], Cabinet Office (July 2010), http://www.caa.go.jp/seikatsu/kojin/gaidorainkentou/kyoutuuka2.pdf.
[10] Ministries' guidelines are *available at* http://www.caa.go.jp/seikatsu/kojin/gaidorainkentou.html (last visited June 5, 2012).
[11] APPI, Act No. 57 of 2003 (May 30, 2003), *last amended by* Act No. 49 of 2009 (June 5, 2009), art. 2, para. 3.
[12] Kojin jōhō no hogo ni kansuru hōritsu shikō rei [Enforcement Order of the Act on the Protection of Personal Information], Cabinet Order No. 507 (Dec. 10, 2003), *last amended by* Cabinet Order No. 166 (May 1, 2008), art. 2.
[13] APPI art. 50, para. 3.
[14] *Id.* art. 2, para. 1.
[15] *Id.* art. 15, para. 1.
[16] *Id.* art. 18, para. 1.
[17] *Id.* art. 16, para. 1.
[18] *Id.* art. 16, para. 3.
[19] *Id.* art. 15, para. 2.

[20] *Id.* art. 17.
[21] *Id.* art. 20.
[22] *Id.* art. 21.
[23] *Id.* art. 22.
[24] Kojin jōhō no hogo ni kansuru hōritsu ni tsuite no keizai sangyō bunya o taishō to suru gaidorain [Guidelines on the Act on Protection of Personal Information in the Areas of Economy and Industry], Ministry of Health, Welfare and Labour and Ministry of Economy, Trade and Industry Ordinance No. 2, Oct. 9, 2009, http://www.meti.go.jp/policy/it_policy/privacy/kaisei-guideline.pdf.
[25] *Id.* at 36–37.
[26] APPI, Act No. 57 of 2003 (May 30, 2003), *last amended by* Act No. 49 of 2009 (June 5, 2009), art. 24, para. 1.
[27] Enforcement Order of the APPI, Cabinet Order No. 507 of 2003 (Dec. 10, 2003), *last amended by* Cabinet Order No. 166 of 2008 (May 1, 2008), art. 5.
[28] APPI art. 25, para. 1.
[29] *Id.*
[30] *Id.* art. 25, para. 2 & art. 28.
[31] *Id.* art. 23, para. 1. One example of the final exception is when hospitals submit certain patient information to the national cancer survey.
[32] *Id.* art. 31, para. 1.
[33] *Id.* art. 31, para. 2.
[34] *Id.* art. 26, para. 1.
[35] *Id.*
[36] *Id.* art. 26, para. 2 & art. 28.
[37] *Id.* art. 27, para. 1.
[38] *Id.*
[39] *Id.* art. 27, para. 2.
[40] *Id.* art. 27, paras. 1 & 2.
[41] *Id.* art. 27, para. 3 & art. 28.
[42] *Id.* art. 29; APPI Enforcement Order, Cabinet Order No. 507 of 2003 (Dec. 10, 2003), *last amended by* Cabinet Order No. 166 of 2008 (May 1, 2008), art. 7.
[43] APPI art. 30.
[44] SHIZUO FUJIWAYA AND KOJIN JOHO HOGO HOSEI KENKYOKAI [PERSONAL INFORMATION LAW RESEARCH STUDY GROUP], KOJIN JOHO HOGO HO NO KAISETSU [COMMENTARY ON THE ACT ON THE PROTECTION OF PERSONAL INFORMATION] 219 (Itsuo Sonobe ed., 2005).
[45] APPI art. 37, para. 1.
[46] *Id.* art. 37, para. 2.
[47] *Id.* art. 39.
[48] *Id.* art. 43.
[49] The Guidelines are available on the Internet Association Japan's website, http://www.iajapan.org/ privacy/ (in Japanese; last visited June 1, 2012).
[50] APPI art. 42, para. 1.
[51] *Id.* art. 42, para. 2.
[52] Tokyo Dist. Ct. Apr. 22, 2008, *cited in* Personal Information Protection Promotion Room, *infra* note 56, at 18.
[53] APPI art. 13.
[54] The Consumer Affairs Agency website lists telephone numbers and addresses of the section of local governments throughout Japan, http://www.caa.go.jp/seikatsu/kojin/kujyomadoguchi.html (in Japanese; last visited May 23, 2012).
[55] The National Consumer Affairs Center's website lists examples of complaints and the Centers' responses, *at* http://www.kokusen.go.jp/jirei/j-top_kojinjoho.html (in Japanese; last visited May 23, 2012).
[56] Kojin jōhō hogo hō ni okeru kujō shori ga saiban tetsuzuki de arasowareta rei ni tsuite [Regarding Lawsuits Where Complaints Concerning the Handling of Personal Information Were Involved], Personal Information Protection Promotion Room, Planning Section, Consumer Affairs Agency (Sept. 29, 2010), http://www.cao.go.jp/consumer/history/01/kabusoshiki/kojin/doc/002_100929_sankou2.pdf.
[57] Kojin jōhō hogo senmon chōsakai hiaringu kōmoku ni taisuru iken chinjutsu no kosshi [Main Points of Statements Regarding Item to Be Heard by Personal Information Protection Special Research Committee], Japan Federation of Bar Associations (May 20, 2011), http://www.cao.go.jp/consumer/history/01/kabusoshiki/kojin/doc/006_110520_shiryou2.pdf.

[58] Fusei akusesu kōi no kinshi ni kansuru hōritsu [Act on the Prohibition of Unauthorized Computer Access], Act No. 128 of 1999 (Aug. 13, 1999), arts. 3, 8.

[59] *Moto kenkyūin ni yūzai hanketsu ACCS fusei akusesu jiken* [*Former Researcher Found Guilty, ACCS Unauthorized Access Case*], IT MEDIA (Mar. 25, 2005), http://www.itmedia.co.jp/news/articles/0503/25/news022.html.

[60] KATSUYA UGA, KOJIN JŌHŌ HOGO HŌ NO CHIKUJŌ KAISETSU [ARTICLE-BY-ARTICLE COMMENTARY OF THE APPI] 37 (2005).

[61] *Outline and Objective*, JIPDEC, http://privacymark.org/privacy_mark/about/outline_and_purpose.html, (last modified Dec. 5, 2011).

[62] *Id.*

[63] *About Conforminity* [sic] *Assessment Body*, JIPDEC, http://privacymark.org/agency/about.html (last modified Dec. 5, 2011).

[64] *Outline and Objective*, JIPDEC, *supra* note 61. Japanese Industrial Standards specify the standards used for industrial activities in Japan. The standardization process is coordinated by the Japanese Industrial Standards Committee (JISC). JIS Q15001 is available in Japanese through the JISC online database, *at* http://www.jisc.go.jp/app/JPS/JPSO0020.html (last visited May 24, 2012).

[65] Puraibashi māku fuyo ni kansuru kiyaku [Agreement on Granting PrivacyMark] 1.2 version (Mar. 1, 2012), arts. 11, 12, 15, http://privacymark.jp/reference/pdf/pmark_guide120401/PMK500.pdf.

[66] Press Release, MIC, Recommendations on the Development of an Environment That Provides Safe and Secure Internet Use – Towards Protection for Minors in the Smartphone Age – "Study Group on Examining Issues Around ICT Services from the User Perspective" (Oct. 28, 2011), http://www.soumu.go.jp/main_sosiki/ joho tsusin/eng/Releases/Telecommunications/111028 f.html.

[67] APPI, Act No. 57 of 2003 (May 30, 2003), *last amended by* Act No. 49 of 2009 (June 5, 2009), art. 36, para. 1.

[68] *Id.*

[69] *Id.* art. 36, para. 3.

[70] *Id.* art. 32.

[71] *Id.* art. 33.

[72] *Id.* art. 34, para. 1.

[73] *Id.* art. 34, para. 2.

[74] *Id.* art. 34, para. 3.

[75] *Id.* art. 16.

[76] *Id.* art. 17.

[77] *Id.* art. 20.

[78] *Id.* art. 21.

[79] *Id.* art. 22.

[80] *Id.* art. 23, para. 1.

[81] News Release, METI, Gūguru kabushiki kaisha ni taisuru chūi kanki bunsho no hasshutsu ni tsuite [Regarding Issuance of a Notice Encouraging Google to Be Careful] (Feb. 29, 2012), http://www.meti.go.jp/press/2011/02/20120229011/20120229011.pdf.

[82] APPI art. 49.

[83] *Id.* art. 46.

[84] *Id.* art. 47.

[85] *Id.* art. 48.

[86] *Id.* art. 57.

[87] *Id.* art. 56.

[88] APPI, Act No. 57 (May 30, 2003), art. 7, para. 3; Kōshin rireki no ichiran (heisei 21nen do) [List of Updates (2009 Fiscal Year)], Consumer Affairs Agency (Sept. 1, 2009), http://www.caa.go.jp/seikatsu/kojin/update2009.html.

[89] Consumer Affairs Agency, *supra* note 88. *See also* Shōhisha chō oyobi shōhisha iinkai secchi hō [Act on Establishment of Consumer Affairs Agency and Consumer Committee], Act No. 48 (June 5, 2009), art. 4, item 23.

[90] Heisei 22nen do ni oketu kojin jōhō no hogo ni kansuru hōritsu no shikō jōkyō no gaiyō ni tsuite [Regarding the Summary of Implementation of the APPI during 2010 Fiscal Year], Consumer Affairs Agency, second page (no page number), http://www.caa.go.jp/seikatsu/kojin/22-sekou.pdf. The annual reports are available on the Agency's website, *at* http://www.caa.go.jp/seikatsu/kojin/index_sub001.html.

[91] *Personal Information Protection*, CONSUMER AFFAIRS AGENCY, http://www.caa.go.jp/seikatsu/kojin/index.html (in Japanese; last visited May 31, 2012).

[92] Personal Information Protection Promotion Room, *supra* note 56.

[93] Tokyo Dist. Ct., June 27, 2007, Hei 18 (wa) no. 18312, HANREI JIHŌ 1978, 27.

[94] Japan Federation of Bar Associations, *supra* note 57.

[95] NIHONKOKU KENPO [CONSTITUTION OF JAPAN] (1946).

[96] Tokyo Dist. Ct., 1962 (wa) 1882 (Sept. 28, 1964), 15 KAMINSHU 9, 2317.

[97] S. Ct., 1965 (A) No. 1187, 23 KEISHU 12, 1625 (Dec. 24, 1969), http://www.courts.go.jp/hanrei/pdf/js_20100319120221050991.pdf; English translation available on Courts of Japan website, *at* http://www.courts.go.jp/english/judgments/text/1969.12.24-1965.-A-.No..1187.html.

[98] *Id.*

[99] Jflmin töroku ho [Resident Registration Law], Act No. 218 of 1951 (June 8, 1951). The registration system changed when the Basic Resident Registry Law was enacted. Jflmin kihon daichO ho, Act No. 81 of 1967 (July 25, 1967).

[100] Basic Resident Registry Law, Act No. 81 of 1967 (July 25, 1967), art. 7.

[101] Act. No. 133 of 1999 (Aug. 18, 1999).

[102] Jūmin kihon daichō nettowāku shisutemu suishin kyōgikai [Basic Resident Registry Network Promotion Council], Jūmin kihon daichō nettowāku no gaiyō [Summary of Basic Resident Registry Network] 1, http://www.soumu.go.jp/main_sosiki/jichi_gyousei/c-gyousei/daityo/old/shousai/02_gaiyo.htm (last visited June 7, 2012).

[103] *Resident Registry Launched in Trial Run for August*, JAPAN TIMES (July 23, 2002), http://www.japantimes.co.jp/text/nn20020723a9.html.

[104] Jūi netto sashitome soshō o shien suru kai [Group Supporting Lawsuits to Suspend Jūki Net], 10gatsu 1tachi Jūki netto sashitome soshō sōkatsu kaigi [Conference to overview Jūki Net suspension lawsuits, October 1st] 11 (Oct. 29, 2011), http://www006.upp.so-net.ne.jp/jukisosho/torikumi/news45p2-p12.pdf.

[105] Kanazawa Dist. Ct., 2002 (wa) No. 836 and 2003 (wa) No. 114 (May 30, 2005), HANREI JIHŌ 1934, 3.

[106] Osaka High Ct. (Nov. 30, 2006). This case was reported in many news articles, but not listed in the court report.

[107] The case was summarized in the Supreme Court decision, *infra* note 108.

[108] S. Ct., 2007 (o) No. 403 (Mar. 6, 2008), 20 MINSHŪ 3, 665, http://www.courts.go.jp/hanrei/pdf/20080306142412.pdf.

[109] Quality of Life Policy Bureau, *supra* note 7, at 1.

[110] JFBA, "KOdo jOhO tsflshin nettowāku shakai" ni okeru puraibashi ken hoshO shisutemu no jitsugen o motomeru ketsugi [Resolution Seeking Realization of Privacy Right Guarantee System in "Advanced Information/Communication Network"] (Oct. 8, 2010), http://www.nichibenren.or.jp/activity/document/civil_liberties/year/2010/2010_2.html.

[111] GyOsei tetsuzuki ni okeru tokutei no kojin o shikibetsu suru tame no bangO no riyO tO ni kansuru hOritsu an [Bill of the Act on Use of Numbers to Identify Individuals in Administrative Procedures], Cabinet Bill No. 32 of 180th Diet Session.

[112] *Id.* art. 1.

[113] ShOhisha iinkai kojin jOhO hogo senmon chOsakai secchi/unei kitei [Rules on Establishment and Management of the Personal Information Protection Special Research Subcommittee, Consumer Committee], Consumer Committee Decision (Dec. 8, 2009), http://www.cao.go.jp/consumer/history/01/kabusoshiki/kojin/__icsFiles/afieldfile/2010/11/24/131 kojinjoho.pdf.

[114] Kojin jöhö hogo senmon chösakai hökokusho [Personal Information Protection Special Research Subcommittee Report], Personal Information Protection Special Research Subcommittee, Consumer Committee (July 2011), http://www.cao.go.jp/consumer/history/01/kabusoshiki/kojin/doc/houkokusho.pdf.

[115] *Id.* at 7.

[116] Bill of the Act on Use of Numbers to Identify Individuals in Administrative Procedures, Cabinet Bill No. 32 of 180th Diet Session, arts. 31–50.

[117] Personal Information Protection Special Research Subcommittee Report, *supra* note 114, at 10–16.

[118] Press Release, MIC, "Riyösha shiten o fumaeta ICT sābisu ni kakaru shomondai ni kansuru kenkyUkai" no kaisai [First Meeting of "Study Group on Consumer Issues with ICT Services"] (Apr. 6, 2009), http://www.soumu.go.jp/menu_news/s-news/02kiban08_000004.html.

[119] STUDY GROUP ON CONSUMER ISSUES WITH ICT SERVICES, AN EXAMINATION OF LIFELOG-MONITORING SERVICES 3 (May 2010), http://www.soumu.go.jp/main_sosiki/joho_tsusin/eng/councilreport/pdf/100526_1.pdf; Japanese version *available at* http://www.soumu.go.jp/main_content/000067551.pdf (*see* Section II of the report).

[120] *Id.*

[121] *Id.* at 17.

[122] "Behavioral advertising and similar applications usually only require (a) logs of Web actions and habits (browsing, purchases, etc.) needed to predict consumer preferences and interests, (b) location information, and (c) IDs generated with cookies needed to acquire action logs and serve advertisements, or (d) subscriber IDs to identify mobile devices." *Id.* at 14.

[123] *Id.* at 14–15.

[124] *Id.* at 17–18.

[125] *Id.* at 23.

[126] *Id.*

[127] *Id.* at 24.

[128] *Id.*

[129] *Id.* at 26.

[130] *Id.* at 33.

[131] *Id.*

[132] *Id.*

[133] *Id.* at 34.

[134] *Id.* at 39.

[135] *Id.*

[136] *Id.* at 40.

[137] The Behavioral Advertising Guidelines were first issued in June 2009. *"Kōdō tāgetingu kōkoku gaidorain" no kaitei ni tsuite* [*Regarding Amendment of the Behavioral Advertising Guidelines*], JIAA, June 24, 2010, at 1, http://www.jiaa.org/dbps_data/_material_/common/release/bta_guideline_release_100624.pdf (Guidelines attached to linked document).

[138] *Id.* The Self-Regulatory Principles for Online Behavioral Advertising are available on the Interactive Advertising Bureau's website, *at* http://www.iab.net/public_policy/behavioral-advertisingprinciples (last visited May 29, 2012).

[139] Telecommunications Bureau, MIC, Dai 2ji teigen go no ugoki to kongo no kentō kadai ni tsuite [Regarding the Movement after the Second Proposal and Agenda], at 5 (Sept. 2010), http://www.soumu.go.jp/main_content /000081042.pdf.

[140] Press Release, MIC, "Sumāto phon / kuraudo sekyuriti kenkyūkai" no kaisai [Opening of "Smartphone / Cloud Security Society"] (Oct. 1, 2011), http://www.soumu.go.jp/menu_news/s-news/01ryutsu03_01000009.html.

[141] Appeal for Opinions on Draft Final Report from 'Smart Phone and Cloud Security Research Society,' MIC, Apr. 27, 2012, http://www.soumu.go.jp/main_sosiki/joho_tsusin/eng/Releases/Telecommunications/ 120427_06. html. The records of the Society's meetings and the final draft report are available in Japanese on the MIC website, *at* http://www.soumu.go.jp/menu_news/s-news/01ryutsu03_02000019.html (last visited May 30, 2012).

[142] The report is available on the MIC website, *at* http://www.soumu.go.jp/main_content/000166095.pdf (in Japanese; last visited June 30, 2012).

[143] Press Release, MIC, 'Working Group on the User Information Sent Through Smartphone' to Be Opened Under Study Group on Consumer Issues with ICT Services (Jan. 18, 2012), http://www.soumu.go.jp/ main sosiki/joho tsusin/eng/Releases/Telecommunications/12011801.html.

[144] Press Release, MIC, Official Announcement of 'Interim Report from Working Group on the User Information Sent through Smartphone' Under Study Group on Consumer Issues with ICT Services (Apr. 11, 2012), http://www.soumu.go.jp/main_sosiki/joho_tsusin/eng/Releases/Telecommunications/120411_01.html.

[145] Sumātophon o keiyu shita riyōsha jōhō no toriatsukai ni kansuru WG chūkan torimatome [Interim Report from Working Group on the User Information Sent Through Smartphone] 33–40 (Apr. 2012), http://www.soumu.go.jp/main_content/000154856.pdf.

[146] The Smartphone Privacy Guide is available at the end of the Interim Report. *Id.* at 45.

[147] Press Release, MIC, Riyōsha shiten o humaeta ICT sābisu ni kakaru shomondai ni kansuru kenkyūkai teigen "sumāatofon puraibashī inishiatibu -riyōsha jōhō no tekisei na toriatsukai to riterashī kōjō ni yoru shin jidai inobēshon-" (an) ni taisuru iken boshū [Public Comments accepted regarding "Smartphone privacy initiative – innovation in a new era by proper handling of user information and improvement of literacy" (Draft) proposed by Study Group on Examining Issues Around ICT Services from the User Perspective] (June 29, 2012), http://www.soumu.go.jp/menu news/s-news/01kiban08 02000081.html.

End Notes for Netherlands

* This report was prepared on the basis of English-language materials, machine-assisted translations, and online Dutch-English dictionaries.

[1] OECD Key ICT Indicators: 6b. Households with Access to the Internet (1), 2000-10 (last updated Nov. 9, 2011), http://www.oecd.org/dataoecd/19/45/34083073.xls (toggle at bottom of page for graph).

[2] OECD Key ICT Indicators: 6c. Households with Broadband Access (1) 2000-10 (last updated Nov. 9, 2011), http://www.oecd.org/dataoecd/23/34/41625794.xls (toggle at bottom of page for graph).

[3] *Netherlands*, NEW MEDIA TREND WATCH (last updated May 9, 2012), http://www.newmediatrend watch.com/markets-by-country/10-europe/76-netherlands.

[4] *Id.* (citing Press Release, comScore, Turkey Has Third Most Engaged Online Audience in Europe (Oct. 18, 2011) (presenting Europe-wide data)).

[5] *Id.* (citing Press Release, Statistics Netherlands, Substantial Growth Mobile Internet Usage (Oct. 25, 2011)).

[6] *Id.*

[7] THE CONSTITUTION OF THE KINGDOM OF THE NETHERLANDS 2008 (as last amended June 27, 2008, in force on July 15, 2008), http://www.rijksoverheid.nl/documenten-en-publicaties/brochures/2008/10/20/the-constitution-of-the-kingdom-of-the-netherlands-2008.html; Grondwet voor het Koninkrijk der Nederlanden van 24 augustus 1815 (as last amended June 27, 2008, in force on July 15, 2008), http://wetten.overheid.nl/BWBR0001840/ geldigheidsdatum_02-05-2012.

[8] *Id.* art. 11.

[9] *Id.* art. 12.

[10] *Id.* art. 13.

[11] Telecommunicatiewet [Telecommunications Act] (Oct. 19, 1998, as last amended by an amendment law in force on June 5, 2012), http://wetten.overheid.nl/BWBR0009950/Hoofdstuk1/Artikel11/geldigheidsdatum_21-05-2012. *See* Wet van 10 mei 2012 tot Wijziging van de Telecommunicatiewet ter Implementatie van de Herziene Telecommunicatierichtlijnen [Act of May 10, 2012, to Amend the Telecommunications Act for Implementation of the Revised Telecommunications Directives], 235 STAATSBLAD (June 4, 2012), https://zoek.officielebekend makingen.nl/stb-2012-235.html.

[12] Directive 2009/136/EC of the European Parliament and of the Council of 25 November 2009 Amending Directive 2002/22/EC on Universal Service and Users' Rights Relating to Electronic Communications Networks and Services, Directive 2002/58/EC Concerning the Processing of Personal Data and the Protection of Privacy in the Electronic Communications Sector and Regulation (EC) No 2006/2004 on Cooperation Between National Authorities Responsible for the Enforcement of Consumer Protection Laws, 2009 O.J. (L 337) 11, http://eur-lex.europa.eu/LexUriServ/LexUriServ.do?uri=OJ:L: 2009:337:0011:0036:En:PDF.

[13] Boekel de Nerée, *Amendments to Dutch Telecoms Law Restricts the Use of Cookies*, THE IN-HOUSE LAWYER (Sept. 1, 2011), http://www.inhouselawyer.co.uk/index.php/the-netherlands/9559-amendments-to-dutch-telecoms-law-restricts-the-use-of-cookies.

[14] Peter van der Veen, *Amendments to Dutch Telecom Law Codify Net Neutrality and Restrict the Use of Cookies,* FUTURE OF COPYRIGHT (June 22, 2011), http://www.futureofcopyright.com/home/blog-post/2011/06/22/amendments-to-dutch-telecom-law-codify-net-neutrality-and-restrict-the-use-of-cookies.html.

[15] Wet bewaarplicht telecommunicatiegegevens [Telecommunications Data Retention Act] (hereinafter TDRA) (July 18, 2009, in force on Sept. 1, 2009), http://wetten.overheid.nl/BWBR0026191/geldigheidsdatum_15- 02-2010.

[16] Mediawet [Media Act] (in force on Jan. 1, 2009) (as last amended May 10, 2012), https://zoek.officielebekendmakingen.nl/stb-2012-235.html; Joost Gerritsen, *Netherlands: Media Act 2008*, IRIS MERLIN 2009-3:18/29 http://merlin.obs.coe.int/iris/2009/3/article29.en.html (last visited June 6, 2012).

[17] Wet bescherming persoonsgegevens (July 6, 2000) (as last amended effective Feb. 9, 2012), http://wetten.overheid.nl/BWBR0011468/geldigheidsdatum_03-05-2012; *see* Wet van 26 januari 2012 tot wijziging van de Wet bescherming persoonsgegevens in verband met de vermindering van administratieve lasten en nalevingskosten, wijzigingen teneinde wetstechnische gebreken te herstellen en enige andere wijzigingen [Act of January 26, 202, Amending the Personal Data Protection Act in Connection with the Reduction of Administrative Charges and Compliance Costs, Amendments to Repair Legal Technical Flaws, and Certain Other Amendments], 33 STAATSBLAD (Feb. 8, 2012), https://zoek.officielebekend makingen.nl/stb-2012-33.html; Personal Data Protection Act (PDPA) (unofficial translation), *available at* Institute for Information Law, http://www.ivir.nl/legislation/nl/personal dataprotectionact.html (updated Dec. 15, 2005).

[18] *Wet bescherming persoonsgegevens (Wbp; Dutch Data Protection Act)*, COLLEGE BESCHERMING PERSOONSGEGEVENS [DATA PROTECTION AUTHORITY, DPA], http://www.dutchdpa.nl/Pages/en_ind_wetten_wbp.aspx (last visited May 3, 2012).

[19] *The Netherlands*, LINKLATERS (last updated Nov. 2011), https://clientsites.linklaters.com/Clients/dataprotected/Pages/TheNetherlands.aspx#nationalleg; Directive 95/46/EC of the European Parliament and of the Council of 24 October 1995 on the Protection of Individuals with Regard to the Processing of Personal Data and on the Free Movement of Such Data, 1995 O.J. (L 281) 31, http://eur-lex.europa.eu/LexUriServ/LexUriServ.do?uri =CELEX:31995L0046:en:HTML.

[20] L.B. Sauerwein & J.J. Linnemann, HANDLEIDING VOOR VERWERKERS VAN PERSOONSGEGEVENS: WET BESCHERMING PERSOONSGEGEVENS (Ministry of Justice, Apr. 2002), http://www.rijksoverheid.nl/documenten-enpublicaties/brochures/2006/07/13/handleiding-wet-bescherming-persoonsgegevens.html.

[21] *New Dutch Notice-and-Take-Down Code Raises Questions*, EUROPEAN DIGITAL RIGHTS (EDRI) (Oct. 22, 2008), http://www.edri.org/edri-gram/number6.20/notice-take-down-netherlands; Esther Janssen, *Netherlands: Dutch Code for Notice-and-Take-Down*, IRIS 2009-1:17/28, http://merlin.obs.coe.int/iris/2009/1/article28.en.html; NOTICE-AND-TAKE-DOWN CODE OF CONDUCT, ECP (Version 1, Oct. 2008), http://www.ecp.nl/sites/default/files/NTD_Gedragscode_Engels_0.pdf.

[22] Telecommunications Act art. 1.1(e)–(h).

[23] PDPA art. 2(1).

[24] *Id.* art. 1(c).

[25] *Id.* art. 3(1).

[26] *Id.* art. 4 (1) & (2).

[27] *Id.* art. 4(3).

[28] *Id.* art. 8(a).

[29] *Id.* art. 8(b)–(f).

[30] *Id.* art. 16.

[31] *Id.* art. 76(1).

[32] *Id.* art. 76(2). This provision was added in the 2012 amendment of the PDPA.

[33] *Id.* art. 76(3).

[34] *Id.* art. 77(1)(a), (b), (e), (g). *See* Directive 95/46/EG of the European Parliament and of the Council of 24 October 1995 on the Protection of Individuals with Regard to the Processing of Personal Data and on the Free Movement of Such Data, 1995 O.J. (L 281) 31, http://ec.europa.eu/justice/policies/privacy/docs/95-46-ce/dir1995- 46_part1_en.pdf.

[35] PDPA art. 77(2).

[36] Telecommunications Act art. 11.2; PETER V. EIJSVOOGEL & HENDRIK JAN DE RU, DUTCH TELECOMMUNICATIONS LAW 169 (2000); Arjen van Rijn, Arnoud Boorsma, Jannetje Bootsma, Michiel Hes, Jeannette van Breugel, & Sandra van Heukelom-Verhage, *Telecommunications Law in the Netherlands*, 30 COMPARATIVE LAW YEARBOOK OF INTERNATIONAL BUSINESS 537 (2008).

[37] Telecommunications Act art. 11.3(1); EIJSVOOGEL & JAN DE RU, *supra* note 36.

[38] *Id.* art. 11.3(2)(b).

[39] *Nieuwe Cookiewetgeving: We Kunnen Er Niet Meer Omheen* [*New Cookie Legislation: We Can No Longer Ignore It*], PERPLEX.NL (May 11, 2012), http://www.perplex.nl/blog/2012/nieuwe-cookiewetgeving-we-kunnen-er-niet-meer-omheen; *Legal Alert – Dutch Senate Finally Adopts New Rules on Cookies, Net Neutrality and Data Security Breach Notifications*, DE BRAUW [law firm] (May 2012), http://www.debrauw.com/News/LegalAlerts/Pages/LegalAlert-DutchSenatefinallyadoptsnewrulesoncookies, netneutralityanddatasecuritybreach notifications.aspx.

[40] Van der Veen, *supra* note 14.

[41] *Id.*

[42] DE BRAUW, *supra* note 39.

[43] *Id.* Despite the delayed date of enforcement, there is some concern, according to van der Veen, that the measure may place Dutch Internet companies at a competitive disadvantage with foreign companies. *See* van der Veen, *supra* note 14.

[44] Directive 2009/136/EC, *supra* note 12.

[45] Directive 2009/140/EC of the European Parliament and of the Council of 25 November 2009 Amending Directives 2002/21/EC on a Common Regulatory Framework for Electronic Communications Networks and Services, 2002/19/EC on Access to, and Interconnection of, Electronic Communications Networks and Associated Facilities, and 2002/20/EC on the Authorisation of Electronic Communications Networks and

Services, 2009 O.J. (L 337) 37, http://eur-lex.europa.eu/LexUriServ/LexUriServ.do? uri=OJ:L:2009:337:0037:0069:EN:PDF.

[46] DE BRAUW, *supra* note 39; *Eerste Kamer Behandelt 'Cookiewet' en Neemt het Voorstel aan* [*The Senate Discussed the 'Cookie Act' and Received a Proposal on It*], LEGAL EXPERIENCE ADVOCATEN (May 9, 2012), http://www.legalexperience.nl/nl/actueel/eerste-kamer-behandelt-cookiewet-en-neemt-het-voorstel-aan.

[47] DE BRAUW, *supra* note 39.

[48] I Motie van het Lid Franken C.S.: Voorgesteld 8 mei 2012 [Motion of the Member C.S. Franken, Introduced 8 May 2012], http://www.eerstekamer.nl/motie/motie_franken_cda_c_s_over_het_2/document/ f=/vizbm2afuxv9.pdf.

[49] Press Release, 2011 OPTA Annual Report and Market Monitor (May 7, 2012), http://www.opta.nl/en/ news/all-publications/publication/?id=3590.

[50] EUROPEAN PARLIAMENT, DOES IT HELP OR HINDER? PROMOTION OF INNOVATION ON THE INTERNET AND CITIZENS' RIGHT TO PRIVACY, IP/A/ITRE/ST/2011-10 (Dec. 2011), at 42, n.61, http://www.euro parl.europa.eu/committees/fr/studiesdownload.html?languageDocument=EN&file=65871.

[51] Telecommunications Act art. 1.1(jj)(1).

[52] *Id.* art. 11.5a(1)(a) & (b).

[53] *Id.* art. 11.5a(3). *See also* van Rijn et al., *supra* note 36, at 538.

[54] Telecommunications Act art. 11.5a(2)(a)–(d).

[55] *Id.* art. 11.5a(4).

[56] PDPA art. 5(1).

[57] *Id.* art. 5(2).

[58] *Id.* art. 37(3), with reference to arts. 35–36. "Responsible party" means "the natural person, legal person, administrative body or any other entity which, alone or in conjunction with others, determines the purpose of and means for processing personal data." *Id.* art. 1(d).

[59] *Id.* art. 37(3).

[60] *Id.* art. 13.

[61] *Id.*

[62] *Id.* art. 14(3) & (5).

[63] *Id.* art. 14(1).

[64] *Id.* art. 14(3)(b).

[65] *Id.* art. 14(4).

[66] Telecommunications Act art. 11.5(1).

[67] *Id.* art. 11.5(3).

[68] PDPA art. 35(1).

[69] *Id.* art. 35(4).

[70] *Id.* art. 36(1). The request is to contain the modifications that should be made.

[71] *Id.* art. 30(3).

[72] *Id.* art. 35(4).

[73] *Id.* art. 36.

[74] *Id.* art. 38(2).

[75] *Id.* art. 46(1).

[76] *Id.* art. 46(2).

[77] *Id.* art. 46(3).

[78] *Id.* art. 46(5) (citing WETBOEK VAN BURGERLIJK RECHTSVORDERING [CODE OF CIVIL PROCEDURE] (as last amended Dec. 22, 2011), Book II, Title 5 (on constraint and its implementation and on penalty payments), § 3, http://wetten.overheid.nl/BWBR0001827/TweedeBoek /Vijfdetitel/geldigheidsdatum_18-05-2012). There are more recent amendments to the Code of Civil Procedure, dated March 15, 2012, but they will not enter into force until July 1, 2012.

[79] *Id.* art. 46(6).

[80] *Id.* art. 47(1).

[81] *Id.* art. 49(1) & (2).

[82] *Id.* art. 49(3).

[83] *Id.* art. 49(4).

[84] *Id.* art. 50(1).

[85] *Id.* art. 50(2).

[86] *Id.* art. 65 (under § 1, "Administrative Measures of Constraint" of Ch. 10, "Sanctions").

[87] *Id.* art. 66. Note that former additional paragraphs of article 66, as well as articles 67–70 and 72–73 of the PDPA, have been repealed.

[88] *Id.* art. 71.

[89] *Id.* art. 75(1). The punishable offenses listed under article 75(1) are petty offenses. *Id.* art. 75(3). As of January 1, 2012, third-category fines are €7,800 (about US$9,752). WETBOEK VAN STRAFRECHT [CRIMINAL CODE] (Mar. 3, 1881, as last amended Apr. 5, 2012), art. 23(4), http://wetten.overheid.nl/BWBR 0001854/EersteBoek/ TitelII/Artikel23/geldigheidsdatum_25-05-2012.

[90] PDPA art. 75(2). The punishable offenses listed under article 75(2) are indictable offenses. *Id.* art. 75(3). As of January 1, 2012, fourth-category fines are €19,500 (about US$24,380). WETBOEK VAN STRAFRECHT art. 23(4), http://wetten.overheid.nl/BWBR0001854/EersteBoek/TitelII/Artikel23/geldigheidsdatum_25-05-2012.

[91] Directive 2006/24/EC of the European Parliament and of the Council of 15 March 2006 on the Retention of Data Generated or Processed in Connection with the Provision of Publicly Available Electronic Communications Services or of Public Communications Networks and Amending Directive 2002/58/EC, 2006 O.J. (L 105) 54, http://eur-lex.europa.eu/LexUriServ/LexUriServ.do?uri=OJ:L: 2006:105:0054:0063:EN:PDF.

[92] TDRA, *supra* note 15. For what appears to be a comparison of retained data under the EU directive and under Dutch law, as well as interpretation and examples, *see Toelichting bewaring gegevens internet* [*Sample Retained Internet Data*], RIJKSOVERHEID [GOVERNMENT OF THE NETHERLANDS] (Dec. 21, 2010), http://www.rijks overheid.nl/documenten-en-publicaties/richtlijnen/2010/12/21/toelichting-bewaring-gegevens-internet.html.

[93] *Report from the Commission to the Council and the European Parliament: Evaluation Report on the Data Retention Directive (Directive 2006/24/EC)* § 4.1, COM (2011) 225 final (Apr. 18, 2011), http://ec.europa.eu/commission_2010-2014/malmstrom/archive/20110418_data_retention_evaluation_en.pdf. According to the TDRA, the relevant articles of the Criminal Procedure Code are 126n, 126na, 126u, and 126ua, 126hh, 126ii, 126nc-126ni, and 126uc-126ui. TDRA, *supra* note 15, arts. 1 D & 1 E(b).

[94] *Report from the Commission to the Council and the European Parliament*, *supra* note 93, § 4.3.

[95] *Id.* § 4.5.

[96] *Id.* § 4.6 (Table 4); TDRA art. 1 F (amending art. 13(5) of the Telecommunications Act, on the obligation of telecom providers of networks and services to protect information on the basis of the Law on the Intelligence and Security Services 2002, as referred to in article 13.2 of the Telecommunications Act).

[97] *Hotels May Be Subject to Strict EU Rules for Providing Wi-Fi*, WHOLESALE ELECTRONICS (May 10, 2012), http://www.ocpol.com/hotels-may-be-subject-to-strict-eu-rules-for-providing-wi-fi_2588.html.

[98] *Id.*

[99] *Id.*

[100] *OPTA Is an IAB*, OPTA, http://www.opta.nl/en/organisation-opta/opta-is-an-iab/ (last modified Nov. 23, 2009) (see left-hand column, "Organisation OPTA").

[101] *Peter Hustinx*, LAW OF THE FUTURE FORUM, http://www.lawofthefuture.org/191/ (last visited May 29, 2012).

[102] PDPA art. 53(1).

[103] *Id.* art. 53(3).

[104] *Id.* art. 56(2).

[105] *Organisation*, DPA, http://www.dutchdpa.nl/Pages/en_ind_cbp_organisatie.aspx (last visited May 29, 2012).

[106] PDPA arts. 62 & 63(3).

[107] Wet Politiegegevens [Police Data Act] (July 21, 2007), art. 34(1) & (4), http://wetten.overheid.nl/ BWBR0022463/geldigheidsdatum_19-05-2012.

[108] PDPA art. 51(1). It also has the authority to institute, on its own initiative, investigations of compliance with the law. *Id.* art. 60.

[109] *Id.* arts. 65, 66, & 75(4).

[110] *Id.* art. 25.

[111] *Id.* arts. 27–30 (notification), 31–32 (preliminary examination).

[112] *Id.* art. 47.

[113] *Id.* art. 64(4); *see also The Dutch DPA's Tasks*, DPA, http://www.dutchdpa.nl/Pages/en_ind_cbp_ taken.aspx (last visited May 29, 2012).

[114] PDPA art. 77(2).

[115] *Id.* art. 58.

[116] *Id.* art. 23.

[117] *Radiocommunications Agency*, RCA, http://www.agentschaptelecom.nl/english (last visited May 31, 2012).

[118] *Id.* For the text of the cooperation protocol, *see* Samenwerkingsovereenkomst Tussen Agentschap Telecom en het College Bescherming Persoonsgegevens met het Oog op de Wijzigingen in de Telecommunicatiewet naar Aanleiding van de Wet Bewaarplicht Telecommunicatiegegevens [Cooperation Agreement Between the Telecommunications Agency and the DPA in View of the Amendments to the Telecommunications Act Following the Data Retention Communications Law] (Sept. 15, 2009), http://www.cbpweb.nl/downloads_pb/pb_20090915_samenwerkingsovereenkomst_at-cbp.pdf.

[119] *Tomorrow Is Made Today*, OPTA, http://www.opta.nl/en/about-opta/tomorrow-is-made-today/ (last visited June 4, 2012).

[120] *Id.*

[121] OPTA, *supra* note 100.

[122] DPA, REPORT OF FINDINGS: OFFICIAL INVESTIGATION BY THE CBP INTO THE PROCESSING OF GEOLOCATION DATA BY TOMTOM N.V. (Dec. 20, 2011), http://www.dutchdpa.nl/downloads_overig/en_pb_20120112_investigation-tomtom.pdf.

[123] *Id.* at 2.

[124] *Id.*

[125] *Id.* at 3.

[126] *Id.* The report cites, by way of examples, CBP, *Ruling on Complaint* [in Dutch], No. z2003-0316 (Apr. 8, 2003), www.cbpweb.nl/downloads_uit/z2003-0163.pdf, & CBP, *Investigation into the Processing of Personal Data by Advance Concepts B.V.* [in Dutch] (Dec. 2009), in particular pp. 27 & 28, http://cbpweb.nl/downloads_pb/pb_20091218_advance_bevindingen.pdf.

[127] DPA, *supra* note 122, at 3.

[128] *Id.* at 24 & 25.

[129] Press Release, DPA, Google Has Complied with Dutch DPA Requirements (Apr. 5, 2012), http://www.dutchdpa.nl/Pages/en_pb_20120405_google-complies-with-Dutch-DPA-requirements.aspx.

[130] *Id.*

[131] *Id.*

[132] *Id.*

[133] Institute for Information Law (IViR), University of Amsterdam, *Netherlands: Internet Service Provider Ordered to Reveal Personal Data of Website Holder* (2006), *available at* http://merlin.obs.coe.int/iris/2006/2/article101.en.html (citing Ruling by the Dutch Supreme Court [*Hoge Raad*], Lycos Netherlands B.V/Pessers of 25 November 2005, C04/234HR, LJN AU4019, http://zoeken.rechtspraak.nl/detailpage.aspx?ljn=AU4019).

[134] Directive 2000/31/EC of the European Parliament and of the Council of 8 June 2000 on Certain Legal Aspects of Information Society Services, in Particular Electronic Commerce, in the Internal Market (Directive on Electronic Commerce), 2000 O.J. (L 178) 1, http://eur-lex.europa.eu/LexUriServ/LexUriServ.do?uri=OJ:L:2000: 178:0001:0001:EN:PDF.

[135] *See* IViR, *supra* note 133.

[136] *Id.*

[137] *Id.*

[138] *Id.*

[139] Ruling by the Dutch Supreme Court, *supra* note 133. The Court considered the applicability of article 8 of the PDPA under section 62.

[140] *Netherlands Likely to Give Green Light to Controversial Web Privacy Law*, INTERNET BUSINESS NEWS (June 22, 2011), *available at* http://www.thefreelibrary.com/-Netherlands+likely+to+give+green+light+to+controversial+web+privacy...-a0259452302.

[141] *Id.*

[142] Belinda van Steijn, *Fired Because of Facebook*, RADIO NETHERLANDS WORLDWIDE (Feb. 12, 2012), http://www.rnw.nl/english/article/fired-because-facebook.

[143] *Id.*

[144] Colin Prins, *Selling My Soul to the Digital World?*, 4:1 AMSTERDAM LAW FORUM 8 (2009), http://www.amsterdamlawforum.org/.

[145] *Id.*

[146] *Id.*

[147] *Id.* at 10.

[148] *Netherlands*, PRIVACY INTERNATIONAL (Jan. 1, 2011), https://www.privacyinternational.org/reports/netherlands. For this information about the new commission, the report cites the Decision of 3 July 2009, No. 09.0018252.

[149] *Senaat wil meer wijzigen in Grondwet* [*Senate Wants More Change in Constitution*], EERSTE KAMER [DUTCH SENATE] (Feb. 8, 2012), http://www.eerstekamer.nl/nieuws/20120208/senaat_wil_meer_wijzigen_in.

[150] *Id.*

[151] *Id.*

[152] *Id.*

[153] Conceptverslag van een Algemeen Overleg over: Kabinetsstandpunt Rapport Staatscommissie Grondwet en Aanpassing Artikel 13 van de Grondwet [Concept Report of a General Discussion About: Cabinet Position Report, State Constitution Commission and Adaptation [of] Article 13 of the Constitution] (May 23, 2012), http://www.tweedekamer.nl/ao_repo/biza/20120523_Kabinetsstandpunt%20rapport%20staatscommissie%20G rond wet%20en%20aanpassing%20artikel%2013%20van%20de%20Grondwet.pdf.

[154] *Kabinetsstandpunt Rapport Staatscommissie Grondwet* [*Cabinet Position Report State Constitution Commission*], TWEEDE KAMER [Dutch House of Representatives], http://www.tweedekamer.nl/kamer stukken/ dossiers/kabinetsstandpunt_rapport_staatscommissie_grondwet.jsp (last visited June 6, 2012). This overview has links to other relevant documents.

[155] Alex Wawro, *What Is Deep Packet Inspection*, PC WORLD (Feb. 1, 2012), http://www.pcworld.com/article/249137/what is deep packet inspection.html.

[156] *Id.*

[157] EUROPEAN PARLIAMENT, *supra* note 50.

[158] *Id.*

[159] *Id.* It is unclear at this time what conclusions were reached by the DPA. However, as indicated above, the Dutch Telecommunications Act now has provisions on net neutrality.

[160] *OPTA en Agentschap Telecom openen meldpunt voor nieuwe meldplichten aanbieders* [*OPTA and Radiocommunications Agency Open Hotline for New Reporting Requirements [for] Providers*], OPTA (Apr. 6, 2012), http://www.opta.nl/nl/actueel/alle-publicaties/publicatie/?id=3593.

[161] Press Release, OPTA, New Dutch Regulator to Be Called ACM, the Netherlands Authority for Consumers and Markets, Merger of Three Regulators to Be Completed January 1, 2013 (Oct. 4, 2011), http://www.opta.nl/en/news/all-publications/publication/?id=3487.

[162] *Id.*

End Notes for Portugal

[1] CONSTITUIÇÃO DA REPÚBLICA PORTUGUESA [C.R.P.] (Constitutional Revision VII (2005)) art. 35, *available at* ASSEMBLEIA DA REPÚBLICA [ASSEMBLY OF THE REPUBLIC], http://www.parlamento.pt/Legislacao/ Paginas/ ConstituicaoRepublicaPortuguesa.aspx.

[2] Lei No. 10/91, de 29 de Abril, *available at* PORTAL DAS FINANÇAS [FINANCE PORTAL], http://info.portaldasfinancas.gov.pt/NR/rdonlyres/54F233C0-FFAA-4C93-B5BA-E4D615916D4C/0/lei_10-91 de 29 de abril i serie a.pdf.

[3] Directive 95/46/EC, of the European Parliament and of the Council of 24 October 1995 on the Protection of Individuals with Regard to the Processing of Personal Data and on the Free Movement of Such Data, 1995 O.J. (L 281) 31, http://eur-lex.europa.eu/LexUriServ/LexUriServ.do?uri=CELEX:31995L0046:en:HTML.

[4] *Id.* arts. 1–4.

[5] QUARTA REVISÃO CONSTITUCIONAL, Lei No. 1/97, de 20 de Setembro, art. 18, *available at* PROCURADORIA-GERAL DISTRITAL DE LISBOA [LISBOA ATTORNEY GENERAL'S OFFICE], http://www.pgdlisboa.pt/ pgdl/leis/lei_mostra_articulado.php?nid=11&tabela=leis&ficha=1&pagina=1.

[6] Lei No. 67/98, de 26 de Outubro, Lei da Protecção de Dados Pessoais [Personal Data Protection Law], http://www.pgdlisboa.pt/pgdl/leis/lei_mostra_articulado.php?nid=156&tabela=leis&ficha=1&pagina=1.

[7] Lei No. 69/98, de 28 de Outubro, *available at* COMISSÃO NACIONAL DE PROTECÇÃO DE DADOS [NATIONAL COMMISSION OF DATA PROTECTION], http://www.cnpd.pt/bin/legis/nacional/lei_6998.htm.

[8] Lei No. 41/2004, de 18 de Agosto, http://www.pgdlisboa.pt/pgdl/leis/lei_mostra_articulado.php?nid=707&tabela=leis&ficha=1&pagina=1.

[9] Directive 2002/58/EC of the European Parliament and of the Council of 12 July 2002 concerning the processing of personal data and the protection of privacy in the electronic communications sector (Directive on privacy and

electronic communications), 2002 O.J. (L 201) 37, http://eur-lex.europa.eu/LexUriServ/LexUriServ.do?uri=CELEX:32002L0058:en:HTML.

[10] C.R.P. art. 26(2).

[11] *Id.* art. 35 (translation by author).

[12] Lei No. 67/98, *supra* note 6.

[13] Lei No. 41/2004, *supra* note 8.

[14] Lei No. 67/98, art. 6 (translation by author).

[15] *Id.* art. 3(a).

[16] *Id.*

[17] *Id.* art. 3(b).

[18] *Id.* art. 3(d).

[19] *Id.* art. 3(h).

[20] Lei No. 41/2004, *supra* note 8, art. 1(2).

[21] Lei No. 67/98, *supra* note 6, art. 2.

[22] *Id.* art. 7(1).

[23] *Id.* art. 7(2). Article 22(1) of Law No. 67/98 determines that CNPD is the national authority charged with the power to supervise and monitor compliance with the laws and regulations in the area of personal data protection, with strict respect for the human rights and the fundamental freedoms and guarantees provided by the Constitution and the law.

[24] *Id.* art. 7(3).

[25] *Id.* art. 7(4).

[26] *Id.* art. 12 (translation by author).

[27] *Id.* art. 5(1) (translation by author).

[28] *Id.* art. 5(2). There is a legitimate interest when it is not contrary to the law and can even be protected by it. JOÃO MELO FRANCO & ANTÓNIO HERLANDER ANTUNES MARTINS, DICIONÁRIO DE CONCEITOS E PRINCÍPIOS JURÍDICOS: NA DOUTRINA E NA JURISPRUDÊNCIA 505 (Coimbra: Livraria Almedina, 1995).

[29] *Id.* art. 5(3).

[30] Lei No. 41/2004, *supra* note 8, art. 7(1).

[31] *Id.* art. 7(2).

[32] *Id.* art. 7(3).

[33] *Id.* art. 7(4).

[34] *Id.* art. 7(5).

[35] *Id.* art. 7(5)(a).

[36] *Id.* art. 7(5)(b).

[37] *Id.* art. 7(6).

[38] *Id.* art. 2(1)(a).

[39] *Id.* art. 2(1)(d).

[40] *Id.* art. 2(1)(e).

[41] Lei No. 67/98, *supra* note 6, art. 14(1).

[42] Lei No. 41/2004, *supra* note 8, art. 3(1).

[43] *Id.* art. 3(3).

[44] *Id.* art. 4(1).

[45] *Id.* art. 9(1).

[46] *Id.* art. 9(7).

[47] *O que é a CNPD*, COMISSÃO NACIONAL DE PROTECÇÃO DE DADOS, http://www.cnpd.pt/bin/cnpd/acnpd.htm (last visited May 15, 2012).

[48] Lei No. 67/98, *supra* note 6, art. 10(1).

[49] *Id.* art. 10(4).

[50] *Id.* art. 11(1)(d).

[51] *Id.* art. 11(1)(e).

[52] *Id.* art. 33.

[53] *Id.* art. 34(1).

[54] Decree-Law No. 433 of October 27, 1982, defines "offense" (contra-ordenação) as any unlawful act that can be characterized as an offense to which a fine is imposed. Decreto-Lei No. 433/82, de 27 de Outubro, art. 1, http://www.pgdlisboa.pt/pgdl/leis/lei_mostra_articulado.php?nid=166&tabela=leis.

[55] Lei No. 67/98, *supra* note 6, art. 38(1).

[56] *Id.* art. 38(2).
[57] Lei No. 67/98, *supra* note 6, art. 41(1).
[58] *Id.* art. 41(2).
[59] *Id.* art. 43.
[60] *Id.* art. 44.
[61] *Id.* art. 45.
[62] *Id.* art. 47.
[63] Directive 2000/31/EC of the European Parliament and of the Council of 8 June 2000 on Certain Legal Aspects of Information Society Services, In Particular Electronic Commerce, in the Internal Market (Directive on Electronic Commerce), 2000 O.J. (L 178) 1, http://eur-lex.europa.eu/LexUriServ/LexUriServ.do?uri=CELEX:32000L0031:EN:HTML.
[64] Decreto-Lei No. 7/2004, de 7 de Janeiro, art. 7(1)(a), http://www.pgdlisboa.pt/pgdl/leis/lei_ mostra_articulado.php?nid=1399&tabela=leis&ficha=1&pagina=1&.
[65] *Id.* art. 3(1).
[66] *Id.* art. 7(2)(a).
[67] *Id.* art. 7(2)(b).
[68] *Id.* art. 7(3).
[69] *Id.* art. 7(4).
[70] Lei No. 32/2008, de 17 de Julho, art. 1(1), http://www.pgdlisboa.pt/pgdl/leis/lei_mostra_articulado.php?nid=1264&tabela=leis&ficha=1&pagina=1&.
[71] Directive 2006/24/EC of the European Parliament and of the Council of 15 March 2006 on the retention of data generated or processed in connection with the provision of publicly available electronic communications services or of public communications networks and amending Directive 2002/58/EC, 2006 O.J. (L 105) 54, http://eur-lex.europa.eu/LexUriServ/LexUriServ.do?uri=OJ:L:2006:105:0054:01:EN:HTML.
[72] Lei No. 32/2008, art. 1(2).
[73] *Id.* art. 3(1).
[74] *Id.* art. 3(2).
[75] *Id.* art. 3(3).
[76] *Id.* art. 3(4).
[77] Lei No. 10/91, *supra* note 2, art. 4(1).
[78] *Id.* art. 4(1).
[79] Lei No. 67/98, *supra* note 6, art. 51.
[80] *Id.* art. 22(1).
[81] *Id.* art. 22(3)(a).
[82] *Id.* art. 22(3)(b).
[83] *Id.* art. 22(3)(c).
[84] *Id.* art. 22(4).
[85] *Id.* art. 22(5).
[86] *Id.* art. 22(2).
[87] *Id.* art. 23(1)(g).
[88] *Id.* art. 23(1)(i).
[89] *Id.* art. 23(1)(j).
[90] *Id.* art. 23(1)(k).
[91] *Id.* art. 23(1)(p).
[92] *Google Impedido de Recolher Imagens em Portugal*, JORNAL DE NOTÍCIAS (Aug. 4, 2010), http://www.jn.pt/PaginaInicial/Tecnologia/Interior.aspx?content_id=1633931&page=-1.
[93] *Id.*
[94] *Id.*
[95] *Id.*
[96] *Dia da Proteção de Dados Assinalado em Portugal*, TEK (Jan. 27, 2011), http://tek.sapo.pt/noticias/computadores/dia_da_proteccao_de_dados_assinalado_em_portu_1124953.html.
[97] *Id.*
[98] *Id.*
[99] *Id.*
[100] *Id.*
[101] Press Release, Europa, Commission Proposes a Comprehensive Reform of Data Protection Rules to Increase Users' Control of Their Data and to Cut Costs for Businesses (Jan. 25, 2012), http://europa.eu/

rapid/pressReleasesAction.do?reference=IP/12/46&format=HTML&aged=0&language=EN&guiLanguage=en
.

[102] *Id. See also* separate report on the European Union, *supra*, at 1.
[103] *Id.*

End Notes for Spain

[1] CONSTITUCIÓN ESPAÑOLA [C.E.], Oct. 31, 1978, BOLETÍN OFICIAL DEL ESTADO [B.O.E.] no. 311, Dec. 29, 1978, http://www.boe.es/buscar/doc.php?id=BOE-A-1978-31229.
[2] *Id.* art. 18.1.
[3] *Id.* art. 18.4.
[4] MARÍA DEL CARMEN GUERRERO PICÓ, EL IMPACTO DE INTERNET EN EL DERECHO FUNDAMENTAL A LA PROTECCIÓN DE DATOS DE CARÁCTER PERSONAL [THE IMPACT OF THE INTERNET ON THE FUNDAMENTAL RIGHT PROTECTING PERSONAL DATA] 134–35 (Thomson-Civitas, Navarre, Spain, 2006).
[5] Ley Orgánica 15/1999, de 13 de diciembre, de protección de datos de carácter personal [LOPDP], B.O.E. no. 298, 43088, Dec. 14, 1999, http://www.boe.es/boe/dias/1999/12/14/pdfs/A43088-43099.pdf.
[6] Directive 95/46/EC of the European Parliament and of the Council of 24 October 1995 on the Protection of Individuals with Regard to the Processing of Personal Data and on the Free Movement of Such Data, 1995 O.J. (L 281) 31, http://eur-lex.europa.eu/LexUriServ/LexUriServ.do?uri=CELEX:31995L0046:EN:HTML.
[7] LOPDP art. 1.
[8] Real Decreto 1720/2007, de 21 de diciembre, por el que se aprueba el Reglamento de desarollo del la Ley Orgánica 15/1999, de protección de datos de carácter personal [RLOPDP], B.O.E. no. 17, 4103, Jan. 19, 2008, http://www.boe.es/aeboe/consultas/bases_datos/doc.php?id=BOE-A-2008-979.
[9] *Id.*
[10] Ley 25/2007, de 18 de octubre, de conservación de datos relativos a las comunicaciones electrónicas y a las redes públicas de comunicaciones, B.O.E. no. 251, 42517, Oct. 19, 2007, http://www.boe.es/boe/dias/2007/10/19/pdfs/A42517-42523.pdf.
[11] Directive 2006/24/EC of the European Parliament and of the Council of 15 March 2006, on the Retention of Data Generated or Processed in Connection with the Provision of Publicly Available Electronic Communications Services or of Public Communications Networks and Amending Directive 2002/58/EC, 2006 O.J. (L 105) 54, http://eur-lex.europa.eu/LexUriServ/LexUriServ.do?uri=OJ:L:2006:105:0054:0063:EN:PDF; *Report from the Commission to the Council and the European Parliament: Evaluation Report on the Data Retention Directive (Directive 2006/24/EC)*, at 9–10, COM (2011) 225 final, http://eur-lex.europa.eu/LexUriServ/LexUriServ.do?uri=CELEX:52011DC0225:EN:HTML.
[12] Directive 2002/58/EC amended by Directive 2009/136/CE of the European Parliament and of the Council of 12 July 2002 Concerning the Processing of Personal Data and the Protection of Privacy in the Electronic Communications Sector (Directive on Privacy and Electronic Communications), 2002 O.J. (L 201) 37, http://eurlex.europa.eu/LexUriServ/LexUriServ.do?uri=CONSLEG:2002L0058:20091219:EN:PDF.
[13] Real Decreto 13/2012, de 30 de marzo, por el que se transponen directivas en materia de mercados interiores de electricidad y gas y en materia de comunicaciones electrónicas, y por el que se adoptan medidas para la corrección de las desviaciones por desajustes entre los costes e ingresos de los sectores eléctrico y gasista [Transposing EU Directive 2009/136], B.O.E. no. 78, 26876, Mar. 31, 2012, http://www.boe.es/boe/dias/2012/03/31/ pdfs/BOE-A-2012-4442.pdf.
[14] LOPDP art. 2.1.
[15] *Id.* art. 1.a–c.
[16] *Id.* art. 35.
[17] *Id.* art. 3.a.
[18] RLOPDP art. 5.1.f.
[19] *Id.*
[20] LOPDP art. 25.
[21] RLOPDP art. 4.
[22] LOPDP art. 11.1; RLOPDP art. 10.1.
[23] RLOPDP art. 10.2.a.

[24] RLOPDP art. 10.3.
[25] RLOPDP art. 10.4.
[26] LOPDP art. 11.2.b, in conjunction with LOPDP art. 21.3.
[27] Real Decreto 13/2012, de 30 de marzo, transposing EU Directive 2009/136, B.O.E. no. 78, 26876, Mar. 31, 2012, http://www.boe.es/boe/dias/2012/03/31/pdfs/BOE-A-2012-4442.pdf.
[28] *Id.* art. 4.
[29] Ley 34/2002, de 11 de julio, de servicios de la sociedad de la información y de comercio electrónico, art. 22.2, B.O.E. no. 166, 25388, July 12, 2002, http://www.boe.es/boe/dias/2002/07/12/pdfs/A25388-25403.pdf.
[30] Javier Fernández-Samaniego, *Spain Implements EU Regulation on Cookies*, BIRD & BIRD (Apr. 26, 2012), http://www.twobirds.com/English/News/Articles/Pages/Spain_implements_EU_regulation_on_cookies_0412.Aspx.
[31] *Id.*
[32] LOPDP art. 14.
[33] *Id.* art. 13.1.
[34] *Id.* art. 13.2.
[35] *Id.* art. 13.3.
[36] *Id.* art. 15.1.
[37] *Id.* art. 16.1–2.
[38] *Id.* art. 16.3.
[39] *Id.* art. 18.
[40] *Id.* art. 19.
[41] *Id.* art. 26.1.
[42] *Id.* art. 26.2.
[43] *Id.* art. 27.
[44] A promotional census is a database based on the information entered into the electoral census, including names and addresses of individuals, which is considered open to the public and may be used for commercial marketing purposes. *Id.* arts. 3.j, 28.
[45] *Id.* art. 28.1.
[46] *Id.* art. 28.2.
[47] *Id.* art. 28.2, para. 2.
[48] C.E. art. 16.2.
[49] LOPDP art. 7.1.
[50] *Id.* art. 7.2.
[51] *Id.* art. 7.4.
[52] *Id.* art. 7.3.
[53] *Id.* art. 7.6.
[54] *Id.* art. 7.6, para. 2.
[55] *Id.* art. 7.5.
[56] INSTITUTO NACIONAL DE TECNOLOGÍAS DE LA COMUNICACIÓN (INTC)/AGENCIA ESPAÑOLA DE PROTECCIÓN DE DATOS PERSONALES (AEPDP) [NATIONAL INSTITUTE OF TECHNOLOGY OF COMMUNICATION/SPANISH AGENCY OF PERSONAL DATA PROTECTION], ESTUDIO SOBRE LA PRIVACIDAD DE LOS DATOS PERSONALES Y LA SEGURIDAD DE LA INFORMACIÓN EN LAS REDES SOCIALES ONLINE [A STUDY ON PERSONAL DATA PRIVACY AND INFORMATION SECURITY IN ONLINE SOCIAL NETWORKS] 117 (undated), http://www.agpd.es/portalweb AGPD/canaldocumentacion/publicaciones/common/Estudios/est_inteco_redesso_022 009.pdf (last visited June 8, 2012).
[57] RLOPDP art. 23.2.b, B.O.E. no. 17, 4103, Jan. 19, 2008, http://www.boe.es/aeboe/consultas/bases_datos/doc.php?id=BOE-A-2008-979.
[58] *Id.* art. 13.1.
[59] *Id.* art. 13.2.
[60] *Id.* art. 13.3.
[61] *Id.* art. 13.4.
[62] INTC/AEPDP, *supra* note 56, at 118.
[63] Ley 25/2007, de 18 de octubre, de conservación de datos relativos a las comunicaciones electrónicas y a las redes públicas de comunicaciones, B.O.E. no. 251, 42517, Oct. 19, 2007, http://www.boe.es/boe/dias/2007/10/19/pdfs/A42517-42523.pdf.

[64] Directive 2006/24/EC of the European Parliament and of the Council of 15 March 2006, on the Retention of Data Generated or Processed in Connection with the Provision of Publicly Available Electronic Communications Services or of Public Communications Networks and Amending Directive 2002/58/EC, 2006 O.J. (L 105) 54, http://eur-lex.europa.eu/LexUriServ/LexUriServ.do?uri=OJ:L:2006:105:0054:0063:EN:PDF.

[65] Ley 25/2007 art. 1.

[66] Marcelo Corrales, *Implementación de la Directiva 2006/24/CE en España*, 23 REVISTA AYS 128 (June 2008), http://www.revista-ays.com/DocsNum23/TemasJuridicos/Corrales.pdf.

[67] Ley 25/2007 art. 5.

[68] *Id.* art. 6.

[69] EDRI is a European privacy and civil rights organization.

[70] XS4ALL is a Dutch Internet service provider.

[71] Corrales, *supra* note 66, at 129.

[72] LOPDP art. 9.1, B.O.E. no. 298, 43088, Dec. 14, 1999, http://www.boe.es/boe/dias/1999/12/14/pdfs/ A43088-43099.pdf.

[73] *Id.* art. 9.2.

[74] RLOPDP arts. 79–114, B.O.E. no. 17, 4103, Jan. 19, 2008, http://www.boe.es/aeboe/consultas/ bases_datos/doc.php?id=BOE-A-2008-979.

[75] LOPDP arts. 43–44.

[76] *Id.* art. 44.2 (translation by the author).

[77] *Id.* art. 44.3 (translation by author).

[78] *Id.* art. 44.4 (translation by author).

[79] *Id.* art. 45.7.

[80] *Id.* art. 45.1–3.

[81] *Id.* art. 45.4.

[82] *Id.* art. 49.

[83] Ley Orgánica 10/1995, de 23 de noviembre, del Código Penal, art. 197, B.O.E. no. 281, 33987, Nov. 24, 1995, http://www.boe.es/boe/dias/1995/11/24/pdfs/A33987-34058.pdf.

[84] *Id.* art. 197.1–3.

[85] *Id.* art. 197.4–6.

[86] LOPDP art. 19.1.

[87] Real Decreto de 24 de julio de 1889 por el que se publica el Código Civil, *as amended*, art. 1902, B.O.E. no. 206, 249 July 25, 1889, http://www.boe.es/aeboe/consultas/bases_datos/act.php?id=BOE-A-1889- 4763&tn =1&p= 20110722&accion=Elegir.

[88] *Id.*

[89] LOPDP art. 35.1.

[90] *Id.* art. 35.4.

[91] *Id.* art. 37.

[92] *Id.* arts. 39 & 32.

[93] RLOPDP arts. 60–64.

[94] Brochure, Spanish Data Protection Agency, http://www.agpd.es/portalwebAGPD/canaldocumentacion/ publicaciones/common/pdfs/AEPD_en.pdf (last visited June 15, 2012).

[95] *Id.*

[96] *Id.*

[97] *Id.*

[98] S. Juz. Prim., Feb. 23, 2012 (No. 32), *available at* LEX NOVA, http://portaljuridico.lexnova. es/jurisprudencia /JURIDICO/128994/sentencia-juz-1-inst-amposta-num-1-32-2012-de-23-de-febrero-derecho-alhonor-demanda-contr.

[99] *Id.*

[100] *Id.*

[101] *Id.*

[102] *Id.*

[103] *España Lleva a Google al Tribunal Europeo por el 'Derecho al Olvido'*, EL PAÍS (Mar. 2, 2012), http://sociedad.elpais.com/sociedad/2012/03/02/actualidad/1330721064 418059.html.

[104] *Id.*

[105] Case C-131/12, Google Spain, S.L., Google Inc. v Agencia Española de Protección de Datos, Mario Costeja González, reference for a preliminary ruling, Mar. 9, 2012, http://curia.europa.eu/juris/fiche.jsf?id= C%3B131%3B12%3BRP%3B1%3BP%3B1%3BC2012%2F0131%2FP&pro=&lgrec=en&nat=&oqp=&lg=&

dates =&language=en&jur=C&cit=none%252CC%252CCJ%252CR%252C2008E%252C%25 2C%252C% 252C%252C% 252C%252C%252C%252C%252Ctrue%252Cfalse%252Cfalse&td=ALL&pcs=O &avg=& mat=or&etat=pend&parti es=Spain&jge=&for=&cid=136854.

[106] EL PAÍS, *supra* note 103.

[107] *Id.*

[108] *Id.*

[109] *Proposal for a Regulation of the European Parliament and of the Council On the Protection of Individuals with Regard to the Processing of Personal Data and on the Free Movement of Such Data (General Data Protection Regulation)*, COM (2012) 11 final (Jan. 15, 2012), 3.4.3.3., http://eur-lex.europa.eu/LexUriServ/Lex UriServ.do?uri=COM:2012:0011:FIN:EN:PDF.

[110] T.S., Sala Tercera, Feb. 8, 2012, *Federación de Comercio Electrónico y Marketing Directo contra Real Decreto 1720/2007 c/ Administración General del Estado, la Asociación de Usuarios de la Comunicación y la Unión General de Trabajadores s/ Recurso Contencioso-Administrativo* 25/08, *available at* http://www.elderecho. com/administrativo/Tribunal-Contencioso-Administrativo-Sentencia-Recurso-EDJ_EDEFIL20120215_0007.pdf.

[111] Directive 95/46/EC, *supra* note 6, art. 7.f.

[112] Juan José García, *Comentarios a la Sentencia del Tribunal Supremo de 8-2-2012 sobre Protección de Datos*, ADARVE ABOGADOS, http://www.adarve.com/prensa/comentarios-la-sentencia-del-tribunal-supremo-de-8-2- 2012-sobre-proteccion-de-datos (last visited June 11, 2012).

[113] Javier Fernández-Samaniego & Antonio Creus, *The Supreme Court Admits 'Legitimate Interest' as a Criterion for the Processing of Personal Data Without Consent*, INTERNATIONAL ASSOCIATION OF PRIVACY PROFESSIONALS (Feb. 16, 2012), https://www.privacyassociation.org/publications/2012_02_16_ the_supreme_ court_admits_legitimate_interest_as_a_criterion_for.

[114] T.S., Sala Tercera, Feb. 8, 2012, *Federación de Comercio Electrónico y Marketing Directo.*

[115] *UK Ranks 21st in Europe for Privacy Protection*, INFORMATION AGE (Jan. 24, 2012), http://www.information-age.com/channels/security-and-continuity/news/1687058/uk-ranks-21st-in-europe-forprivacy-protection-.thtml.

[116] Josh Halliday, *Europe's Highest Court to Rule on Google Privacy Battle in Spain*, THE GUARDIAN (Mar. 1, 2011), http://www.guardian.co.uk/technology/2011/mar/01/google-spain-privacy-court-case.

[117] *Id.*

[118] García, *supra* note 112.

[119] ISABEL DAVARA FERNANDEZ DE MARCOS, HACIA LA ESTANDARIZACIÓN DE LA PROTECCIÓN DE DATOS PERSONALES 35 (Ed. La Ley, Madrid, 2011).

[120] Press Release, Agencia Española de Protección de Datos, La AEPD Destaca la Alta Desconfianza de los Ciudadanos Españoles en la Seguridad de sus Datos en Internet [The AEPD underlines the high confidence of Spanish citizens in the safety of their Internet data] 1 (Sept. 2009), http://www.agpd.es/portalwebAGPD /revista_ prensa/revista prensa/2009/notas prensa/common/oct/151009 nota prensa barometro cis.pdf.

[121] *Id.*

[122] *Id.*

[123] *Id.*

[124] *Id.*

[125] *Id.*

[126] *La Audiencia Pregunta a la UE Cómo Actuar ante las Peticiones de Borrado de Datos en Internet* [*The Audience Asks How the EU Will Deal with the Requests for Deletion of Data on the Internet*], EL MUNDO (Mar. 2, 2012), http://www.elmundo.es/elmundo/2012/03/02/navegante/1330685652.html.

[127] Antonio Viñal & Co. Abogados, *The New EU Data Protection Proposal: Getting Ready with the Spanish Example*, 4 AVCONEWS (Mar. 2012), *available at* http://documents.jdsupra.com/fb0d5d2f-d718-4929- 92ba-567fe7d98b5a.pdf.

[128] *Id; Proposal for a Regulation of the European Parliament and of the Council On the Protection of Individuals with Regard to the Processing of Personal Data and on the Free Movement of Such Data (General Data Protection Regulation)*, COM (2012) 11 final (Jan. 25, 2012), http://eur-lex.europa.eu/LexUriServ/LexUriServ.do? uri=COM:2012:0011:FIN:EN:PDF.

End Notes for Sweden

[1] DATALAG (Svensk författningssamling [SFS] 1973:289); Peter Siepel, *Sweden*, *in* NORDIC DATA PROTECTION LAW 115, 116 (Peter Blume ed., 2001).

[2] REGERINGSFORMEN [RF] [CONSTITUTION] 2:6.

[3] RF 2:3 (SFS 1994:1468), *as amended* 2010.

[4] Proposition [Prop.] 2009/10:80 En reformerad grundlag [A Reformed Constitution] [Government Bill] at 256–57.

[5] *Id.*

[6] PERSONUPPGIFTSLAGEN [PERSONAL DATA ACT] (SFS 2003:389).

[7] Konstitutionsutskottet 1998/99:KU15, Personuppgiftslagen [Personal Data Act], http://www.riksdagen.se/sv/Dokument-Lagar/Utskottens-dokument/Betankanden/Personuppgiftslagen_GM01KU15/.

[8] *Id.*

[9] *See* 2 § PERSONUPPGIFTSLAGEN [PUL] [PERSONAL DATA ACT] (SFS 1998:204), *available at* http://www.riksdagen.se/sv/Dokument-Lagar/Lagar/Svenskforfattningssamling/Personuppgiftslag-1998204_sfs1998-204/?bet=1998:204 (including all amendments to date).

[10] This distinction is mentioned in Siepel, *supra* note 1, at 119.

[11] *See* THOMAS CARLÉN-WENDELS, NÄTJURIDIK - LAG OCH RÄTT PÅ INTERNET 95–98 (3rd ed. 2000).

[12] *Id.*

[13] PUL 10 §.

[14] PUL 10 §.

[15] PUL 10 a–f §§.

[16] PUL 13, 15–19 §§.

[17] PUL 12 §.

[18] *Id.*

[19] PUL 11 §.

[20] DI 280-1999; summary in THOMAS CARLÉN-WENDELS, *supra* note 11, at 95–96.

[21] (SFS 2008:486).

[22] *Personnummer som spärr mot småbarn på chattsajt* [*Personal Identification Numbers as a Barrier Against Small Children's Access to Chat-Site*], DATAINSPEKTIONEN (Dec. 2002), http://www.datainspektionen.se/personuppgiftsombud/samradsyttranden/registrering-av-personuppgifter-fran-barn-/.

[23] LAGEN OM ELEKTRONISK KOMMUNIKATION [LEK] (SFS 2003:389), http://www.riksdagen.se/sv/Dokument-Lagar/Lagar/Svenskforfattningssamling/Lag-2003389-om-elektronisk-_sfs-2003-389/.

[24] LEK ch. 6.

[25] LEK ch. 6:3 §.

[26] *Id.*

[27] LEK ch. 6:5 §.

[28] *Id.*

[29] *Id.*

[30] LEK ch. 6:17 §.

[31] LEK ch. 6:6 §.

[32] LEK ch. 6:9 §.

[33] *See* Post- och telestyrelsen (PTS) website, *at* http://www.pts.se/sv/Regler/Lagar/Lag-om-elektronisk-kommunikation/Cookies-kakor/Fragor-och-svar-om-kakor-for-anvandare/#vad säger lagen (last visited July 5, 2012).

[34] Emanuel Karlsson, *Härmed anmäler jag Riksdagen för brott mot lagen* [*I Hereby Report the Swedish Parliament for Breaching the Law*], EMANUELS RADANMÄRKNINGAR (July 1, 2012), http://emanuelkarlsten.se/07/harmed-anmaler-jag-riksdagen-for-brott-mot-lagen/.

[35] PUL 48 §.

[36] PUL 49 §.

[37] *Id.*

[38] *Id.*

[39] *Id.*

[40] LEK ch. 6:2 §.

[41] Datainspektionen, *Datainspektionen eller PTS – vem ska du vända dig till?* [*Data Inspection Board or the PTS - Who Should You Turn To?*], http://www.datainspektionen.se/om-oss/det-har-gor-vi-inte/lagen-omelektronisk-kommunikation/ (last visited July 5, 2012); PTS, https://www.pts.se (last visited July 5, 2012).

[42] *Datainspektionen 1973–2008* [*Data Inspection Board 1973–2008*], DATAINSPEKTIONEN, http://www.datainspektionen.se/om-oss/historik/ (last visited July 5, 2012).

[43] *Id.*

[44] *About Us*, DATAINSPEKTIONEN, http://www.datainspektionen.se/in-english/about-us/ (last visited July 5, 2012).

[45] INKASSOLAGEN (SFS 1974:182).

[46] KREDITUPPLYSNINGSLAGEN (SFS 1973:1173).

[47] PATIENTDATALAGEN (SFS 2008:355).

[48] *See, e.g.*, Datainspektionen, *Säkerhet för personuppgifter* [*Securing Personal Data*], http://www.datainspektionen.se/Documents/faktabroschyr-allmannarad-sakerhet.pdf (rev'd Nov. 2008).

[49] For a list in English, *see Datainspektionens föreskrifter* [DIFS] [*Data Inspection Board's Regulations*], DATAINSPEKTIONEN, http://www.datainspektionen.se/lagar-och-regler/datainspektionens-foreskrifter/ (last visited July 5, 2012) (scroll to bottom of page).

[50] *Så arbetar Datainspektionen* [*How the Data Inspection Board Works*], DATAINSPEKTIONEN, http://www.datainspektionen.se/om-oss/arbetssatt/ (last visited July 5, 2012).

[51] Prop. 2005/2006:173 Översyn av personuppgiftslagen [Review of the Personal Data Act] [Government Bill], 20 (Mar. 16, 2006), http://www.regeringen.se/content/1/c6/06/08/09/2c0a24ce.pdf.

[52] PUL 47 §.

[53] PUL 44 §.

[54] *Om PTS* [*About PTS*], PTS, http://www.pts.se/sv/OmPTS/ (last visited July 5, 2012).

[55] *Säker kommunikation* [*Secure Communication*], PTS, http://www.pts.se/sv/OmPTS/Verksamhet/Saker-kommunikation/ (last visited July 5, 2012).

[56] *See* Post och Telestyrelsen, https://www.pts.se (last visited July 5, 2012).

[57] Monica Kleja, *Datainspektionen slår ner på molntjänster* [*Data Inspection Board Cracks Down on Cloud Services*], NYTEKNIK.SE (Oct. 3, 2010), http://www.nyteknik.se/nyheter/it_telekom/internet/article3281165.ece (translation by author).

[58] *Facebook svarar de nordiska länderna*, DATAINSPEKTIONEN (Sept. 20, 2011), http://www.data inspektionen.se/press/nyheter/2011/facebook-svarar-de-nordiska-landerna/.

[59] Letter from Richard Allan, Director of Policy for Europe, Africa, and Middle East, Facebook, to Bjorn-Erik Thon, Director, Data Inspectorate of Norway (Sept. 2011), *available at* http://www.datatilsynet.no/Global/english/Facebook_questions_answere2011.pdf.

[60] *See* DATAINSPEKTIONEN, *supra* note 58.

[61] Rättsfall från Hovrätterna [RH] [Court of Appeals] 2004-04-07 p. 51, *available at* https://lagen.nu/dom/rh/2004:51.

[62] Nytt Juridiskt Arkiv [NJA] [Supreme Court] 2001 p. 409; summary in *Vad är straffbart enligt personuppgiftslagen, en vägledning från datainspektionen för polis och åklagare* [*What is Sanctioned Under the Personal Data Act: A Guide from the Data Inspection Board for Police and Prosecutor*], DATAINSPEKTIONEN, at 15 (Jan. 2011), http://www.datainspektionen.se/Documents/vagledning-aklagare.pdf.

[63] NJA 2005-05-26 p. 361.

[64] Summary in DATAINSPEKTIONEN, *supra* note 62, at 18–19.

[65] Decision DNR 684-201 (July 12, 2010), *available at* http://www.datainspektionen.se/Documents/ beslut/2010-07-05-katrineholm.pdf.

[66] Datainspektionen, Diarienr 1288-2009, *Tillsyn enligt personuppgiftslagen (1998:204) – ang. omdömen i en interaktiv tjänst på Internet*, Jan. 11, 2010, http://www.datainspektionen.se/Documents/beslut/2010-01-12-rejtingsajt.pdf.

[67] Dnr 274-2001, summary in DATAINSPEKTIONEN, *supra* note 62, at 14.

[68] DATAINSPEKTIONEN, *supra* note 62, at 10.

[69] *See id.* (referencing Decision Nos. 1658-2008 and 265-2009).

[70] *Id.*

[71] *Id.* at 10–11.

[72] Available online *at* http://curia.europa.eu/juris/liste.jsf?language=en&num=C-461/10 (last visited July 16, 2012).

[73] *See* summary in Stefan Widmark & Evelina Anttila, *ECJ Hands Down Preliminary ePhone Ruling - International Report*, INTELLECTUAL ASSESMENT MANAGEMENT (IAM) (June 13, 2012), http://www.iam-magazine.com/reports/Detail.aspx?g=29765a88-ded7-47ec-9601-c391c513ee89.

[74] *Id.*

75 *See, e.g.*, *Ungdomsförbunden kritiska mot integritetspolitik* [*Youth Parties Critical of Integrity Policies*], SVD.SE, (June 29, 2009; updated July 28, 2009), http://www.svd.se/nyheter/inrikes/politik/valet2010/ungdomsforbunden-kritiska-mot-integritetspolitik 3137721.svd.

76 *Allt fler svenska anonyma på internet* [*Increasing Number of Swedes Anonymous Online*], SVD.SE (May 1, 2012), http://www.svd.se/nyheter/inrikes/allt-fler-svenskar-anonyma-pa-natet_7125265.svd (translation by author).

77 *Sweden Postpones EU Data Retention Directive, Faces Court, Fines*, THE REGISTER (Mar. 18, 2011), http://www.theregister.co.uk/2011/03/18/sweden_postpones_eu_data_retention_directive/.

78 *See* Op-ed, Erik Bengtzboe, *Justitieministern sviker löfte om integritet* [*Minister of Justice Breaks Promise on Integrity*], SVD.SE (June 19, 2012; updated June 20, 2012), http://www.svd.se/opinion/brannpunkt/justitieministern-sviker-lofte-om-integritet_7289849.svd; *see also* Op-ed, Camilla Lindberg & Carl Johan Rehbinder, *Våga vägra datalagringsdirektivet* [*Dare to Refuse the Data Retention Directive*], SVD.SE (Sept. 3, 2010), http://www.svd.se/opinion/brannpunkt/vaga-vagra-datalagringsdirektivet_5242087.svd.

79 For full text of the proposal in Swedish, *see* Prop. 2011/12:55 De brottsbekämpande myndigheternas tillgång till uppgifter om elektronisk kommunikation [Crime Prevention Government Agencies's Access to Information on Electronic Communication][Government Bill] (Feb. 10, 2012), *available at* http://www.regeringen. se/sb/d/108/a/186055.

80 *Sweden Extends Police Eavesdropping Powers*, THELOCAL.SE (May 11, 2012), http://www.thelocal.se/40784/20120511/.

81 *Den framtida regleringen av hemliga tvångsmedel mot allvarliga brott* [*Future Regulation of Secret Surveillance Measures Against Serious Crimes*], REGERINGEN.SE (June 28, 2012), http://www.regeringen.se/sb/d/119/a/195993.

82 *Id.*

83 *Regeringen och Socialdemokraterna överens om signalspaning* [*Swedish Government and Social Democrats Agree on Communication Intelligence*], REGERINGEN.SE (Dec. 15, 2011), http://regeringen.se/sb/d/15434/a/182763.

84 *Ramöverenskommelse mellan regeringen och Socialdemokraterna om Polisens tillgång till signalspaning* [*Frame Agreement Between the Government and the Social Democrats Concerning Police Access to Intelligence*], REGERINGEN.SE (Dec. 15, 2011), http://regeringen.se/content/1/c6/18/27/63/71e7da2c.pdf.

85 Op-ed, Morgan Johansson, *Nätföretagens makt bör regleras* [*The Power of Online Corporations Should be Regulated*], SVD.SE (June 25, 2012), http://www.svd.se/opinion/brannpunkt/natforetagens-makt-borregleras 7299699.svd.

End Notes for United Kingdom

1 European Convention for the Protection of Human Rights and Fundamental Freedoms, *opened for signature* Nov. 4, 1950, 213 U.N.T.S. 222. The European Convention on Human Rights was incorporated into the national legislation of the United Kingdom by the Human Rights Act 1998, c. 42, sch. 1, art. 8.

2 Data Protection Act 1998, c. 29, http://www.opsi.gov.uk/acts/acts1998/ukpga_19980029_en_1. The UK's Data Protection Act was created to implement a European Union Directive that established a set of principles to govern the protection of data throughout the European Economic Area. Directive 95/46/EC of the European Parliament and of the Council of 24 October 1995 on the protection of individuals with regard to the processing of personal data and on the free movement of such data, 1995 O.J. (L 281) 31 (EC), http://eur-lex.europa.eu/LexUriServ/LexUriServ.do?uri=CELEX:31995L0046:EN:HTML.

3 *Data Protection Act Factsheet*, INFORMATION COMMISSIONER, http://www.aimhigher.ac.uk/practitioner/resources/Data_protection_fact_sheet.pdf (last visited June 28, 2012).

4 "Art. 1 of the Data Protection Directive protects the privacy of an individual with respect to the processing of data; on the other hand, there is no mention of the word privacy in the Data Protection Act 1998." DIANE ROWLAND, INFORMATION TECHNOLOGY LAW 151 (2011). *See also* R v. Brown, [1996] 1 All ER 545.

5 Data Protection Act 1998, c. 29, introductory text.

6 Francis G.B. Aldhouse, *Data Protection, Privacy and the Media*, 4 COMM. L. 8, 11 (1999), *cited in* ROWLAND, *supra* note 4, at 152.

7 ROWLAND, *supra* note 4, at 155.

[8] *Id.* at 167.

[9] The Information Commissioner has offered guidance, noting that data is considered to be processed when it is "collected and analysed with the intention of distinguishing one individual from another and to take a particular action in respect of an individual. This can take place even if no obvious identifiers, such as names or addresses, are held." Innovations Mail Order v. DPR, Case DA/92 31/49/1. The Information Commissioner considers that for multi-user devices, such as personal computers in shared households, if it cannot be determined whether the information collected is from an individual user or a group of users it is good practice to treat it all as personal data. Information Commissioner's Office, Personal Information Online Code of Practice 8 (July 2010), http://www.ico.gov.uk/for_organisations/data_protection/topic_guides/~/media /documents/library/Data_Protection/ Detailed_specialist_guides/personal_information_online_cop.ashx.

[10] Data Protection Act 1998, c. 29, sch. 1.

[11] *Id.*, c. 29, § 1.

[12] Durant v. Financial Services Authority, [2003] EWCA Civ. 1746.

[13] *Id.*

[14] Data Protection Act 1998, c. 29, § 5.

[15] *Id.*

[16] ROSEMARY JAY & ANGUS HAMILTON, DATA PROTECTION LAW AND PRACTICE 3.46 (2d ed. 2003).

[17] Information Commissioner's Office, *supra* note 9, at 11.

[18] Directive 2002/58/EC of the European Parliament and of the Council of 12 July 2002 Concerning the Processing of Personal Data and the Protection of Privacy in the Electronic Communications Sector, 2002 O.J. (L 201) 37, http://eur-lex.europa.eu/LexUriServ/LexUriServ.do?uri=CELEX:32002L0058:EN:PDF.

[19] Directive 2009/136/EC on Universal Service and User's Rights Relating to Electronic Communications Networks and Services 2009 O.J. (L 377) 11, http://eur-lex.europa.eu/LexUriServ/LexUriServ.do?uri=OJ:L: 2009:337:0011:0036:EN:PDF.

[20] The Privacy and Electronic Communications (EC Directive) Regulations 2003, SI 2003/2426, 14, http://www.legislation.gov.uk/uksi/2003/2426/regulation/14/made, *as amended by* The Privacy and Electronic Communications (EC Directive) (Amendment) Regulations 2011, SI 2011/1208, http://www.legislation.gov. uk/uksi/2011/1208/contents/made.

[21] *Id.* 6(1)–(2), http://www.legislation.gov.uk/uksi/2003/2426/regulation/6/made.

[22] Information Commissioner's Office, *supra* note 9, at 32.

[23] Data Protection Act 1998, c. 29.

[24] The Privacy and Electronic Communications (EC Directive) Regulations 2003, SI 2003/2426.

[25] Anti-terrorism, Crime and Security Act 2001, c. 24, http://www.legislation.gov.uk/ukpga/ 2001/24/contents.

[26] Home Office, *Retention of Communications Data Under Part 11: Anti-Terrorism, Crime and Security Act 2001, Voluntary Code of Practice*, http://www.opsi.gov.uk/si/si2003/draft/5b.pdf (last visited June 27, 2012).

[27] Anti-terrorism, Crime and Security Act 2001, c. 24, § 103, http://www.legislation.gov.uk/ ukpga/2001/24/contents.

[28] *Id.* § 102.

[29] *Id.* § 104.

[30] The Data Retention (EC Directive) Regulations 2009, SI 2009/859, http://www.legislation.gov.uk/ ukdsi/2009/9780111473894/contents, transposing Directive 2006/24/EC on the Retention of Data Generated or Processed in Connection with the Provision of Publicly Available Electronic Communications Services or of Public Communications Networks, 2006 O.J. (L 105) 54, http://eur-lex.europa.eu/LexUriServ/Lex UriServ.do?uri= CELEX:32006L0024:EN:PDF.

[31] Data Retention (EC Directive) Regulations 2009, *supra* note 30, sched.

[32] Information Commissioner's Office, *supra* note 9, at 12. The UK National Archives has produced guidance on how long data should be retained and when it should be deleted. *Retention and Disposal Schedules*, THE NATIONAL ARCHIVES, http://www.nationalarchives.gov.uk/information-management/projects-and-work/retention-disposal-schedules.htm (last visited May 30, 2012).

[33] Information Commissioner's Office, *supra* note 9, at 12.

[34] *Id.*

[35] The Data Retention (EC Directive) Regulations 2009, SI 2009/859.

[36] Explanatory Memorandum to the Data Retention (EC Directive) Regulations 2009, 2009/859, http://www.legislation.gov.uk/uksi/2009/859/pdfs/uksiem_20090859_en.pdf.

[37] Data Retention (EC Directive) Regulations 2009, SI 2009/859.

[38] *Id.* § 11(1), http://www.legislation.gov.uk/uksi/2009/859/regulation/11/made.

[39] Information Commissioner's Office, *supra* note 9, at 14.

[40] *Id. See also Privacy Notices*, INFORMATION COMMISSIONER'S OFFICE, http://www.ico.gov.uk/for_organisations/data_protection/topic_guides/privacy_notices.aspx (last visited June 27, 2012).

[41] The Privacy and Electronic Communications (EC Directive) Regulations 2003, SI 2426/2003, ¶ 6(1)–(2), http://www.legislation.gov.uk/uksi/2003/2426/regulation/6/made.

[42] Information Commissioner's Office, Privacy and Electronic Communications Regulations: Guidance on the Rules on Use of Cookies and Similar Technologies (May 2012), http://www.ico.gov.uk/for_organisations/privacy_and_electronic_communications/~/media/documents/library/Privacy_and_electronic/Practical_application/ guidance on the new cookies regulations.ashx.

[43] The Privacy and Electronic Communications (EC Directive) Regulations 2003, SI 2426/2003, 6(4).

[44] Data Protection Act 1998, c. 29, § 10, http://www.legislation.gov.uk/ukpga/1998/29/section/10.

[45] *iPhone Apps Exposed for Downloading Users' Data*, WHICH? NEWS (Feb. 16, 2012), http://www.which.co.uk/news/2012/02/iphone-apps-exposed-for-downloading-users-data--279395/.

[46] The Privacy and Electronic Communications (EC Directive) Regulations 2003, SI 2003/2426, 14, http://www.legislation.gov.uk/uksi/2003/2426/regulation/14/made.

[47] *Id.*

[48] *Location Data*, INFORMATION COMMISSIONER'S OFFICE, http://www.ico.gov.uk/for_ organisations /privacy_and_electronic_communications/the_guide/location_data.aspx (last visited June 26, 2012).

[49] The Privacy and Electronic Communications (EC Directive) Regulations 2003, SI 2003/2426, 14(3)(a)–(c), http://www.legislation.gov.uk/uksi/2003/2426/regulation/14/made.

[50] Information Commissioner's Office, *supra* note 46.

[51] The Privacy and Electronic Communications (EC Directive) Regulations 2003, SI 2003/2426, 14.

[52] *Child Internet Safety*, DEPARTMENT FOR EDUCATION, http://www.education.gov.uk/childrenandyoungpeople/healthandwellbeing/safeguardingchildren/a0064981/child-internet-safety (last updated Apr. 12, 2012)

[53] *Id.*

[54] *Study Reveals the UK's 'Under-age' Social Networking Generation*, LONDON SCHOOL OF ECONOMICS AND POLITICAL SCIENCE, http://www2.lse.ac.uk/newsAndMedia/news/archives/2011/04/UKKidsOnline.aspx (last updated Apr. 18, 2011).

[55] Press Release, School of Education, Bath Spa University, Child Protection Conference at Bath Spa University Sparks National Debate (Apr. 24, 2012), http://www.bathspa.ac.uk/about/news/default.asp?article=981.

[56] *See, e.g., Facebook Guidance*, PEEL COMMON JUNIOR SCHOOL, http://www.peelcommon-jun.hants.sch.uk/p_Facebook_.ikml (last visited July 10, 2012).

[57] Data Protection Act 1998, c. 29, sch. 1, pt. 1, ¶ 7.

[58] *Id.* sch. 1, part II, ¶ 9.

[59] *Sending Personal Data Outside the European Economic Area (Principle 8)*, INFORMATION COMMISSIONER'S OFFICE, http://www.ico.gov.uk/for_organisations/data_protection/the_guide/principle_8.aspx (last visited July 9, 2012).

[60] JISC LEGAL INFORMATION, SECURITY, MOBILE DEVICES AND DATA PROTECTION 1 (Key Points) (Feb. 2012), http://www.jisclegal.ac.uk/ManageContent/ViewDetail/ID/2326/Security-Mobile-Devices-and-Data-Protection.aspxhttp://www.jisclegal.ac.uk/Portals/12/Documents/Security%20Mobile%20Devices%20and%20Data %20Protection.pdf.

[61] *New EU Cookie Law (e-Privacy Directive)*, INFORMATION COMMISSIONER'S OFFICE, http://www.ico.gov.uk/for_organisations/privacy_and_electronic_communications/the_guide/cookies.aspx (last visited July 9, 2012).

[62] Data Protection Act 1998, c. 29.

[63] *Id.* pt. II.

[64] *Id.*

[65] *Id.*

[66] Information Commissioner's Office, *supra* note 9, at 32.

[67] Durant v. Financial Services Authority, [2003] EWCA Civ 1746, *cited in* ROWLAND, *supra* note 4, at 175.

[68] Data Protection Act 1998, c. 29, § 7.

[69] *Id.*

[70] *Id.* § 8(2).

[71] *Id.* § 7(4).

[72] ROWLAND, *supra* note 4, at 175.

[73] Data Protection Act 1998, c. 29, § 7.

[74] Ezsias v. Glamorgan NHS Trust, [2007] EWHC 815 (QB) 53–54.
[75] *Id.*
[76] Durant v. Financial Services Authority, [2003] EWCA Civ. 1746, *cited in* ROWLAND, *supra* note 4, at 176.
[77] Data Protection Act 1998, c. 29, part IV & sch. 7.
[78] *Id.*
[79] *Id.* § 7(10).
[80] *Id.* §§ 10–12.
[81] ROWLAND, *supra* note 4, at 176.
[82] Data Protection Act 1998, c. 29, § 14.
[83] Dave Clancy, *The Privacy and Electronic Communications (EC Directive) (Amendment) Regulations 2011*, INFORMATION COMMISSIONER'S OFFICE, http://www.ico.gov.uk/news/blog/2012/~/media/documents/library/Privacy_and_electronic/Notices/cookie_regulations_letter.ashx (last visited June 27, 2012).
[84] Criminal Justice and Immigration Act 2008, c. 4, http://www.legislation.gov.uk/ukpga/2008/4/contents.
[85] Data Protection Act 1998, c. 29, § 40(2).
[86] Information Commissioner's Office, Privacy and Electronic Communications Regulations: Guidance on the Rules on Use of Cookies and Similar Technologies, 2012, 26, http://www.ico.gov.uk/for_organisations/privacy_and_electronic_communications/the_guide/~/media/documents/library/Privacy_and_electronic/Practi cal_ap plication/cookies_guidance_v3.ashx.
[87] *Security Breaches*, INFORMATION COMMISSIONER'S OFFICE, http://www.ico.gov.uk/for_organisations/privacy_and_electronic_communications/the_guide/security_breaches.aspx (last visited June 27, 2012).
[88] The Privacy and Electronic Communications (EC Directive) Regulations 2003, SI 2003/2426, 5C, as amended, http://www.legislation.gov.uk/uksi/2003/2426/contents/made.
[89] *Enforcing the Revised Privacy and Electronic Communications Regulations (PECR)* (May 25, 2012), INFORMATION COMMISSIONER'S OFFICE, http://www.ico.gov.uk/for_organisations/privacy_and_electronic_ communications/~/media/documents/library/Privacy_and_electronic/Practical_ application /enforcing_the_revised_pr ivacy_and_electronic_communication_regulations_v1.pdf.
[90] Data Protection Act 1998, c. 29, § 55.
[91] *Id.* § 55A.
[92] Data Protection Act 1998, c. 29, § 60.
[93] *Data Protection FAQs—for Organisations*, INFORMATION COMMISSIONER'S OFFICE, http://www.ico.gov.uk/Global/faqs/data_protection_for_organisations.aspx#f0CFA8622-7A94-4648-840F0BB40E91C6C5 (last visited June 26, 2012).
[94] *Id.*
[95] Data Protection Act 1998, c. 29, § 55A.
[96] *Id.* sch. 1, Part I, 8.
[97] *Id.* §§ 27–38, sch. 7, 1. There are many exemptions, including national security; crime and taxation; health, education, and social work; regulatory activities; journalism, literature, and art; research history and statistics; and corporate finance.
[98] *Id.* sch. 4.
[99] *About the ICO*, INFORMATION COMMISSIONER'S OFFICE, http://www.ico.gov.uk/about_us.aspx (last visited June 20, 2012).
[100] *History of the ICO*, INFORMATION COMMISSIONER'S OFFICE, http://www.ico.gov.uk/about_us/our_organisation/history.aspx (last visited June 20, 2012).
[101] Data Protection Act 1984, c. 35, http://www.legislation.gov.uk/ukpga/1984/35/enacted.
[102] *Key Facts*, INFORMATION COMMISSIONER'S OFFICE, http://www.ico.gov.uk/about_us/our_organisation/key_facts.aspx (last visited June 20, 2012).
[103] *Id.*
[104] *Id.*
[105] *Id.*
[106] Information Commissioner's Office, *supra* note 9.
[107] *Id.* at 6.
[108] *Id.* at 9.
[109] *Id.* at 8.
[110] *Id.* at 6.
[111] ROWLAND, *supra* note 4, at 182.
[112] *Id*

[113] *Criminal Justice and Immigration Bill – ICO briefing, April 2008*, INFORMATION COMMISSIONER'S OFFICE, http://www.ico.gov.uk/news/current_topics/clause_76_briefing_april_2008.aspx (last visited June 30, 2012).

[114] LEGISLATION.GOV.UK, http://www.legislation.gov.uk/ (last visited June 29, 2012).

[115] *ICO Shows Its Teeth, As the Public's Concern over Illegal Marketing Calls Grows*, INFORMATION COMMISSIONER'S OFFICE (July 5, 2012), http://ico.gov.uk/news/latest_news/2012/ico-shows-its-teeth-as-the-publicconcern-over-illegal-marketing-calls-grows-05072012.asp.

[116] ROWLAND, *supra* note 4, at 187.

[117] Draft Communications Data Bill, 2011–2012, Cm. 8359, http://www.official-documents.gov.uk/document/cm83/8359/8359.pdf.

INDEX

A

B

C

D

T

U

V

W

X

Y